# General Studies Paper-2 (CSAT) Exam

- **Corporate Office :** 45, 2nd Floor, Maharishi Dayanand Marg, Corner Market,
Malviya Nagar, New Delhi-110017
**Tel. :** 011- 49404757/ 49404758/ 49404768

**Typeset by Disha DTP Team**

# DISHA PUBLICATION



**For further information about the books from DISHA,**
Log on to **www.dishapublication.com** or email to **info@dishapublication.com**

# CONTENTS


IAS Prelims Solved Paper-2 2018      2018-1 - 2018-16

IAS Prelims Solved Paper-2 2017      2017-1 - 2017-12


## MOCK TEST


Mock Test-1 with Solutions      1 - 16

Mock Test-2 with Solutions      17 - 30

Mock Test-3 with Solutions      31 - 46

Mock Test-4 with Solutions      47 - 64

Mock Test-5 with Solutions      65 - 80

Mock Test-6 with Solutions      81 - 95

Mock Test-7 with Solutions      96 - 110

Mock Test-8 with Solutions      111 - 123

Mock Test-9 with Solutions      124 - 138

Mock Test-10 with Solutions      139 - 152

New Topics Introduced in IAS Prelims Paper-2      N-1 - N-12

# Classification of Number of Questions of Last Four Years Unit-wise, Chapter-wise and Level-wise [Easy(E), Average (A), Difficult (D)]

| SN | Chapter Name | 2015 | 2016 | 2017 | 2018 |
| --- | --- | --- | --- | --- | --- |
| **UNIT 1 : INTERPERSONAL SKILLS INCLUDING COMMUNICATION SKILLS** | | | | | |
| 1 | Interpersonal Skills and Communication Skills | 0 | 0 | 0 | 0 |
| **UNIT 2 : DECISION MAKING** | | | | | |
| 1 | Administrative Courses of Action | 0 | 0 | 0 | 0 |
| 2 | Decision Making | 0 | 0 | 0 | 0 |
| **UNIT 3 : COMPREHENSION** | | | | | |
| 1 | General Comprehension | 2Qs-E<br>2Qs-A<br>6Qs-D | 1Q-E<br>5Qs-A<br>9Qs-D | 1Q-E<br>2Qs-A<br>2Qs-D | 3Qs-E<br>3Qs-A<br>4Qs-D |
| **UNIT 4 : ENGLISH LANGUAGE COMPREHENSION SKILLS** | | | | | |
| 1 | English Language Comprehension Skills | 0<br>3Qs-A<br>0 | 0<br>0<br>0 | 2Qs-E<br>2Qs-A<br>0 | 1Q-E<br>0<br>0 |
| **UNIT 5 : BASIC NUMERACY** | | | | | |
| 1 | Numbers | 1Q-E | 2Qs-A<br>1Q-D | 2Qs-E<br>1Q-A<br>1Q-D | 3Qs-A |
| 2 | L.C.M. and H.C.F. | 0 | 1Q-A | 1Q-A | 0 |
| 3 | Equations & Inequalities | 1Q-E<br>1Q-A<br>1Q-D | 1Q-E<br>1Q-A | 0 | 2Qs-A<br>1Q-D |
| 4 | Average & Ages | 1Q-A | 2Qs-A | 2Qs-E<br>1Q-D | 0 |
| 5 | Percentage | 1Q-E<br>1Q-A | 2Qs-A<br>1Q-D | 1Q-E<br>1Q-A | 0 |
| 6 | Profit, Loss and Discount | 0 | 1Q-E | 0 | 1Q-A |
| 7 | Simple and Compound Interest | 0 | 0 | 0 | 1Q-A |
| 8 | Ratio, Prop & Partnership | 2Qs-A | 1Q-D | 1Q-A | 0 |
| 9 | Alligation& Mixture | 1Q-A | 1Q-D | 1Q-A | 0 |
| 10 | Time, Work & Wages | 1Q-E | 1Q-A<br>2Qs-D | 1Q-A | 1Q-A |
| 11 | Time, Speed & Distance | 1Q-E<br>1Q-A | 2Qs-A<br>1Q-D | 1Q-A | 1Q-E<br>1Q-D |
| 12 | Time Sequence | 1Q-D | 1Q-A | 1Q-A | 0 |
| 13 | Mensuration –Plane Figures | 0 | 1Q-D | 1Q-A | 1Q-A |
| 14 | Mensuration –Solid Figures | 0 | 2Qs-A | 0 | 0 |
| 15 | Arithmetic Progression | 0 | 1Q-A | 0 | 0 |
| 16 | Set Theory (Include Venn Diagram) | 1Q-E<br>1Q-A<br>1Q-D | 0 | 0 | 1Q-A |
| 17 | Trigonometric Ratio and Height& Distances | 0 | 1Q-A | 0 | 0 |

| SN | Chapter Name | 2015 | 2016 | 2017 | 2018 |
| --- | --- | --- | --- | --- | --- |
| 18 | Permutation & Combination | 2Qs-A<br>1Q-D | 1Q-A | 1Q-E<br>1Q-A<br>2Qs-D | 2Qs-A<br>1Q-D |
| 19 | Probability | 0 | 1Q-A | 0 | 1Q-D |
| **UNIT 6 : DATA INTERPRETATION** | | | | | |
| 1 | Table, Bar, Line, Pie, Mix Graph | 0 | 0 | 0 | 3Qs-A<br>2Qs-D |
| 2 | Miscellaneous graph | 1Q-E<br>1Q-A<br>1Q-D | 0 | 0 | 6Qs-A<br>3Qs-D |
| 3 | Mean, Median & Mode Symmetric& SQSY Distr. | 0 | 0 | 1Q-E<br>1Q-A | 0 |
| **UNIT 7 : GENERAL MENTAL ABILITY** | | | | | |
| 1 | Number Series | 1Q-E | 0 | 0 | 1Q-E |
| 2 | Coding and Decoding | 0 | 1Q-E | 1Q-E | 2Qs-E |
| 3 | Blood Relation | 1Q-E | 0 | 1Q-E<br>1Q-A | 0 |
| 4 | Direction and Distance | 1Q-E | 3Qs-E | 0 | 0 |
| 5 | Ranking and Order | 5Qs-E | 1Q-E | 4Qs-E | 1Q-E<br>1Q-A |
| 6 | Arithmetical Reasoning | 2Qs-E<br>4Qs-A | 1Q-E<br>2Qs-A<br>1Q-D | 1Q-D | 3Qs-A<br>1Q-D |
| 7 | Number Puzzle | 1Q-E | 0 | 0 | 1Q-E |
| 8 | Cube and Dice | 1Q-E | 1Q-E | 1Q-E | 3Qs-E |
| 9 | Non-Verbal Reasoning | 2Qs-E | 0 | 0 | 2Qs-E |
| 10 | Sitting Arrangement | 0 | 1Q-A | 1Q-A | 0 |
| 11 | Puzzles | 1Q-E | 8Qs-A<br>3Qs-D | 2Qs-E<br>7Qs-A | 8Qs-A |
| **UNIT 8 : LOGICAL REASONING AND ANALYTICAL ABILITY** | | | | | |
| 1 | Statement and Assumptions | 0 | 0 | 0 | 0 |
| 2 | Statement and Arguments | 0 | 0 | 0 | 0 |
| 3 | Statement and Conclusions | 4Qs-E<br>1Q-A | 2Qs-E<br>3Qs-A | 4Qs-E<br>1Q-A | 0 |
| 4 | Logical Deduction (Evaluating Inferences) | 0 | 0 | 0 | 0 |
| 5 | Critical Reasoning | 2Qs-E<br>17Qs-A<br>1Q-D | 1Q-E<br>9Qs-A<br>3Qs-D | 2Qs-E<br>8Qs-A<br>4Qs-D | 16Qs-A |
| **UNIT - 9 PROBLEM SOLVING** | | | | | |
| 1 | Problem Solving | 0 | 0 | 0 | 0 |

**'5Qs-E' means 5 Questions of Easy Level**
**'5Qs-A' means 5 Questions of Average Level**
**'5Qs-D' means 5 Questions of Difficult Level**

# Sectionwise and Full paper analysis of CSAT paper-II, 2018.

## 1. Pie-Charts:

### Sectionwise Analysis

**English**

U-1: Interper Skills
U-2: Decision Making
U-3: Comprehension
U-4: English Lang. & Compr. Skills

**Quant**

U-5: Basic Num.
U-6: Data Int.

**Reasoning**

U-7: Gen. Mental Ability
U-8: Logi. and Anal. Ability
U-9: Problem Solving

### Full Paper Analysis

← Easy
← Average
← Difficult

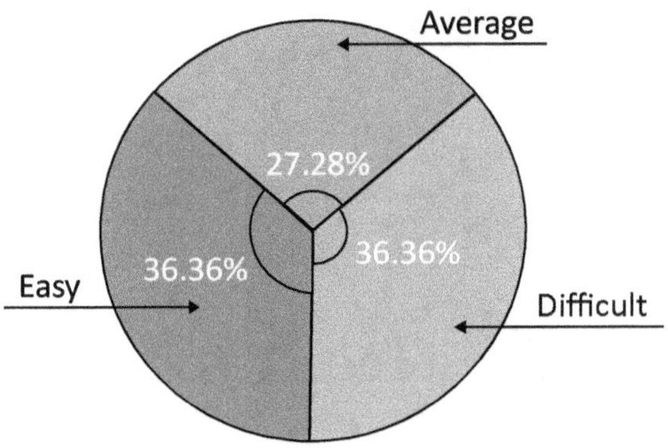

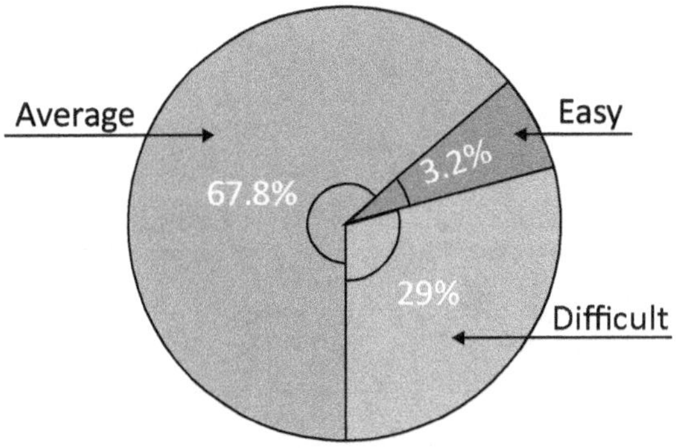

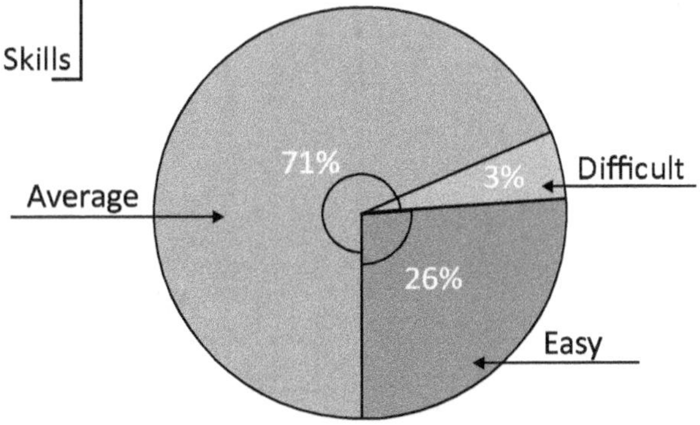

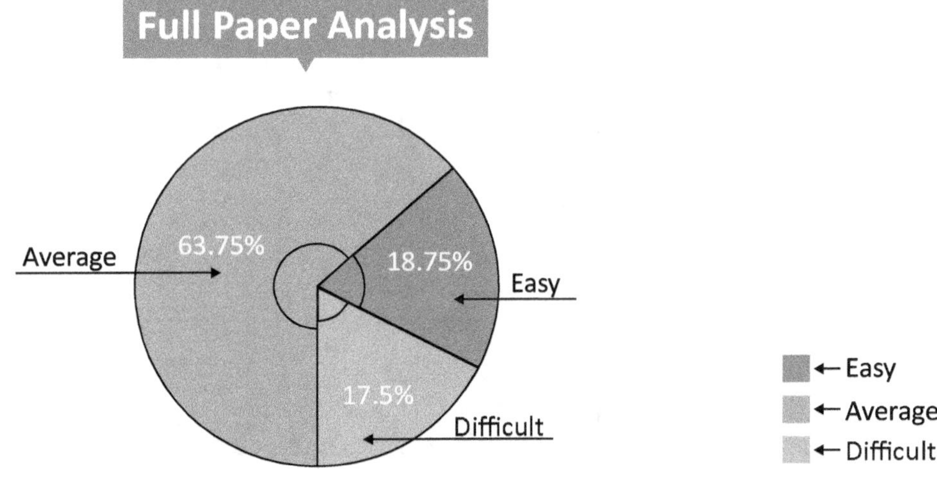

# 2. Bar Graphs:

Sectionwise Analysis
Easy
Average
Difficult
4 Qs
3 Qs
4 Qs
English
U-1: Interper Skills
U-2: Decision Making
U-3: Comprehension
U-4: English Lang. & Compr. Skills
Average
Easy
Difficult
1 Q
21 Qs
9 Qs
Quant
U-5: Basic Num.
U-6: Data Int.
Average
Easy
Difficult
10 Qs
27 Qs
1 Q
Reasoning
U-7: Gen. Mental Ability
U-8: Logi. and Anal. Ability
U-9: Problem Solving
Full Paper Analysis
Average
Easy
Difficult
15 Qs
51 Qs
14 Qs
Easy
Average
Difficult

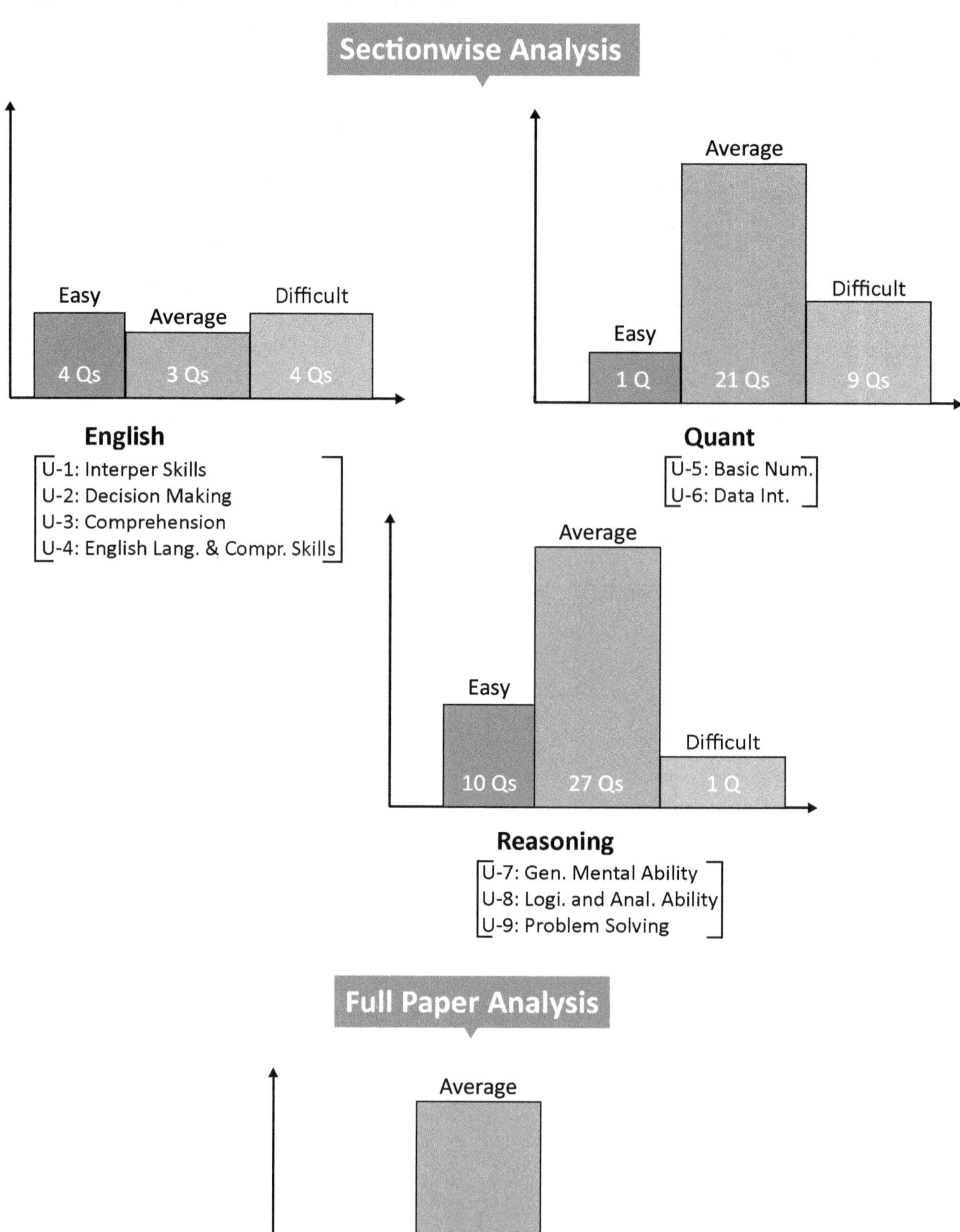

# IAS PRELIMS SOLVED PAPER-2 2018

1. Consider the following graph :

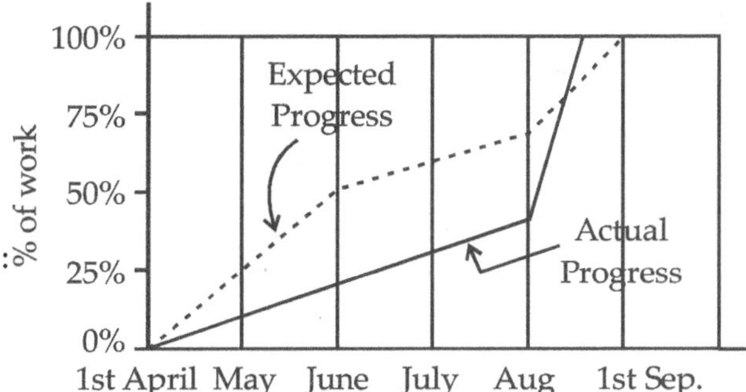


Which one of the following statements is **not** correct with reference to the graph given above?
(a) On 1$^{st}$ June, the actual progress of work was less than expected.
(b) The actual rate of progress of work was the greatest during the month of August.
(c) The work was actually completed before the expected time.
(d) During the period from 1$^{st}$ April to 1$^{st}$ September, at no time was the actual progress more than the expected progress.

2. For a sports meet, a winners' stand comprising three wooden blocks is in the following form :

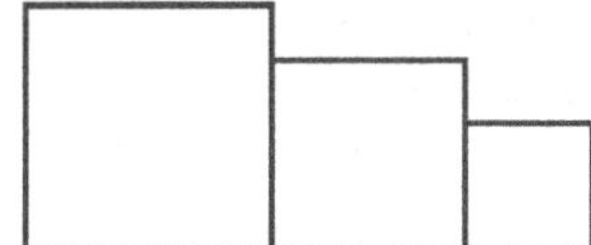

There are six different colours available to choose from and each of the three wooden blocks is to be painted such that no two of them has the same colour. In how many different ways can the winners' stand be painted?
(a) 120      (b) 81
(c) 66      (d) 36

**Directions for the following 2 (two) items :**
Consider the following graph in which the birth rate and death rate of a country are given, and answer the two items that follow.

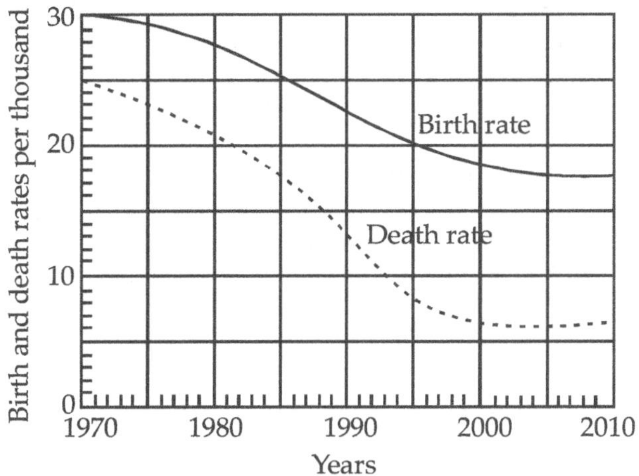


3. Looking at the graph, it can be inferred that from 1990 to 2010
(a) population growth rate has increased
(b) population growth rate has decreased
(c) growth rate of population has remained stable
(d) population growth rate shows no trend

4. With reference to the above graph, consider the following statements considering 1970 as base year :
1. Population has stabilized after 35 years.
2. Population growth rate has stabilized after 35 years.
3. Death rate has fallen by 10% in the first 10 years.
4. Birth rate has stabilized after 35 years.
Which of the above are the **most logical and rational statements** that can be made from the above graph?
(a) 1 and 2 only      (b) 1, 2 and 3
(c) 3 and 4      (d) 2 and 4

5. Average hourly earnings per year (E) of the workers in a firm are represented in figures A and B as follows:

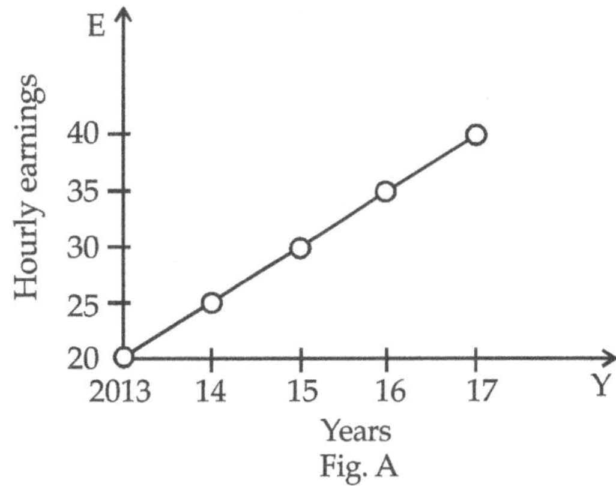


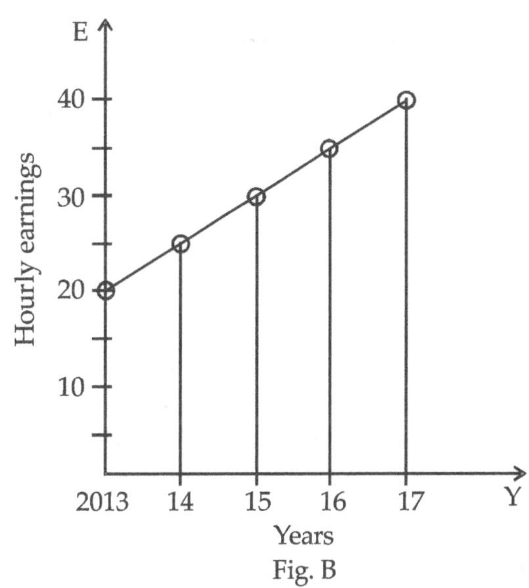

From the figures, it is observed that the
(a) values of $E$ are different
(b) ranges (i.e., the difference between the maximum and the minimum) of $E$ are different
(c) slopes of the graphs are same
(d) rates of increase of $E$ are different

6. Consider the figures given below :

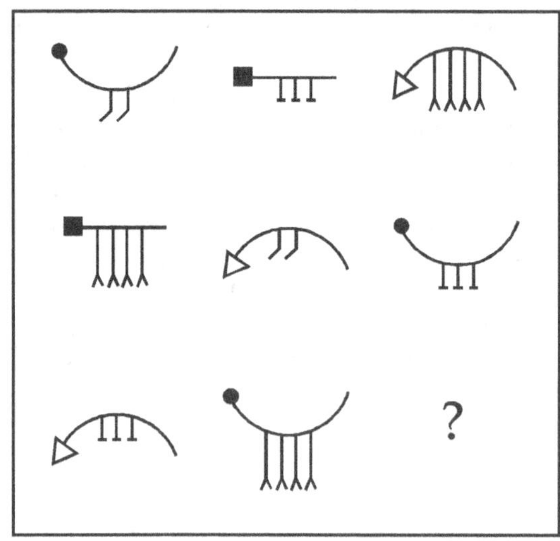

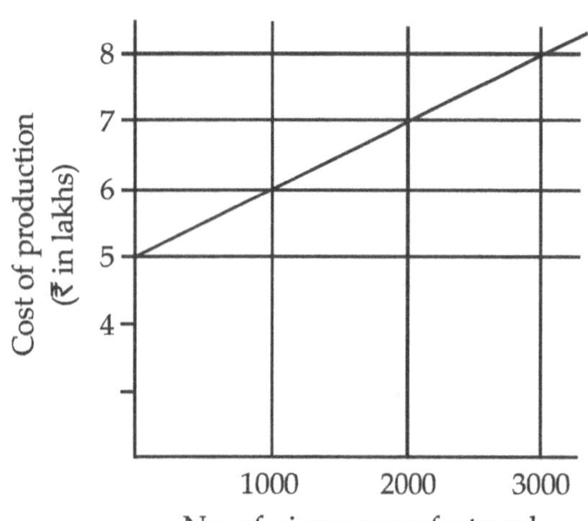

To fit the question mark, the correct answer is

(a)        (b)

(c)        (d)

7. Consider the following figures $A$ and $B$ :

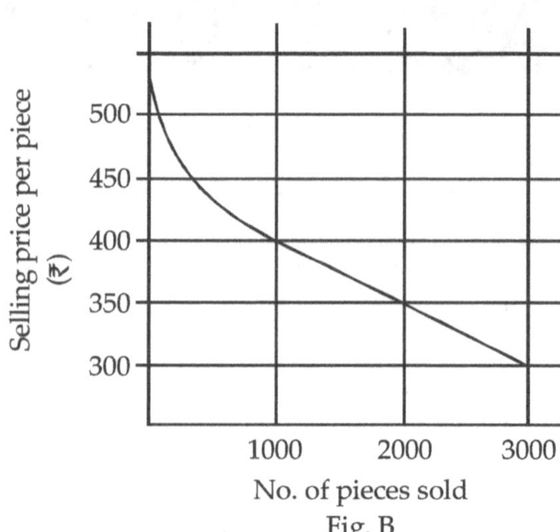

Fig. B

The manufacturing cost and projected sales for a product are shown in the above figures $A$ and $B$ respectively. What is the minimum number of pieces that should be manufactured to avoid a loss?
(a) 2000    (b) 2500    (c) 3000    (d) 3500

8. A lift has the capacity of 18 adults or 30 children. How many children can board the lift with 12 adults?
(a) 6      (b) 10    (c) 12      (d)15

9. A person bought a refrigerater worth ₹ 22,800 with 12.5% interest compounded yearly. At the end of first year he paid ₹ 8,650 and at the end of second year ₹ 9,125. How much will he have to pay at the end of third year to clear the debt?
(a) ₹ 9,990   (b) ₹ 10,000   (c) ₹ 10,590   (d) ₹ 11 ,250

10. Consider the following figures :

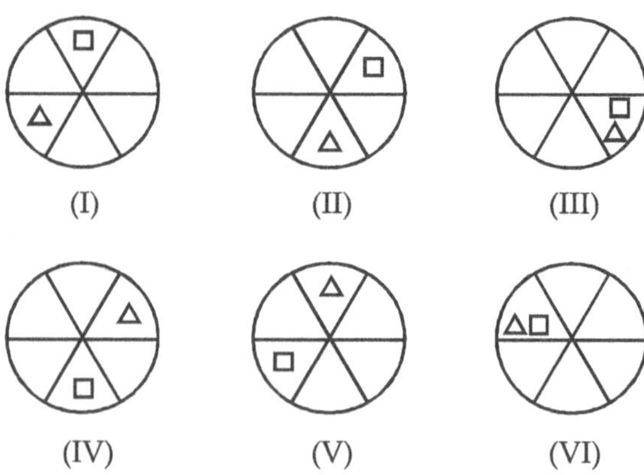

(I)      (II)      (III)

(IV)      (V)      (VI)

In the figures (I) to (VI) above, some parts are shown to change their positions in regular directions. Following the same sequence, which of the figures given below will appear at (VII) stage?

(a) 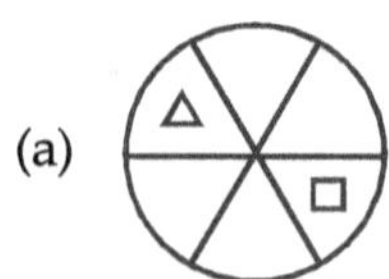      (b) 

Fig. A

(c)

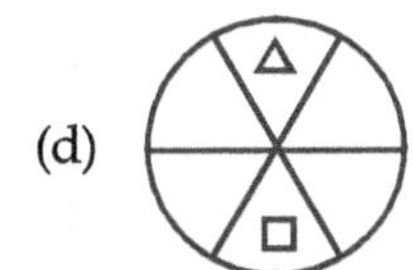

(d)

11. Consider the following graphs. The curves in the graphs indicate different age groups in the populations of two countries *A* and *B* over a period of few decades:

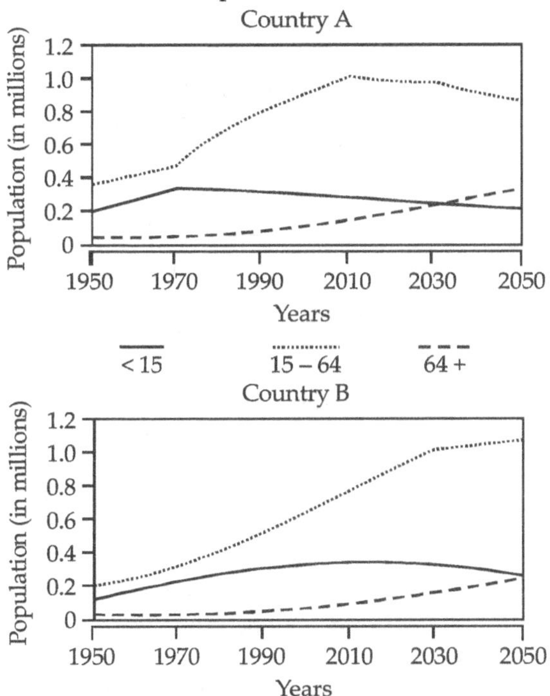


with reference to the above graphs, which of the following are the *most logical and rational inferences* that can be made?

1. Over the last two and a half decades, the dependency ratio for country *B* has decreased.
2. By the end of next two and a half decades, the dependency ratio of country *A* will be much less than that of country *B*.
3. In the next two decades, the work-force relative to its total population will increase in country *B* compared to country *A*.

Select the correct answer using the code given below.

(a) 1 and 2 only
(b) 2 and 3 only
(c) 1 and 3 only
(d) 1, 2 and 3

12. Lakshmi, her brother, her daughter and her son are badminton players. A game of doubles is a bout to begin:
(i) Lakshmi's brother is directly across the net from her daughter.
(ii) Her son is diagonally across the net from the worst player's sibling.
(iii) The best player and the worst player are on the same side of the net.

Who is the best player?
(a) Her brother
(b) Her daughter
(e) Her son
(d) Lakshmi

13. The graph given below indicates the changes in key policy rates made by the Central Bank several times in a year :

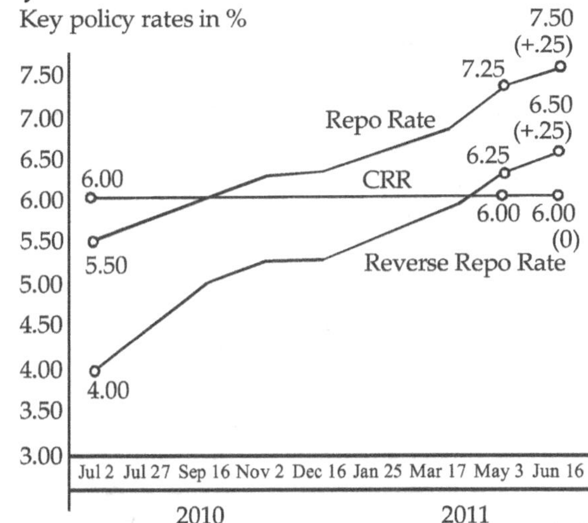


Which one of the following can be the *most likely reason* for the Central Bank for such an action?
(a) Encouraging foreign investment
(b) Increasing the liquidity
(c) Encouraging both public and private savings
(d) Anti-inflationary stance

**Directions for the following 2 (two) items :**
The following table gives the GDP growth rate and Tele-density data of different States of a country in a particular year. Study the table and answer the two items that follow.

| States | Per capita income ($) | GDP growth rate (%) | Tele-density |
|---|---|---|---|
| State 1 | 704 | 9.52 | 70.27 |
| State 2 | 419 | 5.31 | 35.88 |
| State 3 | 254 | 10.83 | 50.07 |
| State 4 | 545 | 9.78 | 5.94 |
| State 5 | 891 | 10.8 | 76.12 |
| State 6 | 1077 | 11.69 | 77.5 |
| State 7 | 900 | 8.88 | 104.86 |
| State 8 | 395 | 5.92 | 6 |
| State 9 | 720 | 7.76 | 82.25 |
| State 10 | 893 | 9.55 | 96.7 |
| State 11 | 363 | 4.7 | 57.7 |
| State 12 | 966 | 7.85 | 63.8 |
| State 13 | 495 | 9.37 | 52.3 |
| State 14 | 864 | 5.46 | 97.9 |
| State 15 | 497 | 7.48 | 62.3 |
| State 16 | 777 | 7.03 | 93.8 |
| State 17 | 335 | 5.8 | 49.9 |
| State 18 | 599 | 7.49 | 47.84 |

14. With reference to the above table, which of the following is/are the *most logical and rational inference/ inferences* that can be made?
    1. Higher per capita income is generally associated with higher Tele-density.
    2. Higher GDP growth rate always ensures higher per capita income.
    3. Higher GDP growth rate does not necessarily ensure higher Tele-density.
    Select the correct answer using the code given below.
    (a) 1 only      (e) 2 and 3
    (b) 1 and 3     (d) 3 only

15. With reference to the above table, the following assumptions have been made :
    1. Nowadays, prosperity of an already high performing State cannot be sustained without making further large investments in its telecom infrastructure.
    2. Nowadays, a very high Tele-density is the most essential condition for promoting the business and economic growth in a State.
    Which of the above assumptions is/are valid?
    (a) 1 only      (b) 2 only
    (c) Both 1 and 2    (d) Neither 1 nor 2

16. The following graph indicates the composition of our tax revenue for a period of two decades :

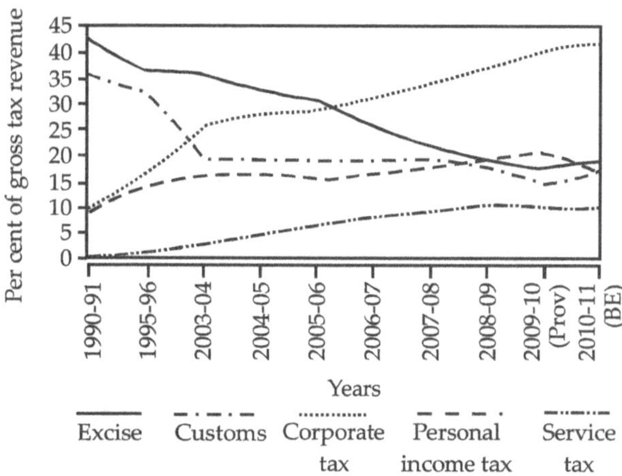


With reference to the above graph, which of the following is/are the *most logical and rational inference/ inferences* that can be made?
1. During the given period, the revenue from Direct Taxes as percentage of gross tax revenue has increased while that of Indirect Taxes decreased.
2. The trend in the revenue from Excise Duty demonstrates that the growth of manufacturing sector has been negative during the given period.
Select the correct answer using the code given below.
(a) 1 only      (b) 2 only
(c) Both 1 and 2    (d) Neither 1 nor 2

17. If $x - y = 8$, then which of the following must be true?
    1. Both $x$ and $y$ must be positive for any value of $x$ and $y$.
    2. If $x$ is positive, $y$ must be negative for any value of $x$ and $y$.
    3. If $x$ is negative, $y$ must be positive for any value of $x$ and $y$.
    Select the correct answer using the code given below.
    (a) 1 only      (b) 2 only
    (c) Both 1 and 2    (d Neither 1 nor 2 nor 3

**Directions for the following 3 (three) items :**
Read the following **two passages** and answer the items that follow. Your answers to these items should be based on the passages only.

### Passage-1

The quest for cheap and plentiful meat has resulted in factory farms where more and more animals are squeezed into smaller lots in cruel and shocking conditions. Such practices have resulted in many of the world's health pandemics such as the avian flu. Worldwide, livestock are increasingly raised in cruel, cramped conditions, where animals spend their short lives under artificial light, pumped full of antibiotics and growth hormones, until the day they are slaughtered. Meat production is water-intensive. 15000 litres of water is needed for every kilogram of meat compared with 3400 litres for rice, 3300 litres for eggs and 255 litres for a kilogram of potatoes.

18. What is the *most rational and crucial message* given by the passage?
    (a) Mass production of meat through industrial farming is cheap and is suitable for providing protein nutrition to poor countries.
    (b) Meat-producing industry violates the laws against cruelty to animals.
    (c) Mass production of meat through industrial farming is undesirable and should be stopped immediately.
    (d) Environmental cost of meat production is unsustainable when it is produced through industrial farming.

### Passage-2

A male tiger was removed from Pench Tiger Reserve and was relocated in Panna National Park. Later, this tiger trekked toward his home 250 miles away. The trek of this solitary tiger highlights a crisis. Many wildlife reserves exist as islands of fragile habitat in a vast sea of humanity, yet tigers can range over a hundred miles, seeking prey, mates and territory. Nearly a third of India's tigers live outside tiger reserves, a situation that is dangerous for both human and animal. Prey and tigers can only disperse if there are recognized corridors of land between protected areas to allow unmolested passage.

19. Which of the following is the *most rational and crucial message* given by the passage?
    (a) The conflict between man and wildlife cannot be resolved, no matter what efforts we make.
    (b) Safe wildlife corridors between protected areas is an essential aspect of conservation efforts.
    (c) India needs to declare more protected areas and set up more tiger reserves.
    (d) India's National Parks and Tiger Reserves need to be professionally managed.

20. With reference to the above passage, the following assumptions have been made:
    1. The strategy of conservation of wildlife by relocating them from one protected area to another is not often successful.
    2. India does not have suitable legislation to save the tigers, and its conservation efforts have failed which forced the tigers to live outside protected areas.
    Which of the above assumptions is/are valid?
    (a) 1 only      (b) 2 only
    (c) Both 1 and 2      (d) Neither 1 nor 2

**Directions for the following 8 (eight) items :**
Read the following **eight passages** and answer the items that follow. Your answers to these items should be based on the passages only.

## Passage-1

All actions to address climate change ultimately involve costs. Funding is vital in order for countries like India to design and implement adaptation and mitigation plans and projects. The problem is more severe for developing countries like India, which would be one of the hardest hit by climate change, given its need to finance development. Most countries do indeed treat climate change as real threat and are striving to address it in a more comprehensive and integrated manner with the limited resources at their disposal.

21. With reference to the above passage, the following assumptions have been made :
    1. Climate change is not a challenge for developed countries.
    2. Climate change is a complex policy issue and also a development issue for many countries.
    3. Ways and means of finance must be found to enable developing countries to enhance their adaptive capacity.
    Which of the above assumptions is/are valid?
    (a) 1 and 2 only      (b) 3 only
    (c) 2 and 3 only      (d) 1, 2 and 3

## Passage-2

Cooking with biomass and coal in India is now recognized to cause major health problems, with women and children in poor populations facing the greatest risk. There are more than 10 lakh premature deaths each year from household air pollution due to polluting cooking fuels with another 1.5 lakh due to their contribution to general outdoor air pollution in the country. Although the fraction of the Indian population using clean cooking fuels, such as LPG natural gas and electricity, is slowly rising, the number using polluting solid fuels as their primary cooking fuel has remained static for nearly 30 years at about 70 crore.

22. Which of the following is the *most crucial and logical inference* that can be made from the above passage?
    (a) Rural people are giving up the use of polluting solid fuels due to their increasing awareness of health hazards.
    (b) Subsidizing the use of clean cooking fuels will solve the problem of India's indoor air pollution.
    (c) India should increase its import of natural gas and produce more electricity.
    (d) Access to cooking gas can reduce premature deaths in poor households.

## Passage-3

Scientific knowledge has its dangers but so has every great thing. Over and beyond the dangers with which it threatens the present, it opens up as nothing else can, the vision of a possible happy world; a world without poverty, without war, with little illness. Science, whatever unpleasant consequences it may have by the way, is in its very nature a liberator.

23. Which one of the following is the *most important implication* of the passage?
    (a) A happy world is a dream of science.
    (b) Science only can build a happy world, but it is also the only major threat.
    (c) A happy world is not possible without science.
    (d) A happy world is not at all possible with or without science.

## Passage-4

The Arctic's vast reserves of fossil fuel, fish and minerals are now accessible for a longer period in a year. But unlike Antarctica, which is protected from exploitation by the Antarctic Treaty framed during the Cold War and is not subject to territorial claims by any country, there is no legal regime protecting the Arctic from industrialization, especially at a time when the world craves for more and more resources. The distinct possibility of ice-free summer has prompted countries with Arctic coastline to scramble for great chunks of the melting ocean.

24. Which one of the following is the *most important implication* of the passage?
    (a) India can have territorial claims in the Arctic territory and free access to its resources.

(b) Melting of summer ice in the Arctic leads to changes in the geopolitics.

(c) The Arctic region will solve the world's future problem of resource crunch.

(d) The Arctic region has more resources than Antarctica.

### Passage-5

Being a member of the WTO, India is bound by the agreements that have been signed and ratified by its members, including itself. According to Article 6 of the Agriculture Agreement, providing minimum support prices for agricultural products is considered distorting and is subject to limits. The subsidy arising from 'minimal supports' cannot exceed 10 per cent of the value of agricultural production for developing countries. PDS in India entails minimum support prices and public stockholding of food grains. It is possible that, in some years, the subsidy to producers will exceed 10 per cent of the value of agricultural production.

25. What is the *crucial message* conveyed by the above passage?
    (a) India should revise its PDS.
    (b) India should not be a member of WTO.
    (c) For India, food security collides with trade.
    (d) India provides food security to its poor.

### Passage-6

India's educational system is modelled on the mass education system that developed in the 19th century in Europe and later spread around the world. The goal of the system is to condition children as 'good' citizens and productive workers. This suited the industrial age that needed the constant supply of a compliant workforce with a narrow set of capabilities. Our educational institutes resemble factories with bells, uniforms and batch-processing of learners, designed to get learners to conform. But, from an economic point of view, the environment today is very different. It is a complex, volatile and globally interconnected world.

26. With reference to the above passage, the following assumptions have been made:
    1. India continues to be a developing country essentially due to its faulty education system.
    2. Today's learners need to acquire new-age skill-sets.
    3. A good number of Indians go to some developed countries for education because the educational systems there are a perfect reflection of the societies in which they function.

    Which of the above assumptions is/are valid?
    (a) 1 and 3 only      (b) 2 only
    (c) 2 and 3 only      (d) 1, 2 and 3

### Passage-7

The practice of dieting has become an epidemic; everyone is looking out for a way to attain that perfect body. We are all different with respect to our ethnicity, genetics, family history, gender, age, physical and mental and spiritual health status, lifestyles and preferences. Thereby we also differ in what foods we tolerate or are sensitive to. So we really cannot reduce so many complexities into one diet or diet book. This explains the failure of diets across the world in curbing obesity. Unless the reasons for weight gain are well understood and addressed and unless habits are changed permanently, no diet is likely to succeed.

27. What is the *most logical and rational inference* that can be made from the above passage?
    (a) Obesity has become an epidemic all over the world.
    (b) A lot of people are obsessed with attaining a perfect body.
    (c) Obesity is essentially an incurable disease.
    (d) There is no perfect diet or one solution for obesity.

### Passage-8

Monoculture carries great risks. A single disease or pest can wipe out swathes of the world's food production, an alarming prospect given that its growing and wealthier population will eat 70% more by 2050. The risks are magnified by the changing climate. As the planet warms and monsoon rains intensify, farmlands in Asia will flood. North America will suffer more intense droughts, and crop diseases will spread to new latitudes.

28. Which of the following is the *most logical, rational and crucial message* given by the passage?
    (a) Preserving crop genetic diversity is an insurance against the effects of climate change.
    (b) Despite great risks, monoculture is the only way to ensure food security in the world.
    (c) More and more genetically modified crops only can save the world from impending shortages of food.
    (d) Asia and North America will be worst sufferers from climate change and the consequent shortage of food.

29. A shopkeeper sells an article at ₹ 40 and gets $X\%$ profit. However, when he sells it at ₹ 20, he faces same percentage of loss. What is the original cost of the article?
    (a) ₹ 10      (b) ₹ 20
    (c) ₹ 30      (d) ₹ 40

30. There are 24 equally spaced points lying on the circumference of a circle. What is the maximum number of equilateral triangles that can be drawn by taking sets of three points as the vertices?
    (a)  4                    (b)  6
    (c)  8                    (d)  12

31. Consider the sequence given below :
    4/12/95, 1/1/96, 29/1/96, 26/2/96, ....
    What is the next term of the series?
    (a)  24/3/96              (b)  25/3/96
    (c)  26/3/96              (d)  27/3/96

32. Twelve equal squares are placed to fit in a rectangle of diagonal 5 cm. There are three rows containing four squares each. No gaps are left between adjacent squares. What is the area of each square?

    (a)  $\dfrac{5}{7}$ sq. cm          (b)  $\dfrac{7}{5}$ sq. cm

    (c)  1 sq. cm                       (d)  $\dfrac{25}{12}$ sq. cm

**Directions for tho following 3 (three) items :**
The following three items are based on the graph given below which shows imports of three different types of steel over a period of six months of a year. Study the graph and answer the three items that follow.

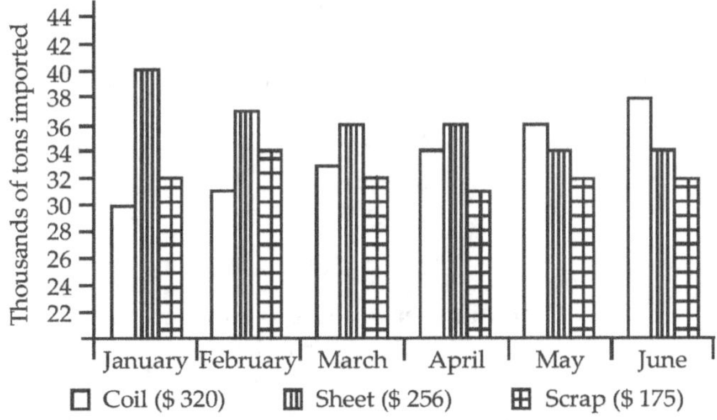


The figures in the brackets indicate the average cost per ton over six months period.

33. By how much (measured in thousands of tons) did the import of sheet steel exceed the import of coil steel in the first three months of the year?
    (a)  11                   (b)  15
    (c)  19                   (d)  23

34. What was the approximate total value (in $) of sheet steel imported over the six months period?
    (a)  45,555              (b)  50,555
    (c)  55,550              (d)  65,750

35. What was the approximate ratio of sheet steel and scrap steel imports in the first three months of the year?
    (a)  1 : 1                (b)  1.2 : 1
    (c)  1.4 : 1              (d)  1.6 : 1

**Directions for the following 3 (three) items :**
Rotated positions of a single solid are shown below. The various faces of the solid are marked with different symbols like dots, cross and line. Answer the three items that follow the given figures.

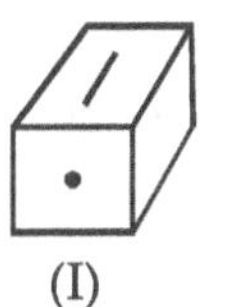

36. What is the symbol on the face opposite to that containing a single dot?
    (a)  Four dots           (b)  Three dots
    (c)  Two dots            (d)  Cross

37. What is the symbol on the face opposite to that containing two dots?
    (a)  Single dot          (b)  Three dots
    (c)  Four dots           (d)  Line

38. What is the symbol on the face opposite to that containing the cross?
    (a)  Single dot          (b)  Two dots
    (c)  Line                (d)  Four dots

**Directions for the following 4 (four) items :**
Read the following **passage** and answer the four items that follow. Your answers to these items should be based on the passage only.

### Passage

It is no longer enough for us to talk about providing for universal access to education. Making available schooling facilities is an essential prerequisite, but is insufficient to ensure that all children attend school and participate in the learning process. The school may be there, but children may not attend or they may drop out after a few months. Through school and social mapping, we must address the entire gamut of social, economic, cultural and indeed linguistic and pedagogic issues, factors that prevent children from weaker sections and disadvantaged groups, as also girls, from regularly attending and complementing elementary education. The focus must be on the poorest and most vulnerable since these groups are the most disempowered and at a greatest risk of violation or denial of their right to education.

The right to education goes beyond free and compulsory education to include quality education for all. Quality is an integral part of the right to education. If the education process lacks quality, children are being denied their right. The Right of Children to Free and Compulsory Education Act lays down that the curriculum should provide for learning through activities, exploration and discovery. This places an obligation on us to change our perception of children as passive receivers of knowledge, and to move beyond the convention of using textbooks as the basis of examinations. The teaching-learning process must become stress-free; and a massive programme for curricular reform should be initiated to provide for a child-friendly learning system, that is more relevant and empowering. Teacher accountability systems and processes must ensure that children are learning, and that their right to learn in a child-friendly environment is not violated. Testing and assessment systems must be reexamined and redesigned to ensure that these do not force children to struggle between school and tuition centres, and bypass childhood.

39. According to the passage, which of the following is/ are of paramount importance under the Right to education?
    1. Sending of children to school by all parents
    2. Provision of adequate physical infrastructure in schools
    3. Curricular reforms for developing child-friendly learning system
    Select the correct answer using the code given below.
    (a) 1 only
    (b) 1 and 2 only
    (c) 3 only
    (d) None of the above

40. With reference to the above passage, the following assumptions have been made:
    1. The Right to Education guarantees teachers' accountability for the learning process of children.
    2. The Right to Education guarantees 100% enrolment of children in the schools.
    3. The Right to Education intends to take full advantage of demographic dividend.
    Which of the above assumptions is/are valid?
    (a) 1 only
    (b) 2 and 3 only
    (c) 3 only
    (d) 1, 2 and 3

41. According to the passage, which one of the following is critical in bringing quality in education?
    (a) Ensuring regular attendance of children as well as teachers in school
    (b) Giving pecuniary benefits to teachers to motivation them
    (c) Understanding the socio-cultural background of children
    (d) Inculcating learning through activities and discovery

42. What is the *essential message* in this passage?
    (a) The Right to Education now is a Fundamental Right.
    (b) The Right to Education enables the children of poor and weaker sections of the society to attend schools.
    (c) The Right to Free and Compulsory Education should include quality education for all.
    (d) The Government as well a parents should ensure that all children attend schools.

43. Consider the following three-dimensional figure:

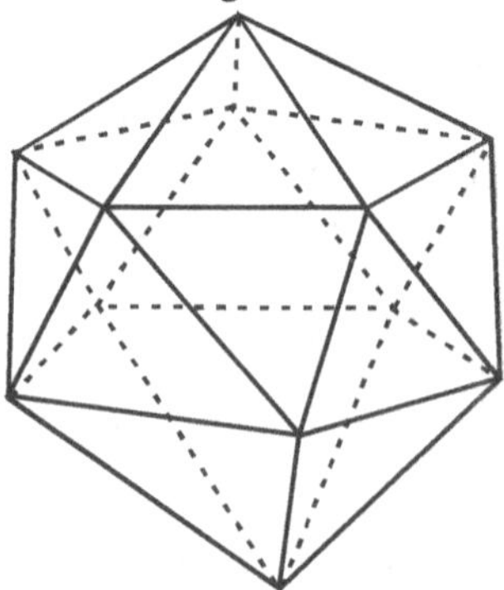

    How many triangles does the above figure have?
    (a) 18
    (b) 20
    (c) 22
    (d) 24

44. Consider the following sum :
    $\bullet + 1\bullet + 2\bullet + \bullet 3 + \bullet 1 = 21\bullet$
    In the above sum, $\bullet$ stands for
    (a) 4
    (b) 5
    (c) 6
    (d) 8

45. Consider the following pattern of numbers:

$$\begin{array}{cccc} 8 & 10 & 15 & 13 \\ 6 & 5 & 7 & 4 \\ \underline{4} & \underline{6} & \underline{8} & \underline{8} \\ 6 & 11 & 16 & ? \end{array}$$

    What is the number at ? in the above pattern?
    (a) 17
    (b) 19
    (c) 21
    (d) 23

46. How many diagonals can be drawn by joining the vertices of an octagon?
    (a) 20
    (b) 24
    (c) 28
    (d) 64

47. The figure drawn below gives the velocity graphs of two vehicles $A$ and $B$. The stright line $OKP$ represents the velocity of vehicle $A$ at any instant, whereas the horizontal straight line. $CKD$ represents the velocity of vehicle $B$ at any instant. In the figure, $D$ is the point where perpendicular from $P$ meets the horizontal line $CKD$ such that $PD = \dfrac{1}{2} LD$ :

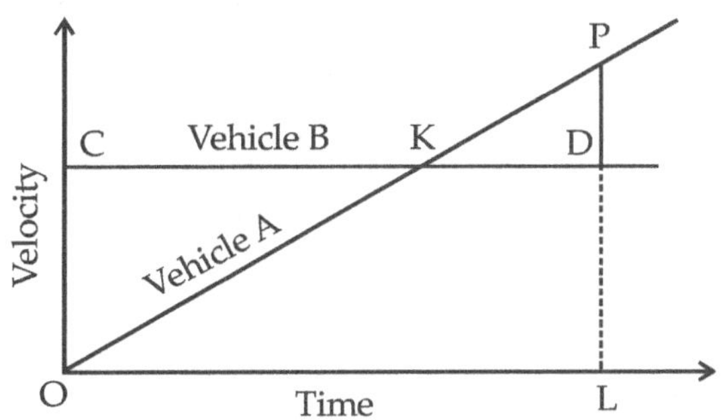


What is the ratio between the distances covered by vehicles *A* and *B* in the time interval *OL*?

(a) 1 : 2
(b) 2 : 3
(c) 3 : 4
(d) 1 : 1

48. A train 200 metres long is moving at the rate of 40 kmph. In how many seconds will it cross a man standing near the railway line?

(a) 12
(b) 15
(c) 16
(d) 18

**Directions for the following 4 (four) items :**
Read the following **four passages** and answer the items that follow. Your answers to these items should be based on the passages only.

### Passage-1

Global population was around 1.6 billion in 1990— today it is around 7.2 billion and growing. Recent estimates on population growth predict a global population of 9.6 billion in 2050 and 10.9 billion in 2100. Unlike Europe and North America, where only three to four percent of population is engaged in agriculture, around 47 percent of India's population is dependent upon agriculture. Even if India continues to do well in the service sector and the manufacturing sector picks up, it is expected that around 2030 when India overtakes China as the world 's most populous country, nearly 42 per cent of India's population will still be predominantly dependent on agriculture.

49. Which of the following is the *most logical and rational inference* that can be made from the above passage?

(a) Prosperity of agriculture sector is of critical importance to India.
(b) Indian economy greatly depends on its agriculture.
(c) India should take strict measures to control its rapid population growth.
(d) India's farming communities should switch over to other occupations to improve their economic conditions.

### Passage-2

Many pathogens that cause food borne illnesses are unknown. Food contamination can occur at any stage from farm to plate. Since most cases of food poisoning go unreported, the true extent of global foodborne illnesses is unknown. Improvements in international monitoring have led to greater public awareness, yet the rapid globalization of food production increases consumers' vulnerability by making food harder to regulate and trace. "We have the world on Our plates", says an official of WHO.

50. Which of the following is the *most logical corollary* to the above passage?

(a) With more options for food come more risks.
(b) Food processing is the source of all foodborne illnesses.
(c) We should depend on locally produced food only.
(d) Globalization of food production should be curtailed.

### Passage-3

I am a scientist, privileged to be some body who tries to understand nature using the tools of science. But it is also clear that there are some really important questions that science cannot really answer, such as : Why is there something instead of nothing? Why are we here? In those domains, I have found that faith provides a better path to answers. I find it oddly anachronistic that in today's culture there seems to be a widespread presumption that scientific and spiritual views are incompatible.

51. Which of the following is the *most logical and rational inference* that can be made from the above passage?

(a) It is the faith and not science that can finally solve all the problems of mankind.
(b) Science and faith can be mutually complementary if their proper domains are understood.
(c) There are some very fundamental questions which cannot be answered by either science or faith.
(d) In today's culture, scientific views are given more importance than spiritual views.

### Passage-4

Though I have discarded much of past tradition and custom, and am anxious that India should rid herself of all shackles that bind and contain her and divide her people, and suppress vast numbers of them, and prevent the free development of the body and the spirit; though I seek all this, yet I do not wish to cut myself off from that past completely. I am proud of that great inheritance that has been and is, ours and I am conscious that I too, like all of us, am a link in that unbroken chain which goes back to the dawn of history in the immemorial past of India.

52. The author wants India to rid herself of certain past bonds because

(a) he is not able to see the relevance of the past
(b) there is not much to be proud of
(c) he is not interested in the history of India
(d) they obstruct her physical and spiritual growth

53. A number consists of three digits of which the middle one is zero and their sum is 4. If the number formed by interchanging first and last digit of the first number is increased by 198, then the difference between the first and last digits is

(a) 1    (b) 2    (c) 3    (d) 4

54. A solid cube of 3 cm side, painted on all its faces, is cut up into small cubes of 1 cm side. How many of the small cubes will have exactly two painted faces.

(a) 12    (b) 8    (c) 6    (d) 4

55. While writing all the numbers from 700 to 1000, how many numbers occur in which the digit at hundred's place is greater than the digit at ten's place, and the digit at ten's place is greater than the digit at unit's place?
    (a) 61
    (b) 64
    (c) 85
    (d) 91

56. If Pen < Pencil, Pencil < Book and Book > Cap, then which one of the following is always true?
    (a) Pen > Cap
    (b) Pen < Book
    (c) Pencil = Cap
    (d) Pencil > Cap

57. A bookseller sold 'a' number of Geography textbooks at the rate of ₹ $x$ per book, 'a + 2' number of History textbooks at the rate of ₹ $(x + 2)$ per book and 'a – 2' number of mathematics textbooks at the rate of ₹ $(x – 2)$ per book. What is his total sale in ₹ ?
    (a) $3x + 3a$
    (b) $3ax + 8$
    (c) $9ax$
    (d) $x^3 a^3$

58. A bag contains 15 red balls and 20 black balls. Each ball is numbered either 1 or 2 or 3. 20% of the red balls are numbered 1 and 40% of them are numbered 2. Similarly, among the black balls, 45% are numbered 2 and 30% are numbered 3. A boy picks a ball at random. He wins if the ball is red and numbered 3 or if it is black and numbered 1 or 2. What are the chances of his winning?

    (a) $\dfrac{1}{2}$
    (b) $\dfrac{4}{7}$

    (c) $\dfrac{5}{9}$
    (d) $\dfrac{12}{13}$

59. Two persons, $A$ and $B$ are running on a circular track. At the start, $B$ is ahead of $A$ and their positions make an angle of 30° at the centre of the circle. When $A$ reaches the point diametrically opposite to his starting point, he meets $B$. What is the ratio of speeds of $A$ and $B$, if they are running with uniform speeds?
    (a) 6 : 5
    (b) 4 : 3
    (c) 6 : 1
    (d) 4 : 2

60. A student has to get 40% marks to pass in an examination. Suppose he gets 30 marks and fails by 30 marks, then what are the maximum marks in the examination?
    (a) 100
    (b) 120
    (c) 150
    (d) 300

61. 19 boys turn out for playing hockey. Of these, 11 are wearing hockey shirts and 14 are wearing hockey pants. There are no boys without shirts and/or pants. What is the number of boys wearing full uniform?
    (a) 3
    (b) 5
    (c) 6
    (d) 8

**Directions for the following 6 (six) Items :**
Read the information given below and answer the six items that follow.
A, B, C and D are students. They are studying in four different cities, viz., P, Q, R and S (not necessarily in that order). They are studying in Science college, Arts college, Commerce college and Engineering college (not necessarily in that order), which are situated in four different States, viz., Gujarat, Rajasthan, Assam and Kerala (not necessarily in that order). Further, it is given that-

(i) $D$ is studying in Assam
(ii) Arts college is located in city S which is in Rajasthan
(iii) A is studying in Commerce college
(iv) $B$ is studying in city $Q$
(v) Science college is located in Kerala

62. $A$ is studying in
    (a) Rajasthan
    (b) Gujarat
    (c) city $Q$
    (d) Kerala

63. Science college is located in
    (a) city $Q$
    (b) city $S$
    (c) city $R$
    (d) city $P$

64. C is studying in
    (a) Science college
    (b) Rajasthan
    (c) Gujarat
    (d) city $Q$

65. Which one of the following statements is correct?
    (a) $D$ is not studying in city $S$.
    (b) $A$ is studying in Science college.
    (c) $A$ is studying in Kerala.
    (d) Engineering college is located in Gujarat.

66. Which one of the following statements is correct regarding Engineering college?
    (a) $C$ is studying there.
    (b) $B$ is studying there.
    (c) It is located in Gujarat.
    (d) $D$ is studying there.

67. Which one of the following statements is correct?
    (a) Engineering college is located in Assam.
    (b) City $Q$ is situated in Assam.
    (c) $C$ is studying in Kerala.
    (d) $B$ is studying in Gujarat.

68. If LSJXVC is the code for MUMBAI, the code for DELHI is
    (a) CCIDD
    (b) CDKGH
    (c) CCJFG
    (d) CCIFE

69. If RAMON is written as 12345 and DINESH as 675849, then HAMAM will be written as
    (a) 92233
    (b) 92323
    (c) 93322
    (d) 93232

70. If $X$ is between – 3 and – 1, and Y is between – 1 and 1, then $X^2 – Y^2$ is in between which of the following?
    (a) – 9 and 1
    (b) – 9 and – 1
    (c) 0 and 8
    (d) 0 and 9

71. $X$ and $Y$ are natural numbers other than 1, and $Y$ is greater than $X$. Which of the following represents the largest number?
    (a) $XY$
    (b) $X/Y$
    (c) $Y/X$
    (d) $(X + Y)/XY$

**Directions for the following 2 (two) items :**
Read the following information and answer the two items that follow.
The plan of an office block for six officers $A$, $B$, $C$, $D$, $E$ and $F$ is as follows : Both $B$ and $C$ occupy offices to the right of the corridor (as one enters the office block) and $A$ occupies on the left of the corridor. $E$ and $F$ occupy offices on opposite sides of the Corridor but their offices do not face each other. The offices of $C$ and $D$ face each other. $E$ does not have a corner office. $F$s office is further down the corridor than $A$'s, but on the same side.

72. If $E$ sits in his office and faces the corridor, whose office is to his left?
    (a) $A$
    (b) $B$
    (c) $C$
    (d) $D$

73. Who is/are Fs immediate neighbour/neighbours?
    (a)  *A* only      (b)  *A* and *D*
    (c)  *C* only      (d)  *B* and *C*

**Directions for the following 7 (seven) items :**
Read the following **four passages** and answer the items that follow. Your answers to these items should be based on the passages only.

## Passage-1

'Desertification' is a term used to explain a process of decline in the biological productivity of an ecosystem, leading to total loss of productivity. While this phenomenon is often linked to the arid, semi-arid and sub-humid ecosystems, even in the humid tropics, the impact could be most dramatic. Impoverishment of human-impacted terrestrial ecosystems may exhibit itself in a variety of ways : accelerated erosion as in the mountain regions of the country, salinization of land as in the semi-arid and arid 'green revolution' areas of the country, e.g., Haryana and western Uttar Pradesh, and site quality decline-a common phenomenon due to general decline in tree cover and monotonous monoculture of rice/wheat across the Indian plains. A major consequence of deforestation is that it relates to adverse alterations in the hydrology and related soil and nutrient losses. The consequences of deforestation invariably arise out of site degradation through erosive losses. Tropical Asia, Africa and South America have the highest levels of erosion. The already high rates for the tropics are increasing at an alarming rate (e.g., through the major river systems-Ganga and Brahmaputra, in the Indian context). due to deforestation and ill-suited land management practices subsequent to forest clearing. In the mountain context, the declining moisture retention of the mountain soils, drying up of the underground springs and smaller rivers in the Himalayan region could be attributed to drastic changes in the forest cover. An indirect consequence is drastic alteration in the upland-lowland interaction, mediated through water. The current concern the tea planter of Assam has is about the damage to tea plantations due to frequent inundation along the flood -plains of Brahmaputra, and the damage to tea plantation and the consequent loss in tea productivity is due to rising level of the river bottom because of siltation and the changing course of the river system. The ultimate consequences of site desertification are soil degradation, alteration in available water and its quality, and the consequent decline in food, fodder and fuelwood yields essential for the economic well-being of rural communities.

74. According to the passage, which of the following are the consequences of decline in forest cover?
    1.  Loss of topsoil
    2.  Loss of smaller rivers
    3.  Adverse effect on agricultural production
    4.  Declining of groundwater
    Select the correct answer using the code given below.
       (a)  1, 2 and 3 only      (b)  2, 3 and 4 only
       (c)  1 and 4 only        (d)  1, 2, 3 and 4

75. Which of the following is/are the *correct inference/inferences* that can be made from the passage?

1.  Deforestation can cause changes in the course of rivers.
2.  Salinization of land takes place due to human activities only.
3.  Intense monoculture practice in plains is a major reason for desertification in Tropical Asia, Africa and South America.
Select the correct answer using the code given below.
(a)  1 only
(b)  1 and 2 only
(c)  2 and 3 only
(d)  None of the above is a correct inference

76. With reference to 'desertification', as described in the passage, the following assumptions have been made:
1.  Desertification is a phenomenon in tropical areas only.
2.  Deforestation invariably leads to floods and desertification.
Which of the above assumptions is/are valid?
(a)  1 only          (b)  2 only
(c)  Both 1 and 2    (d)  Neither 1 nor 2

## Passage-2

A diversity of natural assets will be needed to cope with climate change and ensure productive agriculture, forestry, and fisheries. For example, crop varieties are needed that perform well under drought, heat, and enhanced $CO_2$, But the private-sector and farmer-led process of choosing crops favours homogeneity adapted to past or current conditions, not varieties capable of producing consistently high yields in warmer, wetter, or drier conditions. Accelerated breeding programmes are needed to conserve a wider pool of genetic resources of existing crops, breeds and their wild relatives. Relatively intact ecosystems, such as forested catchments, mangroves, wetlands, can buffer the Impacts of climate change. Under a changing climate, these ecosystems are themselves at risk, and management approaches will need to be more proactive and adaptive. Connections between natural areas, such as migration corridors, may be needed to facilitate species movements to keep up with the change in climate.

77. With reference to the above passage, which of the following would assist us in coping with the climate change?
1.  Conservation of natural water sources
2.  Conservation of wider gene pool
3.  Existing crop management practices
4.  Migration corridors
Select the correct answer using the code given below.
(a)  1, 2 and 3 only     (b)  1, 2 and 4 only
(c)  3 and 4 only        (d)  1, 2, 3 and 4

78. With reference to the above passage, the following assumptions have been made :
1.  Diversification of livelihoods acts as a Coping strategy for climate change.
2.  Adoption of monocropping practice leads to the extinction of plant varieties and their wild relatives.
Which of the above assumptions is/ are valid?
(a)  1 only          (b)  2 only
(c)  Both 1 and 2    (d)  Neither 1 nor 2

### Passage-3

Today, the top environmental challenge is a combination of people and their aspirations. If the aspirations are more like the frugal ones we had after the Second World War, a lot more is possible than if we view the planet as a giant shopping mall. We need to get beyond the fascination with glitter and understand that the planet works as a biological system.

79. Which of the following is the *most crucial and logical Inference* that can be made from the above passage?
    (a) The Earth can meet *only* the basic needs of humans for food, clothing and shelter.
    (b) The only way to meet environmental challenge is to limit human population.
    (c) Reducing our consumerism is very much in our own interest.
    (d) Knowledge of biological systems can *only* help us save this planet.

### Passage-4

Some people belive that leadership is a quality which you have at birth or not at all. This theory is false, for the art of leadership can be acquired and can indeed be taught. This discovery is made in time of war and the results achieved can surprise even the instructors. Faced with the alternatives of going left or right, every soldier soon grasps that a prompt decision either way is better than an endless discussion. A firm choice for direction has an even chance of being right while to do nothing will be almost certainly wrong.

80. The author of the passage holds the view that
    (a) leadership can be taught through war experience only
    (b) leadership can be acquired as well as taught
    (c) the results of training show that more people acquire leadership than are expected
    (d) despite rigorous instruction few leaders are produced

# HINTS & SOLUTIONS

1. (d) According to the given graph, during mid of the August, actual progress was more than expected progress.

2. (a) Required number of ways $= \dfrac{6!}{3!} = 120$

3. (a) According to the graph, death rate is decreased faster than birth rate, therefore population growth rate has increased

4. (d) After 2005 birth rate and population growth has no change.

5. (c) We can see from graph slopes of both graphs are same

6. (a) We can consider each picture formed with an unique body (B) and an unique set of legs (L). Then

    First Row : $\dfrac{B_1}{L_1}\ \dfrac{B_2}{L_2}\ \dfrac{B_3}{L_3}$

    Second Row : $\dfrac{B_2}{L_3}\ \dfrac{B_3}{L_1}\ \dfrac{B_1}{L_2}$

    Third Row : $\dfrac{B_2}{L_3}\ \dfrac{B_1}{L_3}\ \left(\dfrac{B_2}{L_1} = \text{■}\right)$

7. (a) Manufacturing cost of 1000 pieces $= 600000$
    Cost of 1 piece when 1000 pieces manufactured
    $= \dfrac{600000}{1000} = 600$
    Selling price of 1 piece when 1000 pieces manufactured $= 400$
    Manufacturing cost of 2000 pieces $= 700000$
    Cost of 1 piece when 2000 pieces manufactured
    $= \dfrac{700000}{2000} = 350$
    Selling price of 1 piece when 2000 pieces manufactured

    $= 350$
    Hence, required number of pieces $= 2000$

8. (b) 18 Adults $= 30$ children (given)
    3 Adults $= 5$ children $\therefore$ 1 adult $= \dfrac{5}{3}$ children
    12 Adults $+ x$ children $= 18$ Adults
    $12 \times \dfrac{5}{3}$ children $+ x$ children $= 18 \times \dfrac{5}{3}$ children
    $x = 10$ children

9. (d) Amount to be paid after 1 year
    $= 22800 + 22800 \times \dfrac{12.5}{100} = 22800 + 2850 = 25650$
    He paid 8650 then amount left
    $= 25650 - 8650 = 17000$
    Amount to be paid after 2 years
    $= 17000 + 17000 \times \dfrac{12.5}{100} = 17000 + 2125 = 19125$
    He paid 9125 at the end of 2nd year then remaining amount $= 19125 - 9125 = 10000$
    Amount to be paid at the end of 3rd year
    $= 10000 + 10000 \times \dfrac{12.5}{100} = 11250$

10. (b) According to figure.
    Square element moves clockwise direction in each step and triangle element moves anticlockwise direction in each step.
    So, option (b) is correct answer.

11. (c) Dependency Ratio
    $$= \dfrac{\left(\begin{array}{c}\text{Sum of the number of people aged less}\\ \text{than is 15 years and more than 64 years}\end{array}\right)}{(\text{Number of people aged from 15 to 64 years})} \times 100$$

1.  In country B, over the last two and a half decades (2025 to 2050), the sum of the number of people aged less than 15 years and more than 64 years is slightly increased but number of people aged from 15 to 64 years increased tremendeously. Therefore dependency radio of country B has decreased over the last two and half decades.

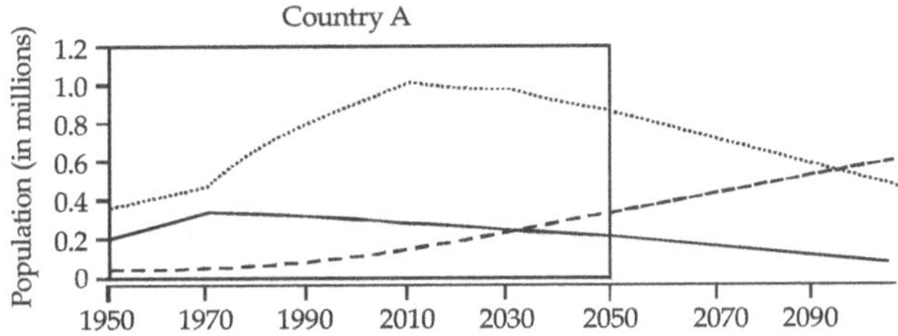


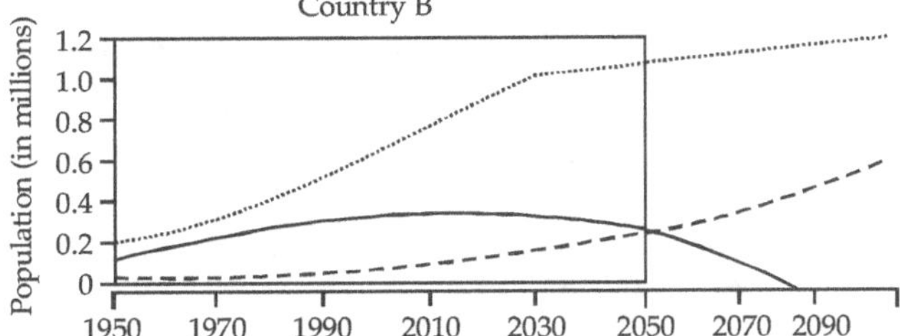


2.  By the end of next two and a half decades (i.e. 2075), sum of the number of people aged less than 15 years and more than 64 years of country A is more than that of country B where as number of people of aged from 15 to 64 years of country A is less than that of country B.
    Hence by the end of next two and a half decades, the dependency ratio of country A will be more than that of country B.

3.  In the next two decades (i.e. 2050-2070), graph of workforce (i.e. population of aged from 15 years to 64 years) of country A is going lower and that of country B is going higher.
    Therefore, in the next two decades, the work-force relative to its total population will increase in country B as compared to country A.

12. (d) Lakshmi herself is the best player

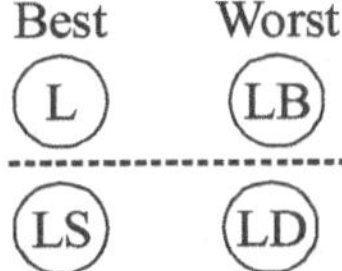


13. (d) Repo rate and reverse repo rate is directly related to Anti-inflationary stance

14. (d) According to the table tele-density is similar to others

15. (d) There are many points related to GDP of state and tele-density is similar to others according to table.

16. (a)
    1.  Corporate tax (......) and personal tax (-----) are direct taxes. From graph it is clear that corporate tax is increasing tremendeously whereas personal tax increased slightly.
        Exercise (——), customs (-·-·-) and service tax (-··-··-) are indirect taxes. From the graph, it is clear that exercise and customs decreased tremendeously whereas service tax is increased.

Therefore, during the given period, the revenue from direct taxes as percentage of gross tax revenue has increased while that of indirect taxes decreased.

2.  From the graph, it is clear that exercise duty is over all decreased tremendeously. But after 2010, exercise duty increases slightly. This traineds of exercise duty has many reasons. One of then may be decreasing rate of exercise duty to promote manufacturing sector thats why after 2010 exercise duty increases slightly.

17. (d) *Checking statement 1*
    $x - y = 8$
    Both $x$ and $y$ must be positive for any value of $x$ and $y$. It is not true because negative values of $x$ and $y$ or positive $x$ and negative $y$ is also possible
    *Checking statement 2*
    If $x$ is positive, $y$ must be negative for any value of $x$ and $y$.
    It is alos not true because positive values of $x$ and $y$ are also possible.
    *Checking statement 3*
    If $x$ is negative, $y$ must be positive for any value of $x$ and $y$.
    Here if $x$ is negative then only negative value of $y$ is possible.
    Hence, neithter 1 nor 2 nor 3

18. (d) Last few lines of the passage state that meat production through industrial farming is water - intensive; it requires 15000 litres of water for every kilogram of meat. We all are aware of the fact that many people in the world strive to get water to drink and for their household works and so, we can't afford to lose such huge amount of water on producing meat in farms thus, it can be said that environmental cost of meat production is unsustainable when it is produced through industrial farming.

19. (b) It is clearly mentioned in the last line of the passage.

20. (a) It is mentioned in the passage how a male tiger that was relocated in Panna National Park trekked toward its home 250 miles away; and that nearly a third of India's tigers live outside tiger reserves. These points indicate that though initiatives have been taken for the conservation of wildlife by relocating them, they have not been often successful. The passage does not say anything about any legistation in this regard.

21. (c) The passage clearly mentions that 'most countries' are 'striving' to address climate change threat. So, it is a complex policy issue and development issue for all. So, 1 is not valid but 2 is.
    Assumption 3 can be made from, 'the problem is more severe ........... finance development. So, the right option is (c).

22. (d) The passage states the fact that household air pollution is hazardous to health of the people living in poor areas to such an extent that more than 10 lakh premature deaths occur every year due to it So, it would be appropriate to say that the access to cooking gas can reduce premature deaths in poor households.

23. (c) It is clearly mentioned in the second sentence of the passage.

24. (b) It is mentioned in the last sentence of the passage that the distinct possibility of ice-free summer has

prompted countries with Arctic coastline to rush to get larger part of the Arctic which thereby leads to changes in the geopolitics.

25. (a) The passage conveys the facts that India provides food security to its poor which collides with its trade. But being a signatory of WTO, it has to revise its PDS, Option (b) is not conveyed.

26. (b) As per the last sentence of the passage, today's educational system is very different i.e. it is a complex, volatile and globally interconnected world; thus, in order to meet these, today's learners need to acquire new-age skill-sets. Assumptions 1 and 3 cannot be made from the passage.

27. (d) The passage conveys that individuals differ in many respects and 'we cannot reduce so many complexities' into one copybook diet plan. So, there is no perfect solution. Options (a), (b) and (c) mention only one aspect each of the discussion and none qualifies as a rational inference.

28. (a) Crop genetic diversification consists in raising a variety of crops depending on suitability to seasonal variations of rainfall and temperatures; and reduces susceptibility to natural disasters like flooding and windstorm, etc., in case of monoculture. Therefore, preserving crop diversity is an insurance against the effects of climate change. Sentence one declares that monoculture carries risk; so, (a) follows.

29. (c) Selling price of article = 40
Profit = x%

$$\text{Cost price} = 40 \times \frac{100}{100+x} = \frac{4000}{100+x}$$

Again
Selling price of article = 20
Loss = x%

$$\text{Cost price} = 20 \times \frac{100}{100-x} = \frac{2000}{100-x}$$

Now

$$\frac{4000}{100+x} = \frac{2000}{100-x}$$

$$\frac{100-x}{100+x} = \frac{1}{2}$$

$$\Rightarrow 100+x = 200-2x$$

$$\Rightarrow 3x = 100 \qquad \therefore x = 33\frac{1}{3}$$

$$\therefore \text{Cost price} = 40 \times \frac{100}{100+\dfrac{100}{3}} = 40 \times \frac{300}{400} = 30$$

30. (c) Each equilateral triangle is made by joining the three points as in the figure given below. Circle is divided into three sectors.

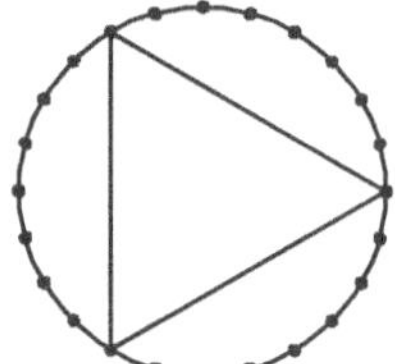

Hence, required number of triangles = $\dfrac{24}{3} = 8$

31. (b) Each next date is given in the series is comes after 28 days from previous date.
Hence next date = 26/2/96 + 28 days = 25/3/96

32. (c) Diagonal of rectangle = 5 cm

$$\sqrt{l^2+b^2} = 5$$

then velue of $l$ and $b$ must be 4 and 3
Area of ractangle = $4 \times 3 = 12$ cm$^2$
Area of square be $a^2$
$12 \times a^2 = 12 \therefore a^2 = 1$

33. (c) Total import of sheet steel in first three months
$= 40+37+36 = 113$
Total import of coil steel in first three months
$= 30+31+33 = 94$
Required velue = $113 - 94 = 19$.

34. (c) Total sheet steel important over six months period
$= 40+37+36+36+34+34 = 217$
Total value = $217 \times 256 = 55552 \approx 55550$

35. (b) Total sheet steel imported in first three months
$= 40+37+36 = 113$
Total scrap steel imported in first three months
$= 32+34+32 = 98$
Required ratio = $113 : 98 = 1.2:1$

**Sol. (36-38)**

36. (b) We can see line, two dots toward one end of the line and three dots toward other end of the line.

37. (c) We can see, two dots, and four dots are on opposite faces.

38. (c) Line and cross are on opposite faces

39. (c) The opening line of the passage says that 'universal access to education' is no longer enough. So, 1 is not of paramount importance. The second sentence says that 'facilities' or infrastructure is a prerequisite but 'insufficient' to fulfil the purpose of education So, 2 is not of paramount importance.
3 is mentioned in the second paragraph as being of paramount importance.

40. (d) Assumption 1 can be made from the sentence, 'Teacher accountability systems...
Assumption 2 follows from 'universal access to education' in the opening line.
Assumption 3 follows from, 'we must address the entire gamut ...,' which implies that India's 'demographic dividend' or 'huge young population across diversities' could be tapped.

41. (d) It is clearly mentioned in the first half of the second paragraph of the passage.

42. (c) The entire passage emphasises on giving quality education to all children. Options (a), (b) and (d) are true, but none conveys the essential message of the passage.

43. (b) For easily count the number of triangles in the given three-dimensional figure, devide the given figure into three parts-top, bottom and middle.
In each of the top and bottom part, there are 5 triangles which are based on a pentagon. In middle part, there are 5 quadrilaterals inclosed between two pentagons. Further each quadrilateral is divided into two triangles. Hence in the middle part, there are 10 triangles.

$\therefore$ Total number of triangles in the given 3D-figure.
= (No. of triangles in top part) + (No. of triangle in bottom part) + (No. of triangle in middle part)
$= 5+5+10 = 20$

44. (d) According to pattern,
when $* = 8$ then,
$8 + 18 + 28 + 83 + 81 = 218$
So, option (d) is correct answer.

45. (a) According to question
As, $(8 + 4) - 6 = 6$
$(10 + 6) - 5 = 11$
$(15 + 8) - 7 = 16$
So, $(13 + 8) - 4 = 17$

46. (a) Number of diagonals in an octagon $= {}^8C_2 - 8$
$$= \frac{8 \times 7}{2} - 8 = 20$$

47. (c) Required Ratio $= \dfrac{1/2\,(\text{PL}) \cdot (\text{OL})}{(\text{OC}) \cdot (\text{OL})} = \dfrac{\text{PL}}{2\,(\text{OC})}$

$$= \frac{\text{PL}}{2 \times \dfrac{2}{3}\,\text{PL}} = \frac{3}{4} = 3 : 4$$

48. (d) Length of train = distance = 200 m

Speed of train $= 40 \times \dfrac{5}{18} = \dfrac{100}{9}$ m/s

Required time $= 200 \div \dfrac{100}{9} = 18$ sec

49. (b) It is stated in the passage that presently, around 47 percent of India's population is dependent on agriculture and it is also expected that around 2030, nearly 42 percent of India's population will still be predominantly dependent on agriculture. Therefore, considering these large percentages, it can be inferred that Indian economy greatly depends on its agriculture.

50. (a) It can be inferred from the line ... rapid globalisation of food... and trace? of the passage.

51. (b) The author states that there are some questions that science cannot really answer while faith provides a better path to answer. Thus, it can be inferred that science and faith can be mutually complementary if their proper domains are understood. Moreover, rest of the options apart from option (b) are irrelevant in the context of the passage.

52. (d) It can be inferred from the first sentence of the passage especially from the part ' India should rid herself ..........development of the body and the spirit'.

53. (b) Let unit digit be $x$ and hundred's digit be y
Number $= x \times 1 + 0 \times 10 + y \times 100 = x + 100\,y$
Aste interchange of digits number $= y \times 1 + 100 \times x = 100\,x + y$
According to the question
$100x + y - x - 100y = 198$
$99\,(x - y) = 198$
$\therefore\ x - y = 2$
Hence disterence = 2

54. (a) Each small cube lying at the middle of each edge of the large cube has exactly two painted faces.
Since there are 12 faces in the given large cube therefore there are exactly 12 small cubes which have exactly two painted faces.

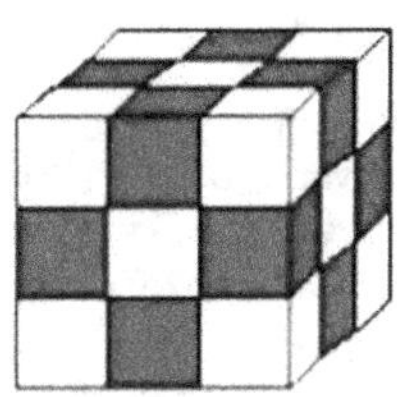

**12 edge cubes**

55. (c)

| Hundred Digit | Corresponding Ten's Digit | Corresponding Unit's Digit | |
|---|---|---|---|
| 7 | 1 | 0 | |
| | 2 | 0, 1 | |
| | 3 | 0, 1, 2 | |
| | 4 | 0, 1, 2, 3 | 21 |
| | 5 | 0, 1, 2, 3, 4 | |
| | 6 | 0, 1, 2, 3, 4, 5 | |
| 8 | 1 | 0 | |
| | 2 | 0, 1 | |
| | 3 | 0, 1, 2 | |
| | 4 | 0, 1, 2, 3 | 28 |
| | 5 | 0, 1, 2, 3, 4 | |
| | 6 | 0, 1, 2, 3, 4, 5 | |
| | 7 | 0, 1, 2, 3, 4, 5, 6 | |
| 9 | 1 | 0 | |
| | 2 | 0, 1 | |
| | 3 | 0, 1, 2 | |
| | 4 | 0, 1, 2, 3 | |
| | 5 | 0, 1, 2, 3, 4 | 36 |
| | 6 | 0, 1, 2, 3, 4, 5 | |
| | 7 | 0, 1, 2, 3, 4, 5, 6 | |
| | 8 | 0, 1, 2, 3, 4, 5, 6, 7 | |

So, total numbers $= 21 + 28 + 36 = 85$

56. (b) According to question.
Pen < Pencil < Book > Cap
So, Pen < Book is always true.

57. (b) Total price of geography textbooks $= a \times x = ₹\,ax$
Total price of History textbooks $= (a + 2)\,(x + 2)$
$= ax + 2a + 2x + 4$
Total Price of Mathematics text books $(a - 2)\,(x - 2)$
$= ax - 2a - 2x + 4$
Total price $= ax + ax + 2a + 2x + 4 + ax - 2a - 2x + 4 = 3ax + 8$

58. (b) Total number of balls $15 + 20 = 35$
Total number of red balls numbered 3
$$= 15 \times \left(\frac{100 - 20 - 40}{100}\right) = 15 \times \frac{40}{100} = 6$$

Total number of black ball numbered 1 or 2
$$= 20 \times \left(\frac{100 - 30}{100}\right) = 20 \times \frac{70}{100} = 14$$

Required chances $= \dfrac{6+14}{35} = \dfrac{4}{7}$

59. (a) B is $30°$ head to A
Total angle covered by A $=180°$
Total angle covered by B $= 180°–30° = 150°$
Required ratio $= 180° : 150 = 6 : 5$

60. (c) Total passing marks $= 30 + 30 = 60$
Percentage of passing marks $= 40\%$
Let total marks be $x$
According to the question

$$x \times \dfrac{40}{100} = 60$$

$$\therefore \ x = \dfrac{60 \times 100}{40} = 150$$

61. (c)

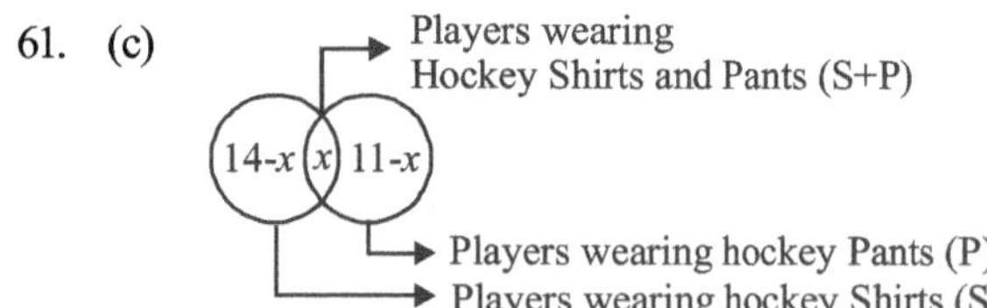


Using venn diagram the given information can be representd as follows:
Let the number of players wearing both hockey shirt and pant be $x$
$\therefore$ n (st+1p) $= x$, n (s) $= 14 – x$
$n$ (p) $= 11 – x$
$n$ (T) $= 19$ ($\therefore$ T = Total number of players)
$\therefore$ $n$ (T) $= n$ (s) $+ n$ (p) $+ n$ (S + P)
$\therefore$ $19 = 14 – x + 11 – x + x$
$\therefore$ $19 = 25 – x$
$\therefore$ $x = 25 – 19 = 6$

Sol. (62– 67):

| Students | Cities | Colleges | States |
| --- | --- | --- | --- |
| A | P/R | Commerce | Gujarat |
| B | Q | Sciences | Kerala |
| C | S | Arts | Rajasthan |
| D | P/R | Engineering | Assam |

62. (b) 63. (a) 64. (b) 65. (a) 66. (d) 67. (a)

68. (a)
As,                                Similarly,

L   S   J   X   V   C           C   C   I   D   D
+1  +2  +3  +4  +5  +6          +1  +2  +3  +4  +5
M   U   M   B   A   I           D   E   L   H   I

69. (b)
As,
R   A   M   O   N           D   I   N   E   S   H
1   2   3   4   5    and     6   7   5   8   4   9

Similarly,
H   A   M   A   M
9   2   3   2   3

70. (d) $–3 < X < –1$     $\Rightarrow 1 < X^2 < 9$
$–1 < Y < 1$     $\Rightarrow 0 < Y^2 < 1$

Min $(X^2 – Y^2) = \min (X^2) – \max (Y^2) = 1 – 1 = 0$
Max $(X^2 – Y^2) = \max (X^2) – \min (Y^2) = 9 – 0 = 9$
$\therefore \ \ 0 < (X^2 – Y^2) < 9$

71. (a) Let X $= 6$, Y $= 8$, then

(a) 48     (b) $\dfrac{3}{4}$     (c) $\dfrac{4}{3}$     (d) $\dfrac{7}{24}$

Sol. (72-73)

```
        D   A   F
        ↓   ↓   ↓
      ┌─────────────┐
  →   │  Corridor   │
Entrance└───────────┘
        ↑   ↑   ↑
        C   E   B
```

72. (c)          73. (a)

74. (d) All the given options are the consequences of decline in forest cover; these can be inferred from the following lines of the passage – "leading to total loss of productivity", "accelerated erosion as in the mountain regions of the country", "adverse alterations in the hydrology and related soil and nutrient losses" and "drying up of the underground springs and smaller rivers in the Himalayan region........".

75. (a) Statement 1 can be drawn from the sentence, 'The current.....and the changing course of the river system'. The sentence, 'Impoverishment of human-impacted...salinization of land...' does not clarify that only human activities cause salinisation of soil. There may be natural causes too. The passage mentions that Tropical Asia, Africa and South America have the highest levels of erosion as a consequence of deforestation. Monoculture is mentioned only in the context of Indian plains.
So, only statement 1 is a correct inference.

76. (b) Assumption 1 is invalid with reference to the line, 'while this phenomenon .... dramatic' which indicates that the phenomenon is not limited to the tropical areas.
Assumption 2 is valid as the passage mentions 'desertification' and 'inundation' as the effects of deforestation.

77. (b) All the points are mentioned in the passage except point 3; these can be inferred from the following lines of the passage – "Accelerated breeding programs are needed to conserve a wider pool of genetic resources of existing crops", "Relatively intact ecosystem, such as forest catchments, mangroves, wetlands....." and "Connections between natural areas, such as migration corridors...".

78. (b) It can be assumed from the discussion of 'monoculture' in the first half of the passage.

79. (c) It can be inferred from the line "If the aspirations are more like the frugal ones we had after the Second World War, a lot more is possible than if we view the planet as a giant shopping mall".

80. (b) It is clearly mentioned in the passage in the line "This theory is false, for the art of leadership can be acquired and can indeed be taught".

# IAS PRELIMS SOLVED PAPER-2 2017

**DIRECTIONS for the following 8 (eight) item :** Read the following eight passages and answer the items that follow the passages. Your answers to these items should be based on the passages only.

## PASSAGE-1

What climate change will undeniably do is cause or amplify events that hasten the reduction of resources. Competition over these diminishing resources would ensue in the form of political or even violent conflict. Resource-based conflicts have rarely been overt and are thus difficult to isolate. Instead they take on veneers that appear more politically palatable. Conflicts over resources like water are often cloaked in the guise of identity or ideology.

1. What does the above passage imply?
   (a) Resource-based conflicts are always politically motivated.
   (b) There are no political solutions to resolve environmental and resource based conflicts.
   (c) Environmental issues contribute to resource stresses and political conflicts.
   (d) Political conflicts based on identity or ideology cannot be resolved.

## PASSAGE-2

The man who is perpetually hesitating which of the two things he will do first, will do neither. The man who resolves, but suffers his resolution to be changed by the first counter-suggestion of a friend-who fluctuates from opinion to opinion and veers from plan to plan-can never accomplish anything. He will at best be stationary and probably retrograde in all. It is only the man who first consults wisely, then resolves firmly and then executes his purpose with inflexible perseverance, undismayed by those petty difficulties which daunt a weaker spirit-that can advance to eminence in any line.

2. The keynote that seems to be emerging from the passage is that
   (a) we should first consult wisely and then resolve firmly
   (b) we should reject suggestions of friends and remain unchanged
   (c) we should always remain broad-minded
   (d) we should be resolute and achievement-oriented

## PASSAGE-3

During the summer in the Arctic Ocean, sea ice has been melting earlier and faster. and the Winter freeze has been coming later. In the last three decades, the extent of summer ice has declined by about 30 per cent. The lengthening period of summer melt threatens to undermine the whole Arctic food web, atop which stand polar bears.

3. Which among the following is the most crucial message conveyed by the above passage?
   (a) Climate change has caused Arctic summer to be short but temperature to be high.
   (b) Polar bears can be shifted to South Pole to ensure their survival.
   (c) Without the presence of polar bears, the food chains in Arctic region will disappear.
   (d) Climate change poses a threat to the survival of polar bears.

## PASSAGE-4

Why do people prefer open defecation and not want toilets or, if they have them, only use them so metimes? Recent research has shown two critical elements : ideas of purity and pollution, and not wanting pits or septic tanks to fill because they have to be emptied. These are the issues that nobody wants to talk about, but if we want to eradicate the practice of open defecation, they have to be confronted and dealt properly.

4. Which among the following is the most crucial message conveyed by the above passage?
   (a) The ideas of purity and pollution are so deep-rooted that they cannot be removed from the minds of the people.
   (b) People have to perceive toilet use and pit-emptying as clean and not polluting.
   (c) People cannot change their old habits.
   (d) People have neither civic sense nor sense of privacy.

## PASSAGE-5

In the last two decades, the world's gross domestic product (GDP) has increased by 50 per cent, whereas inclusive wealth has increased by a mere 6 per cent. In recent decades, GDP-driven economic performance has only harmed inclusive wealth like human capital; and natural capital like forests, land and water. While the world's human capital which stands at 57 per cent of total inclusive wealth grew by only 8 per cent, the natural capital which is 23 per cent of total inclusive wealth declined by 30 per cent worldwide in the last two decades.

5. Which of the following is the most crucial inference from the above passage?
   (a) More emphasis should be laid on the development of natural capital.
   (b) The growth driven by GDP only is neither desirable nor sustainable.
   (c) The economic performance of the countries of the world is not satisfactory.
   (d) The world needs more human capital under the present circumstances.

## PASSAGE-6

By 2020, when the global economy is expected to run short of 56 million young people, India, with its youth surplus of 47 million, could fill the gap. It is in this context that labour reforms are often cited as the way to unlock double-digit growth in India. In 2014, India's labour force was estimated to be about 40 per cent of the population, but 93 per cent of this force was in unorganized sector. Over the last decade, the compound annual growth rate (CAGR) of employment has slowed to 0.5 percent, with about 14 million jobs created during last year when the labour force increased by about 15 million.

6. Which of the following is the most rational inference from the above passage?
   (a) India must control its population growth so as to reduce in unemployment rate.
   (b) Labour reforms are required in India to make optimum use of its vast labour force productively.
   (c) India is poised to achieve the double-digit growth very soon.
   (d) India is capable of supplying the skilled young people to other countries.

## PASSAGE-7

The very first lesson that should be taught to us when we are of enough to understand it, is that complete freedom from the obligation to work is unnatural, and ought to be illegal, as we can escape our share of the burden of work only by throwing it on someone else's shoulders. Nature ordains that the human race shall perish of famine if it stops working. We cannot escape from this tyranny. The question we have to settle is how much leisure we can afford to allow ourselves.

7. The main idea of the passage is that
   (a) it is essential for human beings to work
   (b) there should be a balance between work and leisure
   (c) working is a tyranny which we have to face
   (d) human's understanding of the nature of work is essential

## PASSAGE-8

There is no harm in cultivating habits so long as they are not injurious. Indeed, most of us are little more than bundle of habits. Take away our habits and the residuum would hardly be worth bothering about. We could not get on without them. They simplify the mechanism of life. They enable us to do a multitude of things automatically, which, if we had to give fresh and original thought to them each time, would make existence an impossible confusion.

8. The author suggests that habits
   (a) tend to make our lives difficult
   (b) add precision to our lives
   (c) make it easier for us to live
   (d) tend to mechanize our lives

---

**DIRECTIONS for the following 2 (two) items :** Consider the given information and answer the **two items** that follow.

---

No supporters of 'party X', who knew Z and supported his campaign strategy, agreed for the alliance with 'party Y'; but some of them had friends in 'party Y'.

9. With reference to the above information, which one among the following statements must be true?
   (a) Some supporters of 'party Y' did not agree for the alliance with the 'party X'.
   (b) There is at least one supporter of 'party Y' who knew some supporters of 'party X' as a friend.
   (c) No supporters of 'party X' supported Z's campaign strategy.
   (d) No supporters of 'party X' knew Z.

10. With reference to the above information, consider the following statements :
    1. Some supporters of 'party X' knew Z.
    2. Some supporters of 'party X', who opposed Z's campaign strategy, knew Z.
    3. No supporters of 'party X' supported Z 'S campaign strategy.
    Which of the statements given above is/are **not** correct?
    (a) 1 only           (b) 2 and 3 only
    (c) 3 only           (d) 1, 2 and 3

11. If second and fourth Saturdays and all the Sundays are taken as only holidays for an office, what would be the minimum number of possible working days of any month of any year?
    (a) 23               (b) 22
    (c) 21               (d) 20

12. If there is a policy that 1 / 3rd of a population of a community has migrated every year from one place to some other place, what is the leftover population of that community after the sixth year, if there is no further growth in the population during this period?
    (a) 16/243rd part of the population
    (b) 32/243rd part of the population
    (c) 32 / 729th part of the population
    (d) 64/ 729th part of the population

13. Four tests-Physics, Chemistry, Mathematics and Biology are to be conducted on four consecutive days, not necessarily in the same order. The Physics test is held before the test which is conducted after Biology. Chemistry is conducted exactly after two tests are held. Which is the last test held?
    (d) Physics          (b) Biology
    (c) Mathematics      (d) Chemistry

14. The sum of income of A and B is more than that of C and D taken together. The sum of income of A and C is the same as that of B and D taken together. Moreover, A earns half as much as the sum of the income of B and D. Whose income is the highest?
    (a) A                (b) B
    (c) C                (d) D

15. Consider the following :
    Statement :
    Good voice is a natural gift but one has to keep practising to improve and excel well in the field of music.
    Conclusions :
    1. Natural gifts need nurturing and care.
    II. Even though one's voice is not good, one can keep practising.
    Which one of the following is correct in respect of the above statement and conclusions?
    (a) Only conclusion I follows from the statement.
    (b) Only conclusion II follows from the statement.
    (c) Either conclusion I or conclusion II follows from the statement.
    (d) Neither conclusion I nor conclusion II follows from the statement.

16. There are three pillars, X, Y and Z of different heights. Three spiders A, B and C start to climb on these pillars simultaneously. In one chance. A climbs on X by 6cm but slips down 1 cm. B climbs on Y by 7 cm but slips down 3 cm. C climbs on Z by 6.5 cm but slips down 2 cm. If each of the requires 40 chances to reach the top of the pillars, what is the height of the shortest pillar?
    (a) 161 cm           (b) 163 cm
    (c) 182 cm           (d) 210 cm

17. "Rights are certain advantageous conditions of social well-being indispensable to the true development of the citizen." In the light of this statement, which one of the following is the correct understanding of rights?
    (a) Rights aim at individual good only.
    (b) Rights aim at social good only.
    (c) Rights aim at both individual and social good.
    (d) Rights aim at individual good devoid of social well-being.

18. 15 students failed in a class of 52. After removing the names of failed students, a merit order list has been prepared in which the position of Ramesh is 22nd from the top. What is his position from the bottom?
    (a) 18th             (b) 17th
    (c) 16th             (d) 15th

19. Consider the following :
    A+ B means A is the son of B.
    A− B means A is the wife of B.
    What does the expression P + R - Q mean?

    (a)   Q is the son of P.     (b)   Q is the wife of P.
    (c)   Q is the father of P.   (d)   None of the above

20. Gopal bought a cell phone and sold it to Ram at 10% profit. Then Ram wanted to sell it back to Gopal at 10% loss. What will be Gopal's position if he agreed?
    (a)   Neither loss nor gain   (b)   Loss 1%
    (c)   Gain 1%          (d)   Gain 0.5%

---

**DIRECTIONS for the following 7 (seven) items :** Read the following seven passages and answer the items that follow the passages. Your answers to these items should be based on the passages only.

---

### PASSAGE-1

We have hard work ahead. There is no resting for any of us till we redeem our pledge in full, till we make all the people of India what destiny intends them to be. We are citizens of a great country, on the verge of bold advance, and we have to live up to that high standard. All of us, to whatever religion we may belong are equally the children of India with equal rights, privileges and obligations. We cannot encourage communalism or narrowmindedness, for no nation can be great whose people are narrow in thought or action.

21. The challenge the author of the above passage throws to the public is to achieve.
    (a)   a high standard of living, progress and privileges
    (b)   equal privileges, fulfilment of destiny and political tolerance
    (c)   spirit of adventure and economic parity
    (d)   hard work, brotherhood and national unity

### PASSAGE-2

"The individual, according to Rousseau, parts his person and all his power in common under the supreme direction of the General will and in our corporate capacity we receive each member as an indivisible part of the whole."

22. In the light of the above passage, the nature of General Will is **best described** as
    (a)   the sum total of the private wills of the individuals
    (b)   what is articulated by the elected representatives of the individuals
    (c)   the collective good as distinct from private wills of the individuals
    (d)   the material interests of the community

### PASSAGE-3

In a democratic State, where a high degree of political maturity of the people obtains, the conflict between the will of the sovereign law- making body and the organized will of the people seldom occurs.

23. What does the above passage imply?
    (a)   In a democracy, force is the main phenomenon in the actual exercise of sovereignty.
    (b)   In a mature democracy, force to a great extent is the main phenomenon in the actual exercise of sovereignty.
    (c)   In a mature democracy, use of force is irrelevant in the actual exercise of sovereignty.
    (d)   In a mature democracy, force is narrowed down to a marginal phenomenon in the actual exercise of sovereignty.

### PASSAGE-4

A successful democracy depends upon widespread interest and participation in politics, in which voting is an essential part. To deliberately refrain from taking such an interest, and from voting, is a kind of implied anarchy; it is to refuse one's political responsibility while enjoying the benefits of a free political society.

24. This passage relates to
    (a)   duty to vote
    (b)   right to vote
    (c)   freedom to vote
    (d)   right to participate in politics

### PASSAGE-5

In a free country, the man who reaches the position of leader is usually one of outstanding character and ability. Moreover, it is usually possible to foresee that he will reach such a position, since early in life one can see his qualities of character. But this is not always true in the case of a dictator, often he reaches his position of power through chance, very often through the unhappy state of his country.

25. The passage seems to suggest that
    (a)   a leader foresees his future position
    (b)   a leader is chosen only by a free country
    (c)   a leader must see that his country is free from despair
    (d)   despair in a country sometimes leads to dictatorship

### PASSAGE-6

The greatest blessing that technological progress has in store for mankind is not, of course, an accumulation of material possessions. The amount of these that can be effectively enjoyed by one individual in one lifetime is not great. But there is not the same narrow limit to the possibilities of the enjoyment of leisure. The gift of leisure may be abused by people who have had no experience of making use of it. Yet the creative use of leisure by a minority in societies has been the mainspring of all human progress beyond the primitive level.

26. With reference to the above passage, the following assumptions have been made:
    1.   People always see the leisure time as a gift and use it for acquiring more material possessions.
    2.   Use of leisure by some people to produce new and original things has been the chief source of human progress.

Which of these assumptions is/are valid?
    (a)   1 only         (b)   2 only
    (c)   Both 1 and 2    (d)   Neither 1 nor 2

### PASSAGE-7

There is more than a modicum of truth in the assertion that 'a working knowledge of ancient history is necessary to the intelligent interpretation of current events". But the sage who uttered these words of wisdom might well have added something on the benefits of studying particularly the famous battles of history for the lessons they contain for those of as who lead or aspire to leadership. Such a study will reveal certain qualities and attributes which enabled the winners to win-and certain deficiencies which caused the losers to lose. And the student will see that the same pattern recurs consistently, again and again, throughout the centuries.

27. With reference to the above passage, the following assumptions have been made :
    1.   A study of the famous battles of history would help us understand the modern warfare.
    2.   Studying the history is essential for anyone who aspires to be a leader.

Which of these assumptions is/are valid?
    (a)   1 only         (b)   2 only
    (c)   Both 1 and 2    (d)   Neither 1 nor 2

28. Suppose the average weight of 9 persons is 50 kg. The average weight of the first 5 persons is 45 kg, whereas the

average weight of the last 5 persons is 55 kg, Then the weight of the 5th person will be
- (a) 45 kg
- (b) 47.5 kg
- (c) 50 kg
- (d) 52.5 kg

29. In a group of six women, there are four tennis players, four postgraduates in Sociology, one postgraduate in Commerce and three bank employees. Vimala and Kamla are the bank employees while Amala and Komala are unemployed. Komala and Nimala are among the tennis players. Amala, Kamla, Komala and Nirmala are postgraduates in Sociology of whom two are bank employees. If Shyamala is a postgraduate in Commerce, who among the following is both a tennis player and a bank employee?
- (a) Amala
- (b) Komala
- (c) Nirmala
- (d) Shyamala

30. $P = (40\%$ of $A) + (65\%$ of $B)$ and $Q = (50\%$ of $A) + (50\%$ of $B)$, where A is greater than B.
  In this context, which of the following statements is correct?
- (a) P is greater than Q.
- (b) Q is greater than P.
- (c) P is equal to Q.
- (d) None of the above can be concluded with certainty.

31. A watch loses 2 minutes in every 24 hours. while another watch gains 2 minutes in every 24 hours. At a particular instant, the two watches showed an identical time. Which of the following statements is correct if 24-hour clock is followed?
- (a) The two watches show the identical time again on completion of 30 days.
- (b) The two watches show the identical time again on completion of 90 days.
- (c) The two watches show the identical time again on completion of 120 days.
- (d) None of the above statements is correct.

32. In a city, 12% of households earn less than ₹ 30,000 per year, 6% households earn more than ₹ 2,00,000 per year, 22% households earn more than ₹1,00,000 per year and 990 house-holds earn between ₹ 30,000 and ₹ 1,00,000 per year. How many households cam between ₹ 1,00,000 and ₹ 2,00,000 per year?
- (a) 250
- (b) 240
- (c) 230
- (d) 225

33. A clock strikes once at 1o'clock, twice at 2o'clock and thrice at 3 o'clock, and so on. If it takes 12 seconds to strike at 5 o'clock, what is the time taken by it to strike at 10 o'clock?
- (a) 20 seconds
- (b) 24 seconds
- (c) 28 seconds
- (d) 30 seconds

34. Consider the given statement and the two conclusions that follow:
  Statement:
  Morning walk is good for health.
  Conclusions:
  1. All healthy people go for morning walk.
  2. Morning walk is essential for maintaining good health.
  What is/are the valid conclusion/ conclusions?
- (a) 1 only
- (b) 2 only
- (c) Both 1 and 2
- (d) either 1 nor 2

35. There are thirteen 2-digit consecutive odd numbers. If 39 is the mean of the first five such numbers, then what is the mean of all the thirteen numbers?
- (a) 47
- (b) 49
- (c) 51
- (d) 45

36. Six boys A, B, C, D, E and F play a game of cards. Each has a pack of 10 cards. F borrows 2 cards from A and gives away 5 to C who in turn gives 3 to 8 while B gives 6 to D who passes on 1 to E. Then the number of cards possessed by D and E is equal to the number of cards possessed by
- (a) A, B and C
- (b) B, C and F
- (c) A, B and F
- (d) A, C and F

37. There is a milk sample with 50% water in it. If 1/3rd of this milk is added to equal amount of pure milk, then water in the new mixture will fall down to
- (a) 25%
- (b) 30%
- (c) 35%
- (d) 40%

38. There are 4 horizontal and 4 vertical lines, parallel and equidistant to one another on a board. What is the maximum number of rectangles and squares that can be formed?
- (a) 16
- (b) 24
- (c) 36
- (d) 42

39. A freight train left Delhi for Mumbai at an average speed of 40 km/hr. Two hours later, an express train left Delhi for Mumbai, following the freight train on a parallel track at an average speed of 60 kin/hr. How far from Delhi would the express train meet the freight train?
- (a) 480 km
- (b) 260 km
- (c) 240 km
- (d) 120 km

40. In a test, Randhir obtained more marks than the total marks obtained by Kunal and Debu. The total marks obtained by Kunal and Shankar are more than those of Randhir. Sonal obtained more marks than Shankar, Neha obtained more marks than Randhir. Who amongst them obtained highest marks?
- (a) Randhir
- (b) Neha
- (c) Sonal
- (d) Data are inadequate

**DIRECTIONS for the following 8 (eight) items :** Read the following seven passages and answer the items that follow the passages. Your answers to these items should be based on the passages only.

## PASSAGE-1

Disruption of traditional institutions, identifications and loyalties is likely to lead to ambivalent situations. It is possible that some people may renew their identification with traditional groups whereas others align themselves with new groups and symbols emergent from processes of political development. In addition, political development tends to foster group awareness of a variety of class, tribe, region, clan, language, religion, occupation and others.

41. Which one of the following is the best explanation of the above passage?
- (a) Political development is not a unilinear process for it involves both growth and decay.
- (b) Traditional societies succeed in resisting positive aspects of political development.
- (c) It is impossible for traditional societies to break away from lingering loyalties.
- (d) Sustenance of traditional loyalties is conducive to political development.

## PASSAGE-2

There has been a significant trend worldwide towards regionalism in government, resulting in a widespread transfer of powers downwards towards regions and communities since 1990s. This process, which involves the creation of new political entities and bodies at a sub-national level and an increase in their content and powers, is known as devolution. Devolution has been characterized as being made up of three factors--political legitimacy, decentralization of authority and decentralization of resources. Political legitimacy here means a mass demand from below for the decentralization process, which is able to create a political force for it to take place. In many cases, decentralization is initiated by the upper tier of government without sufficient political mobilization for it at the grassroots level, and in such cases the decentralization process often does not fulfil its objectives.

42. Which among the following is the most logical, rational and critical inference that can be made from the above passage?
    (a) Emergence of powerful mass leaders is essential to create sub-national political entities and thus ensure successful devolution and decentralization.
    (b) The upper tier of government should impose devolution and decentralization on the regional communities by law or otherwise.
    (c) Devolution, to be successful, requires a democracy in which there is free expression of the will of the people at lower level and their active participation at the grass roots level.
    (d) For devolution to take place, a strong feeling of regionalism in the masses is essential.

### PASSAGE-3

We live in digital times. The digital is not just something we use strategically and specifically to do a few tasks. Our very perception of who we are, how we connect to the world around us, and the ways in which we define our domains of life, labour and language are hugely structured by the digital technologies. The digital is everywhere and, like air, invisible. We live within digital systems, we live with intimate gadgets, we interact through digital media, and the very presence and imagination of the digital has dramatically restructured our lives. The digital, far from being a tool, is a condition and context that defines the shapes and boundaries of our understanding of the self, the society, and the structure of governance.

43. Which among the following is the most logical and essential message conveyed by the above passage?
    (a) All problems of governance can be solved by using digital technologies.
    (b) Speaking of digital technologies is speaking of our life and living.
    (c) Our creativity and imagination cannot be expressed without digital media.
    (d) Use of digital systems is imperative for the existence of mankind in future.

### PASSAGE-4

The IMF has pointed out that the fast growing economies of Asia face the risk of falling into 'middle-income trap'. It means that average incomes in these countries, which till now have been growing rapidly, will stop growing beyond a point-a point that is well short of incomes in the developed West. The IMF identifies a number of causes of middle-income trap-none of which is surprising-from infrastructure to weak institutions, to less than favourable macroeconomic conditions. But the broad, overall cause, says IMF, is a collapse in the growth of productivity.

44. Which among the following is the most logical, rational and critical inference that can be made from the above passage?
    (a) Once a country reaches middle-income stage, it runs the risk of falling productivity which leads to stagnant incomes.
    (b) Falling into middle-income trap is a general characteristic of fast growing economies.
    (c) There is no hope at all for emerging Asian economies to sustain the growth momentum.
    (d) As regards growth of productivity, the performance of Asian economies is not satisfactory.

### PASSAGE-5

An innovative India will be inclusive as tell as technologically advanced, improving it lives of all Indians. Innovation and R&D can mitigate increases in social inequality and relieve the pressures created by rapid urbanization. The growing divergence in productivity between agriculture and knowledge-intensive manufacturing and services threatens to increase income inequality. By encouraging India's R&D labs and universities to focus on the needs of poor people and by improving the ability of informal firms to absorb knowledge, an innovation and research agenda can counter this effect. Inclusive innovation can lower the costs of goods and services and create income-earning opportunities for the poor people.

45. Which among the following is the most logical and rational assumption that can be made from the above passage?
    (a) Innovation and R&.D is the only way to reduce rural to urban migration.
    (b) Every rapidly growing country needs to minimize the divergence between productivity in agriculture and other sectors.
    (c) Inclusive innovation and R&D can help create an egalitarian society.
    (d) Rapid urbanization takes place only when a country's economic growth is rapid.

### PASSAGE-6

Climate change is likely to expose a large number of people to increasing environmental risks forcing them to migrate. The international community is yet to recognize this new category of migrants. There is no consensus on the definition and status of climate refugees owing to the distinct meaning the term refugees carry under international laws. There are still gaps in understanding how climate change will work as the root cause of migration. Even if there is recognition of climate refugees, who is going to provide protection? More emphasis has been given to international migration due to climate change. But there is a need to recognize the migration of such people within the countries also so that their problems can be addressed properly.

46. Which of the following is the most rational inference from the above passage?
    (a) The world will not be able to cope with large-scale migration of climate refugees.
    (b) We must find the ways and means to stop further climate change.
    (c) Climate change will be the most important reason for the migration of people in the future.
    (d) Relation between climate change and migration is not yet properly understood.

### PASSAGE-7

Many farmers use synthetic pesticides to kill infesting insects. The consumption of pesticides in some of the developed countries is touching 3000 grams/hectare. Unfortunately, there are reports that these compounds possess inherent toxicities that endanger the health of the farm operators, consumers and the environment. Synthetic pesticides are generally persistent in environment. Entering in food chain they destroy the microbial diversity and cause ecologcal imbalance. Their indiscriminate use has resulted in development of resistance among insects to insecticides, upsetting of balance in nature and resurgence of treated populations. Natural pest control using the botanical pesticides is safer to the user and the environment because they break down into harmless compounds within hours or days in the presence of sunlight Plants with pesticidal properties have been in nature for millions of years without any ill or adverse effects on the ecosystem. They are easily decomposed by many microbes common in most soils. They help in the maintenance of biological diversity of predators and the reduction of environmental contamination and human health hazards. Botanical pesticides formulated from plants are biodegradable and their use in crop protection is a practical sustainable alternative.

47. On the basis of the above passage, the following assumptions have been made :
   1. Synthetic pesticides should never be used in modern agriculture.
   2. One of the aims of sustainable agriculture is to ensure minimal ecological imbalance.
   3. Botanical pesticides are more effective as compared to synthetic pesticides.
   Which of the assumptions given above is/are correct?
   (a) 1 and 2 only      (b) 2 only
   (c) 1 and 3 only      (d) 1, 2 and3

48. Which of the following statements is/are correct regarding biopesticides?
   1. They are not hazardous to human health.
   2. They are persistent in environment.
   3. They are essential to maintain the biodiversity of any ecosystem.
   Select the correct answer using the code given below.
   (a) 1 only      (b) 1 and 2 only
   (c) 1 and 3 only      (d) 1, 2 and 3

49. Certain 3-digit numbers have the following characteristics :
   1. All the three digits are different.
   2. The number is divisible by 7.
   3. The number on reversing the digits is also divisible by 7.
   How many such 3-digit numbers are there?
   (a) 2      (b) 4
   (c) 6      (d) 3

50. Examine the following statements :
   1. All colours are pleasant.
   2. Some colours are pleasant.
   3. No colour is pleasant
   4. Some colours are not pleasant.
   Given that statement 4 is true, what can be de?nitely concluded?
   (a) 1 and 2 are true.      (b) 3 is true.
   (c) 2 is false.      (d) 1 is false.

51. How many numbers are there between 99 and 1000 such that the digit 8 occupies the units place?
   (a) 64      (b) 80
   (c) 90      (d) 104

52. If for a sample data
       Mean < Median < Mode
   then the distribution is
   (a) symmetric
   (b) skewed to the right
   (c) neither symmetric nor skewed
   (d) skewed to the left

53. The age of Mr. X last year was the square of a number and it would be the cube of a number next year. What is the least number of years he must wait for his age to become the cube of a number again ?
   (a) 42      (b) 38
   (c) 25      (d) 16

54. P works thrice as fast as Q, whereas P and Q together can work four times as fast as R. If P, Q and R together work on a job, in what ratio should they share the earnings ?
   (a) 3 : 1 : 1      (b) 3 : 2 : 4
   (c) 4 : 3 : 4      (d) 3 : 1 : 4

55. Consider the following relationships among members of a family of six persons A, B, C, D, E and F:
   1. The number of males equals that of females.
   2. A and E are sons of F.
   3. D is the mother of two, one boy and one girl.
   4. B is the son of A.
   5. There is only one married couple in the family at present.
   Which one of the can be drawn from following inferences the above?
   (a) A, B and C are all females.
   (b) A is the husband of D.
   (c) E and F are children of D.
   (d) D is the daughter of R

56. A bag contains 20 balls. 8 balls are green, 7 are white and 5 are red. What is the minimum number of balls that must be picked up from the bag blindfolded (without replacing any of it) to be assured of picking at least one ball of each colour?
   (a) 17      (b) 16
   (c) 13      (d) 11

57. If 2 boys and 2 girls are to be arranged in a row so that the girls are not next to each other, how many possible arrangements are there?
   (a) 3      (b) 6
   (c) 12      (d) 24

58. The outer surface of a 4 cm × 4 cm × 4 cm cube is painted completely in red. It is sliced parallel to the faces to yield sixty four 1cm × 1cm × 1cm small cubes. How many small cubes do not have painted faces?
   (a) 8      (b) 16
   (c) 24      (d) 36

59. Consider the following :
   A, B, C, D, E, F, G and H are standing in a row facing North.
   B is not neighbour of G.
   F is to the immediate right of G and neighbour of E.
   G is not at the extreme end.
   A is sixth to the left of E.
   H is sixth to the right of C.
   Which one of the following is correct in respect of the above?
   (a) C is to the immediate left of A.
   (b) D is immediate neighbour of B and F.
   (c) G is to the immediate right of D.
   (d) A and E are at the extreme ends.

60. In a certain code, '256' means 'red colour chalk', '589' means "green colour flower' and '254' means 'white colour chalk'. The digit in the code that indicates 'white' is
   (a) 2      (b) 4
   (c) 5      (d) 8

---

**DIRECTIONS for the following 7 (seven) item :** Read the following **seven passages** and answer the items that follow the passages. Your answers to these items should be based on the passages only.

## PASSAGE-1

An air quality index (AQI) is a way to combine measurements of multiple air pollutants into a single number or rating. This index is ideally kept constantly updated and available in different places The AQI is most useful when lots of pollution data are being gathered and when pollution levels are normally, but not always, low. In such cases, if pollution levels spike for a few days, the public can quickly take preventive action (like staying indoors) in response to an air quality warning. Unfortunately, that is not urban India. Pollution levels in many large Indian cities are so high that they remain well above any health or regulatory standard for large part of the year. If our index stays in the 'Red/Dangerous' region day after day, there is not much any one can do, other than getting used to ignoring it.

61.  Which among the following is the **most logical and rational inference** that can be made from the above passage?
     (a)  Our governments are not responsible enough to keep our cities pollution free.
     (b)  There is absolutely no need for air quality indices in our country.
     (c)  Air quality index is not helpful to the residents of many of our large cities.
     (d)  In every city, public awareness about pollution problems should increase.

## PASSAGE-2

Productive jobs are vital for growth and a good job is the best form of inclusion. More than half of our population depends on agriculture, but the experience of other countries suggests that the number of people dependent on agriculture will have to shrink if per capita incomes in agieulture are to go up substantially. While industry is creating jobs, too many such jobs are low-productivity non-contractual jobs in the unorganized sector, offering low incomes, little protection, and no benefits. Service jobs are relatively of high productivity, but employment growth in services has been slow in recent years.

62.  Which among the following is the **most logical and rational inference** that can be made from the above passage?
     (a)  We must create conditions for the faster growth of highly productive service jobs to ensure employment growth and inclusion."
     (b)  We must shift the farm workers to the highly productive manufacturing and service sectors to ensure the economic growth and inclusion.
     (c)  We must create conditions for the faster growth of productive jobs outside of agriculture even while improving the productivity of agriculture.
     (d)  We must emphasize the cultivation of high-yielding hybrid varieties and genetically modified crops to increase the per capita income in agriculture.

## PASSAGE-3

A landscape-scale approach to land use can encourage greater biodiversity outside protected areas. During hurricane 'Mitch' in 1998, farms using ecoagricultural practices suffered 58 per cent, 70 per cent and 99 per cent less damage in Honduras, Nicaragua and Guatemala, respectively, than farms using conventional techniques. In Costa Rica, vegetative windbreaks and fencerows boosted farmers' income from pasture and coffee while also increasing bird diversity. Bee pollination is more effective when agricultural fields are closer to natural or seminatural habitat, a finding that matters because 87 per cent of the world's 107 leading crops depend on animal pollinators. In Costa Rica, Nicaragua and Colombia silvopastoral systems that integrate trees with pastureland are improving the sustainability of cattle production, and diversifying and increasing farmers' income.

63.  Which among the following is the **most logical and rational inference** that can be made from the above passage?
     (a)  Agricultural practices that enhance biodiversity can often increase farm output and reduce the Vulnerability to disasters.
     (b)  All the countries of the world should be encouraged to replace ecoagriculture with conventional agriculture.
     (c)  Ecoagriculture should be permitted in protected areas without destroying the biodiversity there.
     (d)  The yield of food crops will be very high if ecoagricultural practices are adopted to cultivate them.

## PASSAGE-4

The medium term challenge for Indian manufacturing is to move from lower to higher tech sectors, from lower to higher value-added sectors, and from lower to higher productivity sectors. Medium tech industries are primarily capital intensive and resource processing; and high tech industries are mainly capital and technoloy intensive. In order to push the share of manufacturing in overall GDP to the projected 25 per cent, Indian manufacturing needs to capture the global market in sectors showing a rising trend in demand. These sectors are largely high technology and capital intensive.

64.  Which among the following is the **most logical and rational inference** that can be made from the above passage?
     (a)  India's GDP displays high value added and high productivity levels in medium tech and resource processing industries.
     (b)  Promotion of capital and technology intensive manufacturing is not possible in India.
     (c)  India should push up the public investments and encourage the private investments in research and development, technoloy upgradation and skill development.
     (d)  India has already gained a great share in global markets in sectors showing a rising trend in demand.

## PASSAGE-5

Over the last decade, Indian agriculture has become more robust with record production of food grains and oilseeds. Increased procurement, consequently, has added huge stocks of food grains in the granaries. India is one of the world's top producers of rice, wheat, milk, fruits and vegetables. India is still home to a quarter of all undernourished people in the world. On an average, almost half of the total expenditure of nearly half of the households is on food.

65.  Which among the following is the most logical corollary to the above passage?
     (a)  Increasing the efficiency of farm-to-fork value chain is necessary to reduce the poverty and malnutrition.
     (b)  increasing the agricultural productivity will automatically eliminate the poverty and malnutrition in India.
     (c)  India's agricultural productivity is already great and it is not necessary to increase it further.
     (d)  Allocation of more funds for social welfare and poverty alleviation programmes will ultimately eliminate the poverty and malnutrition in India.

## PASSAGE-6

The States are like pearls and the Centre is the thread which turns them into a necklace; if the thread snaps, the pearls are scattered.

66. Which one of the following views corroborates the above statement?
    (a) A strong Centre and strong States make the federation strong.
    (b) A strong Centre is a binding force for national integrity.
    (c) A strong Centre is a hindrance to State autonomy.
    (d) State autonomy is a prerequisite for a federation.

### PASSAGE-7

Really I think that the poorest he that is in England has a life to live, as the greatest he, and therefore truly, I think it is clear that every man that is to live under a government ought first by his own consent to put himself under the government, and I do think that the poorest man in England is not at all bound in a strict sense to that government that he has not had a voice to put himself under.

67. The above statement argues for
    (a) distribution of wealth equally to all
    (b) rule according to the consent of the governed
    (c) rule of the poor
    (d) expropriation of the rich

68. The average rainfall in a city for the first four days was recorded to be 0.40 inch. The rainfall on the last two days was in the ratio of 4:3. The average of six days was 0.50 inch. What was the rainfall on the fifth day?
    (a) 0.60 inch      (b) 0.70 inch
    (c) 0.80 inch      (d) 0.90 inch

---

**DIRECTIONS for the following 3 (three) items :** Consider the given information and answer the three items that follow.

---

A, B, C, D, E, F and G are Lecturers from different cities-Hyderabad, Delhi, Shillong, Kanpur, Chennai, Mumbai and Srinagar (not necessarily in the same order) who participated in a conference. Each one of them ' is specialized in a different subject, viz, Economics, Commerce, History, Sociology, Geography, Mathematics and Statistics (not necessarily in the same order). Further

1. Lecturer from Kanpur is specialized in Geography
2. Lecturer D is from Shillong
3. Lecturer C from Delhi is specialized in Sociology
4. Lecturer B is specialized in neither History nor Mathematics
5. Lecturer A who is specialized in Economics does not belong to Hyderabad
6. Lecturer F who is specialized in Commerce belongs to Srinagar
7. Lecturer G who is specialized in Statistics belongs to Chennai

69. Who is specialized in Geography?
    (a) B
    (b) D
    (c) E
    (d) Cannot be determined as data are inadequate

70. To which city does the Lecturer specialized in Economics belong?
    (a) Hyderabad
    (b) Mumbai
    (c) Neither Hyderabad nor Mumbai
    (d) Cannot be determined as data are inadequate

71. Who of the following belongs to Hyderabad?
    (a) B
    (b) E
    (c) Neither B nor E
    (d) Cannot be determined as data are inadequate

72. In a school, there are five teachers A, B, C, D and E, A and B teach Hindi and English. C and B teach English and Geography. D and A teach Mathematics and Hindi. E and B teach History and French. Who teaches maximum number of subjects.
    (a) A                    (b) B
    (c) D                    (d) E

73. A 2-digit number is reversed. The larger of the two numbers is divided by the smaller one. What is the largest possible remainder
    (a) 9                    (b) 27
    (c) 36                   (d) 45

74. The monthly incomes of X and Y are in the ratio of 4 : 3 and their monthly expenses are in the ratio of 3 : 2. However, each saves ₹ 6,000 per month. What is their total monthly income?
    (a) ₹ 28,000             (b) ₹ 42,000
    (c) ₹ 56,000             (d) ₹ 84,000

75. Two walls and a ceiling of a room meet at right angles at a point P. A fly is in the air 1 m from one wall, 8 m from the other wall and 9 m from the point P. How many meters is the fly from the ceiling ?
    (a) 4                    (b) 6
    (c) 12                   (d) 15

---

**DIRECTIONS for the following 3 (three) items :** Consider the given information and answer the **three items** that follow.

---

Eight railway stations A, B, C, D, E, F, G and H are connected either by two way passages or one way passages. One way passages are from C to A, E to G, B to F, D to H, G to C, E to C and H to G. Two way passages are between A and E, G and B, F and D, and E and D.

76. While travelling from C to H, which one of the following stations must be passed through.
    (a) G                    (b) E
    (c) B                    (d) F

77. In how many different ways can a train travel from F to A without passing through any station more than once?
    (a) 1                    (b) 2
    (c) 3                    (d) 4

78. If the route between G and C is closed, which one of the following stations need not be passed through while travelling from H to C?
    (a) E                    (b) D
    (c) A                    (d) B

79. There are certain 2-digit numbers. The difference between the number and the one obtained on reversing it is always 27. How many such maximum 2-digit numbers are there?
    (a) 3                    (b) 4
    (c) 5                    (d) None of the above

80. What is the total number of digits printed, if a book containing 150 pages is to be numebred from 1 to 150
    (a) 262                  (b) 342
    (c) 360                  (d) 450

# HINTS & SOLUTIONS

1. (c) The passage elucidates the environmental issues contributing to resource stresses and political conflict.

2. (a) The essence of the passage is that one should first consult wisely and then resolve firmly.

3. (d) 'Climate change poses a threat to the survival of polar bears' is the most crucial message conveyed by the passage.

4. (b) People have to understand that toilet use and pit-emptying is a part of cleanliness.

5. (b) The passage infers that the growth driven by GDP only is neither desirable nor sustainable.

6. (b) The passage vindicates that in India the labour reforms are required to make optimum use of its vast labour force productively.

7. (b) The key point of the passage is that there should be a balance between work and leisure.

8. (c) In the paragraph, the author advocates that habits make it easier for us to live.

9. (b) The line " but some of them had Friends in party Y" clearly indicates statement (b) is correct. Best answer is (b)

10. (b) Statement 1 is correct. Statement 2 is incorrect because in the passage there is no mention of people who opposed Z's campaign strategy. Hence the best answer is option (b).

11. (b) Since, the month begins on sunday and if it has 29 days then
1st, 8th, 15th, 22nd and 29th are Sundays. While 14th and 21st days are 2nd and Fourth Saturday. Hence, $29 - (2 + 5) = 22$ working days.

12. (d) Population of the Community after every year $= \dfrac{2}{3}$ of the previous year. Hence, the population of the community after 6 year $= \left(\dfrac{2}{3}\right)^6$ of the original population of the Community.
$$\left(\dfrac{2}{3}\right)^6 = \dfrac{64}{729}\text{th part.}$$

13. (c) Given information can be represented as:-

| Subject | Biology | Physics | Chemistry | Mathematics |
|---------|---------|---------|-----------|-------------|
| DAY | I | II | III | IV |

Hence, Mathermatics was held on the last day.

14. (b) $A + B > C + D$ .....(i)
$A + C = B + D$ .....(ii)
$$A = \dfrac{B + D}{2}$$

So, $C = \dfrac{B + D}{2}$ or, $A = C$ ....(iii)
From (i) and (iii)
$B > D$ ....(iv)
Using (i), (ii), (iii) and (iv),
$B > A = C > D.$
Hence, B's income is highest.

15. (a) Let us apply basic logic. Conclusion I definitely. Follows as that is the main assertion given. Conclusion II is incorrect, as it says "Even though one's voice is not good, one can keep practicing". It is an assumption. Hence best answer is (a).

16. (b) Distance travelled by A in one chance $= (6-1)$ cm $= 5$ cm
Distance travelled by B in one chance $= (7-3)$ cm $= 4$ cm
Distance travelled by C in one chance $= (6.5-2)$ cm $= 4.5$ cm.
Hence, Length of pillar A $= 5 \times 39 + 6 = 201$ cm
Length of pillar B $= 4 \times 39 + 7 = 163$ cm
Length of pillar C $= 4.5 \times 39 + 6.5 = 182$ cm
Length of shortest pillar $\rightarrow$ B. 163 cm.

17. (c) Except (c) other options are absurd.

18. (c) Remaining names after the removal of failed students
$= 52 - 15 = 37.$
Ramesh's position from top $= 22.$
Hence from bottom Ramesh is $(37 + 1 - 22)$th $= 16$th.

19. (c) $P + R - Q$

Hence, Q is the Father of P.

20. (c) Let the original price of phone $= ₹100$
$$\text{SP of Gopal} = 100 \times \dfrac{110}{100} \times ₹110$$
SP of Ram $= 110 - 10\%$ of $110 = ₹99$
Total Profit of gopal $= ₹100 - ₹99 = 1$
But profit was made as CP hence, 1% profit

21. (b) The challenge the author throws to the public is to achieve equal privileges, fulfilment of destiny and political tolerance.

22. (c) The nature of General Will, in the passage, is best described as the collective good as distinct from Private Wills of the individuals.

23. (d) The passage denotes that in a mature democracy, force is narrowed down to a marginal phenomenon in the actual exercise of sovereignty.

24. (a) The passage pertains to duty to vote.

25. (d) The passage denotes that despair sometimes leads to dictatorship in a country.

26. (b) The passage assumes that use of leisure by some people to produce new and original things has been the chief source of human progress.

27. (b) The assumption that the studying the history is essential for anyone who aspires to be a leader is made in the passage.

28. (c) The weight of the 5th persan sum of first 5 person + Sum of last five person–
Sum of weight of 9 persons.
$= 5 \times 45 + 5 \times 55 - 9 \times 50 \, kg = 50 \, kg$

29. (c) The given information can be represented as :-

| Name | Bank Employee | Tennis Player | PG in Commerce | PG in Sociology | In Unemployed |
|---|---|---|---|---|---|
| Vimla | ✓ | | | | |
| Kamla | ✓ | | | ✓ | |
| Amala | | | | ✓ | ✓ |
| Komala | | ✓ | | ✓ | ✓ |
| Nirmala | ✓ | ✓ | | ✓ | |
| Shymala | | | ✓ | | |

Hence, Nirmala is both a tennis player and a bank employee.

30. (d) None of the above can be concluded with certainty.

31. (d) None of the above statement is correct.

32. (b) 12% earn less than ₹ 30,000.
6% earn more than ₹ 2,00,000.
22% earn more than ₹ 1,00,000.
So, between ₹ 30,000 – ₹ 1,00,000 there are $(100 - 22 - 12)\% = 66\%$ household.
66% household is equal to 990
Hence, Number of household = 1500.
Number of household between 1,00,000 and 2,00,000
$= 1500 \times \dfrac{16}{100} = 240.$

33. (*) At 5' o'clock it strikes 5 times. Total gaps between 1 to 5.
$(1-2-3-4-5)$ Total time for 4 gaps.
So, time taken for each gap $= \dfrac{12}{4} = 3 \, sec.$
At 10'o clock, it strikes 10 times. Total gaps = 9
Hence, $9 \times 3 = 27$ seconds.

35. (a) Since 39 is the mean of first five numbers, first five numbers are
$35, 37, 39, 41$ and $43$ and next 8 numbers are $45, 47, 49, 51, 53, 55, 57$ and $59.$
Hence, mean $= \dfrac{(13+1)}{2}$, 7th number or middle number $= 47.$

36. (b)

| A | B | C | D | E | F |
|---|---|---|---|---|---|
| 8 | 7 | 12 | 15 | 11 | 7 |

Hence, $D + E = B + C + F.$

37. (a) Let the original amount be 150 ml.
According to question.
50 ml of mixture + 50ml of pure milk
$\Rightarrow$ 25 ml of Milk + 25ml of water + 50 ml of pure milk.
Hence, % of water in new mixture $= \dfrac{25}{100} \times 100 = 25\%.$

38. (c)

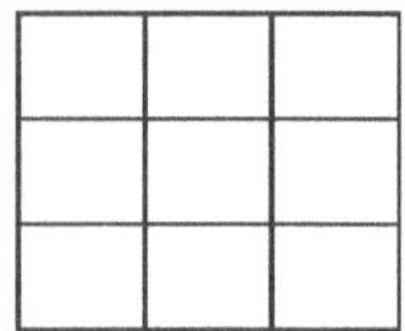

Number of squares and rectangles in a 3 × 3 grid
$= 1^3 + 2^3 + 3^3 = 36.$

39. (c) Distance travelled by freight train in 2 hour $= 2 \times 40 = 80 \, km.$
Relative speed $= 60 \, km - 40 \, km = 20 \, km/hr$
Hence, time taken by express train to meet
Freight train $= \dfrac{80 \, km}{20 \, km/hr} = 4 \, hr.$
So, Distance travelled $= 4 \times 60$ or $6 \times 40 = 240 \, km.$

40. (d) Randheer > (Kunal + Debu) ------ ... (i)
(Kunal + Shankar) > Randheer ------ ... (ii)
Sonal > Shankar       ------ ... (iii)
Neha > Randheer       ------ ... (iv)
From (i), (ii), (iii) and (iv) we can not conclude who optained the highest mark hence, Data are inadequate.

41. (a) The statement that political development is not unilinear process for it involves both growth and decay best explains the passage.

42. (c) 'Devolution, to be successful, requires a democracy in which there is free expression of the will of the people at lower level and their active participation at the grassroots level' is the most logical, rational and critical inference of the passage.

43. (d) The most logical and essential message conveyed by the passage is that the use of digital systems is imperative for the existence of mankind in future.

44. (a) The most logical, rational and critical inference of the passage could be once a country reaches middle-income stage, it runs the risk of falling productivity which leads to stagnant incomes.

45. (c) The passage assumes that inclusive innovation and R&D can help create an egalitarian society.

46. (d) The passage logically infers that relation between climate change and migration is not yet properly understood.

47. (b) The assumption that one of the aims of sustainable agriculture is to ensure minimal ecological imbalance can be made from the passage.

48. (c) Biopesticides are not hazardous to human health and they are essential to maintain the biodiversity of any ecosystem.

49. (b) Let the numbers are of the form abc.
So, According to question,
$100a + 10b + c = 7K$       ....(i)
$100c + 10b + a = 7m$       .....(ii)

From, (i) − (ii)

$99a − 99c = 7(k–m)$

$99(a − c) = 7n$

$a − c = 7$

$a = 9, c = 2$

$a = 8, c = 1$

Hence, 4 numbers, 259, 952, 168 and 861.

50. (d)

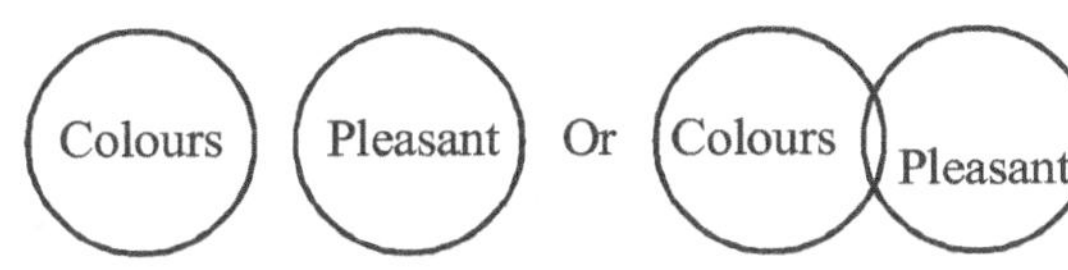


1. False
2. Can't say
3. Can't say

Hence (i) is false.

51. (c) — —8

There are 9 values (1 to 9) for hundreds place digit.

While 10 values (0 to 10) for ten's place digit.

Hence, $9 × 10 = 90$ Numbers.

52. (d) Skewed to the left.

53. (b) Mr. x's present age 26, because 25 was a perfect square and the next year would be a perfect cube.

Next cube number → 64

Hence, minimum years required $= 64 − 26 = 38$ years.

54. (a) Let the work done by Q in 1 day = x units.

So the work done by P in 1 day = 3x units

$$\text{Work done by R in 1 day} = \frac{3x + x}{4} = x \text{ units}$$

$$\text{Hence, the ratio of earnings} = \overset{P}{3x} : \overset{Q}{x} : \overset{R}{x}$$

$$= 3 : 1 : 1.$$

55. (b) A is the husband of D.

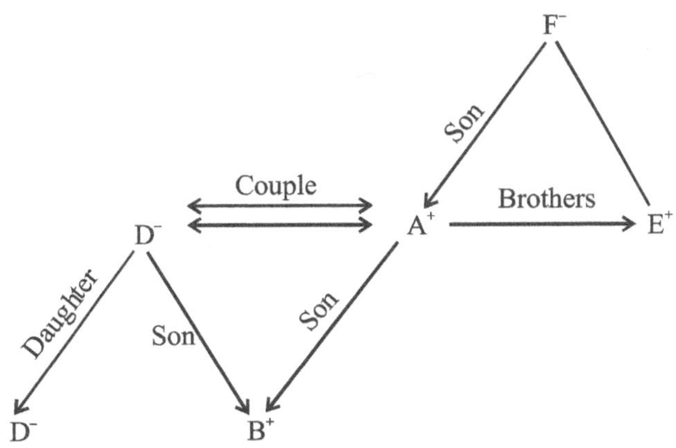


56. (b) Considering the worst case First 15 picked balls are red and white. Hence in 16th time it is assured that 3 different colour balls exist.

57. (c) — $B_1$ — $B_2$ —

2 boys can take their seats in 2! ways and 3 girls can take the remaining 3 seats in $3_{C_2} × 2!$ ways.

Hence, $2! × 3_{C_2} × 2! = 12$ ways.

58. (a) Number of Colour less cubes $= (4 − 2)^3 = 8$.

59. (c) The given information can be represented as −

A C B D G F E H

Hence, G is the immediate right of D.



60. (b)

Red ⟶ 6

White ⟶ 4

61. (c) The most logical and rational inference that can be made from the passage is the air quality index is not helpful to the residents of many of our large cities.

62. (c) Creating conditions for the faster growth of productive jobs outside of agriculture even while improving the productivity of agriculture is the most logical and rational inference made from the passage.

63. (a) The most logical and rational inference that can be made from the passage is agricultural practices that enhance biodiversity can many a time increase farm output and reduce the vulnerability to disasters.

64. (c) India should boost up the public investments and encourage the private investments in research and development, technology upgradation and skill development.

65. (a) The most logical corollary to the passage can be the increasing the efficiency of farm-to-fork value chain is necessary to reduce the poverty and malnutrition.

66. (b) 'A strong Centre is a binding force for national integrity' correctly corroborates the given statement.

67. (b) The passage argues for the rule according to the consent of those who are governed.

68. (c) The sum of rainfall for the first four days $= 4 × 0.40 = 1.60$ inch

The Sum of rainfall for six days $= 0.50 × 6 = 3.00$ inch

$⇒$ Sum of rainfall for last two days $= 3.00 − 1.06 = 1.40$ inch

$$\text{Rainfall on 5th day} = \frac{4}{7} × 1.40 \text{ inch} = 0.80 \text{ inch.}$$

Solution (69-71)

| City | Subject | Lecturers |
|---|---|---|
| Kanpur | Geography | B |
| Shillong | | D |
| Delhi | Sociology | C |
| Mumbai | Economics | A |
| Srinagar | Commerce | F |
| Chennai | Statistics | G |
| Hyderabad | | E |

69. (a)　　70. (b)　　71. (b)

**Solutions (72)**

| Teachers \ Subject | Hindi | English | Math | History | French | Geography |
|---|---|---|---|---|---|---|
| A | ✓ | ✓ | ✓ | | | |
| B | ✓ | ✓ | | ✓ | ✓ | ✓ |
| C | | ✓ | | | | ✓ |
| D | ✓ | | ✓ | | | |
| E | | | | ✓ | ✓ | |

72. (b)

73. (d) 94 divided by 49 leaves the largest remainder 45.

74. (b) Let the monthly incomes of x and y be 4x and 3x.

So, $\dfrac{4x - 6000}{3x - 6000} = \dfrac{3}{2}$

$\Rightarrow \quad 8x - 12000 = 9x - 18000$

$\therefore \quad x = ₹\,6,000$

Total income of x and y $= (3 + 4)x$
$= ₹\,6,000 \times 7 = ₹\,42,000$

75. (a) $9 = \sqrt{(8)^2 + (1)^2 + (d)^2}$

$\Rightarrow \quad 81 = 64 + 1 + (d)^2$

$\Rightarrow \quad (d)^2 = 16$

$d = 4.$

**Solutions (76 -78)**

' $\leftrightarrow$ ' Denotes one way, ' $\Leftrightarrow$ ' Denotes two way.

$C \leftrightarrow A, \ E \leftrightarrow C, \ E \leftrightarrow G, \ H \leftrightarrow G$

$B \leftrightarrow F, \ A \Leftrightarrow E, \ D \leftrightarrow H, \ G \Leftrightarrow B$

$G \leftrightarrow C, \ F \Leftrightarrow D, \ E \Leftrightarrow D$

76. (b)

77. (d) F — D — E — C — A or F — D — H — G — C – A,
or
F — D — E — A or F — D — E — G — C – A.
So, 4 ways.

78. (c) H — G — E — C and H — G — B — F — D — E – C.
So, nowhere we have to travel through A.

79. (d) Let the two digit numbers are of the form ab.
So, $10a + b - (10b + a) = 27$

$\Rightarrow \quad 9a - 9b = 27$

$\Rightarrow \quad a - b = 3$

$(a, b) \Rightarrow (9, 6), (8, 5), (7, 4)\,(6, 3)\,(4, 1), (5, 2)$
Hence, 96 , 85 , 74 , 63 , 41, 52 and 25, 14, 36, 47, 58, 69
are the required numbers.

80. (b) Number of digits used For $1 - 9 = 9 \times 1 = 9$
Number of digits used For $10 - 99 = 90 \times 2 = 180$
Number of digits used for $100 - 150 = 51 \times 3 = 153$
Hence, $153 + 180 + 9 = 342$ digits.

# 1 MOCK TEST

1. There is a close co-relation between India's culture and its nature. The "Barahmasa" paintings are famous in this context.
   What is the main theme of Barahmasa paintings.
   (a) The twelve battles of Ashoka period
   (b) The seasonal cycle
   (c) Different forces of nature
   (d) Twelve Buddhist Jatakas

2. With reference to the Gulf of Mannar Biosphere Reserve; consider the following statements:
   1. It is the first marine biosphere reserve in Asia.
   2. One can find sea cow, sea horse and several species of whales in Gulf of Mannar.
   Select the correct answer from the codes given below:
   (a) 1 only        (b) 2 only
   (c) Both 1 and 2    (d) Neither 1 nor 2

3. With reference to the Balance of Payments, which of the following constitute/constitutes the Capital Account?
   1. External assistance.
   2. External Commercial Borrowings (net).
   3. Balance of trade.
   4. Banking Capital.
   Select the correct answer using the codes given below:
   (a) 1 and 2        (b) 2, 3 and 4
   (c) 1, 2 and 4     (d) 1, 2, 3 and 4

4. Consider the following statements with reference to Project "Stree Swabhiman"
   (1) It aims to provide the adolescent girls and women; access to affordable sanitary products in rural areas.
   (2) This project is undertaken by Ministry of Electronics and information technology.
   Which of the above statements/statements is/are correct?
   (a) only (1)       (b) only (2)
   (c) Both (1) and (2)   (d) Neither (1) nor (2)

5. Which among the following were the news papers having advocacy for revolutionary terrorism:
   1. Sandhya
   2. Ugantar
   3. The Bengal Gazettee
   4. Kal.
   In the context of the Indian National movement select the correct answer from the codes given below:
   (a) 1 and 2 only     (b) 1, 2 and 4 only
   (c) 2, 3, and 4 only   (d) 1, 2, 3 and 4 all

6. Consider the following statements:
   1. The constitution empowers the president to promulgate ordinances during the recess of parliament.
   2. The power of the president to legislate by ordinance is a parallel power of legislation.
   3. President can promulgate an ordinance even when any one of house of the parliament is not in session.
   Choose the correct statement/statements using the codes given below:
   (a) 1 and 2 only     (b) 1 and 3 only
   (c) 2 and 3 only     (d) 1, 2 and 3

7. E-Nose is used for the purpose of,
   (a) Monitoring of Industrial noises.
   (b) Monitoring of Particulate matters from industries.
   (c) Monitoring of emitted Green House gases from Industries.
   (d) Monitoring of obnoxious odours from Industries.

8. Which of the following ranges is not a part of the lesser Himalayas or the Himachal Range?
   (a) Pir Panjal Range    (b) Mahabharata Range
   (c) Zaskar Range      (d) Dhauladhar Range

9. With reference to the history of ancient India, which of the following was/were common to both Buddhism and Jainism?
   1. Inclination towards peace and celibacy.
   2. Indifference to the authority of Vedas
   3. Denial of efficacy of rituals.
   Select the correct answer using the codes given below:
   (a) 1 only        (b) 2 and 3 only
   (c) 1 and 3 only    (d) 1, 2 and 3

10. The Verma Committee on Fundamental Duties of the citizens (1999) identified the existence of legal provisions for the implementation of some of the fundamental duties. Which among the following is not one among them.
    (a) The protection of Civil Rights Act (1955)
    (b) The Indian Penal Code (IPC)
    (c) The representation of People Act (1951)
    (d) The Government of India Act (1935)

11. Kyanite is a heat resistant mineral. It is used in glass, cement and china clay industries. The largest producer of kyanite in India is
    (a) Maharashtra     (b) Karnataka
    (c) Jharkhand       (d) Assam

12. Consider the following statements:
    1. Finance Commission is a 5 member body (including the chairman)
    2. Finance Commission submits its report to parliament.
    Which of the above statements is/are correct.
    (a) 1 only
    (b) 2 only
    (c) Both 1 and 2
    (d) None of the above

13. The terms thisra, chatusra, misra, khanda are associated with:
    (a) Different terms of Mughal painting
    (b) Different types of Musical instruments.
    (c) The fundamental units of the Indian rhythmic structure (Talas)
    (d) None of the above

14. Which of the following statements best describes the process of respiration and respiratory organs in frogs and mammals?
    1. Frogs and mammals both contain a pair of lungs
    2. Exchange of gases takes place through skin in frog but not in human
    Select the correct answer using the codes given below:
    (a) 1 only
    (b) 2 only
    (c) Both 1 and 2
    (d) Neither 1 nor 2

15. With reference to Vijay Nagara Empire which of following statements stands true about Amara-Nayaka
    1. The Amara-Nayakas were military commanders who were given territories to govern by the raya.
    2. They sent tribute to the king annually to express their loyalty.
    3. King could transfer them from one place to other.
    Select the correct answer using the code given below:
    (a) 1 only
    (b) 2 and 3 only
    (c) 1 and 3 only
    (d) 1, 2 and 3

16. Consider the following statements:
    1. Resistivity of a conductor is smaller than that of Insulator
    2. Resistivity of an alloy is greater than its constituent metals
    Select the correct answer using the code given below:
    (a) 1 only
    (b) 2 only
    (c) 1 and 2 only
    (d) Neither 1 nor 2

17. According to a group of scientists, aeroplanes may be ejecting significant amounts of black carbon (BC) and this may be depleting the ozone layer:
    In this context consider the following statements:
    1. Black carbon cannot be produced naturally.
    2. It is known to be more potent than carbon dioxide in whetting global warming.
    3. Black carbon is emitted directly into the atmosphere in the form of fine particles (PM 2.5)
    Select the correct statement/statements using the codes given below:
    (a) 1 and 2 only
    (b) 2 and 3 only
    (c) 1 and 3 only
    (d) 3 only

18. Regarding the Loksabha and Assembly elections in India consider the following statements:
    1. The winning candidate need not secure a majority of the votes.
    2. Constitution prescribes a plurality system as the method of election.

Which of the above is/are correct.
(a) 1 only
(b) 2 only
(c) Both 1 and 2
(d) None of the above

19. Consider the following statements with reference to ALGAL BLOOMS:
    1. A bloom often results in a colour change in the water.
    2. Algal blooms can be of any colour.
    3. All algal blooms are harmful for the water ecosystem.
    Select the correct answer from the codes given below:
    (a) 1 and 3 only
    (b) 2 and 3 only
    (c) 1, 2 and 3
    (d) 1 and 2 only

20. Consider the following statements:
    (1) The Urban HUNGaMA survey was conducted in ten largest cities of India
    (2) The Urban HUNGaMA survey collected data on reading ability of primary school students
    Select the correct statement/statements using the codes given below:
    (a) only (1)
    (b) only (2)
    (c) both (1) and (2)
    (d) Neither (1) nor (2)

21. Which of the following vector borne disease has not been targeted under National vector borne disease control programme?
    (1) Kala azar
    (2) Yellow fever
    (3) Japanese Encephalitis
    (4) Plague
    Select the correct answer using the codes given below.
    (a) only (2)
    (b) only (1)
    (c) (2) and (4)
    (d) (1) and (3)

22. Consider the following statements with reference to the Brazzaville declaration signed in March/2018.
    1. It was signed to promote world's largest Peatlands.
    2. Peatlands are wetlands that contain mixture of decomposed organic material,partially submerged in layer of water, lacking oxygen.
    Select the correct answer from the codes given below:
    (a) 1 only
    (b) 2 only
    (c) Both 1 and 2
    (d) Neither 1 nor 2

23. Consider the following statements:
    1. "Word Development Report" is published by World Bank.
    2. The World Development Report, 2018 has warned of a learning crisis in global education.
    Select the correct statement/statements using the codes given below:
    (a) 1 only
    (b) 2 only
    (c) Both 1 and 2
    (d) Neither 1 nor 2

24. Which among the following is the correct decreasing order of statewise coal production in India?
    (a) Odisha > MP > Chhattisgarh > Jharkhand
    (b) Chhattisgarh > Jharkhand > Odisha > MP
    (c) Jharkhand > Chhattisgarh > MP > Odisha
    (d) MP > Odisha > Chhattisgarh > Jharkhand

25. With reference to the Cabinet Committee which of the following is/are correct:
    1. Standing committee is of permanent nature.
    2. Adhoc committee is of temporary nature.
    3. All cabinet committees are set up by prime minister.
    (a) 1 and 2 only
    (b) 2 and 3 only
    (c) 1, 2 and 3
    (d) 1 and 3 only

26. Gandhi set up Tolstoy Farm in South Africa in 1910. What was the objective behind establishment of the Tolstoy Farm:
    (a) To arrange the marriage certificates for Indians.
    (b) To house the Indian windows.
    (c) To promote Social reform among Indians residing in South Africa.
    (d) To house the families of the Satyagrahis.

27. Stockholm convention pertains to
    (a) Prohibition of the use in war of Asphyxiating, poisonous or other gases.
    (b) Eliminate or restrict the production and use of persistent organic pollutants (POPs).
    (c) Prior informed consent procedure for certain hazardous chemicals and pesticides in International Trade.
    (d) None of the above.

28. Which of the following reports is/are released by World Economic Forum?
    1. Global Competitiveness Index
    2. Networked Readiness Index
    3. Global Innovation Index
    Select the correct statement/statements using the code given below:
    (a) 1 only
    (b) 1 and 2 only
    (c) 2 and 3 only
    (d) 1, 2 and 3

29. Consider the following statements:
    1. Under Lead Bank Scheme, a particular bank is designated as Lead Bank of the district.
    2. Service area approach is operated under lead Bank Scheme.
    Select the correct statement/statements using the codes given below:
    (a) 1 only
    (b) Both 1 and 2
    (c) 2 only
    (d) Neither 1 nor 2

30. Consider the following statements.
    1. The Thar link express connects Jodhpur (India) and Lahore (Pakistan)
    2. It carries only passengers
    Select the correct statement/statements using the codes given below
    (a) 1 only
    (b) 2 only
    (c) Both 1 and 2
    (d) Neither 1 nor 2

31. Which of the following is/are among the areas of low rainfall in India?
    1. Parts of western coast.
    2. Western Rajasthan.
    3. Interior of the Deccan plateau.
    4. East of the Sahyadris.
    Select the correct answer from the codes given below:
    (a) 1, 2 and 3 only
    (b) 2, 3 and 4 only
    (c) 1, 3 and 4 only
    (d) 1, 2, 3 and 4

32. In context of Fundamental Rights consider the following statements:
    1. Fundamental Rights are absolute Rights.
    2. Government can put reasonable restrictions on the exercise of fundamental rights.
    Select the correct statements.
    (a) 1 only
    (b) 2 only
    (c) Both 1 and 2
    (d) None of the above

33. Read the following statements about Superconductivity,
    1. It is the state of matter in which materials lose their electrical resistance
    2. The phenomenon takes place generally at higher temperature
    Select the correct answer using the codes given below:
    (a) 1 only
    (b) 2 only
    (c) Both 1 and 2
    (d) Neither 1 nor 2

34. Which of the following best explains the Lisbon Treaty?
    (a) It is an international treaty which amended Maastricht Treaty and Treaty of Rome to form European Union on constitutional basis.
    (b) It is a treaty to develop defence capabilities and make then available for European military operations.
    (c) It is a treaty on sustainable development in which European Union member European Union States committed to cooperate internationally to facilitate safe, orderly and regular migration.
    (d) None of these

35. Consider the following statements:
    1. Lord Dalhousie is known as the father of local self government in India.
    2. Govt of India Act 1919 provided for the establishment of village panchayats.
    Select the correct statement/statements using the code given below:
    (a) 1 only
    (b) 2 only
    (c) Both 1 and 2
    (d) Neither 1 nor 2

36. Consider the following statements with reference to "Cyber Surakshit Bharat Initiative."
    (1) It has been launched by the Ministry of communications.
    (2) It aims to strengthen cybersecurity ecosystem in India.
    Which of the above statement/statements is/are correct?
    (a) only (1)
    (b) only (2)
    (c) both (1) and (2)
    (d) Neither (1) nor (2)

37. Which among the following is/are threat to the healthy sustainability of mangroves:
    1. Channel dredging
    2. Production forestry
    3. Land clearance
    4. Sewage
    Select the correct answer from the codes given below:
    (a) 1, 2 and 3 only
    (b) 2, 3 and 4 only
    (c) 1, 3 and 4 only
    (d) 1, 2, 3 and 4

38. With reference to the Mughal period the term 'Jizya' refers to
    (a) Religious tax on Muslims
    (b) Religious tax on Non-Muslims
    (c) Land tax
    (d) Trade tax

39. Which of the following statements are correct in context of Indian judiciary:
    1. Supreme court has recently ordered to install CCTV cameras with audio recording in all district courts.
    2. 20th Law commission has recommended for audio visual recording of court proceedings.
    (a) 1 only
    (b) 2 only
    (c) Both 1 and 2
    (d) None of the Above

40. The Financial Stability Report, 2017 has been released by
    (a) Ministry of Finance
    (b) Reserve Bank of India
    (c) Asian Development Bank
    (d) IMF

41. Jawara, Matki, Phulpati are the folk dances of
    (a) Rajasthan
    (b) Himachal Pradesh
    (c) Madhya Pradesh
    (d) Haryana

42. Which among the following is/are characteristics of Ecotone:
    1. It is a zone of tension.
    2. It may contain certain species which are entirely different from that of the adjoining communities.
    3. An Ecotone is always a narrow zone.
    Select the correct answer from the codes given below:
    (a) 1 and 3 only
    (b) 1 and 2 only
    (c) 2 and 3 only
    (d) 1, 2 and 3

43. Which of the following is/are characteristics of Mediterranean climate?
    1. A dry, warm summer.
    2. Bright sunny weather with hot dry summers and wet mild winter.
    3. Prominence of local winds around the Mediterranean sea.
    Select the correct statement/statements using the codes given below:
    (a) 1 and 2 only
    (b) 2 and 3 only
    (c) 1 and 3 only
    (d) 1, 2 and 3 only

44. Select the most appropriate statements with reference to 'Multiple Burn Technology',
    1. It is related to usage of solid, liquid and cryogenic propellants in the same system.
    2. It is used during launching of satellites into multiple orbits using burning of different fuels.
    3. It refers to Switching 'off' and switching 'on' of engine to control height.
    Select the correct answer using the codes given below:
    (a) 1 only
    (b) 2 only
    (c) 3 only
    (d) Both 2 and 3

45. Air pollution that is the result of the interaction of Sun light with certain chemicals in the atmosphere is known as
    (a) Mist
    (b) Dew
    (c) Haze
    (d) Smog

46. Which of the following can be considered as the "National Income" of an economy?
    (a) Net National Product at Market Price ($NNP_{MP}$)
    (b) Net National Product at Factor Cost ($NNP_{FC}$)
    (c) Gross Domestic Product
    (d) Net Domestic Product

47. Which of the following United Nations Member States are not signatories of the Chemical Weapons Convention (CWC)?
    (a) Iraq, Palestine, Sudan
    (b) Palestine, Libya and Syria
    (c) Egypt, North Korea, Palestine and Sudan
    (d) Sudan, South Korea, Egypt

48. With reference to the Election Commission of India, consider the following statements:
    1. The Chief Election Commissioner (CEC) has more powers than the other Election Commissioners.
    2. CEC and Election Commissioners are appointed for a six year term or continue till the age of 65 years.
    3. CEC can be removed before the expiry of term by the president.
    Which of the statements given above is/are correct?
    (a) 1 and 2 only
    (b) 2 and 3 only
    (c) 2 only
    (d) All 1, 2 and 3.

49. In 2017, "Earth Overshoot Day" fell on August 2, with reference to the Earth Overshoot Day, consider the following statements.
    1. It is the date when humanity annual demand on nature exceeds, what Earth can regenerate over the entire year.
    2. It is calculated by World Economic Forum (WEF).
    Select the correct answer from the codes given below:
    (a) 1 only
    (b) 2 only
    (c) Both 1 and 2
    (d) Neither 1 nor 2

50. Chaiti, Phag, Kajari etc. can be usually heard in Indian Society. With reference to the rich and composite culture of India, what these terms pertain to-
    (a) Folk dancers
    (b) Regional dialects
    (c) Seasonal festivals
    (d) Musical modes/ragas

51. Which of the following sources releases Sulphur in the environment:
    (a) Weathering of rocks
    (b) Erosional runoff
    (c) Decomposition of organic matter
    (d) All the above

52. Consider the following statements about Trans-pacific partnership-11.
    (1) Its members include USA and 11 other pacific Rim nations.
    (2) The agreement has been renamed as comprehensive and progressive agreement for Trans-pacific partnership which of the above statement/statements is/are correct?
    (a) only 1
    (b) only (2)
    (c) Both (1) and (2)
    (d) Neither (1) nor (2)

53. Which of the following body manages the Dam Rehabilitation and Improvement Project (DRIP) with the financial assistance from World Bank to rehabilitate about 225 dams in India?
    (a) National Disaster Management Authority
    (b) Damodar Valley Corporation
    (c) Central Water Commission (CWC)
    (d) None of the above

54. Which of the following are the implications of Rupee Depreciation on the Indian economy?
    (a) All imports become expensive
    (b) It widens the current account deficit
    (c) Both (a) and (b)
    (d) Neither (a) nor (b)

55. Consider the following statements :
    1. A retired judge of High court can be appointed as a judge of Supreme court.
    2. Ad hoc judges to the Supreme court are appointed by the chief justice of India.
    3. An Ad hoc judge of Supreme court enjoys same power and privileges as enjoyed by other judges of Supreme court.
    Choose the correct statement from the above.
    (a) 2 & 3　　　　　　　(b) 1 & 3
    (c) only 3　　　　　　 (d) All 1, 2, & 3

56. Consider the following statements:
    1. The stagnation in agriculture during the colonial rule was permanently broken by the green revolution.
    2. In the first phase of green revolution (1960s-1970s), the use of HYV seeds was restricted to more affluent states such as Punjab, Andhra Pradesh and Tamilnadu.
    3. Use of pesticides and insecticides was an essential component of Green Revolution.
    Select the correct statement/statements using the codes give below:
    (a) 1 and 2 only　　　 (b) 1, 2 and 3
    (c) 2 and 3 only　　　 (d) 1 and 3 only

57. Which of the following is not correct with reference to "Mission Parivar Vikas?"
    (a) It aims for increasing the access to contraceptives and family planning service in the high fertility districs.
    (b) It includes provision of Home delivery of contraceptives by ASHAs.
    (c) It is launched by the Union Ministry of Health and family welfare.
    (d) All the above statements are correct

58. Rock salt is produced mainly in
    (a) Rohtas (Bihar)
    (b) Mandi (Himachal Pradesh)
    (c) Purulia (West Bengal)
    (d) None of the above

59. Which among the following represents an ecosystem:
    1. A banyan tree
    2. A rainforest
    3. A well

Select the correct answer from the codes given below
    (a) 2 only　　　　　　 (b) 2 and 3 only
    (c) 1 and 3 only　　　 (d) 1, 2 and 3

60. Which of the following statements about the reasons for Separation of the Railway Budget from the general budget is/are correct:
    1. To introduce flexibility in railway finance management.
    2. To facilitate a business approach to the railway policy.
    3. To secure stability of the general revenues by providing an assured annual contribution from railway revenues.
    4. To give financial autonomy to railways.
    Select the correct statement/statements using the codes given below :
    (a) 1, 2 & 3 only　　　(b) 1, 3 & 4 only
    (c) 1 & 3 only　　　　 (d) 1, 2, 3 and 4

61. With reference to state legislature, which of the following statements is/are correct
    1. A minister cannot participate in the proceedings of a house of which he is not a member.
    2. A minister who is not a member of either house, can participate in the proceedings of both the houses.
    (a) 1 only　　　　　　 (b) 2 only
    (c) Both 1 and 2　　　 (d) Neither 1 nor 2

62. Consider the following statements:
    1. Lactation period is the transition time between calving and halting of milk removal
    2. Exotic breeds are used for cross-breeding with local breeds to decrease the lactation period
    Select the correct answer using the codes given below:
    (a) 1 only　　　　　　 (b) 2 only
    (c) Both 1 and 2　　　 (d) Neither 1 nor 2

63. Consider the following statements:
    1. Earth rotates from west to east.
    2. All the planets orbit around the sun in a clockwise direction from east to west.
    Select the correct statement/statements using the codes given below:
    (a) 1 only　　　　　　 (b) 2 only
    (c) Both 1 and 2　　　 (d) Neither 1 nor 2

64. Which among the following is/are among ways to remove the excess nutrients from a lake:
    1. Flushing with nutrient poor water
    2. Deep water abstraction
    3. Removal of fishes and Macrophytes
    4. Sludge removal
    Select the correct answer from the codes given below:
    (a) 1, 2 and 3　　　　 (b) 1, 2 and 4
    (c) 2, 3 and 4　　　　 (d) 1, 2, 3 and 4

65. Which of the following is/are true with respect to HT cotton:
    1. It can transform weeds into super weeds on large-scale.
    2. It will threaten growth and yields of all crops in future.
    Select the correct answer from the codes given below:
    (a) 1 only　　　　　　 (b) 2 only
    (c) Both 1 and 2　　　 (d) Neither 1 nor 2

66. The base year for the computation of National Accounts Statistics has been revised from 2004-05 to:
  (a) 2007-08        (b) 2009-10
  (c) 2010-11        (d) 2011-12

67. Consider the following events:
  1. Chauri-Chaura incident.
  2. Moplah rebellion in Kerala.
  3. Kakori train robbery.
  The above given events took place under the Viceroy ship of
  (a) Lord Chelmsford        (b) Lord Reading
  (c) Lord Irwin.        (d) Lord Hardinge II

68. Who is known as pioneer of modern Hindi literature?
  (a) Gopal Hari Deshmukh
  (b) Bhartendu Harishchandra
  (c) Raja Ram Mohan Roy
  (d) Ishwar Chandra Vidyasagar

69. Consider the following statements:
  1. The first seven five year plans gave importance to self-reliance.
  2. The Green revolution was introduced in and around the third five year plan.
  3. 14 Largest commercial banks were nationalised in the fourth five year plan.
  Select the correct statement/statements using the codes given below:
  (a) 1 and 2 only        (b) 2 and 3 only
  (c) 1 and 3 only        (d) 1, 2 and 3 only

70. Which of the following is/are evidences that earth is a sphere?
  1. The circular horizon.
  2. Mast of the ship is seen before the hull.
  3. Circum-navigation of the earth.
  4. Different timings of sunrise and sunset across the world.
  Select the correct statement/statements using the codes given below:
  (a) 1, 2 and 3 only.        (b) 2, 3 and 4 only.
  (c) 1, 3 and 4 only.        (d) All the above.

71. With reference to the constitution of India consider the following statements:
  1. Constitution gives us a moral identity.
  2. The Indian constitution was never subjected to a referendum.
  Which of the above given statement is/are correct.
  (a) 1 only        (b) 2 only
  (c) Both 1 and 2 only        (d) None of the above

72. Read the following statements with reference to properties of nano $CO_2$ harvester?
  1. It can suck CO and $CO_2$ from atmosphere and convert them into ethanol
  2. It can suck only $CO_2$ from the atmosphere and convert it into ethanol
  Select the correct statement/statements using the codes given below:
  (a) 1 only        (b) 2 only
  (c) Both 1 and 2        (d) Neither 1 nor 2

73. Read the following statements with reference to "National Health Protection Scheme," (NHPS)
  (1) It will provide medical cover of up to ₹ 5 lakh per year per person
  (2) Uttar Pradesh became the first state to opt out of centre's (NHPS).
  Select the correct answer using the codes given below:
  (a) only (1)        (b) only (2)
  (c) both (1) and (2        (d) Neither (1) nor (2)

74. Which of the following states does not share the boundary with Telangana?
  (a) Andhra Pradesh        (b) Jharkhand
  (c) Maharashtra        (d) Karnataka

75. In context of "electoral bonds" which of the following statements is/are correct:
  1. Donors can buy new electoral bonds from the state bank of India only.
  2. The electoral bonds would be valid for 15 days only.
  3. The electoral bonds will not carry any interest.
  (a) 1 and 2 only        (b) 2 only
  (c) All 1, 2 and 3 are correct. (d) All 1, 2 and 3 are wrong.

76. Lead is a major air pollutant. Which among the following is/are sources of lead:
  1. Petrol        2. Lead batteries
  3. Pencil lead        4. Hair dye
  Select the correct answer from the codes given below:
  (a) 1, 2 and 3 only        (b) 2, 3 and 4 only
  (c) 1, 2 and 4 only        (d) 1, 2, 3 and 4

77. Which among the following is not a characteristics of the Unorganised Sector in India?
  (a) Small and Scattered units largely outside the government's control.
  (b) Low paying and irregular jobs.
  (c) Provision for overtime, paid leave, holidays and sick leave.
  (d) Insecure employment.

78. The north-western part of India receives mild rainfall. These light showers are much needed for the winter crops and are locally known as 'Mahawat':
  These light showers are caused by –
  (a) Retreating monsoon        (b) Cyclonic depression
  (c) Western disturbances        (d) South-west monsoon

79. The term "Green box" is related to
  (a) World Bank        (b) UNFCC
  (c) WTO        (d) IMF

80. Which of the following is/are true about reverse charge mechanism in the GST regime?
  (a) The liability to pay tax is on the recipient of goods and services rather than on the supplier of the goods and services
  (b) It is applicable only in case of unregistered person.
  (c) GST council has specified 12 categories of services for reverse charge mechanism
  (d) All are correct

81. Which of the following statements are correct:
    1. Directive principles of state policy have no legal force behind them.
    2. Directive principles are supplementary to the fundamental rights of the citizens.
    (a) 1 only
    (b) 2 only
    (c) Both 1 and 2
    (d) None of the above

82. The amount of Nitrogen fixed by man through industrial process has far exceeded the amount fixed by the Natural cycle. As a result Nitrogen has become a pollutant which can disrupt the balance of nitrogen. Excess of Nitrogen on the earth may lead to
    1. Acid rain
    2. Eutrophication
    3. Harmful Algal Blooms
    Select the correct answer from the codes given below:
    (a) 1 and 2 only
    (b) 2 and 3 only
    (c) 1 and 3 only
    (d) 1, 2 and 3

83. Consider the following statements:
    1. Executive council of four members to assist the governor general of Bengal.
    2. Establishment of a supreme court at Calcutta.
    3. Establishment of dyarchy in provinces.
    Which of the above statements is/are among the provisions of Regulating Act of 1773:
    (a) 1 and 2 only
    (b) 2 and 3 only
    (c) 1 and 3 only
    (d) 1, 2, and 3 all

84. What is the main purpose behind fortification of foods?
    1. To prevent malnutrition
    2. To increase the shelf life
    3. To maintain the nutritive value of food
    Select the correct answer using the codes given below:
    (a) 1 only
    (b) 2 only
    (c) 3 only
    (d) 1, 2 and 3

85. Consider the following statements with reference to India BPO Promotion Scheme (IBPS):
    (1) It aims at setting up of BPO units in rural areas to secure balanced regional growth of the industry.
    (2) It provides capital support along with special incentives up to ₹ 1 Lakh to companies to create BPO units.
    (3) It is under the Make in India Programme for the promotion of BPO operations.
    Select the correct statement/statements using the codes given below:
    (a) Only (1) is correct.
    (b) (1) and (3) are correct.
    (c) (1) and (2) are correct.
    (d) All are correct.

86. For which of the following the term "Paper Gold" is used:
    (a) United States Dollar
    (b) Gold Reserved with International Monetary Fund
    (c) Gold reserved with the Central Bank
    (d) Special Drawing Rights (SDR) of IMF

87. The constitution confers the some rights previleges on citizens of India. Which of the following rights it denies to aliens?
    1. Right against discrimination on grounds of sex or place of birth.
    2. Cultural and educational rights.
    3. Right to contest for membership of Parliament.
    Select the correct answer using the code given below:
    (a) 1 and 2 only
    (b) 2 and 3 only
    (c) 1 and 3 only
    (d) 1, 2 and 3

88. In regard with Citizenship Act, which of the following is/are the correct statements?
    1. The provision for the common wealth citizenship was replaced by citizenship (Amendment) Act 2005.
    2. The citizenship Act (1955) has been amended four times so far.
    3. The Citizenship Act of 1955 prescribes five ways of acquiring citizenship.
    Select the correct answer using the code given below:
    (a) 1 and 2 only
    (b) 2 and 3 only
    (c) 1 and 3 only
    (d) 1, 2 and 3

89. Consider the following statements:
    1. The constitution deals with the citizenship under part II. However, it contains neither any permanent nor any elaborate provisions in this regard.
    2. Constitution deal with the problem of acquisition or loss of citizenship subsequent to its commencement.
    3. The constitution of India empowers the parliament to enact a law to provide for such matters and any other matter relating to citizenship.
    Which of the following statement is/are correct?
    (a) 1 and 2 only
    (b) 2 and 3 only
    (c) 1 and 3 only
    (d) 1, 2 and 3

90. Government of India and World Bank sign $375 Million Loan to Help India Develop its First Modern Waterway. Consider the following statements about the Project:
    1. The project has been launched for water transport fairway on the Ganga River.
    2. The 1,360 km-stretch of the waterway between Patna and seaport of Haldia are included in the Project.
    3. The Project will help the Inland Waterways Authority of India (IWAI) to National Waterway 1.
    Which of the statement given above is/are correct?
    (a) 1 and 2 only
    (b) 2 and 3 only
    (c) 1 and 3 only
    (d) 1, 2 and 3

91. Consider the following statements about Pradhan Mantri LPG Panchayats:
    1. Each such panchayat brings together about a hundred women LPG customers on an interactive platform to discuss about safe and sustainable usage of LPG.
    2. One lakh such panchayats will be conducted across India before 31st March 2019.
    Which of the statements given above is/are correct?
    (a) 1 only
    (b) 2 only
    (c) Both 1 and 2
    (d) Neither 1 nor 2

92. Consider the following statements about "The 'Startup India Yatra":
    1. It is for the search of entrepreneurial talent in Tier-2 and Tier-3 cities.
    2. It is an awareness workshop on the Startup India Initiative being held at technical universities across the country.
    3. Startup Yatra in Uttarakhand has been started on 2 April.
    Which of the statements given above is/are correct?
    (a) 1 and 2 only      (b) 2 and 3 only
    (c) 1 and 3 only      (d) 1, 2 and 3

93. Consider the following statements about Ujwal Discom Assurance Yojana (UDAY):
    1. It targets reducing the aggregate losses from power theft to 15% by 2019.
    2. An envisaged impact of the scheme is increased demand for power.
    3. The Central Government will not include the discom debt taken over by States as per the above scheme in the calculation of fiscal deficit of respective States for the financial years 2015-16 to 2019-20.
    Which of the statements given above is/are correct?
    (a) 1 and 2 only      (b) 2 and 3 only
    (c) 1 and 3 only      (d) 1, 2 and 3

94. With reference to "Gram Uday se Bharat Uday Abhiyan", which of the following statement is/are correct?
    1. It was launched to make nationwide efforts to strengthen Panchayati Raj institution in India.
    2. The scheme will promote rural development and foster farmers'welfare & livelihoods of the poor.
    3. It was launched on 125th Birth Anniversary of Mahatma Gandhi.
    Select the correct answer using the code given below
    (a) 1 and 2 only      (b) 2 and 3 only
    (c) 1 and 3 only      (d) 1, 2 and 3

95. Consider the following statement:
    1. As per the standard practice, India's external debt statistics are released with a lag of one quarter.
    2. At end-September 2018, India's external debt witnessed a decline of 3.6 % over its level at end-March 2018
    3. The external debt to GDP ratio stood at 20.8 % at end-September 2018, higher than its level of 20.5 % at end-March 2018.
    Select the correct answer using the code given below
    (a) 1 and 2 only      (b) 2 and 3 only
    (c) 1 and 3 only      (d) 1, 2 and 3

96. Consider the following statements:
    1. Viruses were discovered during the first decade of 19th century.
    2. Giant viruses, which are more than twice the size of typical viruses, have complex genomes.
    3. The neurons of animal brains, including human brains, hold the genetic remnants of an ancient viral infection that may be key to how thought processes work
    Select the correct answer using the code given below
    (a) 1 and 2 only      (b) 2 and 3 only
    (c) 1 and 3 only      (d) 1, 2 and 3

97. Consider the following statements about the proteins that have designed by the scientist in the lab to zip together:
    1. It has the same characteristic as DNA molecules zip up to form a double helix.
    2. In the past, researchers interested in designing biomolecular nanomachines have often used DNA as a major component.
    Which of the statements given above is/are correct?
    (a) 1 only            (b) 2 only
    (c) Both 1 and 2      (d) Neither 1 nor 2

98. With reference to the Election Commission of India, consider the following statements:
    1. It is a permanent and independent body
    2. It is responsible for getting conduct the elections of President, Vice President and Municipal Corporations
    3. Article 324 of the Constitution envisages the provisions relating to the Election Commission
    Select the correct answer using the code given below
    (a) 1 and 2 only      (b) 2 and 3 only
    (c) 1 and 3 only      (d) 1, 2 and 3

99. In context to Election Commission of India, consider the following statements:
    1. The term of the Election Commissioners is up to 6 years or 65 years of age.
    2. He Decides the disqualification of a Member of Parliament by using his discretion power
    3. Chief Election Commissioner can be removed by the same procedure as it is followed to remove the Judge of the Supreme Court
    Select the correct answer using the code given below
    (a) 1 and 2 only      (b) 2 and 3 only
    (c) 1 and 3 only      (d) 1, 2 and 3

100. Which of the following is not one of the grounds for disqualification for being elected as a Member of Parliament?
    1. If the person holds an office of an office of profit under the State Government.
    2. If the person has voluntarily acquired citizenship of a foreign State.
    3. If the person has/had been detained under the Preventive Detention Law.
    Select the correct answer using the code given below
    (a) 1 only
    (b) 3 only
    (c) 1 and 3
    (d) 1, 2 and 3

## RESPONSE SHEET

| | | | | | | | | | |
|---|---|---|---|---|---|---|---|---|---|
| 1. | ⓐⓑⓒⓓ | 2. | ⓐⓑⓒⓓ | 3. | ⓐⓑⓒⓓ | 4. | ⓐⓑⓒⓓ | 5. | ⓐⓑⓒⓓ |
| 6. | ⓐⓑⓒⓓ | 7. | ⓐⓑⓒⓓ | 8. | ⓐⓑⓒⓓ | 9. | ⓐⓑⓒⓓ | 10. | ⓐⓑⓒⓓ |
| 11. | ⓐⓑⓒⓓ | 12. | ⓐⓑⓒⓓ | 13. | ⓐⓑⓒⓓ | 14. | ⓐⓑⓒⓓ | 15. | ⓐⓑⓒⓓ |
| 16. | ⓐⓑⓒⓓ | 17. | ⓐⓑⓒⓓ | 18. | ⓐⓑⓒⓓ | 19. | ⓐⓑⓒⓓ | 20. | ⓐⓑⓒⓓ |
| 21. | ⓐⓑⓒⓓ | 22. | ⓐⓑⓒⓓ | 23. | ⓐⓑⓒⓓ | 24. | ⓐⓑⓒⓓ | 25. | ⓐⓑⓒⓓ |
| 26. | ⓐⓑⓒⓓ | 27. | ⓐⓑⓒⓓ | 28. | ⓐⓑⓒⓓ | 29. | ⓐⓑⓒⓓ | 30. | ⓐⓑⓒⓓ |
| 31. | ⓐⓑⓒⓓ | 32. | ⓐⓑⓒⓓ | 33. | ⓐⓑⓒⓓ | 34. | ⓐⓑⓒⓓ | 35. | ⓐⓑⓒⓓ |
| 36. | ⓐⓑⓒⓓ | 37. | ⓐⓑⓒⓓ | 38. | ⓐⓑⓒⓓ | 39. | ⓐⓑⓒⓓ | 40. | ⓐⓑⓒⓓ |
| 41. | ⓐⓑⓒⓓ | 42. | ⓐⓑⓒⓓ | 43. | ⓐⓑⓒⓓ | 44. | ⓐⓑⓒⓓ | 45. | ⓐⓑⓒⓓ |
| 46. | ⓐⓑⓒⓓ | 47. | ⓐⓑⓒⓓ | 48. | ⓐⓑⓒⓓ | 49. | ⓐⓑⓒⓓ | 50. | ⓐⓑⓒⓓ |
| 51. | ⓐⓑⓒⓓ | 52. | ⓐⓑⓒⓓ | 53. | ⓐⓑⓒⓓ | 54. | ⓐⓑⓒⓓ | 55. | ⓐⓑⓒⓓ |
| 56. | ⓐⓑⓒⓓ | 57. | ⓐⓑⓒⓓ | 58. | ⓐⓑⓒⓓ | 59. | ⓐⓑⓒⓓ | 60. | ⓐⓑⓒⓓ |
| 61. | ⓐⓑⓒⓓ | 62. | ⓐⓑⓒⓓ | 63. | ⓐⓑⓒⓓ | 64. | ⓐⓑⓒⓓ | 65. | ⓐⓑⓒⓓ |
| 66. | ⓐⓑⓒⓓ | 67. | ⓐⓑⓒⓓ | 68. | ⓐⓑⓒⓓ | 69. | ⓐⓑⓒⓓ | 70. | ⓐⓑⓒⓓ |
| 71. | ⓐⓑⓒⓓ | 72. | ⓐⓑⓒⓓ | 73. | ⓐⓑⓒⓓ | 74. | ⓐⓑⓒⓓ | 75. | ⓐⓑⓒⓓ |
| 76. | ⓐⓑⓒⓓ | 77. | ⓐⓑⓒⓓ | 78. | ⓐⓑⓒⓓ | 79. | ⓐⓑⓒⓓ | 80. | ⓐⓑⓒⓓ |
| 81. | ⓐⓑⓒⓓ | 82. | ⓐⓑⓒⓓ | 83. | ⓐⓑⓒⓓ | 84. | ⓐⓑⓒⓓ | 85. | ⓐⓑⓒⓓ |
| 86. | ⓐⓑⓒⓓ | 87. | ⓐⓑⓒⓓ | 88. | ⓐⓑⓒⓓ | 89. | ⓐⓑⓒⓓ | 90. | ⓐⓑⓒⓓ |
| 91. | ⓐⓑⓒⓓ | 92. | ⓐⓑⓒⓓ | 93. | ⓐⓑⓒⓓ | 94. | ⓐⓑⓒⓓ | 95. | ⓐⓑⓒⓓ |
| 96. | ⓐⓑⓒⓓ | 97. | ⓐⓑⓒⓓ | 98. | ⓐⓑⓒⓓ | 99. | ⓐⓑⓒⓓ | 100. | ⓐⓑⓒⓓ |

# HINTS & EXPLANATIONS

1. **(b)** The Indian Seasons have been the subject of beautiful descriptions in poetry, prose and drama since ancient times and the relationship between man and nature has been fundamental to India's worldview.

   The paintings of barahmasa (the depiction of twelve months in painting) appear to be modest attempts to correlate the artistic and literary endeavours of Indian poets and painters, portraying the cycle of seasons.

   **Source:** NCERT : Natural Heritage

2. **(c)** Gulf of Mannar is the first Bio-sphere Reserve in Asia. It lies between the South eastern tip of India and the west coast of Sri Lanka, in the coromandal coast region.

   Fauna found in Gulf of Mannar–Endangered Dugong (sea cow) three species of endangered sea turtles, sea horses, several species of dolphins and whales etc.

   – It is a part of UNESCO MAB (MAN and Biosphere) programme.

3. **(c)** Capital account transactions are two way and multiple transactions. It means paid money can be recovered through periodical income and/or by disposal of the asset created.

   The Capital Account Constitutes of
   1. External assistance (Net).
   2. Net External Commercial Borrowings.
   3. Short term debt.
   4. Banking Capital.
   5. Foreign Investment.
   6. Foreign Direct Investment (FDI)

   **Source:** Key concepts- Shankar ganesh.

4. **(c)** Under the Project Stree Swabhiman, sanitary napkin micro manufacturing units (semi-automatic and manual process production unit) are being set up at CSCs across India, particularly those operated by women entreprenuers.

5. **(b)** Ugantar was published from Bengal and Kal from Maharashtra.

   Sandhya, Ugantar and Kal were the news paper that advocated revolutionary terrorism during the National Freedom struggle.

6. **(b)** Article-123 of the constitution empowers the president to promulgate ordinance during the recess of Parliament. These ordinances have the same force and effect & as an act of Parliament, but are in nature temporary laws.

   – He can promulgate an ordinance only when both the Houses of parliament are not in session or when either of the two houses of parliament is not in session.

   An ordinance made when both the houses are in session is void. Thus the power of the president to legislate by ordinance is not a parallel power of legislation.

7. **(d)** E-nose or electronic nose is used for monitoring of obnoxious odours released from industries. An E-nose or electronic nose is a device that identifies the specific components of an odor and analyzes its chemical makeup to identify it. An electronic nose consists of a mechanism for chemical detection, such as an array of electronic sensors and a mechanism for pattern recognition such as a neural network.

8. **(c)** The lesser Himalayas or the Himachal Range is in the South of the Great Himalayas.

   There are several small ranges under the lesser Himalayas which are– Pir Panjal Range, Dhauladhar Range, Nag-Tibba Range, Mahabharata Range.

9. **(d)** Both are inclined towards peace, denied the efficacy of rituals in difference to the authority of Vedas and follow Celibacy.

10. **(d)** The Government of India Act is not relevant in this context.

    Besides the legal provisions given in the question, there are certain other provisions like
    – The wildlife (protection) Act of 1972
    – The forest (conservation) Act of 1980
    – The unlawful Activities (prevention) Act of 1967

11. **(c)** The largest producer of kyanite is Jharkhand (83%) followed by Maharashtra (16).

12. **(a)** Finance Commission consists of a chairman and four other members to be appointed by the president.
    – The commission submits its report to the president. He lays it before both the houses of parliament.

13. **(c)** Talas are rhythmic cycles. They have a universal unity, besides being quite complicated. The fundamental units of the Indian rhythmic structure are thisra (three), chatusra (four), khanda (five), misra (seven) and sankeertana (nine)

14. **(c)** Frog and mammals both contains a pair of lungs. The exchange of gases in both of them takes place in lungs. In addition frogs also respire through their moist skin.

15. **(d)** The Nayaka System was a major political innovation of Vijaynagara Empire. Many features of this system were derived from the Iqta system of Delhi-Sultanate. The Amara-Nayaka were military commanders who were given territories to govern by the raya. They sent tribute to the King annually and personally. Kings occasionally asserted their control over Amara Nayaka by transferring them from one place to another.

16. **(c)** Resistivity of conductor is smaller than that of Insulator. Resistivity of an alloy is greater than its constituent metals.

17. **(d)** Black carbon is produced both naturally and by human activities as a result of the incomplete combustion of fossil fuels, bio fuels and biomass.

– It is known to be one-fourth as potent as carbon dioxide in whetting global warming.

– Black carbon particles strongly absorb sunlight and give soot its black colour.

18. (c) In India the method of election followed for the General elections and assembly elections is First Past the Post (FPTP) system. In this system whoever has more votes than all other candidates is declared elected. The winning candidate need not secure a majority of the votes.

– This method of election is also called the plurality system.

– This is the method of election prescribed by the constitution.

**Source:** N.C.E.R.T. (Std. XI$^{th}$) (Chapter 3)

19. (d) Algae or phytoplankton are microscopic organisms that can be found naturally in coastal waters. They are major producers of oxygen and food for many of the animals that live in these waters.

– When environmental conditions are favourable for their development, these cells may multiply rapidly and form high number of cells and this is called algal bloom.

– A bloom often results in a color change in the water. Algal blooms can be of any color, but the most common ones are red or brown. These blooms are commonly referred to as red or brown tides.

– Most algal blooms are not harmful but some produce toxins and do affect fish, birds, marine mammals and humans.

20. (b) The Urban HUNGaMA (Hunger and Malnutrition) survey collected data on Urban Nutrition. The survey was conducted to capture nutritional data of children between 0-59 months in ten largest cities of India.

21. (c) National vector borne disease control programme is an umbrella programme for prevention and control of vector borne diseases and is subsumed under National Health Mission. Vector borne diseases that are being targeted are Malaria, Dengue, Lymphatic filariasis, Kala-azar, Japenese Encephalitis and chikungunya.

22. (c) The Brazzaville declaration was signed to promote better management and conservation of world's largest tropical peatlands-Cuvette centrale region in Congo basin from unregulated land use and prevent its drainage and degradation. It was signed jointly by Democratic Republic of Congo (DRC), Republic of Congo and Indonesia on the sidelines of Third Partners Meeting of Global Peatlands Initiative held in Brazzaville, Republic of Congo.

– Peatlands are globally important carbon store.

23. (c) The World Development Report is published by World Bank or the International Bank for Reconstruction and Development (IBRD). The 2018 report was titled. "Learning to Realize Education's Promise".

The report has warned of a learning crisis in global education particularly in low and middle income countries like India.

– The World Development Report is an annual report and the first report was published in 1978.

**Source:** The Hindu.

24. (b) As of 2017, Chhattisgarh is the largest coal producing state followed by Jharkhand, Odisha & Madhya Pradesh.

25. (c) All the above given statements are correct. Cabinet committees are extra-constitutional as they are not mentioned in the constitution.

They are of two types-standing and adhoc. The former are of a permanent nature while the latter are of a temporary nature.

In case the prime minister is a member of a committee he invariably presides over it.

26. (d) When it became rather difficult to Sustain the high pitch of the struggle, Gandhi decided to devote all his attention to the Struggle. The Tolstoy Farm was meant to house the families of the Satyagrahis and to give them a way to sustain themselves.

27. (b) Stockholm convention aims to contain use of persistent organic pollutant (POPs.) DDT is allowed to used publicy for control of malaria (this is an exception).

28. (b) The Global Innovation Index is an annual ranking of countries by their capacity for and success in innovation. It is published by INSEAD; World Intellectual property organisation.

29. (b) Under Lead Bank Scheme a particular bank is designated as Lead Bank of the district. It co-ordinates the activities of all banks in that district to avoid duplication of banking works, to ensure same person does not get loans from different Banks.

30. (b) The Thar link express connects Jodhpur and Karachi. India and Pakistan have extended agreement of Thar Link Express, Second Solitary Rail Service between both countries for three years. It carries only passengers.

31. (b) Parts of western coast and north east India receive over about 400 cm of rainfall annually. However it is less than 60 cm in western

Rajasthan and adjoining parts of Gujarat, Haryana and Punjab.

– Rainfall is equally low in the interiors of the Deccan plateau, and east of the Sahyadris.

– A third area of low precipitation is around Leh in Jammu and Kashmir.

– The rest of the country receives moderate rainfall.

– Snowfall is restricted to the Himalayan region.

32. (b) Judiciary has the powers and responsibility to protect the fundamental rights from violations by actions of the government.

Executive as well as legislative actions can be declared illegal by the judiciary if these violate the fundamental rights or restrict them in an unreasonable manners.

However fundamental rights are not absolute or unlimited rights. Govt. can put reasonable restrictions on the exercise of our fundamental rights.

33. (a) Superconductivity is the state of matter displayed by certain materials to conduct electric current without any resistance. The phenomenon takes place at low temperature.

34. (a) Lisbon Treaty is an international treaty which amended maastricht treaty and treaty of Rome to form European Union on constitutional basis. It was signed by EU member States in 2007.

35. (b) In modern times, elected local government bodies were created after 1882. Lord Ripon, who was the viceroy of India at that time, took the initiative in creating these bodies. They were called local boards.
    Government of India Act 1919 (Montagu Chelmsford) reforms provided for the establishment of village panchayats. Consequently village panchayats were established in a number of provinces. This trend continued after the government of India Act of 1935.

36. (b) Cyber Surakshit Bharat Initative has been launched by Ministry of Electronics and Information Technology in association with National e-Governace Division (NeGD) and industry partners to strengthen cyber Security ecosystem in India. It aims to spread awarness about cybercrime and build capacity of chief information security officers (CISOs) and frontline IT staff across all government departments.

37. (d) Mangroves are medium height shrubs, found in Saline Coastal regions. Mangroves are mainly found in tropical and sub-tropical region. Mangroves are Salt-tolerant halophytes. Mangroves flourish well in anaerobic conditions.
    The following posses threat to healthy sustainability of mangroves:
    – Production forestry
    – Land clearance
    – Introduced species
    – Agriculture
    – Marine farming
    – Infilling and reclamation
    – Channel dredging

38. (b) Jizya, Zakat, Khams, Kharaj, Ushr, Trade tax, House tax, Horse tax, Mines tax were the main sources of revenue during medieval period. Jizya was a tax on Non-Muslims. Women Children, beggars, priests, Brahmans etc and all those who had no source of income were exempted from this tax Firoz Tughlaq levied this tax on Brahmans also. Zakat was a religious tax which was imposed only on rich Muslims and it was 2.5% of their income. Ushr was the Land tax which was collected from the peasant.

39. (b) Chairman of 20th Law commission Ajit Prakash Shah has recommended for audio-visual recording of court proceedings.
    – Recently Supreme court ordered installation of CCTV cameras in courtrooms and its premises without audio recordings in at leasts two districts of all states.

– Supreme court made it clear that footage of CCTV cameras will not be available under RTI.
    **Source:** The Hindu

40. (b) The Financial Stability Report, 2017 is released by the RBI. It stated that India's NPA stands at 9.6%.

41. (c) Jawara is performed in the Bundelkhand area on wedding occassions, the countryside women of Malwa perform the Matki dance with an earthen pot balanced on the head.
    The phulpati is exclusively for unmarried girls. It is a dance of the semi-rural women folk.

42. (b) Ecotone is a zone of junction between two or more diverse ecosystems. For example the mangrove forests represent an ecotone between marine and terrestrial ecosystem.
    Ecotone may be very narrow or quite wide. It has conditions intermediate to the adjacent ecosystems. Hence it is a zone of tension.
    A well developed ecotone contains some organisms which are entirely different from that of the adjoining communities.
    Sometimes the number of species and the population density of some of the species is much greater in this zone than either community. This is called edge effect.

43. (d) The Mediterranean type of climate is characterized by very distinctive climatic features.
    – All the above given are true regarding Mediterranean climate.

44. (c) Under Multiple burn technology during satellite launch, the rocket's engine is switched off and then switched on to control its height. It is used to place satellites in two different orbits.

45. (d) Photo chemical smog (smog) is a term used to describe air pollution that is a result of the interaction of sunlight with certain chemicals in the atmosphere.

46. (b) There are four concepts in the output of an economy - GNP, GDP, NNP and NDP. The NNP is the best method to measure growth of an economy as it covers all the nationals of a country and is also a net increase after depreciation. It is also called as "National Income" of an economy.

47. (c) Chemical weapons convention is a multilateral treaty that bans chemical weapons and requires their destruction within a specified period of time. Egypt, North Korea, Palestine and Sudan are the only countries that have not signed the convention.

48. (b)
    – The Chief Election Commissioner (CEC) presides over the Election Commission, but does not have more powers than the other Election Commissioners.
    – The CEC and the two Election Commissioners have equal powers to take all decisions relating to elections as a collective body.
    – For the conduct of free and fair elections an independent Election Commission has been provided for in Art 324.

- The constitution ensures the security of the tenure of the CEC and Election Commissioners. They are appointed for a six year term or continue till the age of 65 years, whichever is earlier.
- The CEC can be removed before the expiry of the term, by the president if both houses of parliament make such a recommendation with a special majority. This is done to ensure that a ruling party cannot remove a CEC who refuses to favour it in elections.

49. (a) The Earth Overshoot Day is calculated by World Wide Fund for Nature (WWF) and Global Footprint Network. It signifies that we have emitted more carbon than the Oceans and forests can absorb in a year.

50. (d) Intimate connection with nature and the seasons can also be seen in our music, both classical and folk. Some of the classical ragas are based on seasons or moods of the day.
Musical modes like Chaiti, Phag, Kajari etc. are essentially seasonal. Songs poetic compositions, festivals and even paintings have nature and the cycle of seasons as their theme.
**Source:** NCERT : Heritage of India

51. (d) The sulphur reservoir is in the soil and sediments where it is locked in organic (coal, oil and peat) and inorganic deposits (pyrite rock and sulphur rock) in the form of sulphates, sulphides and organic sulphur.
It is released by weathering of rocks, erosional runoff and decomposition of organic matter and is carried to terrestrial and aquatic ecosystem in salt solution.
The sulphur cycle is mostly sedimentary except two of its compounds hydrogen sulphide ($H_2S$) and sulphur dioxide ($SO_2$) add a gaseous component to its normal sedimentary cycle.

52. (b) Transpacific partnership was a free trade agreement between USA and 11 other pacific Rim nations i.e. Australia, New zealand, Singapore, Malaysia, Brunei, Veitnam, Japan, Canada, Mexico, Peru ad Chile and was signed in 2016. However, USA withdraw from it.

53. (c) CWC is managing DRIP (i.e. Dam Rehabilitation and Improvement Project)

54. (c) India's imports comprise of essentials such as crude petroleum, machineries and fertilizers which become expensive raising their prices facilitating 'import' of inflation.
All imports become expensive including raw materials, goods and machineries which further push up domestic costs. Rupee Depreciation widens the current account deficit, which may require dipping into scarce foreign exchange reserve.

55. (d) – At any given time, the chief justice of India can request a retired judge of the Supreme court or High court to act as an Ad hoc judge of the Supreme court.
– When there is a lack of Quorum in the Supreme court, the chief justice of India can appoint a judge of High court as Ad hoc judge to the Supreme court.

– Quorum: It is the minimum strength of the Supreme court which is required for Supreme court to function efficiently.
– The Ad hoc judges enjoy all the jurisdiction, powers and privileges of a judge of the Supreme court.

56. (b) All the above given statements are true with reference to the Green Revolution.
Components of Green revolution:
– High Yielding Varieties (HYV) of seeds.
– Irrigation.
– Use of fertilizers.
– Use of Insecticides and Pesticides.
– Command Area Development (CAD)
– Consolidation of Holdings.
– Land Reforms.
**Note:** The use of HYV seeds was restricted to the more affluent states such as Punjab, Andhra Pradesh and Tamilnadu. In the second phase of Green Revolution (Mid 1970s to Mid-1980s), the HYV technology spread to a large number of states.
**Source:** N.C.E.R.T. 11th Economics.

57. (b) The objective of mission parivar vikas is to accelerate access to high quality family planning choices based on information, reliable services and supplies within a rights-based framework. The districts are located in the seven high focus states of Uttar Pradesh, Bihar, Rajasthan, Madhya Pradesh, Chattisgarh, Jharkhand and Assam.

58. (b) In Mandi district, rock salt beds are found in association with the limestone, shale and sandstone belonging to the Sabathu or the Krol group of rocks.

59. (d) An ecosystem is defined as a structural and functional unit of biosphere consisting of community of living beings and the physical environment, both interacting and enchanging materials between them.
Ecosystem can be as small as a single tree or as large as entire forests.
eg. A well represents a complete ecosystem in itself as the amphibians in the well depends on phytoplanktons and zoo planktons present in the well.
Similarly a single tree can also be considered as an ecosystem.

60. (d) All the above statements are correct.
In September 2016, Government of India approved the merging of the Railway Budget with the Union budget of India and thus came to end a 92 year old practice of separate rail and general budgets.

61. (b) In addition to the members of a house, every minister and the advocate general of the state have the right to speak and take part in the proceedings of either house or any of its committees of which he is named a member, without being entitled to vote.
– Also A minister can participate in the proceedings of a house, of which he is not a member.
– A minister who is not a member of either house, can participate in the proceedings of both the houses.

62. (a) Exotic breeds are used for cross-breeding with local breeds to increase the lactation period. Lactation period is the duration of milk production after calving.

63. (a) The sun rises and sets at different times at different places. As the earth rotates from west to east, places in the east see the sun earlier than those in the west.
    – Unlike other planets, uranus orbits around the sun in a clockwise direction from east to west with five satellites revolving round it.

64. (b) Excess of the nutrients from a lake can be removed by following methods:
    – Flushing with nutrient-poor waters.
    – Deep water abstraction.
    – On-site algae swimming and separator thickening.
    – Harvest of fishes and macrophytes.
    – Sludge removal.
    – Artificial Mixing/Destratification

65. (c) Herbicide-Tolerant (HT) cotton also known as BG-III cotton is innovation in Bt cotton as it takes care of weeds problem at much lower cost as compared to physical labour required for weeding.

66. (d) The recent introduction of new series of national accounts by Central Statistics Office (CSO) revised the base for National Accounts Statistics to 2011-12 from 2004-05. Along with the revision of base, a number of Methodological changes have also been made.

67. (b) The above given events took place during the viceroy ship of Lord Reading (1921-1926)

68. (b) Gopal Hari Deshmukh, Raja Rammohan Ray and Ishwar Chandra Vidyasagar made inportant contribution to the growth of literature in their respective languages. Bhartendu Harishchandra was the pioneer of modern Hindi literature.

69. (a) The first seven five year plans gave importance to self-reliance which means avoiding imports of those goods which could be produced in India itself. This policy was considered a necessity in order to reduce our dependence on foreign countries, especially for food.
    The Government of India issued an ordinance (Banking Companies Acquisition and Transfer of undertaking ordinance, 1969) and nationalised the 14 largest commercial banks with effect from the midnight of 19 July 1969. These banks contained 85 percent of bank deposits in the country. (1966-69) Period of Plan Holidays). The years 1965-66 ushered India into Green Revolution and advanced agriculture. M.S. Swaminathan is considered as the architect of Green Revolution in India.
    **Source:** N.C.E.R.T 11th Economics.

70. (d) All the above mentioned are evidences of the fact that earth is a sphere:
    The early voyagers feared to venture deep into the sea because, it was believed that earth is flat like a table and if the ship reaches the edge, it will fall down.
    But now it is established well beyond doubt that earth is a sphere. Following are the evidences:

1. Modern air routes and ocean navigation are based on the assumption that the earth is round.
2. The distant horizon viewed from the deck of a ship at sea is always and everywhere circular in shape.
3. When a ship appears over the distant horizon, the top of the mast is seen first before the hull.
4. The sun rises and sets at different times at different places. As the earth rotates from west to east, places in the east see the sun earlier than those in the west.

71. (c) Some countries have subjected their constitution to a full-fledged referendum, where all the people vote on the desirability of a constitution.
    The Indian constitution was never subjected to such a referendum, but nevertheless carried enormous public authority because it had the consensus and backing of leaders who were themselves popular.
    Therefore the authority of people who enact the constitution helps determine in part its prospects for success.
    – Constitutional norms are the overarching framework within which one pursues individual aspirations, goals and freedoms.
    – The constitution sets authoritative constraints upon what one may or may not do. It defines the fundamental values that we may not trespass. So the constitution also gives one a moral identity.

72. (b) Nano $CO_2$ harvester can suck $CO_2$ from the atmosphere and convert it into Methanol. The converted methanol can further be used as vehicular fuel.

73. (d) National Health Protection Scheme will provide medical cover up to ₹ 5 lakh per year per household for secondary and tertiary health care. The premium will be shared in 60:40 ratio between centre and states. West bengal became the first state to opt out of the centre's National Health Protection Scheme (NHPS)

74. (b) Telangana is the 29th state of India. It is a land-locked state surrounded by four states–Andhra Pradesh, Chattisgarh, Maharashtra and Karnataka.

75. (c) The idea of "electoral bonds" was first announced in the Budget 2017-18 to make political funding more transparent.
    – The Donors can buy electoral bonds from specified branches of State Bank of India (SBI) for 10 days each in months of Jan., April, July and October.
    – The bonds would be valid for 15 days and will not carry the donor's name.
    – Although called a bond, the banking instruments resembling promissory note will not carry any interest.
    – Electoral bonds will allow donors to pay political parties using banks as an intermediary.
    **Source:** The Hindu

76. (c) Lead is present in petrol, diesel, lead batteries, paints, hair dye products etc. Lead affects children in particular.
    – It can cause nervous system damage and digestive problems and in some cases causes cancer.
    – The main component of Pencil lead is graphite.

77. (c) The Unorganised Sector is characterised by small and scattered units which are largely outside the control of the government. There are rules and regulations but these are not followed. Jobs here are low-paid and often not regular. There is no provision for overtime, paid leave, holidays, leave due to sickness etc. Employment is not secure. People can be asked to leave without any reason. Unorganised sector includes a large number of people who are employed on their own doing small jobs such as selling on the streets or doing repair work. Similarly farmers work on their own and hire labourers as and when they require.

     **Source:** N.C.E.R.T 10<sup>th</sup> Economics.

78. (c) A characteristic feature of the cold weather season over the northern plains is the inflow of cyclonic disturbances from the west and the north west.

     – These low pressure systems, originate over the mediterranean sea and western Asia and move into India, along with the westerly flow.

     – They cause the much-needed winter rains over the plains and snowfall in the mountains.

     – Although the total amount of winter rainfall locally known as 'Mahawat' is small, they are of immense importance for the cultivation of 'rabi' crops.

79. (c) Agriculture related subsidies that fit in WTO's green box are policies that are not restricted by the trade agreement because they are not considered trade distorting. To qualify for the Green box, subsidy must not distort trade or at most cause minimal distortion. The other two boxes are Amber box and Blue box.

80. (d) All the options (a), (b) and (c) are correct. Besides this, if the supply of goods or services or both are exempt under GST, then the recipient is not liable to pay tax under the reverse charge mechanism. The C GST law mandates registration for those who are required to pay tax under reverse charge, even if their turnover is less than the threshold limit of ₹ 20 Lakh.

81. (c) D.P.S.P have no legal force behind them as they are non-justiciable and not enforceable in the court of law. D.P.S.P are supplementary to fundamental Rights as these also include rights (although non-justiciable).

82. (d) All the above statements are correct.

     As a result of Industrial Manufacturing of nitrogen, it has become a pollutant which can disrupt the balance of nitrogen. It may lead to Acid rain, Eutrophication and Harmful Algal Blooms.

     Nitrogen is mainly manufactured by industrial method in the fertilizer sector.

83. (a) Dyarchy or the Act of devolution was introduced by Govt. of India Act of 1919.

The Regulating Act of 1773 also strengthened the control of the British Government over the company by requiring the Court of Directors (governing body of the company) to report on its revenue, civil & military affairs in India.

     – Remember: The Regulating Act of 1773 was the first step taken by the British Government to control and regulate the affairs of the East India company.

     **Source:** M. Lakshmikant

84. (a) Fortification is the process of adding vitamins/minerals to foods for prevention of malnutrition.

85. (c) Statement (i) and (ii) are correct. Besides this, the objective of the program is to create opportunities for the youth living in these areas so that they do not migrate to urban clusters. It is under the Digital India Programme. Metro cities such as Bengaluru, Chennai, Hyderabad, Kolkata, Mumbai, National Capital Region (NCR), and Pune, along with their urban agglomeration are excluded.

86. (d) As a loan arrangement, the Member Countries are entitled to get loan from IMF's Special Drawing Account. This loan is amount with IMF. It is also known as paper Gold. In this arrangement IMF does not lend directly. It is the member countries who are in strong position lend their SDR holdings to member countries who are in Balance of Payment Problem.

87. (d) The constitution confers the following rights and privileges on the citizens of India and denies the same to aliens.

1. Right against discrimination on grounds of religion, race, caste, sex or place of birth (Article 15).

2. Right to equality of opportunity in the matter of public employment (Article 16).

3. Right to freedom of speech and expression, assembly, association, movement, residence and profession (Article 19).

4. Cultural and educational rights (Articles 29 and 30).

5. Right to vote in elections to the Lok Sabha and state legislative assembly.

6. Right to contest for the membership of the Parliament and the state legislature.

7. Eligibility to hold certain public offices, that is President of India, Vice-President of India, judges of the Supreme Court and the high courts, governor of states, attorney general of India and advocate general of states.

88. (b) The Citizenship Act (1955) provides for acquisition and loss of citizenship after the commencement of the constitution. Originally, the Act also provided for

the commonwealth citizenship. But this provision was replaced by Citizenship (Amendment) Act, 2003.

89. (c) The constitution of India deals with the citizenship from Articles 5 to 11 under Part II. However, it does not contain any permanent or any elaborate provisions in this regard. It does not deal with the problems of acquision or loss of citizenship. The constition empowers the Parliament to enact a law to provide for such matters and any other matter relating to citizenship. Accordingly, the Parliament has enacted the citizenship Act, 1955, which has been amended in 1986, 1992, 2003 and 2005.

90. (d) The Government of India and the World Bank on 2nd February, 2018 signed a $375 million loan agreement to support India develop its first modern inland water transport fairway on the Ganga river between Varanasi and the seaport of Haldia. National Waterway-1 is an inland water transport route between Haldia in West Bengal to Prayagraj in Uttar Pradesh.

91. (b) PM LPG Panchayats consist of meetings of Ujjwala beneficiaries. These meetings will serve as platforms for the government to interface with the beneficiaries, harness their experiences and integrate them to create a knowledge base for triggering a sustainable and viable movement around Ujjwala. Such panchayats bring together about 100 (women) LPG customers together near their living areas on an interactive platform to discuss about safe and sustainable usage of LPG, it's benefits and the linkage between use of clean fuel for cooking and women empowerment.

92. (c) The Startup India Yatra is an initiative that travels to Tier 2 and Tier-3 cities of India to search for entrepreneurial talent and help develop Startup ecosystem. The Startup Yatras have covered the States of Gujarat, Uttar Pradesh and Odisha where more than 18000 young entrepreneurs were supported through mentorship. Startup Yatra in Uttarakhand has recently been started on 2 April.

93. (a) As per the provisions of UDAY: States shall take over 75% of DISCOM debt as on 30 September 2015 over two years – 50% of DISCOM debt shall be taken over in 2015-16 and 25% in 2016-17. Government of India will not include the debt taken over by the States as per the above scheme in the calculation of fiscal deficit of respective States in the financial years 2015-16 and 2016-17.

94. (a) The Central Government, in collaboration with State Governments and Panchayats, launched the 'Gramoday se Bharat Uday Abhiyan'. The campaign began with Dr. Bhimrao Ambedkar's 125th Birth Anniversary on 14th April 2016, and culminates with the Panchayati Raj Day on 24th April 2016.

95. (d) As per RBI press release, at end-September 2018, India's external debt witnessed a decline of 3.6 % over its level at end-March 2018, on account of a decrease in commercial borrowings and non-resident Indian (NRI) deposits. The decrease in the magnitude of external debt was primarily due to valuation gains resulting from the appreciation of the US dollar against the Indian rupee and major currencies.

96. (b) Scientist discovered Viruses in 1892, and yet even in 2018, researchers are still uncovering new secrets about these infectious invaders

97. (c) Proteins have now been designed in the lab to zip together in much the same way that DNA molecules zip up to form a double helix. The technique, whose development was led by University of Washington School of Medicine scientists, could enable the design of protein nano machines that can potentially help diagnose and treat disease, allow for the more exact engineering of cells and perform a wide variety of other tasks.

98. (c) The election commission is not concerned with the election to Panchayats and Municipalities in the State. For this, the constitution of India provides for a separate State Election Commission.

99. (c) The Election Commission shall seek the approval of the president in deciding the disqualification of a Member of Parliament.

100. (b) As per the provision of the Article 102; Disqualifications for being elected as an MP:

(1) A person shall be disqualified for being chosen as, and for being, a member of either House of Parliament-

(a) If he holds any office of profit under the Government of India or the Government of any State, other than an office declared by Parliament by law not to disqualify its holder;

(b) If he is of unsound mind and stands so declared by a competent court;

(c) If he is an undischarged insolvent;

(d) If he is not a citizen of India, or has voluntarily acquired the citizenship of a foreign State, or is under any acknowledgement of allegiance or adherence to a foreign State;

(e) If he is so disqualified by or under any law made b by Parliament, explanation For the purposes of this clause a person shall not be deemed to hold an office of profit under the Government of India or the Government of any State by reason only that he is a Minister either for the Union or for such State.

(2) A person shall be disqualified for being a member of either House of Parliament if he is so disqualified under the Tenth Schedule.

# 2 MOCK TEST

1. In the wake of alleged data breaches of Aadhaar, Unique. Identification Authority of India (UIDAI) has introduced virtual IDs.
   Which of the following is/are, incorrect with reference to virtual IDs?
   (1) It is a 10 digit permanent number:
   (2) It can be generated only one by Aadhaar holders.
   (3) It is compulsory for all agencies that undertake authentication to accept virtual ID from their users.
   Select the correct answer using the codes given below.
   (a) (1) and (2) only.   (b) (2) and (3) only.
   (c) (1) and (3) only.   (d) (3) only.

2. Which of the following is not among the 10 Indicators of Multidimensional Poverty Index:
   (a) Nutrition       (b) Water
   (c) Electricity     (d) Housing

3. Consider the following statements:
   1. A minister can only be a member of the Lok Sabha.
   2. The ministers are collectively responsible to the Parliament.
   Select the correct statement/statements using the codes given below.
   (a) 1 only          (b) 2 only
   (c) Both 1 and 2    (d) Neither 1 nor 2.

4. Which of the following desert has become the first desert in the world to achieve large-scale desertification control?
   (a) Sonoran Desert     (b) Mojave Desert
   (c) Chihuahuan Desert  (d) Kubuqi Desert

5. The largest and most spectacular rock shelter is located in the Vindhya hills in Madhya Pradesh. With reference to the themes of these paintings; consider the following.
   1. Mundane events of daily life
   2. Hunting and dancing
   3. Animal fight
   4. Royal and Sacred images
   Select the correct answer using codes given below.
   (a) 1, 2 and 3 only    (b) 2, 3 and 4 only
   (c) 1, 2, 3 and 4      (d) 1 and 3 only

6. Which among the following are examples of traditional theatre forms:
   (1) Yakshagana      (2) Thumri
   (3) Teyyam          (4) Phitlam
   Select the correct answer from the codes given below.
   (a) (1) and (2) only   (b) (2) and (3) only
   (c) (1) and (3) only   (d) All the above

7. With reference to Mahalwari system, consider the following statements:
   1. Ownership rights were vested with Zamindars.
   2. It was an amalgamation of both the Zamindari system and Ryotwari system.

Which of the statements given above is/are correct?
   (a) 1 only          (b) 2 only
   (c) Both 1 and 2    (d) Neither 1 nor 2

8. Consider the following statements with reference to lakes in India.
   1. In India, Natural lakes mostly lie in the peninsula region.
   2. On the basis of their nutrient content, vast majority of lakes are Eutrophic or mesotrophic.
   Select the correct statement/statements using codes given below:
   (a) 1 only          (b) 2 only
   (c) Both 1 and 2    (d) Neither 1 nor 2

9. Consider the following statements with reference to the National Human Rights Commission (NHRC):
   1. The chairman should be a retired chief justice of India.
   2. The chairman and members are not eligible for further employment under the central/state government post retirement.
   Select the correct statement/statements using the codes given below:
   (a) 1 only          (b) 2 only
   (c) Both 1 and 2    (d) Neither 1 nor 2

10. Which of the following is/are not among the features of "Khelo India" programme.
   (1) Each athlete selected under the programme will get a scholarship of ₹ 5 lakh per annum for eight years.
   (2) Government aims to set up 20 universities across the country as hubs of sporting excellence.
   (3) It subsumed earlier three different sports schemes into one namely: Rajiv Gandhi Khel Abhiyan, (RGKA) National Sports Talent Search Scheme (NSTSS) and urban sports infrastructure scheme (USIS).
   Select the correct answer using the codes given below:
   (a) All are correct.   (b) (1) and (2)
   (c) (1) and (3)        (d) (2) and (3)

11. Which among the following is/are not Jain literature
   1. Kalp Sutra        2. Angutar Nikaya
   3. Acharang Sutra    4. Milanda Panho
   Select the correct answer from the codes given below.
   (a) 1 and 3 only     (b) 2 and 4 only
   (c) 1 and 4 only     (d) 2 and 3 only

12. Consider the following statements :
   1. Supreme court has power to review its own judgement.
   2. All authorities, civil and judicial shall act in aid of the Supreme court.
   Choose the correct statement/statements –
   (a) 1 only           (b) 2 only
   (c) Both 1 & 2       (d) None of the Above

13. Bioindicators, sometimes seen in the news, are related to
    (a) Health of few endangered species
    (b) Health of the patient
    (c) Health of the ecosystem
    (d) Health of the plant
14. The process of burning waste in large furnaces at high temperature is known as:
    (a) Incineration        (b) Pyrolysis
    (c) Composting          (d) None of the above
15. Consider the following statements with reference to Indian Economy:
    1. The share of agriculture sector in GDP has consistently declined since 1950.
    2. Services Sector has maximum contribution in GDP in present times.
    Select the correct statement/ statements using the codes given below:
    (a) 1 only              (b) 2 only
    (c) Both 1 and 2        (d) Neither 1 nor 2
16. Consider the following statements
    1. The constitution has given the states the option of establishing either a unicameral or bicameral legislature.
    2. At present only 5 states have bicameral legislature.
    Select the correct statement/statements using the codes given below.
    (a) 1 only              (b) 2 only
    (c) Both 1 and 2        (d) Neither 1 nor 2
17. Consider the following statements with reference to Pradhan Mantri MUDRA Yojana
    (1) It is a program launched to give access to cheap credit to poor and small fledgling businesspersons.
    (2) Under the program, loans are given to non-farm income generating enterprises whose credit needs are below ₹10 lakh
    (3) Micro Units Development and Refinance Agency Ltd. (MUDRA) is an NBFC.
    Which of the above statement/statements is/are correct?
    (a) (1) and (2)         (b) (2) and (3)
    (c) All are correct     (d) (1) and (3)
18. Consider the following statements.
    (1) G-4 nations comprises of India, South Africa, Brazil and Canada.
    (2) G-4 nations support each other's bids for permanent seats in the UN Security council
    Which of the statement/statements given above is/are correct.
    (a) (1) only            (b) (2) only
    (c) Both (1) and (2)    (d) Neither (1) nor (2)
19. With reference to the Prehistoric Rock painting, consider the following statements.
    1. Animals were painted in a naturalistic style.
    2. Humans were depicted only in a stylistic manner.
    3. There were as many as 20 layers of paintings, one on top of another.
    Select the correct statements from the codes given below.
    (a) 1 and 2 only        (b) 2 and 3 only
    (c) 1 and 3 only        (d) 1, 2 and 3
20. Which of the following is are true regarding the Intended Nationally Determined Contribution (INDC) of India:
    1. 40% electric power installed capacity from non-fossil fuel based energy resources by 2030.

    2. Additional carbon sink of 2.5 to 3 billion tonnes of $CO_2$ equivalent.
    Select the correct answer using the codes given below:
    (a) 1 only              (b) 2 only
    (c) Both 1 and 2        (d) Neither 1 nor 2
21. Consider the following statements:
    1. In the original constitution the subject of local government was assigned to the states.
    2. Local government was mentioned in DPSP as one of the policy directives to all governments in the country.
    Select the correct statement/statements using the codes given below:
    (a) 1 only              (b) 2 only
    (c) Both 1 and 2        (d) Neither 1 nor 2
22. Arrange the following rivers of northeast India in the order from east to west.
    1. Raidak               2. Jaldhaka
    3. Kamneng              4. Manas
    Select the correct answer from the codes given below:
    (a) 1, 3, 2, 4          (b) 3, 4, 1, 2
    (c) 4, 3, 2, 1          (d) 1, 2, 3, 4
23. Consider the following statements:
    1. Mankidia are classified as scheduled caste in Odisha
    2. Mankidia people are trained in hunting the birds
    Which of the statements given above is/are correct?
    (a) 1 only              (b) 2 only
    (c) Both 1 and 2        (d) Neither 1 nor 2
24. With reference to the Jain Philosophy, consider the following statements:
    1. The doctrines of Jainism were similar from the period of Rishabhnatha to Mahavira.
    2. Jainism recognized the existence of god as a supreme.
    Which of the statements given above is/are correct?
    (a) 1 only              (b) 2 only
    (c) Both 1 and 2        (d) Neither 1 nor 2
25. Read the following statements with reference to MIMO.
    1. It is a type of Antenna-free technology.
    2. It is a type of Video communications technology.
    Select the correct answer using the code given below.
    (a) 1 only              (b) 2 only
    (c) 1 and 2 only        (d) Neither 1 nor 2
26. With reference to the veto powers of the President of India, consider the following statements:
    1. He possess suspensive veto in the case of money bills.
    2. President has no veto power in respect of a constitutional amendment bill.
    Select the correct statement/statements using the codes given below:
    (a) 1 only              (b) 2 only
    (c) Both 1 and 2        (d) Neither 1 nor 2
27. The use of microorganisms (bacteria and fungi) to degrade the environmental contaminants into less toxic forms is known as
    (a) Bio-magnification   (b) Bio-Remediation
    (c) Both (a) and (b)    (d) None of the above

28. Read the following statements with reference to division of cells.
    1. Mitosis is equational division.
    2. Mitosis is restricted to haploid cells.
    3. Some of the haploid cells also divide by meiosis.
    Select the correct answer using the codes given below.
    (a) 1 only
    (b) 2 only
    (c) 2 and 3 only
    (d) 1 , 2 and 3

29. Which of the following is not among the arguments in favour of India's bid for UN Security Council membership?
    (a) India is the founding member of UN.
    (b) India is the second largest contributor to UN peacekeeping operations.
    (c) Strong Political will of Permanent members to change the composition of the P5.
    (d) None of these

30. If one has to travel through the horn of Africa to reach Turkey, which of the following countries will come in the way:
    1. Saudi Arabia       2. Yemen
    3. Iran               4. Sudan
    Select the correct answer from the codes given below.
    (a) 1, 2 and 3 only
    (b) 2, 3 and 4 only
    (c) 1, 2 and 4 only
    (d) All the above

31. Consider the following statements:
    1. No two biomes are alike.
    2. Aquatic systems are not called biomes.
    Select the correct answer from the codes given below:
    (a) 1 only
    (b) 2 only
    (c) Both 1 and 2
    (d) Neither 1 nor 2

32. Which among the following is/are correct for the cold weather season in India:
    1. The peninsular region has a well defined cold season.
    2. North-east trade winds prevail over the country.
    3. The temperature decreases from south to the north.
    4. In flow of cyclonic disturbances from the west in the southern India.
    Select the correct answer using the codes given below:
    (a) 1, 2 and 3 only
    (b) 2 and 3 only
    (c) 1, 3 and 4 only
    (d) 2, 3 and 4 only

33. Which of the following statements stands true with reference to the constitution of India?
    1. The policy of reservation shall not be seen as a violation of the right to equality.
    2. Right to shelter and livelihood is a Fundamental Right.
    Select the correct answer using the codes given below:
    (a) 1 only
    (b) 2 only
    (c) Both 1 and 2
    (d) None of the above

34. Consider the following statements:
    1. The savanna is confined within the tropics.
    2. Trade winds are the prevailing winds in Savanna.
    3. Savanna witnesses moderate diurnal range of temperature.
    Select the correct answer from the codes given below:
    (a) 1 and 2 only
    (b) 2 and 3 only
    (c) 2 and 3 only
    (d) 1, 2 and 3

35. Which among the following is/are Scorpene-class Submarines?
    (1) INS Khanderi
    (2) INS Kalvari
    (3) INS Ranvijay
    (4) INS Karanj
    Select the correct answer using the codes given below.
    (a) (1) and (2)
    (b) (1), (2) and (3)
    (c) (1) and (3)
    (d) (1), (2) and (4)

36. With reference to Al.-Biruni's description of the caste system, consider the following statements:
    1 He explained Indian cast system by looking for parallels in other societies.
    2 Social divisions were not unique to India.
    Which of the above statements is/are correct?
    (a) 1 only
    (b) 2 only
    (c) Both 1 and 2
    (d) Neither 1 nor 2

37. The relationship between the percentage of income or wealth earned and percentage of people who earned that particular percentage of income/wealth is best described by–
    (a) Kuznets curve
    (b) Gini coefficient
    (c) Lorenz curve
    (d) Engel's law

38. Consider the following statements:
    1. Hindi written in Devanagari Script is to be the official language of the union.
    2. The constitution does not specify the official language of different states.
    Select the correct statement/statements using the codes given below:
    (a) 1 only
    (b) 2 only
    (c) Both 1 and 2
    (d) Neither 1 nor 2

39. Consider the following statements.
    (1) The government has set up the target to double the farmer's income by 2020.
    (2) Government has restricted the export of certain types of pulses.
    (3) Various state governments have launched price deficiency payment (PDP) schemes to pay the difference between the Minimum Support Price (MSP) and the market-determined price.
    Which of the above statement/statements is/are correct?
    (a) (1) and (2)
    (b) (2) and (3)
    (c) Only (3)
    (d) All are correct

40. Least distance of distinct vision and near point of eye,
    1. is same for young adults with normal vision.
    2. is same for senior citizens with normal vision.
    3. is same for young adults with vision defect.
    Select the correct answer using the codes given below:
    (a) 1 only
    (b) 2 only
    (c) 3 only
    (d) 1, 2 and 3

41. Which nutrient is considered to be the main cause of excessive growth of rooted and free-floating microscopic plants in lakes?
    (a) Phosphorus
    (b) Sulphur
    (c) Nitrogen
    (d) Carbon

42. Consider the following statements with reference to the Central Bureau of Investigation (CBI).
    1. CBI comes under the ministry of Home Affairs.
    2. CBI is a constitutional body.
    Select the correct answer from the codes given below:
    (a) 1 only
    (b) 2 only
    (c) Both 1 and 2
    (d) Neither 1 nor 2

43. Which of the following is the correct order of the given plateaus from east to west.
    (1) Malwa plateau
    (2) Bhander plateau
    (3) Chota Nagpur plateau
    (4) Baghelkhand plateau

Codes:
(a)  (2), (3), (4), (1)    (b)  (3), (4), (2), (1)
(c)  (4) (2) (3) (1)    (d)  (3), (2), (4), (1)

44.  Which of the following correctly explains the purpose of "EoTT equipment" proposed by Indian Railways?
(a)  Prevention of collision of train bogies
(b)  It is wireless communication between stations and train
(c)  Communication system driver and last wagon of train
(d)  Facility to run the train in low visibility conditions like fog

45.  The Ghadr Party was a revolutionary group organised around a weekly newspaper 'The Ghadr'. The Ghadrites intended to bring about a revolt in India. Their plans were encouraged by
1.  The split in two factions of congress.
2.  The Komagata maru incident.
3.  The outbreak of the first world war.
4.  The launch of Home Rule movement.
Select the correct answer from the codes given below.
(a)  1 and 2 only    (b)  2 and 3 only
(c)  3 and 4 only    (d)  1 and 4 only

46.  Black Revolution pertains to the production of
(a)  Tobacco    (b)  Petroleum
(c)  Solar Energy    (d)  Jute

47.  Holographic technology can be used in which of the following fields
1.  Engineering and Architecture
2.  Health and medicine
3.  Tradeshows
Select the correct answer using the codes given below:
(a)  1 and 2 only    (b)  2 and 3 only
(c)  3 only    (d)  1, 2 and 3

48.  Governor of a state can promulgate ordinances when the state legislature is not in session. After the re-assembly of state legislature, these ordinances must be approved by it within
(a)  1 month    (b)  Six months
(c)  2 months    (d)  Three weeks

49.  Which of the following is the correct order of the given hills from north to south
(1)  Gawilgarh Hills    (2)  Shevaroy Hills
(2)  Javadi Hills    (4)  Cardamom Hills
Codes
(a)  (1), (3), (2), (4)    (b)  (1), (3), (2), (4)
(c)  (3), (1), (4) (2)    (d)  (3), (4), (1), (2)

50.  Consider the following statements with reference to "Ashgabat Agreement".
(1)  It aims to establish international transport and transit corridor linking Central Asia with the Persion Gulf.
(2)  Kazakhstan and Pakistan are not the part of this agreement
Which of the above Statement/Statements is/are correct?
(a)  Only (1)    (b)  Only (2)
(c)  Both (1) and (2)    (d)  Neither (1) nor (2)

51.  Before formally Launching the Civil Disobedience Movement (CDM), Gandhi put forward eleven demands before the British Government.
Which the following is/are not among those eleven demands?
1.  Introduce total prohibition.
2.  Dominion status for India.
3.  Universal adult-franchise.
4.  Reserve Coastal Shipping for Indians.
Select the correct answer using the codes given below:
(a)  1 and 2 only    (b)  1 and 3 only
(c)  1 and 4 only    (d)  3 and 4 only

52.  Which among the following is/are a source of Capital Receipts:
1.  External borrowings
2.  Net Market Loans
3.  Treasury Bills issued to RBI
4.  Ways and Means Advances
Select the correct answer from the codes given below:
(a)  1, 2 and 3 only    (b)  2, 3 and 4 only
(c)  1, 3 and 4 only    (d)  All 1, 2, 3, 4

53.  With reference to hydrogen as a fuel read the following statements,
1.  It can be extracted from any of hydrogen containing compound.
2.  Production cost of hydrogen based fuel is very less.
3.  In comparison to fossil fuels it generates lower nitric oxide.
4.  Energy content per unit weight of hydrogen based fuel is highest among all known fuels.
Which of the statements given above is/are correct?
(a)  1 and 2 only    (b)  2 and 3 only
(c)  3 and 4 only    (d)  1 and 4 only

54.  Which of the following statements is are true regarding Proportional Representation System of election:
1.  Voters exercise their preference for a party and not a candidate.
2.  More than one representative may be elected from one constituency
(a)  1 only    (b)  2 only
(c)  Both 1 and 2    (d)  None of the above

55.  Consider the following statements in context of conservation of elephants in India:
1.  Under the wildlife (protection) Act, 1972, Elephant is a schedule III animals.
2.  Asian elephants are listed as "Threatened" in the IUCN Red List of threatened species.
Select the correct statement/statements using the codes given below:
(a)  1 only    (b)  2 only
(c)  Both 1 and 2    (d)  Neither 1 nor 2

56.  Which of the following industry releases Inorganic pollutants like sulphuric acid, hydrogen sulphide, ferric hydroxide, suspended solids and heavy metals.
(a)  Iron and steel    (b)  Mining
(c)  Soop and detergent (d)  Paper and Pulp

57.  Reef formation in India can be witnessed in
(a)  Gulf of Kutch only.
(b)  Gulf of Mannar only.
(c)  Lakshadweep Islands only.
(d)  All the above.

58.  Consider the following statements:
1.  The centre of curvature of a convex mirror lies in front of it.
2.  Convex lens is also known as converging lens.
3.  Focal length is the distance between pole and principal focus of a spherical mirror.

Select the correct answer using the code given below.
(a)  2 only (b)  1 and 2 only
(c)  2 and 3 only (d)  1, 2 and 3

59. Which committee suggested the incorporation of eight fundamental duties in the constitution?
(a)  Balwant Rai Mehta Committee
(b)  Justice Shah Committee.
(c)  Sardar Swaran Singh Committee
(d)  None of the above

60. Consider the following statements with reference to government's expenditure on education.
1.  Elementary education takes a major share of total education expenditure.
2.  During 1952-2010, education expenditure as percentage of total government expenditure has increased uniformly.
Select the correct statement/statements using the codes given below:
(a)  1 only (b)  2 only
(c)  Both 1 and 2 (d)  Neither 1 nor 2

61. Which among the following is a major reason for desertification in India.
(a)  Wind erosion
(b)  Salinity
(c)  Vegetation degradation
(d)  Water erosion

62. During the Quit India Movement, the parallel governments were established at
(a)  Ballia (b)  Tamluk
(c)  Satara (d)  All the above

63. The tendency of toxic substances to increase in concentration progressively at higher levels of the food chain is known as
(a)  Bio-remediation (b)  Bio-magnification
(c)  Symbiosis (d)  Homeostasis

64. Which of the following features of the Constitution was described by Dr. B.R. Ambedkar as "Novel features" of the Indian Constitution–
(a)  Fundamental Rights.
(b)  Fundamental Duties.
(c)  Directive Principles of State Policy.
(d)  Right to Constitution remedy.

65. Consider the following statements with reference to International Monetary Fund (IMF), Special Drawing Rights (SDR):
1.  SDR's main function is to cater to the problem of balance of payment.
2.  In India SDR is held with the central government.
Select the correct statement/statements using the codes given below:
(a)  1 only (b)  2 only
(c)  Both 1 and 2 (d)  Neither 1 nor 2

66. Consider the following statements:
1.  Tundra biome is devoid of trees except stunted shrubs.
2.  The dominating vegetation of Taiga biome is coniferous evergreen mostly spruce.
Select the correct answer from the codes given below:
(a)  1 only (b)  2 only
(c)  Both 1 and 2 (d)  Neither 1 nor 2

67. With reference to Government of India Act; 1858; consider the following statements:
1.  It abolished the East India Company.
2.  It ended the system of double government.
3.  It created a new office, secretary of state for India.
4.  It established new legislative council for Bengal.
Which of the following is/are correct.
(a)  All 1, 2, 3 and 4 (b)  1, 2 and 4 only
(c)  1, 2 and 3 only (d)  1, 3 and 4 only

68. All loans raised by government of India by the issue of treasury bills, loans or ways and means advances shall be deposited in
(a)  Consolidated Fund of India
(b)  Public Account of India
(c)  Contingency Fund of India
(d)  None of the above

69. There is an inexhaustible supply of nitrogen in the atmosphere but the elemental form cannot be used directly by most of the living organism. Nitrogen needs to be 'fixed' that is converted to ammonia, nitrites or nitrates, before it can be taken up by plants.
By which of the following way nitrogen can be fixed on earth
1.  By micro-organism.
2.  By industrial process.
3.  By atmospheric phenomenon such as lighting.
Select the correct answer from the codes given below:
(a)  1 and 2 only (b)  2 and 3 only
(c)  1 and 3 only (d)  1, 2 and 3 all

70. Consider the following statements with reference to the Maratha Empire of 18th century.
1.  The Maratha raids in Delhi were not conducted for conquest.
2.  The Peshwaship of Baji Rao was the period of the greatest expansion of the Maratha power.
Select the correct statements from the codes given below.
(a)  1 only (b)  2 only
(c)  Both 1 and 2 (d)  Neither 1 nor 2

71. Which of the following statements can be considered as a reason behind judicial delays in India.
1.  Poor judge-population ratio.
2.  Impasses over appointment of judges.
3.  Liberal adjournment of cases.
4.  Police lack scientific training.
Select the correct answer using the codes given below:
(a)  1, 2, 4 only (b)  1, 2, 3 only
(c)  2, 3, 4 only (d)  1, 2, 3, 4 All

72. Biosphere is absent at:
(a)  Deepest oceans
(b)  Highest mountains
(c)  Extremes of the North and South poles
(d)  All the above

73. Consider the following statements:
1.  The northern hemisphere will have its longest day in Summer Solstice.
2.  On equinoxes, all parts of the world have equal days and nights.
Select the correct statement/statements using the codes given below:
(a)  1 only (b)  2 only
(c)  Both 1 and 2 (d)  Neither 1 nor 2

74. The Global Multidimensional Poverty Index (MPI) was developed by
(a)  Oxford Poverty and Human Development Initiative (OPHI)
(b)  United Nation Development Programme (UNDP)
(c)  Both (OPHI) and UNDP
(d)  WORLD Bank

75. In 1913, under the leadership of Gandhi, Indians in South Africa protested by illegally migrating from Natal into Transvaal. What was the main cause of discontent among Indians in South Africa?
    (a) Cancellation of suffrage rights of Indians.
    (b) A supreme court order which invalidated all marriages not conducted according to Christian rites.
    (c) Mass arrest of Indians protesting against colonial regime.
    (d) British regime not giving constitutional concessions.

76. Consider the following statements:
    1. Naturalised citizens are not eligible for the office of President in India.
    2. Cultural and educational rights are available only to citizens in India.
    Which of the above given statements is/are true.
    (a) 1 only          (b) 2 only
    (c) Both 1 and 2     (d) Neither 1 nor 2

77. Which of the following is not among the India's Maritime Initiatives?
    (a) SOLAS Convention
    (b) Seafarers' Identity Documents Convention 2003
    (c) Maritime labour convention, 2006.
    (d) None of the above

78. The Genetic Engineering Appraisal Committee (GEAC) recently made recommendation on "GM crops and its impact on environment".
    With reference to the Impact of GM crops on Environment consider the following statements.
    1. GM crops do not contaminate the soil and water.
    2. GM products being sold in the country have no labeling.
    Select the correct statement/statements using the codes given below:
    (a) 1 only          (b) 2 only
    (c) Both 1 and 2     (d) Neither 1 nor 2

79. With reference to Water Audit, consider the following statements.
    (1) The purpose of a water audit is to accurately determine the amount of unaccounted-for-water (UAW) in a water distribution system.
    (2) Water quality of the distribution system is monitored regularly in the Audit.
    (3) Central government shall form water audit cells in the water resource department of the concerned states,
    Which of the statement/statements given above is/are correct?
    (a) (1) and (3)      (b) (2) and (3)
    (c) (1) and (2)      (d) All are correct.

80. Consider the following statements:
    1. Betwa is the only big river that joins the Ganga directly from the Southern plateau.
    2. Ambala is located on the water divide between the Indus and the Ganga river system.
    Select the correct answer from the codes given below:
    (a) 1 only          (b) 2 only
    (c) Both 1 and 2     (d) Neither 1 nor 2

81. Which among the following is/are located in Assam:
    (a) Kaziranga National Park
    (b) Manas National Park
    (c) Sirohi National Park
    (d) Both (a) and (b)

82. In India the earliest paintings have been reported from the
    (a) Neolithic age
    (b) Mesolithic age
    (c) Upper palaeolithic age
    (d) Lower palaeolithic age

83. Which of the following ingredients or components is/are revealed by The Preamble of the Constitution.
    1. Nature of Indian State.
    2. Source of authority of the constitution.
    3. Objectives of the constitution.
    4. Date of adoption of the constitution.
    (a) 1, 2 and 3 only      (b) 2, 3 and 4 only
    (c) 1, 3 and 4 only      (d) All the above

84. Which among the following is/are counted in Revenue Receipts:
    1. Customs Duties
    2. Dividends and Profits
    3. Receipts from Social Services
    4. External Borrowings
    5. Securities against small savings.
    Select the correct answer using codes given below.
    (a) 1, 2 and 3 only      (b) 3, 4 and 5 only
    (c) 2, 3 and 4 only      (d) All 1, 2, 3, 4 and 5

85. If one has to travel from Gulf of Oman to Caspian Sea by crossing over just one country then it can be done by travelling through:
    (a) Saudi Arabia      (b) Iran
    (c) Turkey            (d) Yemen

86. To acquire citizenship by registration a person must have been resident in India for how many years immediately before making an application.
    (a) One year          (b) Two year
    (c) Four year         (d) Five year

87. With reference to Central Bureau of Investigation (CBI), which of the following statements is/are correct?
    1. It is a constitutional body
    2. It was established on the recommendation of the Santhanam Committee (1962-64)
    3. Appointment of the director of CBI is done for 2 years as per the Central Vigilance Commission Act, 2003.
    Select the correct answer using the code given below:
    (a) 1 and 2 only      (b) 2 and 3 only
    (c) 1 and 3 only      (d) 1, 2 and 3

88. In context with Central Bureau of Investigation, which of the following statement is/are not correct?
    1. The CBI comes under the Ministry of Home Affairs.
    2. Central Bureau of Investigation acts as the Central Bureau of INTERPOL in India.
    3. Metrological branch belongs to CBI.
    Choose the answer from the code given below?
    (a) 1 and 2           (b) 2 and 3
    (c) 1 and 3           (d) None of the above

89. Consider the following statements:
    1. The post of the Comptroller and Auditor General of India has been envisaged in the Article 76 of Indian Constitution.
    2. Comptroller and Auditor General of India, is called the guardian of the public fund.
    Which of the statements given above is/are correct?
    (a) 1 only          (b) 2 only
    (c) Both 1 and 2     (d) Neither 1 nor 2

90. Consider the following statements:
    1. National Waterway-1 is an inland water transport route between Haldia in West Bengal to Prayagraj in Uttar Pradesh.
    2. The Haldia-Varanasi stretch of the National Waterway-1 has been developed with technical assistance and investment support from the World Bank with the cost assistance of 50:50 ratio.
    3. The Varanasi inland port on Ganga River is the second after Haldia, multi-modal terminal on the Ganga.
    Which of the statement given above is/are correct?
    (a) 1 and 2 only        (b) 2 and 3 only
    (c) 1 and 3 only        (d) 1, 2 and 3

91. In context with Jal Marg Vikas project (JMVP), Consider the following statements:
    1. JMVP was announced by Government in 2018-19 Budgets to enable commercial navigation of at least 1500 tonne vessels on the River Ganga.
    2. The project envisages the development of waterway between Allahabad and Haldia on Ganga River that will cover a distance of 1620 km.
    3. The project is completed with the technical assistance and investment support of the World Bank and is expected to complete by 2023.
    Which of the statements given above are correct?
    (a) 1 and 2 only        (b) 2 and 3 only
    (c) 1 and 3 only        (d) 1, 2 and 3

92. Consider the following statements about Ayushman Bharat-National Health Protection Mission which was launched by Central Govt. recently?
    1. It is a scheme of the Central government which focuses on the wellness of the poor families and providing medical benefits to them.
    2. Rashtriya Swasthya Bima Yojana (RSBY) and the Senior Citizen Health Insurance Scheme (SCHIS) will be merged under this scheme.
    3. In September 2018, Ayushman Bharat Yojana was finally launched as Pradhan Mantri Jan Arogya Abhiyan.
    Which of the statements given above is/are correct?
    (a) 1 and 2 only        (b) 2 and 3 only
    (c) 1 and 3 only        (d) 1, 2 and 3

93. With reference to 'The Pradhan Mantri Ujjwala Yojana (PMUY), which of the following statement is/are correct?
    1. Pradhan Mantri Ujjwala Yojana (PMUY) was launched in May 2016.
    2. The initial target set for the scheme was to provide 80 million LPG connections to below poverty line (BPL) families by 2019.
    3. The PMUY scheme targets to reach out to provide free LPG connections to 80 million families by 2020.
    Select the correct answer using the code given below
    (a) 1 and 2 only        (b) 2 and 3 only
    (c) 1 and 3 only        (d) 1, 2 and 3

94. Consider the following statements about Atal Bhujal Yojana:
    1. It is conceived to arrest the rampant overuse of groundwater in India
    2. It is supported by the Word Bank
    3. It is a sub-scheme under National Groundwater Management Improvement Scheme (NGMIS)

Select the correct statements
(a) 1 and 2        (b) 2 and 3
(c) 1 and 3        (d) All of the above

95. Regarding the functions of RBI, which of the following statements is/are correct?
    1. It Formulates implements and monitors the monetary policy.
    2. It maintains banking accounts of all scheduled banks.
    3. It is the Manager of Foreign Exchange and it manages it according to the Foreign Exchange Management Act, 1934.
    Select the correct answer using the code given below
    (a) 1 and 2 only        (b) 2 and 3 only
    (c) 1 and 3 only        (d) 1, 2 and 3

96. Which of the following statements are correct about 'Ledumahadi mafube' that was in news recently?
    1. It is a fossil of a new dinosaur species which is discovered in South Africa.
    2. It is believed that 'Ledumahadi mafube' were the relative of the brontosaurus that weighed 26,000 pounds, equal to the size of a large African elephant.
    Which of the statements given above is/are correct?
    (a) 1 only        (b) 2 only
    (c) Both 1 and 2        (d) Neither 1 nor 2

97. Consider the following statements:
    1. The Govt. is celebrating the Diamond Jubilee celebration of Subhash Chandra Bose's declaration of the formation of the Azad Hind government.
    2. To commemorate the day of declaration of the formation of the Azad Hind government, Govt. has renamed the Ross Island as Netaji Subhash Chandra Bose Island.
    3. Ross, Neil and Havelock Island are located at northern part of Lakshdweep Islands.
    Select the correct answer using the code given below
    (a) 1 and 2 only        (b) 2 and 3 only
    (c) 1 and 3 only        (d) 1, 2 and 3

98. Which of the following are voluntary provisions as per the 73rd Constitutional Amendment Act of 1992?
    1. Providing representation to members of the Parliament and State Legislature in the Panchayats.
    2. Devolution of powers and responsibilities upon Panchayats.
    3. Organization of Gram Sabha.
    Select the correct answer using the code given below
    (a) 1 and 2 only        (b) 2 and 3 only
    (c) 1 and 3 only        (d) 1, 2 and 3

99. Which of the following is/are true?
    1. The composition of the state finance commission may be provided by the state government.
    2. Article 280 deals with State finance Commission
    Which of the statements given above is/are correct?
    (a) 1 only        (b) 2 only
    (c) Both 1 and 2        (d) Neither 1 nor 2

100. Consider the following statements.
    1. Balwant Rai Mehta Committee was appointed in 1957.
    2. Ashok Mehta Committee was set up in 1977.
    3. G.V.K. Rao committee was set up in 1989.
    Select the correct answer using the code given below
    (a) 1 and 2 only        (b) 2 and 3 only
    (c) 1 and 3 only        (d) 1, 2 and 3

## RESPONSE SHEET

| | | | | |
|---|---|---|---|---|
| 1. ⓐⓑⓒⓓ | 2. ⓐⓑⓒⓓ | 3. ⓐⓑⓒⓓ | 4. ⓐⓑⓒⓓ | 5. ⓐⓑⓒⓓ |
| 6. ⓐⓑⓒⓓ | 7. ⓐⓑⓒⓓ | 8. ⓐⓑⓒⓓ | 9. ⓐⓑⓒⓓ | 10. ⓐⓑⓒⓓ |
| 11. ⓐⓑⓒⓓ | 12. ⓐⓑⓒⓓ | 13. ⓐⓑⓒⓓ | 14. ⓐⓑⓒⓓ | 15. ⓐⓑⓒⓓ |
| 16. ⓐⓑⓒⓓ | 17. ⓐⓑⓒⓓ | 18. ⓐⓑⓒⓓ | 19. ⓐⓑⓒⓓ | 20. ⓐⓑⓒⓓ |
| 21. ⓐⓑⓒⓓ | 22. ⓐⓑⓒⓓ | 23. ⓐⓑⓒⓓ | 24. ⓐⓑⓒⓓ | 25. ⓐⓑⓒⓓ |
| 26. ⓐⓑⓒⓓ | 27. ⓐⓑⓒⓓ | 28. ⓐⓑⓒⓓ | 29. ⓐⓑⓒⓓ | 30. ⓐⓑⓒⓓ |
| 31. ⓐⓑⓒⓓ | 32. ⓐⓑⓒⓓ | 33. ⓐⓑⓒⓓ | 34. ⓐⓑⓒⓓ | 35. ⓐⓑⓒⓓ |
| 36. ⓐⓑⓒⓓ | 37. ⓐⓑⓒⓓ | 38. ⓐⓑⓒⓓ | 39. ⓐⓑⓒⓓ | 40. ⓐⓑⓒⓓ |
| 41. ⓐⓑⓒⓓ | 42. ⓐⓑⓒⓓ | 43. ⓐⓑⓒⓓ | 44. ⓐⓑⓒⓓ | 45. ⓐⓑⓒⓓ |
| 46. ⓐⓑⓒⓓ | 47. ⓐⓑⓒⓓ | 48. ⓐⓑⓒⓓ | 49. ⓐⓑⓒⓓ | 50. ⓐⓑⓒⓓ |
| 51. ⓐⓑⓒⓓ | 52. ⓐⓑⓒⓓ | 53. ⓐⓑⓒⓓ | 54. ⓐⓑⓒⓓ | 55. ⓐⓑⓒⓓ |
| 56. ⓐⓑⓒⓓ | 57. ⓐⓑⓒⓓ | 58. ⓐⓑⓒⓓ | 59. ⓐⓑⓒⓓ | 60. ⓐⓑⓒⓓ |
| 61. ⓐⓑⓒⓓ | 62. ⓐⓑⓒⓓ | 63. ⓐⓑⓒⓓ | 64. ⓐⓑⓒⓓ | 65. ⓐⓑⓒⓓ |
| 66. ⓐⓑⓒⓓ | 67. ⓐⓑⓒⓓ | 68. ⓐⓑⓒⓓ | 69. ⓐⓑⓒⓓ | 70. ⓐⓑⓒⓓ |
| 71. ⓐⓑⓒⓓ | 72. ⓐⓑⓒⓓ | 73. ⓐⓑⓒⓓ | 74. ⓐⓑⓒⓓ | 75. ⓐⓑⓒⓓ |
| 76. ⓐⓑⓒⓓ | 77. ⓐⓑⓒⓓ | 78. ⓐⓑⓒⓓ | 79. ⓐⓑⓒⓓ | 80. ⓐⓑⓒⓓ |
| 81. ⓐⓑⓒⓓ | 82. ⓐⓑⓒⓓ | 83. ⓐⓑⓒⓓ | 84. ⓐⓑⓒⓓ | 85. ⓐⓑⓒⓓ |
| 86. ⓐⓑⓒⓓ | 87. ⓐⓑⓒⓓ | 88. ⓐⓑⓒⓓ | 89. ⓐⓑⓒⓓ | 90. ⓐⓑⓒⓓ |
| 91. ⓐⓑⓒⓓ | 92. ⓐⓑⓒⓓ | 93. ⓐⓑⓒⓓ | 94. ⓐⓑⓒⓓ | 95. ⓐⓑⓒⓓ |
| 96. ⓐⓑⓒⓓ | 97. ⓐⓑⓒⓓ | 98. ⓐⓑⓒⓓ | 99. ⓐⓑⓒⓓ | 100. ⓐⓑⓒⓓ |

# HINTS & EXPLANATIONS

1. (a) Virtual IDs is a 16 digit temporary number (like an OTP) which can only be generated by Aadhaar holders in place of Aadhaar numbers to validate their identity. Users can generate as many virtual IDs as he or she wants. The older ID gets automatically canceled once a fresh one is generated. Agencies that do not migrate to the new system by the stipulated deadline will face financial disincentives.

2. (d)

**Multi-Dimensional Poverty Index**

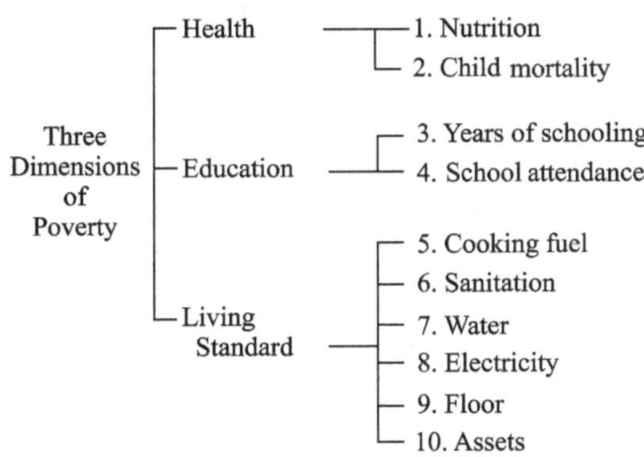


**Source:** The Hindu

3. (b) A minister can be a member of either of the two houses i.e. Lok-Sabha and Rajya Sabha. A person cannot be a minister without being a member of the parliament. The constitution stipulates that a minister who is not a member of the parliament for a period of 6 consecutive months ceases to be a minister.

   – The Ministers are collectively responsible to the parliament in general and to the Lok Sabha in particular (Art.-75). They act as a team and Swim and Sink together.

4. (d) Kubuqi Desert in Ordos, Inner Mongolia has become the first desert in the world to achieve large-scale desertification control.

   Kubuqi model can be implemented in India to improve the land status, as an estimated 32 percent of India's total land area is affected by land degradation (of which desertification is a major component).

5. (c) The themes of paintings found here are of great variety, ranging from Mundane events of daily life in those times to sacred and royal images. These include hunting, dancing, music, horse and elephant riders, animal fighting, honey collection, decoration of bodies and other household scenes.

   The rock art of Bhimbetka has been classified into various groups on the bases of style, technique and superimposition.

   **Source:** Indian Art : XI[th]

6. (c) The Indian theatre has a tradition of at least 5000 years. Theatre in India started as a narrative elements made our theatre essentially theatrical right from the beginning. That is why the theatre in India has encompassed all the other forms of literature and fine arts into its physical presentation.

   Some of the traditional theatre forms in India are

   – Yakshagana (Karnataka)

   – Teyyam (Kerala)

   – Koodiyattam (Kerala)

   – Bhand Pather (Kashmir)

   – Swang (Haryana)

   – Nautanki (UP)

7. (b) Mahal wari system was introduced in 1833 during the period of William Bentick. In this system owner ship rights were vested with the peasants. It had many provisions of both the Zamindari system and Ryotwari system. In this system, the land was divided into Mahals. Each Mahal comprised of one or more villages.

8. (b) In India, natural lakes (relatively few) mostly lie in the Himalayan region, the flood plains of Indus, Ganga and Brahmaputra.

   – On the basis of their nutrient content, they are categorized as oligotrophic (very low nutrient), mesotrophic (moderate nutrients) and Eutrophic (highly nutrient rich).

   – Vast majority of lakes in India are either eutrophic or mesotrophic because of the nutrients derived from their surroundings or organic wastes entering them.

9. (c) The NHRC is a multi-member body consisting of a chairman and four members. The chairman should be a retired chief justice of India and other members should be a serving or retired judge of the Supreme Court or of High Court.

   The chairman and members hold office for a term of 5 years or until they attain the age of 70 years, whichever is earlier. After their tenure, the chairman and members are not eligible for further employment under the central or a state government.

10. (a) All the statements given in the question are correct. It is a National Programme for Development of Sports, which aims to enable a pathway from school to Olympics.

11. (b) Buddhist Literature: Sutta Pitaks, Vinay Pitaks, Abhidhamma Pitaks, Milanda Panho, Angular Nikaya.

    Jain Literature: Kalp Sutra, Nayadhamma Kaha, Acharang Sutra.

12. (c) **Article - 137**: Supreme court shall have the power to review any judgement pronounced or order made by it.

  **Article - 144**: All authorities, civil and judicial, in the territory of India shall act in aid of the Supreme court.

13. (c) Bioindicators are living organisms that indicate health of the ecosystem.

14. (a) The process of burning waste in large furnaces at high temperature is known as incineration. In these plants the recyclable material is segregated and the rest of the material is burnt and ash is produced.

15. (c) On the eve of Independence, Industry (manufacturing) sector had minimum share in GDP (around 15%) and agriculture sector had maximum share (around 53%). The share of Agriculture has consistently declined while that of services sector has consistently increased over the years.

  The share of services sector in GDP was around (33%) in 1950-51, while it has risen to around (55%) in 2013-14.

  While the share of Agriculture sector (primary sector) has decreased, the dependency of population on agriculture for the employment has increased. This is a big reason to worry for Government of India.

  **Source:** The Hindu

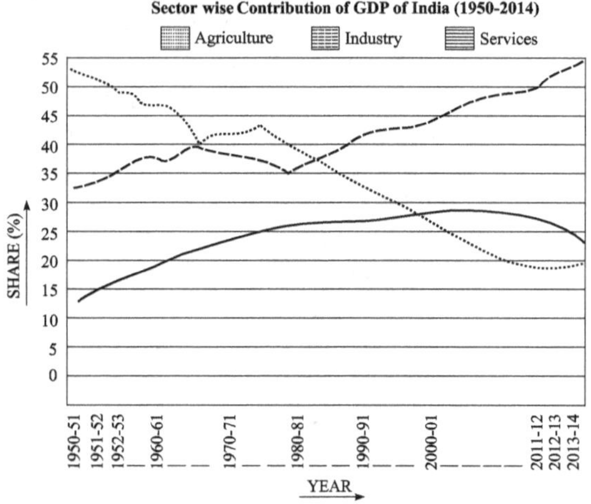



16. (a) At present only seven states have a bicameral legislature.

  State having a bicameral legislature.

  – Andhra Pradesh

  – Bihar

  – Jammu & Kashmir

  – Karnataka

  – Maharashtra

  – Telangana

  – Uttar Pradesh

  – The parliament can abolish a legislative council or create it if the legislative assembly of the concerned State passes a resolution to that effect.

  – Such a specific resolution must be passed by the state assembly by a special majority.

17. (c) All the statements (1), (2) and (3) are correct. Mudra debit cards are issued to borrowers. Using these, they can withdraw the loan from any ATM in India, as and when they need the money.

18. (b) G-4 nations comprises of Brazil, Germany, India and Japan. They recently demanded an 'early reform' and enhanced role for developing countries and improvement of working methods in UNSC.

19. (d) Though animals were painted in a naturalistic style, humans were depicted only in a stylistic manner. The artists of Bhimbetka used many colours, including various shades of white, yellow, orange, red, green and black. The paints were made by grinding various rocks and minerals. At many rock art sites a new painting is painted on top of an older painting.

  At Bhimbetka, in some places, there are as many as 20 layers of paintings, one on top of another.

  **Source:** N.C.E.R.T : Indian Art-XI

20. (c) India has announced its Intended Nationally Determined Contribution (INDC) in respect of climate change inclusive of following aspects:

  – To achieve about 40 percent amulative electric power installed capacity from non-fossil fuel based energy resources by 2030 with the help of transfer of technology and low cost international finance.

  – To create an additional carbon sink of 2.5 to 3 billion tonnes of $CO_2$ equivalent.

  – To better adapt to climate change by enhancing in-vestments in development programmes in sectors vulnerable to climate change.

  – To mobilize domestic, new and additional funds from developed countries.

  – To build capacities for the quick diffusion of cutting-edge climate technology in India and for joint collaborative R and D.

  **Source:** The Indian Economy – Sanjeev Verma

21. (c) When the constitution was prepared, the subject of local government was assigned to the states. It was also mentioned in the directive principles as one of the policy directives to all governments in the country (Article-40).

  However the Directive Principles of State Policy being non-justiciable, the establishment of Panchayati Raj institutions remain primarily advisory in nature.

22. (b) Kamneng, Manas, Raidak and Jaldhaka are tributaries of Brahmaputra.

23. (d) Mankidia are classified as particularly Vulnerable Tribal Groups in Odisha. These are expert in monkey hunting and the state's Forest department has asked it s personnel to learn hunting techniques to contain the monkey menace.

24. (d) Jainism taught five doctrines. It is believed that only the fifth doctrine, observe continence, was added by Mahavira and the other four were taken over by him from Previous teachers. In Jaina Philosophy the existence of God is accepted but it placed the god lower than Jina.

25. (d) MIMO or Multiple In-Multiple out is a smart Antenna based technology which is a type of Radio communications technology.

26. (b) Suspensive veto-when president returns a bill for reconsideration of the parliament.

    President does not possess suspensive veto in the case of money bills. The president can either give his assent to a money bill or withhold his assent to a money bill but cannot return it for the reconsideration of the parliament.

    President has no veto power in respect of a constitutional amendment bill. The $24^{th}$ constitutional Amendment Act of 1971 made it obligatory for the president to give his assent to a constitutional amendment bill.

27. (b) The microorganisms may be indigenous to a contaminated area or they may be isolated from elsewhere and brought to the contaminated site.

28. (a) Mitosis is the division in which daughter cells are formed with equal number of chromosomes to that of the parental cells. This type of division is known as equational division. Mitosis is usually restricted to diploid cells but with few exceptions where some haploid cells also undergo mitosis.

29. (c) The UN's rules state that changing the composition of the P5 involves changing the UN's charter which will further require the backing of two thirds of the General Assembly including the current P5 which is difficult to obtain due to lack of political will and conflicting national interest of different countries.

30. (c) Refer to Map of World

31. (c) No two biomes are alike. The climate determines the boundaries of a biome and abundance of plants animals found in each one of them. The most important climatic factors are temperature and precipitation.

    Aquatic systems are not called biomes, however they are divided into distinct life zone, with regions of relatively distinct plant and animal life.

    The major differences between the various aquatic zones are due to salinity, levels of dissolved nutrients, water temperature, depth of sunlight penetration.

32. (b) The cold weather season begins from Mid-November in northern India and stays till February.

    – The temperature decreases from south to the north.

    – Frost is common in the north and the higher slopes of the Himalayas experience snowfall.

    – During this season, the northeast trade winds prevail over the country. They blow from land to sea and hence, for most part of the country, it is a dry season.

    – A characteristic feature of the cold weather season over the northern plains is the inflow of cyclonic disturbances from the west and the northwest.

33. (c) Article 16(4) of the constitution explicitly clarifies that a policy like reservation will not be seen as a violation of right to equality.

    The supreme court has ruled that (Article-21) also includes right to live with human dignity, free from exploitation.

    – The court has held that right to shelter and livelihood is also included in the right to life because no person can live without the means of living, that is means of livelihood.

34. (a) The Savanna or Sudan climate is a transitional type of climate found between the equatorial forests and the trade wind hot deserts. It is confined within the tropics and is best developed in the Sudan where the dry and wet seasons are most distinct.

    The Savanna type of climate is characterized by an alternate hot, rainy season and cool, dry season.

    The extreme diurnal range of temperature is another characteristic feature of the Savanna climate.

    The prevailing winds of the region are the Trade winds which bring rain to the coastal districts.

35. (d) Scorpene-class Submarines includes INS Kalvari, INS Khanderi and INS Karanj. The Scorpene Submarines can undertake various missions such as anti-surface warfare, anti-submarine warfare, intelligence gathering, mine laying and area surveillance. INS Karanj has been recently launched by Indian Navy.

36. (c) Al-Biruni in his Kitab-Ul-hind, tried to explain the caste system by looking for parallels in other societies. He noted that in ancient Persia, four social categories were recognised; those of knights and princes; monks; fire-priests and lawyers; Physicians, astronomers and other scientists; and finally peas ants and artisans. In other words, he attempted to suggest that social divisions were not unique to India.

37. (c) Lorenz curve explains the relationship between the percentage of income or wealth earned or appropriated and percentage of people who earned that particular percentage of income or wealth.

    The cumulative percentage of income is measured on the y-axis and the cumulative percentage of people is measured on x-axis.

    **Source:** Key Concepts – Shankarganesh

38. (c)

    – Hindi written in Devanagari Script to be the official language of the union. But the form of numerals to be used for the official purpose of the union has to be the international form of Indian numerals.

    – The constitution does not specify the official language of different states.

–      The legislature of a state may adopt any one or more of the languages in use in the state or Hindi as the official language of that state.

39.   (c)   The Government has set up the target to double the farmer's income by 2022. Government has recently opened up the export of all types of pulses. Various PDP schemes launched by states are Bhavantar Bhugtan Yojana (BBY) by MP, incentive of ₹ 5-per-litre to milk farmers in Karnataka etc.

40.   (d)   Least distance of distinct vision and near point is the same. It is therefore same for all individuals.

41.   (a)   Phosphorus plays a central role in aquatic ecosystem and water quality. Unlike carbon and nitrogen which come primarily from the atmosphere, phosphorus occurs in large amounts as a mineral in phosphate rocks and enters the cycle from erosion and mining activities. This is the nutrient considered to be the main cause of excessive growth of rooted and free-floating microscopic plants in lakes.

42.   (d)   The CBI was set up in 1963 by a resolution of the Ministry of Home Affairs. Later it was transferred to the Ministry of personnel and now it enjoys the status of an attached office.

      **Source:** M. Lakshmikant

43.   (b)   Malwa plateau is located in the north of Vindhya ranges and Bhander plateau to the north of Mahadeo Hills.

      The correct order of the given plateaus from east to west is Chota Nagpur plateau → Baghelkhand →Bhander plateau → Malwa plateau

44.   (c)   The EoTT equipment proposed by Indian Railways will act as a communication system between driver and last wagon of train. This will ensure that the train is running with all coaches as a complete unit.

45.   (b)   The Plans of Ghadr Party were encouraged by two events in 1914 the Komagata Maru incident and the outbreak of the first world war.

      Komagata Maru was the name of a ship which was carrying 370 passengers, mainly Sikh and Punjabi Muslims would be immigrants from Singapore to vancouver

46.   (b)   Black revolution pertains to the increased production of petroleum and petroleum products.

      **Source:** The Indian Economy – Sanjeev Verma

47.   (d)   Holographic Technology is being used in different fields like Health and medicine, Engineering and Technology, tradeshows, telepresence etc.

      A 3-D holographic model of buildings and architectural designs gives a real time experience. Holographic imaging is used in medicine to create a 3D image of interior organs of a patient's body. Holographic display is useful during tradeshows to launch and present any product without actually transporting the product at the site. Similarly, holographic telepresence is used to address people at different places simultaneously.

48.   (b)

49.   (a)

50.   (a)   Recently, India Joined "Ashgabat Agreement" Kazakhstan and Pakistan joined this agreement in 2016. The agreement also aims to Synchronize with the Eurasian railway connectivity project and international North - South Transport Corridor.

51.   (c)   The demands put forward by Gandhi were as follows:
      –      Reduce expenditure on Army.
      –      Introduce total prohibition.
      –      Carry out reforms in criminal Investigation Department (CID)
      –      Accept postal Reservation Bill.
      –      Reduce land revenue by 50 percent.
      –      Abolish Salt tax and government's salt monopoly.
      –      Reserve coastal shipping for Indians.
      –      Change Arms Act allowing popular control of issue of firearms licences.

52.   (b)   Capital Receipts are essentially a two way transactions. It means once disbursed money will come in the form of regular income or at the time of disposal if any asset was created out of the disbursed money.

      Source of Capital Receipts are:
      – Market loans (net)
      – Treasury Bills Issued to RBI and Banks
      – Funded Securities
      – Other special securities issued to RBI
      – Ways and Means Advance
      – Special floating and other loans
      – Securities against small savings
      – Small saving scheme
      – Provident funds
      – Non-debt capital receipts

53.   (d)   Hydrogen can be extracted from any of the hydrogen containing compounds. It produces water vapour mixed with warm air as waste products. Presently the production cost of hydrogen fuel based vehicles is high.

54.   (c)   In Proportional Representation System voters exercise their preference for a party and not a candidate. The seats in a constituency are distributed on the basis of

votes polled by a party. Thus, representatives from a constituency would and do belong to different parties. And more than one candidate can be elected from one constituency.

**Source:** N.C.E.R.T. (Std. XI[th]) (Polity–Chapter 3)

55. (d) Under the wildlife (protection) Act, 1972, elephant is a schedule I animal.

Also Asian elephants are listed as "endangered" in the IUCN Red List of threatened Species.

56. (b) Mining industry releases inorganic pollutants like mine wastes: chlorides, various metals, ferrous sulphate, sulphuric acid, hydrogen sulphide, ferric hydroxide, surface wash offs, suspended solids, chlorides and heavy metals.

57. (d) The major reef formations in India are restricted to the Gulf of Mannar, Palk bay, Gulf of kutch, Andaman and Nicobar Islands and the Lakshadweep islands. While the Lakshadweep reefs are atolls, the others are all fringing reefs. Patchy coral is present in the inter-tidal areas of the central west coast of the country.

58. (c) The centre of curvature of a convex mirror lies behind it. The convex lens is also known as converging lens and focal length is the distance between pole and principal focus of a spherical mirror.

59. (c) In 1976, the Congress Party set up the Sardar Swaran Singh Committee to make recommendations about fundamental duties.

Though the Swaran Singh Committee suggested the incorporation of eight fundamental duties in the constitution, the 42$^{nd}$ Constitutional Amendment Act (1976) included ten fundamental duties.

60. (a) The percentage of education expenditure of total government expenditure indicates the importance of education in the Scheme of things before the government.

– During 1952-2010, education expenditure as percentage of total governments expenditure increased from 7.92 to 11.1 and as percentage of GDP increased from 0.64 to 3.25.

– Throughout this period the increase in education expenditure has not been uniform and there has been irregular rise and fall.

– Elementary education takes a major share of total education expenditure and the share of the higher/tertiary education is the least.

61. (d) Water erosion is the major cause of desertification in India. It is responsible for 10.98% desertification. Other reasons for desertification are:

| | | |
|---|---|---|
| Wind erosion | — | 5.55% |
| Vegetation degradation | — | 8.91% |
| Salinity | — | 1.12% |
| Others | — | 2.7% |
| Human–Made settlement | — | 0.69% |

62. (d) Parallel governments were established at Ballia (in Aug. 1942) for a week, at Tamluk ( in 1944) and at satara (mid 1943 to 1945)

**Source:** Spectrum's Modern India.

63. (b)

64. (c) The framers of the constitution borrowed D.P.S.P from the Irish constitution of 1937. Dr. B.R. Ambedkar described D.P.S.P as 'novel features' of the constitution.

65. (a) SDR is a reserve created by International Monetary Fund (IMF), to help countries that have Balance of Payment Problem.

The member countries have to contribute to this account. The contribution is in proportion of their IMF quota. It is held with the government or the central bank of the member countries. In India SDR is held with RBI's exchange reserve.

**Source:** Key Concepts – Shankarganesh

66. (c) Tundra biome is devoid of trees except stunted shrubs in the southern part of tundra biome, ground flora includes lichen, mosses and sedges.

The dominating vegetation of Taiga/Boreal biome is coniferous evergreen mostly spruce with some pine and firs.

The Tundra biome is found in Northern and Southern most region of world adjoining the ice bound poles. The Taiga / boreal biome is found in Northern Europe, Asia and North America.

67. (c) The Govt. of India Act: 1858 was enacted in the wake of the Revolt of 1857. Important features of the Act:

– Governor General of India was made Viceroy of India.

– It ended the system of double government by abolishing the Board of control and court of directors.

– It abolished the East India Company.

– It established a 15 member council of India to assist the Secretary of State for India.

**Note:** Indian Councils Act of 1861 provided for establishment of new legislative councils for Bengal, NWFP and Punjab.

68. (a) The Consolidated Fund has been defined in Article – 226(1) of the constitution.

Accordingly, all revenues received by the Government of India, all loans raised by that government by the issue of treasury bills, loans or ways and means advances and all moneys received by that government in repayment of loans shall form one consolidated fund to be entitled "The Consolidated Fund of India."

**Source:** Key Concepts – Sankarganesh

69. (d) The amount of Nitrogen fixed by man through industrial process has far exceeded the amount fixed by the Natural Cycle. As a result Nitrogen has become a pollutant which can disrupt the balance of Nitrogen. It may lead to Acid rain, Eutrophication and Harmful Algal Blooms.

70. (a) Baji Rao I conquered Malwa, Southern Gujarat and Bundelkhand and conducted raids up to the very gates of Delhi. However he didnot occupy Delhi as the Mughal emperor still carried considerable prestige.

The Maratha raids were not conducted for conquest. They were primarily interested laying their hand on a major part of the land revenue of these areas.

Baji Rao's son Balaji Baji Rao continued the forward policy of his father. During his peshwaship, the Maratha reached as far as Bihar and Orissa in the east and the Punjab in the north. This was the period of the greatest expansion of the Maratha power

**Source:** N.C.E.R.T :8th – (old): Modern India

71. (d)

1. India has only 17 judges per 10 lakh population which is very poor as compared to other European and American countries. eg. USA has 151 and China 170 judges per 10 lakh population.

2. Vacancies in High courts have reached nearly 50% of their sanctioned strength. Lower courts too have huge unfilled posts.

3. In efficient and time consuming procedures must be avoided.

4. Police often fail to collect vital evidences because of lack of scientific training.

Source – The Hindu.

72. (d) Life in the biosphere is abundant between 200 metres (660 feet) below the surface of the ocean and about 6000 metres (20,000 feet) above sea level.

Biosphere is absent at extremes of the North and South poles, the highest mountains and the deepest oceans, since existing hostile conditions there do not support life. Occasionally spores of fungi and bacteria do occur at great height beyond 8000 metres, but they are not metabolically active and hence represent only dormant life.

73. (c) The Sun is vertically overhead at the equator on two days each year. These are usually 21 March and 21 September though the date changes because a year is not exactly of 365 days.

These two days are termed equinoxes meaning "equal nights" because on these two days all parts of the world have equal days and nights.

– After the March equinox the sun appears to move north and is vertically overhead at the Tropic of Cancer on about 21 June. This is known as June or Summer Solstice, when the northern hemisphere will have its longest day and shortest night.

By about 22 December, the Sun will be overhead at the Tropic of Capricorn. This is the winter solstice when the Southern hemisphere will have its longest day and shortest hight.

74. (c) The Global Multidimensional Poverty Index (MPI) was developed in 2010 by the Oxford Poverty and Human Development Initiative (OPHI) and the United Nations Development Programme; it uses different factors to determine poverty beyond income based lists. It replaced the previous Human Poverty Index.

**Source:** The Hindu

75. (b) A supreme court order invalidated all marriages not conducted according to Christian rites and registered by the registrar of marriage. By implication, Hindu, Muslim and Parsi marriages were illegal and children born out of such marriages illegitimate.

**Source:** Spectrum's Modern India.

76. (b) In India both a citizen by birth as well as a naturalised citizen are eligible for the office of president while in USA, only a citizen by birth and not a naturalised citizen is eligible for the office of president.

– Cultural and educational rights are available only to citizens in India and not to aliens (Article-29 and Art.-30).

77. (d) All the initiatives given in the question are among the India's Maritime initiatives. Besides this, India has been re-elected to the Council of the International Maritime Organization (IMO) under category "B" for two years recently

78. (c) GM crops contaminate and cross–pollinate with non-GM crops and create super weeds. GM crops do impact unintended organism including beneficial organisms like bees and butterflies along with predators.

- No is house scientific study has been carried out till date to study the impact of GM crops on human health.

- Bt toxin produced in GM Bt crops is present in every part of the plant, so when the parts that have not been harvested decompose, a considerable amount of the toxin may reach the soil.

79. (c) State governments (not central government) should form water audit cells under monitoring units in their water resource department Besides this, water quality of the distribution system is also monitored regularly at strategic points to find out the level and nature of contaminants present in the supplied water.

80. (b) The Son is the only big river to join the Ganga directly from the southern plateau. Son is the right bank tributary of Ganga and it joins Ganga near Patna.

Ambala is located on the water divide between the Indus and the Ganga river system. The plains from Ambala in the northwest to Sunderbans in the east stretch over nearly 1800 km. During its entire stretch from Haryana to Bangladesh, there is a fall of hardly 300 metres in its slope.

81 (d) Sirohi National Park is located in Manipur.

82. (c) Indian cave paintings are regarded as the earliest evidences of Indian paintings which are made on cave walls and palaces while miniature paintings are small-sized colourful intricate illumination. This starts from prehistoric cave painting of bhimbetka and flourishes through cave paintings of Ajanta Caves, Ellora Caves and Bagh. In India the earliest paintings have been reported from the Upper Palaeolithic times.

We do not really know if lower palaeolithic people ever produced any art objects. But by the upper palaeolithic times we see a proliferation of artistic activities.

Around the world the walls of many caves of this time are full of finely carved and painted pictures of animals which the cave dwellers hunted.

**Source:** N.C.E.R.T : Indian Art-XI

83. (d)

1. The preamble states that the constitution derives its authority from the people of the India.

2. It declares India to be a Sovereign, Socialist, Secular democratic and republican polity.

3. It specifies justice, liberty, equality and fraternity as the objectives.

84. (a) The Sources of Revenue Receipts are:

1. Tax Revenue : Union Excise Duty

        : Customs Duties

        : Corporate Tax

        : Income Tax

        : Service Tax

        : Taxes of UTs

        : Other Taxes & Duties.

2. Non Tax Revenues : Interest Receipts

        : Dividends and Profits

3. Other Non-Tax Receipts

– Fiscal Services – currency, coinage, mint

– Other General Services

– Social Services like education, health, culture

– Economic Services

– Grants in Aid Contributions

85. (b) Refer to Map of Asia.

86. (a) A person of full age and capacity who, or either of his parents was earlier citizen of Independent ndia, and has been residing in India for one year immediately before making an application for registration.

87. (b) The Central Bureau of Investigation was established in 1963 on the basis of a resolution of the Home Ministry and the recommendation of Santhanam Committee.

88. (c) The Central Bureau of Investigation was established under the Home Ministry but later on it was put under the supervision of Ministry of Personel and training. Metrological branch does not belong to the Central Bureau of Investigation, but it is related to the metrological department.

89. (b) As per the provision of Article 148 of Indian Constitution, the post of the Comptroller and Auditor General has been envisaged. The Attorney general of India is appointed by the President as per Article 76(1) of the Indian Constitution.

90. (c) Recently PM Modi has received the container vessel at the Varanasi inland port on Ganga River which has been newly developed and is the first multi-modal terminal on the Ganga.

91. (b) JMVP was announced by Government in 2014-15 Budget to enable commercial navigation of at least 1500 tonne vessels on River Ganga. The project covers Uttar Pradesh, Bihar, Jharkhand and West Bengal. The major districts under its ambit are Varanasi, Ballia, Ghazipur, Chhapra, Buxar Patna, Vaishali, Khagaria, Begusarai, Munger, Bhagalpur, Sahibganj, Murshidabad, Pakur, Hooghly and Kolkata.

92. (d) Ayushman Bharat Yojana is a scheme of the Central government which provides medical benefits to poor. The scheme will include the on-going centrally sponsored schemes-Rashtriya Swasthya Bima Yojana (RSBY) and the Senior Citizen Health Insurance Scheme (SCHIS. On 23rd September 2018, Ayushman Bharat Yojana was finally launched as Pradhan Mantri Jan Arogya Abhiyan.

93. (c) The initial target set for the The Pradhan Mantri Ujjwala Yojana (PMUY) was to provide 50 million LPG connections to below poverty line (BPL) families by 2019, by giving financial assistance of Rs 1600 per family.

94. (a) Atal Bhoojal Yojana is an ambitious plan aimed at efficient management of available water resources. The emphasis of the scheme will be on recharge of ground water sources and efficient use of water by involving people at the local level. The half of the fund of 6000 crore will be supported by a World Bank loan of 3000 crore and the rest will be funded by central government. It would initially be implemented with community participation in Gujarat, Maharashtra, Haryana, Karnataka, Rajasthan, Uttar Pradesh and Madhya Pradesh.

95. (a) RBI is the manager of Foreign Exchange and it manages it as per the provision of the Foreign Exchange Management Act, 1999.

96. (a) Scientist have recently discovered fossil of a new dinosaur species in South Africa that is believed to a relative of the brontosaurus that weighed 26,000 pounds, about double the size of a large African elephant.

97. (a) PM hoisted a 150-feet-high national flag at Port Blair to mark the 75th anniversary of freedom fighter Subhash Chandra Bose's declaration of the formation of the Azad Hind government in 1943. He also renamed three islands in Andaman & Nicobar. The three islands — Ross Island, Neil Island and Havelock Island — will now be called Netaji Subhash Chandra Bose Island, Shaheed Dweep and Swaraj Dweep, respectively.

98. (a) The Act has several provisions. Some of them are compulsory that means that they need to be included in the state laws related to New Panchayati Raj system. Others are voluntary provisions. Their inclusion is on the discretion of the State government. Voluntary provisions are at the discretion because they let the state take into account various local factors like geography, administration, etc. into consideration while adopting the new system. Thus act translates representative democracy into participatory democracy, helping build democracy at the grassroots of the country.

99. (a) Article 243 I - The governor of a state shall constitute a finance commission to review the financial position of the Panchayats. The commission will be constituted every five years. As per the provision of Article 243 H - The state legislature may - authorize a Panchayat to levy, collect and appropriate taxes, duties, tolls and fees; assign to a panchayat taxes, duties, tolls and fees levied and collected by the state government; provide for making grants-in-aid to the Panchayats from the consolidated fund of the state; and provide for constitution of funds for crediting all moneys received by or on behalf of the Panchayats.

100. (a) GVK Rao committee was appointed by Planning Commission in 1985. The committee comes to Final conclusion that development process was gradually Bureaucratised and Divorced from the Panchayat Raj.

1. Which among the following Indian Philosophy belongs to the Heterodox school of Philosophy/Nastika school.
   1. Vaisesika
   2. Jain
   3. Purva mimansa
   4. Buddhist
   5. Carvaka
   Select the correct answer from the codes given below.
   (a) 1, 2 and 3 only
   (b) 3, 4 and 5 only
   (c) 2, 4 and 5 only
   (d) 1, 3 and 5 only

2. Which of the following is/are among the reasons behind stagnation of Agricultural sector during the colonial period:
   1. Land Revenue System.
   2. Exploitative nature of zamindars.
   3. Lack of irrigation facilities.
   4. Negligible use of fertilizers.
   5. Commercialisation of Agriculture.
   Select the correct answers from the codes given below
   (a) 1, 2, 3 and 5 only
   (b) 2, 3, 4 and 5 only
   (c) 1, 2, 3 and 4 only
   (d) 1, 2, 3, 4 and 5 only

3. Consider the following statements:
   1. The Fundamental Duties are confined to citizens only and do not extend to foreigners.
   2. Fundamental Duties are non-justiciable.
   3. There is no legal sanction against the violation of fundamental duties.
   Select the correct statement/statements using the codes given below:
   (a) 1 and 2 only
   (b) 2 and 3 only
   (c) 1 and 3 only
   (d) 1, 2 and 3 all

4. Consider the following statements:
   1. Sulphur dioxide ($SO_2$) is a major contributor to smog and acid rain.
   2. Paper industry releases ($SO_2$) in the environment.
   Select the correct statement/statements using the codes given below:
   (a) 1 only
   (b) 2 only
   (c) Both 1 and 2
   (d) Neither 1 nor 2

5. Consider the following statements with reference to the Veerashaiva Lingayats.
   1. They were followers of Basavanna
   2. They worship Shiva in his manifestation as a Linga.
   3. They believed in the theory of rebirth.
   Which of the statements given above is/are correct
   (a) 1 only
   (b) 1 and 2 only
   (c) 2 and 3 only
   (d) 1, 2 and 3

6. Which of the following is/are characteristics of the hot, wet Equatorial Climate:
   1. Uniformity of temperature throughout the year.
   2. Well defined winter season.
   3. Heavy precipitation.

Select the correct answer using the codes given below:
(a) 1 and 2 only
(b) 1 and 3 only
(c) 2 and 3 only
(d) 1, 2 and 3 only

7. Consider the following statements:
   1. Inflation benefits the debtors.
   2. Inflation benefits the bond-holders.
   Which of the statements given above is/are correct?
   (a) 1 only
   (b) Both 1 and 2
   (c) 2 only
   (d) Neither 1 nor 2

8. Consider the following statements:
   1. Maximum strength of state legislative council is fixed at two-third of the total strength of the legislative assembly of concerned state.
   2. 5/6th of the total members of a legislative council are indirectly elected.
   3. 1/6th of the total members of a legislative council are nominated by the governor.
   Select the correct statement/statements using the codes given below:
   (a) 1 only
   (b) 2 and 3 only
   (c) 1 and 3 only
   (d) 1 and 2 only

9. Consider the following statements:
   1. Estuaries are the most productive water bodies in the world.
   2. An estuary has very little wave action
   3. Estuaries are located at the higher end of a river and are not subjected to wave fluctuations.
   Select the correct answer from the codes given below:
   (a) 1 and 2 only
   (b) 2 and 3 only
   (c) 1 and 3 only
   (d) All the above

10. Consider the following statements with reference to the Faraizi Movement:
    1. Its scene of action was in East Bengal.
    2. It aimed at promoting social innovations current among the Muslims of the region.
    Select the correct statement/statements using the codes given below.
    (a) 1 only
    (b) 2 only
    (c) Both 1 and 2
    (d) Neither 1 nor 2.

11. Read the following statements with reference to National Achievement Survey?
    1. The survey was conducted by NCERT for students of class 3rd to class 8th.
    2. It was based on performance of students in 5 major subjects
    3. As per findings of the survey, rural students performed better than their urban counter parts.

Select the correct statement/statements using he codes given below:
(a) 1 only       (b) 3 only
(c) 2 and 3 only       (d) 1, 2 and 3

12. With reference to elections in India, consider the following statements.
1. Election commission allocates sharing of time on the cable television network to different political parties.
2. Election commission allots election symbols to political partis.
3. Registers political parties for the purpose of elections.
Which of the above statements is/are correct?
(a) 1 and 2 only       (b) 2 and 3 only
(c) All 1, 2 and 3       (d) 1 and 3 only

13. Which of the following is/are not a subject listed in the eleventh schedule of the constitution:
1. Poverty alleviation programme
2. Markets and fairs
3. Fire services
4. Slum improvement and upgradation
5. Burials and burial grounds
Select the correct answer using the codes given below:
(a) 1 and 2 only       (b) 2, 3 and 4 only
(c) 3, 4 and 5 only       (d) 1 and 4 only

14. Consider the following statements with reference to peninsular rivers.
(i) These rivers flow over soft, resistant and easily erodable bed rocks.
(ii) These rivers form wide U shaped valleys.
(iii) There flood plains are narrow, senile and lateral erosion is absent in them.
Which of the above mentioned statements are correct?
(a) (i) and (ii)       (b) only ii
(c) (ii) and (iii)       (d) all are correct

15. Read the following statements about Super Pressure Balloon Technology,
1. Super Pressure Balloon Technology serves as low-cost, near-space access for scientific payloads
2. The Super Pressure Balloon is made up of **polyethylene** film
Select the correct statement/statements using the codes given below:
(a) 1 only       (b) 2 only
(c) Both 1 and 2       (d) Neither 1 nor 2

16. Consider the following statements:
1. The president can pardon sentences inflicted by court martial while governor cannot.
2. Both president and governor can pardon death sentence.
Select the correct statement/statements using the codes given below:
(a) 1 only       (b) 2 only
(c) Both 1 and 2       (d) Neither 1 nor 2

17. Which of the following factors limit the productivity of Aquatic ecosystems:
1. Sunlight
2. Amount of oxygen dissolved in water.
3. Moisture.
4. Transparency
5. Temperature
Select the correct answer from the codes given below:
(a) 1, 2, 3 and 4       (b) 2, 3, 4 and 5
(c) 1, 2, 4 and 5       (d) All the above

18. Consider the following statements with reference to the Government of India Act. 1919
1. Dyarchy was introduced in provinces.
2. Provincial Legislative councils were expanded.
3. Voting rights was further curtailed.
Select the correct answer from the codes given below.
(a) 1 and 2 only       (b) 2 and 3 only
(c) 1 and 3 only       (d) 1, 2 and 3 all

19. Consider the following statements with reference to the Vermin animals.
1. They pose a threat to human and their livelihood.
2. They are schedule II animals under Wildlife (protection) Act, 1972.
3. States have no rights in declaring an animal as Vermin.
Select the correct answer from the codes given below:
(a) 1 only       (b) 2 and 3 only
(c) 1 and 3 only       (d) 1, 2 and 3 all

20. The Indian civil services was opened for all through which of the following legislation:
(a) Charter Act of 1833
(b) Charter Act of 1853
(c) Charter Act 1858
(d) Indian councils Act 1861

21. Article - 74 speaks of a council of minister to aid and advise president of India. Such a ministerial advice has been made binding on the president through:
(a) 44th Constitutional Amendment
(b) 42nd Constitutional Amendment
(c) 91st Constitutional Amendment
(d) 61st Constitutional Amendment

22. Which among the following are/is sources of Eutrophication:
1. Chemical fertilizers
2. Manure
3. Aquaculture
4. Fossil fuel combustion
Select the correct answer using the codes given below:
(a) 1, 2 and 3       (b) 2, 3 and 4
(c) 1, 3 and 4       (d) All of the above

23. Consider the following statements:
1. Spines of cactus are modified leaves.
2. Edible parts of onions are Modified leaves.
3. Modified leaves of saffron called threads are used as seasoning agent in food.
Which of the statements given above is/are correct?
(a) 1 and 2 only       (b) 2 and 3 only
(c) 1 and 3 only       (d) 1, 2 and 3

24. Which of the following does not pertains to the Israel-Palestine conflict.
(a) OSPO Accord, 1991
(b) The Madrid conference of 1991
(c) Hawke's Bay Regional council
(d) UNSC Resolution 1397

25. Consider the following statements:
1. The caves of Ajanta were excavated mainly during the time of Vakatakas.
2. The caves of Ajanta have sculptures and paintings on ceilings and walls.
Select the correct answer from the codes given below.
(a) 1 only       (b) 2 only
(c) Both 1 and 2       (d) Neither 1 nor 2

26. Which among the following is not related to estimation of poverty in India:
    (a) Dr. V.M. Dandekar.
    (b) Lakdawala Formula
    (c) Suresh Tendulkar Committee
    (d) All the above are related to estimation of poverty in India

27. Read the following statements with reference to institute of Eminence panel constituted by Government of India,
    1. The Panel will identify top 10 best higher educational Institutions in the country.
    2. The identified institute will enjoy autonomy in salaries, fees, courses etc.
    Select the correct answer using the codes given below:
    (a) 1 and 2          (b) 2 only
    (c) 1 only           (d) Neither 1 nor 2.

28. Consider the following statements:
    1. The western cyclonic disturbances are weather phenomena of the summer months.
    2. They usually influence the weather of the north and north-western regions of India.
    With reference to the Climatic phenomenons of India, which of the above statements stands true?
    (a) 1 only           (b) 2 only
    (c) Both 1 and 2     (d) Neither 1 nor 2

29. Consider the following statements:
    1. The Sun is vertically overhead at tropic of cancer on winter solstice.
    2. The Sun is vertically overhead at tropic of Capricorn in Summer Solstice.
    3. Beyond the tropics the sun is never overhead at any time of the year.
    Select the correct statement/statements using the codes given below:
    (a) 1 and 2 only     (b) 3 only
    (c) 1 and 3 only     (d) 2 and 3 only

30. Which of the following is/are not iniatives of the Government specifically meant for the welfare of Minorities:
    (i) USTTAD: (Upgrading the Skills and Training in Traditional Arts/crafts for Development)
    (ii) MANAS (Maulana Azad National Academy for Skills)
    (iii) Pradhan Mantri Vidya Shakti Yojana.
    Select the correct answer using the codes given below:
    (a) (i) and (ii)     (b) (ii) and (iii)
    (c) Only (i)         (d) (iii) and (i)

31. Which among the following is\are examples of Direct Taxes:
    1. Income Tax
    2. Wealth Tax
    3. Minimum Alternate Tax (MAT)
    Select the correct answer from the codes given below:
    (a) 1 & 2 only       (b) 2 & 3 only
    (c) 1 & 3 only       (d) All the above.

32. A stupa is mainly a tumulus or mound containing the relics of the Buddha. In this context consider the following statements.
    1. The largest concentration of stupas is in Andhra Pradesh.
    2. The best preserved examples of stupas are at Sanchi in Madhya Pradesh and Sarnath.
    Select the correct answer from the codes given below:
    (a) 1 only           (b) 2 only
    (c) Both 1 and 2     (d) Neither 1 nor 2

33. Which provision of the Present Indian Constitution resembles closely to the "Instrument of Instructions" enumerated in the Government of India Act of 1935–
    (a) Fundamental Rights
    (b) Emergency Provisions
    (c) Directive Principles of State Policy
    (d) Other than those given in the options

34. Which among the following pertains to "the prohibition of the use in war of Asphyxiating, Poisonous or other gases and of Bacteriological Methods of warfare?
    (a) Stockholm Convention
    (b) Geneva Protocol
    (c) Rotterdam Convention
    (d) The Vienna Convention

35. With reference to Inter State Council, which among the following statements stands false?
    (a) Its functions are complementary to Supreme Court's Jurisdiction under Art 131 to decide a legal controversy between the state governments.
    (b) Composition of Inter State Council also includes Six Central Cabinet Ministers, including Home Minister.
    (c) It is a recommendatory body and not a permanent constitutional body.
    (d) All the Chief Ministers except those of Union Territories are included in the composition of Inter State Council.

36. Government has Constituted Empowered Expert Committee (EEC) to select 20 Institutions of Eminence from among 104 institutions (public or private) that have applied for the status:
    Which among the following committee has been discussed above:
    (a) Malegon Committee
    (b) Justice Shah Committee
    (c) N Gopalswami Committee
    (d) None of the above

37. The Lucknow Session: 1916 of Indian national congress is significant as it is remembered for the reunion of the moderate and extremist factions of the congress.
    Who presided over the Lucknow session:
    (a) S.P. Sinha        (b) A.C. Majumdar
    (c) Annie Besant      (d) C.R Das

38. Consider the following statements with reference to fundamental rights:
    1. There is a clear tension between right to life and personal liberty and the provision for preventive detention.
    2. Any genuine protest against an act or policy of government by the people can not be denied permission.
    Choose the correct statements using the codes given below.
    (a) 1 only           (b) 2 only
    (c) Both 1 and 2     (d) None of these

39. Consider the following statements:
    1. Montreux Record is a register of wetland sites.
    2. It is maintained as part of the Ramsar List.
    Select the correct statement/statements using the codes given below:
    (a) 1 only           (b) 2 only
    (c) Both 1 and 2     (d) Neither 1 nor 2

40. In the context of Vedic Period consider the following statements.
    1. The basic and the highest political unit of Vedic period were Kula and Jana respectively.
    2. Monogamy and polygamy were generally practiced.
    Which of the statement/statements given above is/are correct.
    (a) 1 only      (b) 2 only
    (c) Both 1 and 2      (d) Neither 1 nor 2.

41. If one travels from Kolkata to Aizawal by road without crossing any international boundary, through how many states one has to pass to including the origin and destination States:
    (a) 4      (b) 5
    (c) 6      (d) 7

42. Which State Government has rolled out 'Asmita Yojana' on the International Women's Day to provide affordable sanitary Pads to school girls and women:
    (a) Gujarat      (b) Maharashtra
    (c) Kerala      (d) Tamilnadu

43. Consider the following statements:
    1. The width of the Himalayas decreases from west to east.
    2. The height of eastern half is greater than the western half.
    With reference to the himalayas, select the correct statement/statements using the codes given below:
    (a) 1 only      (b) 2 only
    (c) Both 1 and 2      (d) Neither 1 nor 2

44. "Project Brainwave" deep Learning acceleration platform for real-time Artificial Intelligence has been launched by,
    (a) Google      (b) Microsoft
    (c) IBM      (d) Apple

45. Which among the following found place in the Motilal Nehru Report, 1928;
    1. Dominion status for India.
    2. Separate electorates for Muslims
    3. Linguistic provinces.
    4. Certain fundamental rights.
    Select the correct answer from the codes given below.
    (a) 1 and 2 only      (b) 2 and 3only
    (c) 1, 3 and 4 only      (d) All the above

46. Which of the following is the method for converting files from Binary to ASCII?
    (a) BNCODE      (b) BIASCODE
    (c) UDECODE      (d) UUENCODE

47. With reference to "Budapest Convention", which of the following stands false?
    (a) It is the only binding international instrument on cyber crime.
    (b) It is supplemented by a protocol on Xenophobia and Racism.
    (c) It aims to pursue a common criminal policy.
    (d) It is the convention of the United Nations Security Council.

48. Which of the following constitutes capital account.
    1. Foreign Loans
    2. Foreign Direct Investment.
    3. Private Remittances.
    4. Portfolio Investment.
    Select the correct answer using the codes given below:
    (a) 1, 2 and 3      (b) 1, 2 and 4
    (c) 2, 3 and 4      (d) 1, 3 and 4

49. Which of the following is the correct order of the given peaks from south to north.
    (i) Guru Shikhar      (ii) Mahabaleshwar
    (iii) Doda Betta      (iv) Kalsubai
    **Codes:**
    (a) (iii), (ii), (iv), (i)      (b) (iii), (ii), (i), (iv)
    (c) (ii), (iii), (iv), (i)      (d) (i), (iv), (iii), (ii)

50. With reference to "National Commission for Scheduled Tribes" consider the following questions.
    1. It found place in the original constitution as imple-mented on 26-Jan 1950.
    2. It consists of a chairperson, a vice-chairperson and 3 other members.
    3. The commission is vested with the power to regulate its own procedure.
    Which of the above statement is/are true.
    (a) 1 and 2 only
    (b) 2 and 3 only
    (c) 1 and 3 only
    (d) 1, 2 and 3 all

51. Which of the following statements is /are correct regarding the concept of Force and Momentum?
    1. The momentum is the product of mass and velocity
    2. Force can be expressed in Kg metre per second squared
    3. Force is vector while momentum is scalar quantity
    Select the correct answer using the codes given below:
    (a) 1 and 2 only      (b) 2 and 3 only
    (c) 1 and 3 only      (d) 1, 2 and 3

52. Consider the following pairs with reference to the types of flood and the regions vulnerable to it.
    1. Flash Floods : Uttarakhand, J & K, Bangalore.
    2. Cyclone Flooding : Assam, West Bengal, Bihar.
    3. River Flooding : Coastal areas of Odisha, Andhra Pradesh, Tamil Nadu and Gujarat.
    Select the correct answer from the codes given below:
    (a) 1 only      (b) 1 and 2 only
    (c) 2 and 3 only      (d) All the above

53. Consider the following statements with reference to the Olive Ridley turtles:
    1. They are smallest and most abundant of all the sea turtles.
    2. They are carnivorous.
    3. They are found only in warmer waters.
    Select the correct answer from the codes given below:
    (a) 1 only      (b) 1 and 3 only
    (c) 1 and 2 only      (d) 1, 2 and 3 only

54. With reference to "Pradhan Mantri Bhartiya Janaushadhi Pariyojana" Consider the following statements.
    (i) It aims to provide quality medicines at affordable prices through special Jan Aushadhi Kendras.
    (ii) Jan Aushadhi Kendra can only be opened by any Government agency in any Government building owned by Government bodies.
    (iii) Recently, Railway ministry has given an in-principle approval to opening up of Jan Aushadhi Kendras at railway stations.
    Which of the above statement/statements is/are correct?
    (a) Only (i)      (b) (i) and (iii)
    (c) (i) and (ii)      (d) All are correct.

55. With reference to the Foreign Investment, which of the following constitutes portfolio investment:
    1. Foreign Institutional investment (FII)
    2. Depository Receipts
    3. Shares acquired by way of IPO
    4. Offshore funds
    Select the correct answer using the codes given below
    (a) 1, 2 and a3       (b) 1, 2 and 4.
    (c) 2, 3 and 4        (d) 1, 2, 3, and 4

56. Which of the followings were among the modern industries that were first set up during the colonial period.
    1. Cotton & Jute textile mills.
    2. Shipping.
    3. Chemical industry.
    4. Iron and steel industry.
    5. Sugar industry.
    6. Cement industry.
    Choose the correct answer using the codes given below:
    (a) 1, 2 and 3 only       (b) 1, 4, 5 and 6 only
    (c) 2, 3, 4, and 6 only   (d) 2, 3, 5 and 6 only

57. Which of the following statements best represents characteristics of Antibodies?
    1. These are produced by immune system to neutralize alien objects
    2. Bacteria and viruses are also neutralized by antibodies
    3. Antibody are V-shaped proteins
    4. Antibody binds with specific antigens
    Select the correct answer using the codes given below:
    (a) 1, 3 and 4 only       (b) 2, 3 and 4 only
    (c) 1, 2 and 4 only       (d) 1, 2, 3 and 4

58. Which of the following language is not listed in the eighth Schedule of the constitution.
    (a) Konkani       (b) Kashmiri
    (c) Himachali     (d) Santhali

59. Which among the following is/are ecological cause/causes of Coral bleaching:
    1. Temperature
    2. Solar Irradiance
    3. Sedimentation
    4. Sub aerial Exposure
    Select the correct answer from the codes given below:
    (a) 1 and 2 only       (b) 3 and 4 only
    (c) 1, 3 and 4 only    (d) All the above

60. With which of the following country/countries china does not have free trade agreement?
    (i) Maldives       (ii) India
    (iii) Pakistan     (iv) Sri Lanka
    Select the correct answer using the codes given below.
    (a) (ii) and (iv)     (b) only (iv)
    (c) (iii) and (iv)    (d) only (iii)

61. Which among the following is/are favourable condition/conditions for the formation of tropical cyclones:
    1. A source of warm, moist air derived from tropical oceans.
    2. Winds near the ocean surface blowing from different directions.
    3. Winds which do not very greatly with height.
    4. Coriolis force.
    Select the correct answer using the codes given below:
    (a) 1, 2 and 3 only       (b) 2, 3 and 4 only
    (c) 1, 3 and 4 only       (d) 1, 2, 3 and 4

62. Consider the following statements with reference to the economic crisis of 1991:
    1. The government was not able to generate sufficient revenue from the internal sources.
    2. No attempt was made to reduce the profligate spending.
    3. Prices of many essential goods rose sharply.
    4. Exports grew at a very high rate without matching growth of exports.
    Select the correct statements from the codes given below:
    (a) 1, 2 and 3 only       (b) 1, 2 and 4 only
    (c) 2, 3 and 4 only       (d) 1, 2, 3 and 4 only

63. Consider the following statements regarding the functioning of National Human Rights Commission (NHRC):
    1. It has all the powers of a civil court and its proceedings have a judicial character.
    2. It has power to punish the violators of human rights.
    3. It can award any relief including monitory relief to the victim.
    Select the correct statement/statements using the codes given below:
    (a) 1 and 2 only       (b) 2 and 3 only
    (c) 1 only             (d) 3 only

64. Consider the following statements with reference to metamorphosis in insects:
    1. Metamorphosis is a non-essential event in the life cycle of insects except butterfly
    2. It is controlled by thyroxine hormone
    Which of the statements given above is/are correct?
    (a) 1 only            (b) 2 only
    (c) Both 1 and 2      (d) Neither 1 nor 2

65. With reference to Foreign Investment, which of the following constitutes Foreign Direct Investment (FDI):
    1. Shares acquired by way of IPO
    2. Shares acquired by way of preferential allotment.
    3. Off shore funds.
    4. Depositry Receipts.
    Select the correct answer using the codes below:
    (a) 1 and 2 only       (b) 2 and 4 only
    (c) 3 and 4 only       (d) 1 and 3 only

66. Consider the following statements with reference to the Statutory Liquidity Ratio (SLR):
    1. Scheduled Banks are required to keep SLR in their vault itself.
    2. SLR has to be kept in the form of cash only.
    Select the Incorrect answer from the codes given below:
    (a) 1 only            (b) Both 1 and 2
    (c) 2 only            (d) Neither 1 nor 2

67. 1. The $15^{th}$ Finance Commission has been constituted under the chairmanship of N.K. Singh.
    2. The term of $15^{th}$ Finance Commission will from 2020–2025.
    Choose the correct statements.
    (a) 1 only            (b) 2 only
    (c) Both 1 and 2      (d) None of these

68. Selling goods in foreign countries at a price lower than the cost of production is known as:
    (a) Price dumping      (b) Cost dumping
    (c) Predatory dumping  (d) Both (b) and (c)

69. With reference to self Help Groups (SHGs) in India. Consider the following statements:
    1. Any SHG must have at least 50 members.
    2. SHGs can exist with or without registration.
    3. 90% of SHGs in India consist exclusively of women.
    Select the correct answer using the codes given below:
    (a) 1 only           (b) 2 only
    (c) 1 and 3 only     (d) 1, 2 and 3

70. Consider the following statements with reference to preamble of the constitution.
    1. The preamble to the Indian Constitution is based on the 'Objective Resolution' drafted and moved by Pandit Nehru.
    2. Three new words secular, integrity and fraternity were added by 42$^{nd}$ Constitutional Amendment Act (1976).
    Which of the above given statement is are correct.
    (a) 1 only           (b) 2 only
    (c) Both 1 and 2     (d) None of these

71. Montreux Record highlights are those sites where adverse changes in ecological character have occurred or are occurring. Certain Indian sites have been placed on the Montreux Record.
    In this context consider the following statements.
    1. Chilika lake was added due to Siltation.
    2. Loktak lake was added due to deforestation in the catchment area.
    3. Keoladeo national park was added due to damage caused by forest fires.
    Select the correct statement/statements using the codes given below:
    (a) 1 and 3 only     (b) 1 and 2 only
    (c) 2 and 3 only     (d) All the above

72. Which among the following is not true in context of the significance of perma-culture:
    (a) It is environment friendly.
    (b) It helps in checking global warming.
    (c) Cost benefit ratio is less as compared to Mono culture.
    (d) It promotes traditional practices.

73. Consider the following statements.
    (i) India's Higher Education Sector is largest in the world.
    (ii) Maharashtra tops in student enrolment in Universities.
    Which of the above statement is/are correct with reference to All India Survey on Higher Education 2016-2017?
    (a) Only (i)         (b) Only (ii)
    (c) Both (i) and (ii)   (d) Neither (i) nor (ii)

74. The Sangeet Natak Akademi recognises eight Indian Classical Dances. "Kathak" is one of them. With reference to "Kathak"; consider the following statements.
    1. It ends with a dramatic climax.
    2. It starts with invocation of Gods.
    Select the correct answer from the codes given below:
    (a) 1 only           (b) 2 only
    (c) Both 1 and 2     (d) Neither 1 nor 2

75. The new form of matter discovered by scientists recently has been named as
    (a) Excito-onicum     (b) ExStonium
    (c) Excitonicum      (d) Excitonium

76. Which among the following is/are demerits of the parliamentary system:
    1. No guarantee of a stable government.
    2. Not conducive for the formulation and implementation of long-term policies.
    3. The cabinet exercises nearly unlimited powers.
    4. It is against separation of powers between legislature and the executive.
    Select the correct answer using the codes given below.
    (a) 1, 2 and 3 only    (b) 2, 3 and 4 only
    (c) 1, 2 and 4 only    (d) All 1, 2, 3 and 4

77. In order for biomagnification to occur, the pollutant must be
    1. Long-lived
    2. Mobile
    3. Soluble in water
    4. Biologically active
    Select the correct answer from the codes given below:
    (a) 1, 2 and 3 only    (b) 2, 3 and 4 only
    (c) 1, 2 and 4 only    (d) 1, 2, 3 and 4

78. Consider the following statements:
    1. Calcium carbonate changes into calcium oxide and carbon dioxide on cooling. It is a decomposition reaction.
    2. Burning of coal to form carbon dioxide is a type of combination reaction
    Which of the statements given above is/are correct?
    (a) 1 only           (b) 2 only
    (c) Both 1 and 2     (d) Neither 1 nor 2

79. With reference to Agricultural and processed Food Export Development Authority (APEDA), Consider the following statements.
    (i) It is under Ministry of Agriculture and farmers welfare.
    (ii) It is mandated with the responsibility of promotion and development of the export of its scheduled products.
    Which of the following options are correct?
    (a) Only (i).        (b) Only (ii)
    (c) Both (i) and (ii).   (d) Neither (i) and (ii)

80. Consider the following questions:
    1. Proportional Representation System is a complicated system and more suitable for a small country.
    2. The First Post the Post system offers voters a choice not simply between parties but between specific candidates also.
    Select the correct statement/statements using the codes given below.
    (a) 1 only           (b) 2 only
    (c) Both 1 and 2     (d) None of these

81. The Faizpur session ; 1936 of the Indian National Congress is unique in itself. what was so remarkable about the Faizpur session?
    (a) Nehru urged congress to adopt Socialism as its goal.
    (b) The session held in a village for the first time.
    (c) Rajendra Prasad took over as president after Subhas Chandra Bose resigned.
    (d) The Swarajya party was formed.

82. Which of the following is not among the reasons for large number of drug addicts in India?
   (a) Rise of virtual currencies
   (b) Presence of Golden Crescent and Golden Triangle in the border regions up Myanmar, Laos and Thailand.
   (c) Abuse of pharmaceutical preparations like codeine based cough syrups and pain killers like 'Proxivon'.
   (d) Availability of Pucca Roads along the International Border and adequate infrastructure.

83. Consider the following statements:
   1. The citizens in India owns allegiance only to the Union.
   2. The right of outsiders to enter, reside and settle in tribal areas is restricted.
   Which of the above statements is/are correct:
   (a) 1 only     (b) 2 only
   (c) Both 1 and 2     (d) Neither 1 nor 2

84. Which among the following is/are source of air pollution?
   1. Tobacco smoking
   2. Pollen from plants
   3. Pesticides
   4. Hair from pets
   Select the correct answer using the codes given below:
   (a) 1, 2, 3 and 4     (b) 1, 2 and 3 only
   (c) 2, 3 and 4 only     (d) 1, 2 and 4 only

85. With reference to the Ajanta and Ellora Caves; consider the following statements:
   1. The Ajanta Caves are entirely Buddhist Caves.
   2. These Caves combine 3 art forms i.e. architecture, sculpture and painting.
   3. The paintings in these caves are inspired from Jataka stories.
   Select the correct answer from the codes given below:
   (a) 1 and 2 only     (b) 2 and 3 only
   (c) 1, 2 and 3 all     (d) 1 and 3 only

86. Which of the following statements regarding the comptroller and Auditor-General is/are correct?
   1. The Comptroller and Auditor General of India have the authority to audits the accounts of consolidated fund of India only.
   2. He audits all the institutions which receive fund from the central government.
   3. Auditor-General can be removed from his post by the same process as the judge of the Supreme Court removed.
   Which of the following statement is/are correct?
   (a) 1 and 2 only     (b) 2 and 3 only
   (c) 1 and 3 only     (d) 1, 2 and 3

87. Consider the following statements about Public Accounts Committee (PAC):
   1. The committee was set up first in 1921 under the provisions of Govt. of India Act of 1919.
   2. It has 22 members at present and all parties get due representation in it.
   3. A minister cannot be elected as a member of the committee.
   Which of the statements given above is/are correct?
   (a) 1 and 2 only     (b) 2 and 3 only
   (c) 1 and 3 only     (d) 1, 2 and 3

88. Regarding Public Accounts Committee, consider the following statements:
   1. It examine the annual audit reports of CAG, which are laid before the Parliament by the President.
   2. The Committee examines public expenditure to discover technical and economical irregularities.
   Which of the statements given above is/are correct?
   (a) 1 only     (b) 2 only
   (c) Both 1 and 2     (d) Neither 1 nor 2

89. Consider the following statements about the Parliamentary Committee on public accounts:
   1. It consists of not more than 25 members of the Loksabha.
   2. It scrutinises appropriation and finance accounts of the government.
   3. Examines the report of the comptroller and Auditor General of India.
   Which of the statements given above is/are correct?
   (a) 1 and 2     (b) 2 and 3
   (c) 1 and 3     (d) 1, 2 and 3

90. With reference to The World Development Report 2018 (WDR 2018), consider the following:
   1. The report is prepared by World Bank.
   2. The 2018 WDR explores four main themes and is the first ever devoted entirely to education.
   3. How to make systems work for learning, is one of the theme of WDR 2018
   Which of the following statement is/are correct?
   (a) 1 and 2 only     (b) 2 and 3 only
   (c) 1 and 3 only     (d) 1, 2 and 3

91. Consider the following statement:
   1. National Nutrition Mission was launched as an extension to the Beti bachao Beti Padhao programme.
   2. POSHAN Abhiyan was launched at Ahmadabad Gujarat on the occasion of the International Women's Day on March 8, 2018
   Which of the statements given above is/are correct?
   (a) 1 only     (b) 2 only
   (c) Both 1 and 2     (d) Neither 1 nor 2

92. Regarding the Operation Green that Finance Minister Arun Jaitley has announced in Union Budget 2018, which of the following statements is/are true?
   1. The scheme aims to double the farmers' income by end of the year 2022.
   2. The Scheme will be in line with the operation flood.
   3. The scheme was sanctioned with the budget allocation of Rs. 1000 crore.
   Select the correct answer using the code given below
   (a) 1 and 2     (b) 2 and 3
   (c) 1 and 3     (d) All of the above

93. With reference to Kandhamal Haldi (turmeric) which is in news recently, which of the following statements is/are correct?
   1. It is found in Odisha and will soon get Geographical Indications (GI) tag.
   2. It is of golden yellow colour and is famous for spice quality.
   Select the correct answer using the code given below
   (a) 1 only     (b) 2 only
   (c) Both 1 and 2     (d) Neither 1 nor 2

94. Consider the following statements:
    1. LaQshya program will benefit every pregnant woman and newborn delivering in public health institutions.
    2. The maternal death in India was 225 in 2001-03
    3. India reported an impressive decline of maternity death by 70% in a decade.
    Select the correct answer using the code given below
    (a) 1 and 2
    (b) 2 and 3
    (c) 1 and 3
    (d) All of the above

95. Regarding the Reserve Bank of India (RBI), which of the following statements is not correct?
    (a) The Reserve Bank of India was established on April 1, 1935 in accordance with the provisions of the Govt. of India Act, 1935.
    (b) The Central Office of the Reserve Bank was initially established in Calcutta but was permanently moved to Mumbai in 1937.
    (c) The Preamble of the Reserve Bank of India describes the basic functions of the Reserve Bank
    (d) The Reserve Bank's affairs are governed by a central board of directors that is appointed by the Government of India in keeping with the Reserve Bank of India Act.

96. Consider the following pairs

| | Arts | Regions |
|---|---|---|
| 1. | Warli | Western ghat |
| 2. | Phad | Rajasthan |
| 3. | Pahari Painting | Uttrakhand |

    Which of the pair given above is/are correct?
    (a) 1 only
    (b) 1 and 2 only
    (c) 3 only
    (d) 2 and 3 only

97. Which of the following statements are correct about Indian Railway Scheme 'buy tickets now and pay later'?
    1. This service is for only Rajdhani trains

2. Under this scheme passengers would be able to buy tickets from the IRCTC website and pay later.
3. This scheme option is valid only on e-tickets.
Which of the statements given above are correct?
(a) 1 and 2 only
(b) 2 and 3 only
(c) 1 and 3 only
(d) 1, 2 and 3

98. Consider the following statements:
    1. Pothos ivy is a common house plant that genetically modified by researchers to remove chloroform from air.
    2. HEPA filter is used to trap harmful particles such as pollen, pet dander, dust mites, and tobacco smoke.
    Which of the statements given above is/are correct?
    (a) 1 only
    (b) 2 only
    (c) Both 1 and 2
    (d) Neither 1 nor 2

99. Which of the following statements are correct about 'Himalayan marmots' that are recently in news?
    1. These creatures can survive at altitudes up to 5,000 meters in the Himalayan regions.
    2. The Himalayan marmot is chronically exposed to cold temperature, hypoxia, and intense UV radiation
    3. They mostly hibernate during the night.
    Select the correct answer using the code given below
    (a) 1 and 2 only
    (b) 2 and 3 only
    (c) 1 and 3 only
    (d) 1, 2 and 3

100. Cabinet has approved the creation of which agency for educational testing under the Indian Societies Registration Act, 1860?
    (a) National Testing Agency
    (b) National Educational Agency
    (c) National Education Testing Agency
    (d) National Higher Education Testing Agency

# RESPONSE SHEET

| | | | | |
|---|---|---|---|---|
| 1. ⓐⓑⓒⓓ | 2. ⓐⓑⓒⓓ | 3. ⓐⓑⓒⓓ | 4. ⓐⓑⓒⓓ | 5. ⓐⓑⓒⓓ |
| 6. ⓐⓑⓒⓓ | 7. ⓐⓑⓒⓓ | 8. ⓐⓑⓒⓓ | 9. ⓐⓑⓒⓓ | 10. ⓐⓑⓒⓓ |
| 11. ⓐⓑⓒⓓ | 12. ⓐⓑⓒⓓ | 13. ⓐⓑⓒⓓ | 14. ⓐⓑⓒⓓ | 15. ⓐⓑⓒⓓ |
| 16. ⓐⓑⓒⓓ | 17. ⓐⓑⓒⓓ | 18. ⓐⓑⓒⓓ | 19. ⓐⓑⓒⓓ | 20. ⓐⓑⓒⓓ |
| 21. ⓐⓑⓒⓓ | 22. ⓐⓑⓒⓓ | 23. ⓐⓑⓒⓓ | 24. ⓐⓑⓒⓓ | 25. ⓐⓑⓒⓓ |
| 26. ⓐⓑⓒⓓ | 27. ⓐⓑⓒⓓ | 28. ⓐⓑⓒⓓ | 29. ⓐⓑⓒⓓ | 30. ⓐⓑⓒⓓ |
| 31. ⓐⓑⓒⓓ | 32. ⓐⓑⓒⓓ | 33. ⓐⓑⓒⓓ | 34. ⓐⓑⓒⓓ | 35. ⓐⓑⓒⓓ |
| 36. ⓐⓑⓒⓓ | 37. ⓐⓑⓒⓓ | 38. ⓐⓑⓒⓓ | 39. ⓐⓑⓒⓓ | 40. ⓐⓑⓒⓓ |
| 41. ⓐⓑⓒⓓ | 42. ⓐⓑⓒⓓ | 43. ⓐⓑⓒⓓ | 44. ⓐⓑⓒⓓ | 45. ⓐⓑⓒⓓ |
| 46. ⓐⓑⓒⓓ | 47. ⓐⓑⓒⓓ | 48. ⓐⓑⓒⓓ | 49. ⓐⓑⓒⓓ | 50. ⓐⓑⓒⓓ |
| 51. ⓐⓑⓒⓓ | 52. ⓐⓑⓒⓓ | 53. ⓐⓑⓒⓓ | 54. ⓐⓑⓒⓓ | 55. ⓐⓑⓒⓓ |
| 56. ⓐⓑⓒⓓ | 57. ⓐⓑⓒⓓ | 58. ⓐⓑⓒⓓ | 59. ⓐⓑⓒⓓ | 60. ⓐⓑⓒⓓ |
| 61. ⓐⓑⓒⓓ | 62. ⓐⓑⓒⓓ | 63. ⓐⓑⓒⓓ | 64. ⓐⓑⓒⓓ | 65. ⓐⓑⓒⓓ |
| 66. ⓐⓑⓒⓓ | 67. ⓐⓑⓒⓓ | 68. ⓐⓑⓒⓓ | 69. ⓐⓑⓒⓓ | 70. ⓐⓑⓒⓓ |
| 71. ⓐⓑⓒⓓ | 72. ⓐⓑⓒⓓ | 73. ⓐⓑⓒⓓ | 74. ⓐⓑⓒⓓ | 75. ⓐⓑⓒⓓ |
| 76. ⓐⓑⓒⓓ | 77. ⓐⓑⓒⓓ | 78. ⓐⓑⓒⓓ | 79. ⓐⓑⓒⓓ | 80. ⓐⓑⓒⓓ |
| 81. ⓐⓑⓒⓓ | 82. ⓐⓑⓒⓓ | 83. ⓐⓑⓒⓓ | 84. ⓐⓑⓒⓓ | 85. ⓐⓑⓒⓓ |
| 86. ⓐⓑⓒⓓ | 87. ⓐⓑⓒⓓ | 88. ⓐⓑⓒⓓ | 89. ⓐⓑⓒⓓ | 90. ⓐⓑⓒⓓ |
| 91. ⓐⓑⓒⓓ | 92. ⓐⓑⓒⓓ | 93. ⓐⓑⓒⓓ | 94. ⓐⓑⓒⓓ | 95. ⓐⓑⓒⓓ |
| 96. ⓐⓑⓒⓓ | 97. ⓐⓑⓒⓓ | 98. ⓐⓑⓒⓓ | 99. ⓐⓑⓒⓓ | 100. ⓐⓑⓒⓓ |

## HINTS & EXPLANATIONS

1.  (c)  Six orthodox schools : Nyaya, Vaisesika, Samkhya, Yoga, Purva Mimansa and Vedanta. The Heterodox are Jain, Buddhist and Materialist (Carvaka) school of philosophy.

2.  (c)  The stagnation in the agricultural sector was caused mainly because of the various systems of land settlement that were introduced by the colonial government.
    – The main interest of the zamindars was only to collect rent regardless of the economic condition of the cultivators.
    – The teams of the revenue settlement were also responsible for the zamindars adopting such an attitude.
    – Besides this low levels of technology lack of irrigation facilities and negligible use of fertilizers, all added up to aggravate the plight of the farmers and contributed to the dismal level of agricultural productivity.
    – There are however certain evidence of a relatively higher yield of cash crops in certain areas of the country due to commercialisation of agriculture.

    **Source:** N.C.E.R.T - 11$^{th}$ - Economics.

3.  (d)  All the above given statements are true regarding the fundamental duties. There is no legal sanction against the violation of fundamental duties. Howver parliament is free to enforce them by suitable legislation. Also fundamental duties are non-justiciable that is they are not enforceable in the court.

4.  (c)  Sulphur dioxide ($SO_2$) is a gas produced from burning coal, mainly in thermal power plants. Some industrial processes, such as production of paper and smelting of metals, produce Sulphur dioxide. It is a major contributor to smog and acid rain. Sulfur dioxide can lead to lung diseases.

5.  (b)  In twelfth century, a new movement was emerged in Karnataka. It was led by a Brahmana named Basavanna. The followers of Basavanna were known as Veerashaiva or Lingayats. Lingayats believe that on death the devotee will be united with Shiva and will not return to this world.

6.  (b)  The most outstanding feature of the equatorial climate is its great uniformity of temperature throughout the year.
    There is no winter. Cloudiness and heavy precipitation help to moderate the daily temperature, so that even at the equator itself, the climate is not unbearable.
    In addition regular land and sea breezes assist in maintaining a truly equable climate.

7.  (a)  In the case of inflation the value of money decreases and so the particular asset held by an investor will not yield much revenue. Inflation will harm the bond-holders.

8.  (b)  The members of the legislative council are indirectly elected. The maximum strength of the council is fixed at one-third of the total strength of the assembly and the minimum strength is fixed at 40.
    It means that the size of the council depends on the size of the assembly of the concerned state.

9.  (a)  Estuaries are located where river meets the sea. Estuaries are water bodies where the flow of freshwater from river mixes with salt water transported by tide from the ocean.
    – Estuaries are the most productive water bodies in the world. They are located at the lower end of a river and are subject to tidal fluctuations.
    – An estuary has very little wave action, so it provides a calm refuge from the open sea. It provides the shelter for some of the animals.

10. (a)  The movement also called the Fairaizi Movement because of its emphasis on the Islamic pillars of faith was founded by Haji Shariat-Allah.
    Its Scene of action was East Bengal and it aimed at the eradication of social innovations current among the Muslims of the region.

11. (c)  National Achievement Survey was conducted by NCERT for students in class 3$^{rd}$, class 5$^{th}$ and class 8$^{th}$ to assess performance in subjects English, Mathematics, Science, Social Science and Modern Indian Languages. One of the findings of the survey was better performance of rural students than those from urban regions.

12. (c)  Under a 2003 provision, the Election Commission should allocate equitable sharing of time on the cable television network and other electronic media during elections to display or propagate any matter or to address public.
    – Allotting election symbols and Registering political parties comes under functions of election commission besides many other functions.

13. (c)  Eleventh Schedule of the Constitution deals with the establishment of local self government in rural areas. It contains 29 functional items placed within the preview of panchayats. Some of them are–
    – Agriculture
    – Land reforms
    – Minor forest producer
    – Rural housing
    – Drinking water
    – Non-conventional energy etc.

    **Note:** Fire Services, Slum improvement and burial grounds are listed in 12$^{th}$ Schedule which deals with establishment of local self government in urban areas.

14. (c)  Peninsular rivers are rain-fed rivers. The rivers flow over hard and resistant rocks. The bed rocks of these rocks are not easily erodable. These rivers have poor development of stream order and form wide

U shaped valleys. These flood plains are narrow, senile and lateral erosion is absent in them. These are non-perennial rivers and most of their channel dry up during the summer season.

15. (d) Super Pressure Balloon Technology serves as low-cost, near-space access for scientific payloads. The Super Pressure Balloon is made up of long durable Polyethylene film.

16. (a) Article - 72; Pardoning power of the president.
Article - (161); Pardoning power of the governor.
The pardoning power of the governor differs from that of the president in following two respects.
   – The President can pardon sentences inflicted by court martial (Military courts) while the governor cannot.
   – The president can pardon death sentence while governor cannot.
However governor can suspend, remit or commute a death sentence.

17. (c) Sunlight and oxygen are most important limiting factors of the aquatic ecosystems whereas moisture and temperature are the main limiting factors of terrestrial ecosystems.
   – The factors limiting the productivity of Aquatic Habitats are:
   – Sunlight based on light penetration and plant distribution aquatic ecosystem is categorised into photic and aphotic zones.
   – Dissolved oxygen
   – Transparency
   – Temperature.

18. (a) Voting rights were also given to womens through the Governments of India Act. 1919. Thus the scope of franchise was expanded.
Dyarchy ie rule of Two-executive councillors and popular ministers was introduced. The governor was to be the executive head in the province.

19. (a) Any animal which pose a threat to human and their livelihood especially farming can be declared Vermin. They are Schedule V animals under Wildlife (protection) Act, 1972.
   – States can send a list of wild animals to the centre requesting it to declare them Vermin for selective slaughter.

20. (b) The Charter Act of 1853 was last of the Charter Acts. It opened up the civil services for all. For the first time, the legislature was given the right to frame its own rules of procedure.

21. (b) After the 42$^{nd}$ Constitutional Amendment (1976), ministerial advice has been made binding on the president, but no such provision has been made with respect to the governor.

22. (d) Eutrophication is a syndrome of ecosystem, response to the addition of artificial or natural nutrients such as nitrates and phosphates through fertilizers, sewage etc that fertilize the aquatic ecosystem.

It is primarily caused by the leaching of phosphate or nitrate containing fertilizers from agricultural lands into lakes or rivers.
   – The growth of green algae which we see in the lake surface layer is the physical identification of an Eutrophication.
   – All the above mentioned are the sources of the eutrophication.

23. (d) Leaves are modified into spines in case of cactus and into fleshy edible leaves in onion. Stigma and style of saffron plants commonly called threads are used as seasoning agent in food

24. (c) Hawke's Bay Biodiversity strategy was launched in march 2016. This is a regional approach to improve habitats and support native species.

25. (c) The caves of Ajanta were excavated mainly during the time of Vakatakas. The caves at Ajanta are famous for beautiful sculptures and paintings on ceilings and walls. Bagh caves in Dhar district of Madhya Pradesh are also known for paintings, but most of these have unfortunately deteriorated.
**Source:** N.C.E.R.T : Heritage of India

26. (d) The history of poverty estimation in India goes back to 19th century when Dadabhai Naroji's efforts and careful study led him to conclude subsistence based poverty line.
Other efforts in this regard are:
   – 1938; National Planning Committee
   – Y. K. Alagh Committee 1979.
   – Lakdawala Formula 1993.
   – Suresh Tendulkar Committee:2005
   – Arvind Panagariya Task Force.
   – Rangarajan Formula.
**Source:** Key concepts ; Shankarganesh

27. (b) Government of India constituted a panel for identification of top 20 best higher education institutions in the country. The panel will be headed by N Gopalaswami former CEC. The Institute of Eminence will enjoy autonomy in faculty and staff salaries, students, courses etc.

28. (b) The western cyclonic disturbances are weather phenomena of the winter months brought in by the westerly flow from the Mediterranean region. They usually influence the weather of the north and north-western regions of India.

29. (b) The Sun is vertically overhead at tropic of cancer (23'/2°N) on June/21, this is known as summer solstice.
   – The Sun is vertically overhead at tropic of Capricorn (23"2°S) on 22/December, this is known as winter Solstice.
   – The tropics thus mark the limits of the overhead Sun, because beyond these, the Sun is never overhead at any time of the years.

30. (a) Pradhan Mantri Vidya Shakti Yojana is an existing scheme of construction of Hostels for SC girl students and setting up of residential schools for Scheduled

Caste girls studying in class VI to class XII with the objective of reducing the dropout rate of Scheduled Caste girls.

31. (d) Direct Taxes are:
- Incomes Tax
- Corporate Tax.
- Wealth Tax.
- Securities Transaction Tax.
- Commodities Transaction Tax
- Minimum Alternate Tax.

32. (c) A stupa is mainly a tumulus or mound containing the relics of the Buddha. The largest concentration of stupas is in Andhra Pradesh where these were erected mainly between the third century BC and the third century A.D.

The stupas at Nagarjunakonda and Amaravati were covered with beautiful sculptured slabs. The best preserved examples of stupas are at Sanchi in Madhya Pradesh and Sarnath in Uttar Pradesh. Sanchi is famous for its gateways.

**Source:** N.C.E.R.T : Heritage of India

33. (c) In the words of Dr. B.R. Ambedkar 'The Directive principles are like the "instrument of instructions", which were issued to the Governor-General and to the Governors of the colonies of India by the British Government under the Government of India Act, 1935.

34. (b)

35. (d) Inter State Council is a recommendatory body on issues relating to inter-state, centre-state and centre and Union Territory relations, composition of Inter State Council includes Prime Minister as the Chairman, Chief Ministers of all states, Chief Ministers of Union Territories having legislative Assemblies, Governors of the States under the President's rule and Six Central Cabinet Ministers, including Home Minister to be nominated by the P.M.

36. (c) The Committee will be headed by former Chief Election Commissioner (CEC) N Gopalswami. The Scheme of Institutions of Eminence was rolled out by University Grants Commission (UGC).

37. (b) A.C Majumdar presided over the Lucknow session of Indian national congress.

38. (a) According to the provision of the preventive detention (Art-22), a person can be arrested simply out of an apprehension that he or she is likely to engage in unlawful activity and imprisoned for some time without following the established procedure. Therefore it comes in conflict with the right to life and personal liberty.

The Rights provided by Art-19(i) i.e. right to freedom of speech and expression is subjected to certain restrictions. Such as public order, peace and morality etc.

Therefore any genuine protest against an act or policy of government by the people may be denied permission.

**Source:** N.C.E.R.T XI[th] [Indian Constitution at Work]

39. (c) Montreux Record is the principal tool under the Ramsar Convention, is a register of wetland sites on the list of wetlands of International Importance.

It is maintained as part of the Ramsar List.

Montreux Record highlights those sites where adverse changes in ecological character have occurred are occurring or are likely to occur as a result of technological developments, pollution or other human interference and which are therefore in need of priority conservation attention.

40. (a) Monogamy was generally practiced while polygamy was prevalent among the royal and noble families.

41. (b) Refer the Map of India.

42. (b) Under the Scheme, school girls studying in Zilla Parishad Schools will get sanitary napkin packet at ₹ 5 while rural women can avail it at subsidised rate of ₹ 24 and ₹ 29.

43. (c) The Himalayas extend from the Indus in the west to the Brahmaputra in the east. They form an arc between these two extremes, covering a distance of 2,500 km. The width of the Himalayas varies from 400 km in the west to 150 km in the east.

Himalayas are wide in Kashmir and become narrow towards the east. The height of the eastern half is greater than the western half.

44. (b) Project Brainwave, deep Learning acceleration platform for real-time Artificial Intelligence is launched by Microsoft using the field-programmable gate array infrastructure.

45. (c) In 1928, the congress appointed a sub committee under the chairmanship of Motilal Nehru to draft a Constitution.

The major recommendation of the Nehru Report were:
- Dominion status on lines of self governing dominions as the form of government desired by Indians.
- Rejection of separate electorates which had been the basis of constitutional reforms so far, instead it demanded for joint electorates with reservation of seats for Muslims
- Linguistic provinces.
- Nineteen fundamental rights including equal rights for women right to form unions and universal adult suffrage.
- Responsible government at the centre and in provinces.

46. (d) UUENCODE- is a method for converting files from Binary to ASCII for the purpose of transfer across the Internet.

47. (d) Budapest Convention on Cyber crime is the convention of the council of Europe. It is the first international treaty on crimes committed via the internet and other computer networks and deals with issues such as infringements of copyright, computer related fraud, child pornography and violations of network security.

48. (b) A capital account shows the net change in physical or financial asset ownership for a nation and together with the current account, constitutes a nation's balance of payments.

   The capital account includes foreign direct investment - (FDI), portfolio and other investments, plus changes in the reserve account.

49. (a)

50. (b) In order to Safeguard the interests of the STs more effectively, it was proposed to set up a separate National Commission for STs by bifurcating the existing combined National Commission for SCs and STs.

   This was done by passing the $89^{th}$ constitutional Amendment Act of 2003.

   – It consists of a chairperson, a vice-chairperson and 3 other members, all appointed by president.

   – The commission is vested with the power to regulate its own procedure.

51. (a) The momentum is the product of mass and Velocity. Both momentum and force are vectors. Force can be expressed in Kg metre per Second Square or Newton.

52. (a) According to the National Commission on floods set up in 1976, around 40 million hectare area in India is prove to floods.

   River flooding – Assam, West Bengal, Bihar and Eastern UP

   Cyclone Flooding – Coastal areas of Odisha, Andhra Pradesh, Tamil Nadu and Gujarat.

   Flash Floods – Haryana, Uttarakhand, J & K, Bangalore etc.

53. (b) Olive Ridley turtles are smallest and most abundant of all the sea turtles. They are omnivorous. They are found only in warmer waters, including the Southern Atlantic, Pacific and Indian Oceans.

54. (b) Pradhan Mantri Bhartiya Janaushadhi Pariyojana is a Campaign Launched by the Department of Pharmaceuticals, to provide quality medicines at affordable prices to the masses through special Jan Aushadhi Kendra. These kendras can also be opened by any NGOs/Charitable Society/Institution/self help Group/Individual Entrepreneurs/pharmacist/Doctor outside of the hospital premises or any suitable place. Government also provides grants up to ₹ 2.5 lakh.

55. (b) Investment through stock on exchange that is through secondary market is called investment. Portfolio investment refers to investment in various financial instruments like shares, debentures of a company through secondary market. There are three major types of investment. They are

   1. Foreign Institutional Investment (FII)
   2. Depository Receipts.
   3. Offshore funds.

56. (b) During the second half of the nineteenth century modern industry began to take root in India but its progress remained very slow. Initially this development was confined to the setting up of cotton and jute textile mills.

   Subsequently the iron and steel industries began coming up in the beginning of the twentieth century. A few other industries in the fields of sugar, cement, paper etc. come up after the second world war.

   However there was hardly any capital good industry to help promote further industrialisation in India.

   **Source:** N.C.E.R.T - $11^{th}$ - Economics

57. (c) Antibodies are produced by immune system to neutralize foreign objects like bacteria, viruses etc. **These are Y-shaped** proteins which bind with specific antigens and signal the other cells of immune system.

58. (c) At present the eighth schedule of the constitution specifies 22 languages (originally 14 languages). These are

   | | | | |
   |---|---|---|---|
   | 1. | Assamese | 12. | Manipuri |
   | 2. | Bengali | 13. | Marathi |
   | 3. | Bodo | 14. | Nepali |
   | 4. | Dogri (Dongri) | 15. | Oriya |
   | 5. | Gujarati | 16. | Punjabi |
   | 6. | Hindi | 17. | Sanskrit |
   | 7. | Kannada | 18. | Santhali |
   | 8. | Kashmiri | 19. | Sindhi |
   | 9. | Konkani | 20. | Tamil |
   | 10. | Mathili (Maithili) | 21. | Telugu |
   | 11. | Malayalam | 22. | Urdu |

59. (d) A Coral reef bleaching can be caused by a variety of factors:

   – Anomalously low and high sea temperatures can induce Coral bleaching.

   – Solar radiation has been suspected to play a role in Coral bleaching.

   – Relatively few instances of coral bleaching have been linked solely to sediment.

   – Rapid dilution of reef waters from storm-generated precipitation and runoff has been demonstrated to cause Coral reef bleaching.

   – Sudden exposure of reef flat Corals to the atmosphere during events such as extreme low tides can potentially induce bleaching.

60. (b) China has Free Trade Agreement with Pakistan, and is exploring or negotiating Free Trade Agreements with Bangladesh, Sri Lanka and Nepal.

61. (d) According to the Indian Meteorological Centre, Tropical cyclones require certain conditions for their formation. All the above mentioned conditions are favourable for the formation of tropical cyclones.

62. (d) The origin of the financial crisis can be traced from the inefficient management of the Indian economy in the 1980s.

   – The continued spending on development programmes of the government did not generate additional revenue. Moreover the government was not able to generate sufficiently from internal sources such as taxation.

At times our foreign exchange borrowed from other countries and international financial institutions was spent on meeting consumption needs. Neither was an attempt made to reduce such profligate spending nor sufficient attention was given to boost exports to pay for the growing imports.

– Prices of many essential goods rose sharply. Imports grew at a very high rate without matching growth of exports.

– Also no country or international funder was willing to lend to India.

**Source:** N.C.E.R.T - 11th - Economics.

63. (c) NHRC is vested with the power to regulate its own procedure. It has all the powers of a civil court and its proceedings have a judicial character.

Functions of NHRC are mainly recommendatory in nature. It has no power to punish the violators of human rights, nor to award any relief including monetory relief to the victim.

The recommendations of NHRC are not binding on the concerned government or authority.

64. (d) Metamorphosis is an essential stage in life cycle of insects and controlled by insect hormones.

65. (a) Investment through the mode other than the stock exchange is called foreign direct investment in India. There is prescribed size to treat an investment as foreign direct investment. FDI includes the following:

– Shares acquired by way of IPO.

– Shares acquired by way of preferential allotment.

– Shares acquired by way of offer for sale through private arrangement.

– Transfer of shares by way of offer for sale through private arrangement.

– In all these purchases there is direct contact between the securities buyer and the seller company.

**Source:** Key concept- Shanker Ganesh

66. (b) Scheduled banks are required to keep certain percentage of their net time and demand deposits in their vault itself. It need not be deposited with RBI. This reserve is a precautionary measure. It prevents bank from lending all its deposits which is too risky and it is mandatory under Banking Regulation Act 1949. The ratio is 25 - 40% of net. Time and Demand deposit.

This reserve has to be kept in the form of cash, gold and bond.

67. (c) The 15th finance commission has been set up by the government under the chairmanship of N.K. Singh. The Operational Duration of the commission will be 2020-2025.

68. (d) Cost dumping means selling goods in foreign countries at a price lower than cost of production. It is mainly aimed at wiping out the domestic producers from the market. It is also called Predatory Dumping.

69. (b) A typical SHG has 15-20 members, usually belonging to one neighbourhood, who meet? save regularly,

– Members can take small loans from the group itself to meet their needs.

– Self Help Groups can exist with or without registration.

– Also 90% of SHGs, in India consist exclusively of women.

– SHGs in India often work in association with Banks (SHG - Bank Linkage Programme)

**Source:** N.C.E.R.T - 10th - Economics

70. (a) – Statement 1 is correct Pt. Nehru introduced the "Objective Resolution" in the constituent Assembly which on Dec.13, 1946. This resolution as accepted by the constituent Assembly forms the basis of the Indian Political System. It guided the constitution making process.

71. (b) Keoladeo national park, Rajasthan was placed on the Montreux Record in 1990 due to water shortage and un-balanced grazing regime around it.

72. (c) Permaculture is the conscious design and maintenance of agriculturally productive ecosystems which have the diversity, stability and resilience of natural ecosystems. Permaculture improves income. Instead of Mono culture, permaculture uses polyculture where a diverse range of vegetation and animals are utilised to support each other to create a self-sustaining systems.

73. (a) As per, All India Survey on Higher Education (2016-17), Uttar Pradesh tops in student enrolment in Universities followed by Maharashtra and Tamil Nadu.

74. (c) Kathak is a pure dance. It progresses in tempo from slow to fast, ending with a dramatic climax. It start with Vandana (in vocation of Gods), a short dance composition is known as a tukra, a longer one as a toda. Bols are vocals from tabla.

75. (d) Recently scientists have proven the existence of new form of matter-Excitonium. It is made up of excitons and exhibits macroscopic quantum phenomena similar to a superconductor.

76. (d) All the above given statements are among demerits of the parliamentary system. Also the parliamentary system is not conducive to administrative efficiency as the ministers are not experts in their fields.

77. (c) Biomagnification refers to the tendency of pollutants to concentrate as they move from one tropic level to the next.

Thus in biomagnification there is an increase in concentration of a pollutant from one link in a food chain to another.

In order for bio-magnification to occur, the pollutant must be long-lived, mobile, soluble in fats and biologically active.

If the pollutant is soluble in, it will be excreted by the organism. Pollutants that dissolve in fats, however may be retained for a long time.

78. (b) Burning of coal to form carbon dioxide from carbon and oxygen is an example of combination reaction. Calcium carbonate on heating dissociates into calcium oxide and carbon dioxide, it is a type of decomposition reaction.

79. (b) Agricultural and processed food Export Development Authority (APED) is an export promotion organization under ministry of commerce and Industries. It was established under the Agricultural and Processed Food Products Export Development Authority Act.

80. (c) Proportional Representation is a complicated system which may work in a small country, but would be difficult to work in a sub-continental country like India. The reason for the popularity and success of the FPTP system is its simplicity.

    Also the FPTP system offers voters a choice not simply between parties but between specific candidates.

81. (b) The faizpur session was held in Dec. 1936. The session was headed by Jawahar Lal Nehru. It was the first annual session of the Indian National Congress that was held in a village.

82. (d) Non-Availability of Pucca roads along the International Border in Punjab, suitable observation posts & obsolete infrastructure for border floodlights has worked in favour of smugglers.

83. (c) Though the Indian constitution is federal and envisages a dual polity (centre and states), it provides for only a single citizenship, that is Indian citizenship. The citizens in India are allegiance only to the union. There is no separate state citizenship.
    – The freedom of movement and residence (under Article-19) is subjected to the protection of interests of any schedule tribe.
    – In other words, the right of outsiders to enter, reside and settle in tribal areas is restricted. This is door to protect the distinctive culture, language, customs and manners of schedule tribes and to safeguard their traditional vocation and property against exploitation.

84. (a) Sources of air pollutants are:
    – Volatile organic compounds.
    – Tobacco
    – Biological pollutants
    – Formaldehyde
    – Radon
    – Asbestos
    – Pesticides

85. (c) The Ajanta caves are entirely Buddhist and date from about 200 BC to approximately 650 AD. These caves are unique in that they combine three forms of art- architecture, sculpture and painting.

    The colours used were local pigments and all the colours except blue could be obtained from neighbouring hills. The paintings sought their inspiration from the Jatakas, legendary Buddhist Stories.
    **Source:** Spectrum's : Indian Culture

86. (b) The comptroller and Auditor General of India have the authority to audit the accounts of 911 institutions which recieved funds from Central Govt. He also audit the accounts of consolidated fund of India, The accumulated fund of the state and the accounts of Each Union Territory which have Legislative Assembly.

87. (d) Public Accounts Committee (PAC) was set up under the provisions of the Government of India Act of 1919 and has since been existed. At present it consists of 22 members (15 from the Loksabha and 7 from Rajyasabha). The members are elected by the Parliament every year from amongst its member according to the Principle of proportional representation by means of the single transferable vote.

88. (c) The CAG submits three audit reports to the President, namely, audit report on appropriation accounts, audit report on finance accounts and audit report on public undertaking. The committee examines public expenditure not only from legal and formal points of view to discover technical irregularities but also from the point of view of economy, prudence, wisdom and propriety to bring out the cases of waste, loss, corruption, extravagance, inefficiency and nugatory expences.

89. (b) At present Public Accounts Committee consists of 22 members, 15 from Loksabha and 7 from the Rajyasabha.

90. (d) The World Development Report is prepared by World Bank. The 2018 WDR explores four main themes: Education's promise; The need to shine a light on learning; How to make schools work for learners; and How to make systems work for learning.

91. (a) National Nutrition Mission (POSHAN Abhiyan) was launched at Jhunjhunu in Rajasthan on the occasion of the International Women's Day on March 8, 2018 by Prime Minister Narendra Modi. The main objectives of this scheme are to attain proper nutritional status among children from 0-6 years, adolescent girls, pregnant women and lactating mothers in a timely manner; reduce stunting, under-nutrition, and anemia among young children, women, and adolescent girls; and lowering low birth weight by at least 2% per annum.

92. (a). With the budget allocation of Rs. 500 Cr, Finance Minister Arun Jaitley has announced about the Operation Green in Union Budget 2018. This scheme will facilitate the farmers of the nation. This will be in line with the operation flood. To reduce the fluctuation in the pricing of Onion, Tomatoes and Potatoes the scheme has been launched.

93. (a) Odisha's Kandhamal Haldi (turmeric) will soon get Geographical Indications (GI) tag. Its registration was moved by Kandhamal Apex Spices Association for Marketing and was accepted under sub-section (1) of Section 13 of Geographical Indications of Goods (Registration and Protection) Act, 1999. Kandhamal Haldi is famous for its healing properties. Apart from domestic use, it is also used for cosmetic and medicinal purposes.

94. (b) India has come a long way in improving maternal survival as Maternal Mortality Ratio (MMR) has reduced from 301 maternal deaths in 2001-03 to 167 in year 2011-13, an impressive decline of 45% in a decade. India is further committed to ensuring safe motherhood to every pregnant woman in the country.

95. (a) The Reserve Bank of India was established on April 1, 1935 in accordance with the provisions of the Reserve Bank of India Act, 1934.

96. (b) Pahari painting is the name given to Rajput paintings, made in the in the Himachal Pradesh and Jammu & Kashmir states of India. These painting developed as well as flourished during the period of 17th to 19th century. Indian Pahadi paintings have been done mostly in miniature forms. Warli is a form of Art originated by the Warli tribes from the Western Ghat of India, in 2500 BCE, this is easily one of the oldest art forms of India. Phad is mainly a religious form of scroll painting depicting folk deities Pabuji or Devnarayan. It was originated in Rajasthan.

97. (b) Indian Railway Catering and Tourism Corporation Ltd. (IRCTC) has recently introduced a Scheme of booking e-ticket online and making payment after 15 days through 'e-Paylater'. This Scheme is powered by M/s Arthashastra Fintech Pvt. Ltd. Under this scheme, a customer has the option to pay after 15 days of booking e-tickets of any train through IRCTC website. The service charge levied on using 'ePaylater' scheme is 3.50% of transaction amount and applicable taxes.

98. (c) Researchers at the University of Washington have genetically modified a common houseplant -- pothos ivy -- to remove chloroform and benzene from the air around it. HEPA air filters are used to keep offending allergens and dust particles at bay.

99. (a) Himalayan marmots can survive at altitudes up to 5,000 meters in the Himalayan regions of India, Nepal, and Pakistan and on the Qinghai-Tibetan Plateau of China, where many of them face extreme cold, little oxygen, and few other resources. According to a scientist, Enqi Liu of Xi'an Jiaotong University Health Science Center in China, Himalayan marmots hibernate for more than six months during the wintertime.

100. (a) In November, 2017, the Union Cabinet chaired by Prime Minister has approved creation of National Testing Agency (NTA) as a Society registered under the Indian Societies Registration Act, 1860. The NTA would initially conduct those entrance examinations which are currently being conducted by the CBSE.

# 4 MOCK TEST

1. Consider the following statements:
   1. The Governor cannot return a Money Bill for re-consideration of the state legislature.
   2. When a money bill is reserved for consideration of president, he/she can return the bill for the re-consideration of the state legislature.

   With reference to state-legislature, which of the above given statement is/are correct.
   (a) 1 only
   (b) 2 only
   (c) Both 1 and 2
   (d) Neither 1 nor 2

2. With reference to Satavahana rulers, consider the following statements:
   1. They were identified through metronymics
   2. Succession to the throne was generally Patrilineal.
   3. Many Chaityas were cut out of the solid rock in the north-western Deccan.

   Select the correct statement/statements using the code given below:
   (a) 1 only
   (b) 2 and 3 only
   (c) 1 and 3 only
   (d) 1, 2 and 3

3. Which of the following best describes the Biodigester technology in Indian context?
   (a) Different enzymes are added for digestion process to complete
   (b) Organic wastes are converted into methane and water
   (c) Methane and Carbon dioxide is liberated during the process which is stored and used for running the Biodigester
   (d) Organic wastes as well as Industrial wastes are converted into bio-degradable products

4. What does venture capital mean?:
   (a) A short-term capital provided to industries.
   (b) A long term start up capital provided to new entrepreneurs.
   (c) Funds provided to industries at times of incurring losses.
   (d) Funds provided for replacement and renovation of industries.

5. Consider the following statements with reference to Indian Classical Music:
   1. Talas are rhythmic cycles.
   2. Raga is a series of five notes only.

   Select the correct statement/statements using the codes given below:
   (a) 1 only
   (b) 2 only
   (c) 1 and 2 both
   (d) Neither 1 nor 2

6. Consider the following statements with respect to the Sendai Framework (2015-2030).
   (1) It is a voluntary and non-binding agreement.
   (2) It is the successor instrument to the Hyogo Framework for Action (HFA).
   (3) It aims to lower average per 100,000 global mortality rate in the decade 2020-2030 compared to the period 2005-2015.

   Which of the above statement/statements is/are correct?
   (a) (3) and (1)
   (b) (2) and (1)
   (c) (2) and (3)
   (d) (1), (2) and (3)

7. Increasing Sea Salinity is a major concern for the environmentalists. In this context, consider the following statements.
   1. Change in temperature influences the salinity of sea.
   2. Change in density influences the salinity.
   3. Major source of Sea Salinity is terrestrial discharge by rivers.

   Which of the statement/statements given above are correct?
   (a) 1 and 2 only
   (b) 2 and 3 only
   (c) 1 and 3 only
   (d) All the above

8. Consider the following statements with reference to North East Rural Livelihood Project (NERLP).
   1. It is implemented only in four North-Eastern States namely Mizoram, Nagaland, Sikkim and Tripura.
   2. It is a central sector scheme externally aided by World Bank.

   Which of the above statement/statements is/are correct?
   (a) Only (1)
   (b) Only (2)
   (c) Both (1) and (2)
   (d) Neither (1) and (2)

9. Consider the following rivers:
   1. Indravati
   2. Barakar
   3. Hasdeo

   Which of the above flows/flow through Chhattisgarh?
   (a) 1 and 2 only
   (b) 1 only
   (c) 1 and 3 only
   (d) 2 and 3 only

10. Which of the following is/are instrument through which legislature holds executive accountable:
    1. Deliberation and discussion.
    2. Approval or Refusal of laws
    3. Financial control.
    4. No confidence motion
    5. Question Hour.

    Select the correct answer using the codes given below:
    (a) 1, 2 and 3 only
    (b) 2, 3 and 4 only
    (c) 1, 2, 3 and 4
    (d) 1, 2, 3, 4 and 5

11. In context of the Gupta period consider the following statements;
    1. Women were allowed to listen epics and the Puranas.
    2. The members of the higher order were polygamous.
    3. Women were not allowed to worship.

    Select the correct statement/statements using the code given below :
    (a) 1 only
    (b) 2 and 3 only
    (c) 1 and 2 only
    (d) 1 , 2 and 3

12. Consider the following statements:
    1. Reaction of a metal with acid produces hydrogen gas.
    2. Salt is produced following reaction of metal with acid.
    3. Metals are electropositive.
    Which of the statements given above is/are correct?
    (a)  1 only                  (b)  1 and 2 only
    (c)  2 and 3 only            (d)  1, 2 and 3

13. Which of the following statements best describes the Supercluster of galaxies discovered by Indian Scientists?
    1. The Supercluster spans over 650 million light years
    2. The total mass is equal to 20 times the mass of Sun
    3. The supercluster contains about 100 galaxies
    Select the correct answer using the codes given below:
    (a)  1 only                  (b)  2 only
    (c)  3 only                  (d)  1 and 3 only

14. Which among the following is/are measures to control inflation?
    1. Demonetisation of Currency
    2. Surplus Budget
    3. Rational Wage Policy
    4. Increase in Indirect taxes
    Select the correct answer using the codes given below:
    (a)  1, 2, 4                 (b)  1, 2 and 3
    (c)  2, 3 and 4             (d)  1, 2, 3 and 4

15. 1. Parliament can establish a tribunal for the adjudication of election disputes.
    2. Orders of Delimitation Commission can be challenged in court.
    Choose the correct statements:
    (a)  1 only                  (b)  2 only
    (c)  Both 1 and 2           (d)  Neither 1 nor 2

16. Consider the following statements:
    1. There are no active volcanoes in Himalayas.
    2. Active volcanoes are common in the interior of the continents.
    3. The only active volcano of west Africa is Mt. Kilimanjaro.
    Select the correct statement/statements using the codes given below:
    (a)  3 only                  (b)  1 and 2 only
    (c)  1 only                  (d)  2 and 3 only

17. Which of the following is not among the arguments against settlement of Rohingya's in India?
    (a)  India is not the signatory of the 1951 convention relating to the status of Refugees.
    (b)  Foreigners Act of 1946, empowers the central government to deport a person who is an illegal immigrant.
    (c)  India is the signatory of the 1967 protocol relating to status of refugees.
    (d)  None of the above

18. Consider the following statements:
    1. A formal impeachment is not required for removal of vice-president.
    2. No ground has been mentioned in the constitution for removal of vice-president.
    Select the correct statement/statements using the codes given below:
    (a)  1 only                  (b)  2 only
    (c)  Both 1 and 2           (d)  Neither 1 nor 2

19. With reference to the Government of India Act of 1858, Consider the following statements :
    1. The British Governor-General of India was given the title of viceroy.
    2. It established 20 member council which was an advisory body.
    3. It abolished the Board of control and court of Directors.
    Select the correct statement/statements using the code given below:
    (a)  1 only                  (b)  2 and 3 only
    (c)  1 and 3 only           (d)  1 , 2 and 3

20. Select the range of sound frequency which can be emitted by Bats
    (a)  0.02 kHz to 20 kHz
    (b)  0.002 kHz to 20000 Hz
    (c)  0.0025 kHz and above
    (d)  22kHz and above

21. With reference to the Balance of Payments, which of the following constitute/constitutes the Invisibles:
    1. Non-factor services.
    2. Income
    3. Private Transfers
    Select the correct answer using the codes given below:
    (a)  1 and 2                 (b)  2 and 3
    (c)  1 and 3                 (d)  1, 2 and 3

22. Haws bill Turtle has been placed in the wildlife protection act 1972's critically endangered category. Which among the following is true with reference to its habitat.
    (a)  Highly migratory, broad habitat during life time
    (b)  Throughout tropical water
    (c)  Larger extent subtropical, Atlantic & Pacific Ocean.
    (d)  All the above

23. With reference to August offer 1940, Consider the following statements:
    1. It proposed dominion status for India.
    2. It proposed the expansion of Viceroy council.
    3. It proposed the appointment of a constitution making body, immediately after war.
    Select the correct statement/statements using the code given below:
    (a)  1 only                  (b)  2 and 3 only
    (c)  1 and 3 only           (d)  1 , 2 and 3

24. Which of the following is/are the characteristic/characteristics of Anthracite grade of coal?
    1. It is the hard coal and best grade of coal
    2. It has 80 to 95 per cent carbon
    3. It has semi-metallic luster and negligible proportion of carbon
    4. In India, It is found only in Odisha and that too in small quantity.
    Select the correct statement/statements using the codes given below:
    (a)  (1), (2) and (3)        (b)  (1) and (2)
    (c)  (2), (3) and (4)        (d)  All are correct

25. The size of council of ministers of the central government is determined by
    (a)  Constitution            (b)  President
    (c)  Prime Minister          (d)  Parliament

26. Read the following statements with reference to gravitational force
    1. The force between any two objects is equal to the sum of their masses
    2. It is inversely proportional to the root square of the distance between the objects
    3. It is a weak force
    Select the correct answer using the codes given below:
    (a)   2 only              (b)   3 only
    (c)   1 and 2 only        (d)   1, 2 and 3
27. Which of the following is/are among the "Terms of Credit".
    1. Interest rate
    2. Collateral requirement
    3. Mode of re-payment
    Select the correct answer using the codes given below:
    (a)   1 and 3 only        (b)   1 and 2 only
    (c)   2 and 3 only        (d)   1, 2 and 3
28. Consider the following statements with reference to the "Right to Internet Access".
    1. Right to access internet comes under fundamental right of expression and cannot be curtailed at any cost.
    2. Mumbai is the first state to declare availability of internet as a basic right for every citizen.
    3. Nodal officers have been appointed at the state level to keep tabs on the net for offensive material.
    Which of the statement/statements given above is/are correct?
    (a)   (1) and (3)         (b)   (2) and (3)
    (c)   (1) and (2)         (d)   All are correct
29. Which of the following is not among the features of National Lok Adalat?
    (a)   There is no court fee payable when a matter is filed in a Lok Adalat.
    (b)   Lok Adalats resolve disputes through mutul settlements of parties.
    (c)   Mobile Lok Adalats are also organized in various parts of the country which travel from one location to another to resolve disputes.
    (d)   The decision of Lok Adalat is final and binding on all the parties.
30. Which of the following books were authored by Dr. B.R. Ambedkar?
    1. The evolution of provincial finance in British India.
    2. The Law and The Lawyers.
    3. Pakistan or Partition of India.
    Select the correct answer using the code given below:
    (a)   1 only              (b)   2 and 3 only
    (c)   1 and 3 only        (d)   1 , 2 and 3
31. Which of the following is the correct decreasing order of availability of ports in the given states:
    (a)   Andhra Pradesh > Maharashtra > Gujarat.
    (b)   Maharashtra > Gujarat > Andhra Pradesh.
    (c)   Andhra Pradesh > Gujarat > Maharashtra.
    (d)   None of the above.
32. Consider the following statements:
    1. Rajasthan was the first state to establish Panchayati Raj.
    2. Formation of Panchayats depend on the will of the state government.
    Select the correct statement/statements using the codes given below:
    (a)   1 only              (b)   2 only
    (c)   Both 1 and 2        (d)   Neither 1 nor 2

33. Consider the following statements:
    1. Angel investors invest only in big start ups.
    2. The capital provided by angel investors is a one-time investment.
    Select the correct statement/statements from the codes given below:
    (a)   1 only              (b)   2 only
    (c)   Both 1 and 2        (d)   Neither 1 nor 2
34. Consider the following statements with reference to Central Pollution Board.
    1. It is a statutory body under Ministry of Environment, Forests and Climate Change.
    2. It was constituted under water (Prevention and Control of Pollution) Act, 1974.
    3. It advises the Central Government on any matter concerning prevention and control of water and air pollution and improvement of the quality of air.
    Which of the above statements is/are correct?
    (a)   (1) and (3)         (b)   (2) and (3)
    (c)   (3) only            (d)   all are correct
35. Stalactites and Stalagamites are features of which of the following types of topography.
    (a)   Volcanic Topography
    (b)   Glacial Topography
    (c)   Karst Topography
    (d)   Fluvial Topography
36. Which of the following is not welfare scheme programme for women?
    1. Shakti
    2. Pradhan Mantri Ujjwala Yojana.
    3. SWADHAR,
    Choose the correct answer using the codes given below:
    (a)   Only (1)            (b)   Only (3)
    (c)   (1) and (3)         (d)   Only (2)
37. Consider the following statements:
    1. Corporate tax is levied on the company's profit income.
    2. Corporate tax is not an income tax.
    Select the correct statement/statements using the codes given below:
    (a)   1 only              (b)   Both 1 and 2
    (c)   2 only              (d)   Neither 1 nor 2
38. Consider the following statements with reference to the miniature paintings of the medieval times:
    1. The Lepakshi paintings are characterised by the absence of primary colours in general.
    2. Realism is the keynote of the Mughal School of painting.
    Select the correct statement/statements using the codes given below:
    (a)   1 only
    (b)   2 only
    (c)   Both 1 and 2
    (d)   Neither 1 nor 2
39. Which among the following is/are reasons for development of cotton Textile Industry in TamilNadu:
    (a)   Availability of cheap hydro-electricity
    (b)   Availability of cheap labour
    (c)   Availability of internal market.
    (d)   All the above.

40. Consider the following statements related of Olympic Task Force:
    1. It was formed with an aim to improve the performance of Indian Sportspersons in Olympic, Commonwealth, Asian as well as other International Games.
    2. Pullela Gopichand and Abhhinav Bindra are members of this Tast force.
    3. One of the recommendations submitted by task force is for restructuring of Sports Authority of India.
    Select the correct statement/statements using the codes given below:
    (a) 1 only      (b) 2 only
    (c) 2 and 3 only      (d) 1, 2 and 3

41. Consider the following statements:
    1. All states have constituted respective State Human Rights Commissions.
    2. A State Human Rights Commission can inquire into violation of human rights only in respect of subjects mentioned in the State List of the Seventh Schedule of the Constitution.
    Select the correct statement/statements using the codes given below:
    (a) 1 only      (b) 2 only
    (c) Both 1 and 2      (d) Neither 1 nor 2

42. Consider the following statements:
    1. Mercury is most common and most toxic substance found in water bodies.
    2. Most industrial effluents have mercury.
    Select the correct statement/statements using the codes given below:
    (a) 1 only      (b) 2 only
    (c) Both 1 and 2      (d) Neither 1 nor 2

43. Which of the following statements explains Circadian Rhythm?
    1. It is associated with Day and night cycle
    2. It is synchronized with silence and noise phase
    3. It influences physiology of the body
    Select the correct statements using the codes given below:
    (a) 1 and 2 only      (b) 2 and 3 only
    (c) 1 and 3 only      (d) 1, 2 and 3

44. The puppet theatre of India has a long and old tradition. String, rod, glove and shadow puppets were well known. In this context consider the following statements.
    1. Shadow puppets are flat, leather puppets are made translucent.
    2. Rod puppets are smaller than glove puppets.
    Select the correct statement/statements using the codes given below:
    (a) 1 only      (b) 2 only
    (c) Both 1 and 2      (d) Neither 1 nor 2

45. Consider the following statements with reference to elections in India:
    1. The chief election commissioner may appoint such "Regional Commissioners" as he may consider necessary to assist the election commission.
    2. The conditions of service and tenure of regional commissioners shall be determined by the president.
    Select the correct statement/statements.
    (a) Only 1      (b) Only 2
    (c) Both 1 and 2      (d) None of the above

46. Which of the following was major observation of the Karve committee set up by government of India in 1955.
    (a) Strengthening the institution of local government.
    (b) Possibility of using small-scale industries for promoting rural development.
    (c) Privatisation of Railways
    (d) Imposition of greater trade barriers

47. Which of the following could be considered as a cause for weathering of mountains:
    1. Carbonation
    2. Rainfall
    3. Snowfall
    4. Burrowing by rodents.
    Select the correct answer using the codes given below
    (a) 1, 2 and 3 only
    (b) 2, 3 and 4 only
    (c) 1, 3 and 4 only
    (d) 1, 2, 3 and 4.

48. Read the following statements with reference to SUNREF Project.
    1. It is an environmental project jointly launched by Ministry of Environment & Forests with UNEP.
    2. It is a housing project jointly launched by National Housing Bank, French Development Agency & European Union.
    3. The project is a joint initiative of members of International Solar Alliance as per "New Delhi Declaration".
    Select the correct statement/statements using the codes given below:
    (a) 1 only      (b) 2 only
    (c) 3 only      (d) None of 1, 2 and 3

49. Consider the following statements:
    1. State election commissioner is appointed by the president.
    2. State election commissioner can be removed by the governor only.
    Select the correct statement/statements using the codes given below:
    (a) 1 and 2 both      (b) 1 only
    (c) 2 only      (d) Neither 1 nor 2.

50. Which among the following explains the habitat areas of "Chiru"?
    (a) Open Sal with grassland farms
    (b) High altitude plain, hill plateau & Montane Valley
    (c) Open terrain plains, alpine meadows
    (d) Coastal areas with Muddy, brackish water at river mouth

51. In the context of Swadeshi Movement, consider the following statements:
    1. The Swadeshi Movement had its genesis in anti partition movement.
    2. Syed Haidar Raza led the Swadeshi Movement in Delhi.
    3. Swadesh Bandhab Samiti was set up by Lokmanya Tilak.
    Select the correct statement/statements using the code given below:
    (a) 1 only      (b) 1 and 2 only
    (c) 2 and 3 only      (d) 1 , 2 and 3

52. Which of the following is/are among the international initiatives taken to contain Nitrogen Pollution?
    1. Gothenburg Protocol
    2. Kyoto Protocol
    3. Minamata Convention
    Select the correct answer using the codes given below.
    (a) Only (1)          (b) Only (2)
    (c) (1) and (2) only    (d) (2) and (3) only

53. Read the following statements with reference to auditory ossicles,
    1. Inside human body three pairs of ossicles are present in each ear
    2. These are helpful in increasing the efficiency of transmission of sound waves to the ear.
    Select the correct statement/statements using the codes given below:
    (a) 1 only          (b) 2 only
    (c) Both 1 and 2    (d) Neither 1 nor 2

54. Article-32 gives Supreme court the right to issue writs for the restoration of fundamental rights of an aggrieved person. On which of the following grounds, a writ can be issued:
    1. An arrested person is not presented before court.
    2. A particular office holder is not doing legal duty.
    3. When a lower court has considered a case going beyond its jurisdiction.
    4. A person is holding office but is not entitled to hold that office.
    (a) 1, 2 and 3 only    (b) 2, 3 and 4 only
    (c) 1, 2 and 4 only    (d) All 1, 2, 3 and 4 are correct

55. Consider the following statements with reference to the Socio Economic Caste Census; 2011 (SECC).
    1. SECC; 2011 was conducted by Ministry of Law and Justice.
    2. SECC; 2011 was the first paperless census in India.
    3. SECC; 2011 data will also be used to identify beneficiary and expand the direct benefit transfer scheme.
    Select the correct statement/statements using the codes given below:
    (a) 1 and 2 only    (b) 2 and 3 only
    (c) 1 and 3 only    (d) 1, 2 and 3

56. India's environment ministry is considering doubling the number of protected areas such as national parks and wildlife sanctuaries.
    Which of the following is/are among the reasons behind it?
    1. India's network of protected areas is far below the 'Aichi Target'.
    2. Protected areas are the last refuge of endangered wildlife.
    3. Climate change and global warming effects.
    4. Increasing population of wildlife animals.
    Select the correct answer using the codes given below.
    (a) (1) and (2) are correct
    (b) (1), (2) and (3) are correct
    (c) (1), (2) and (4) are correct
    (d) All are correct

57. A situation in which people are thrown out from job due to a recession in the economy is known as–
    (a) Disguised unemployment
    (b) Cyclical unemployment
    (c) Open unemployment
    (d) Educated unemployment

58. Which among the following states fall in the drainage basin of River Mahanadi:
    1. Madhya Pradesh    2. Chhattisgarh.
    3. Andhra Pradesh.   4. Jharkhand.
    5. Odisha
    Select the correct answer using the codes given below:
    (a) 1, 3 and 4 only.    (b) 2, 4 and 5 only
    (c) 3, 4 and 5 only.    (d) 1, 2 and 3 only.

59. Which of the following is true with reference to the Martial Law:
    1. It suspends the government and ordinary law courts.
    2. It is imposed to restore the breakdown of law and order due to any reason.
    3. It has specific provision in the constitution.
    Select the correct answer using the codes given below:
    (a) 1 and 2 only    (b) 2 and 3 only
    (c) 1 and 3 only    (d) All 1, 2 and 3

60. Which of the following is/are among the four pillars of Zero Budget Natural farming?
    1. Bijamrita (Seed treatment)
    2. Mulching (Soil, straw and live)
    3. Waaphasa (Soil moisture)
    4. Jiwamrita (No fertilizers, No Pesticides)
    Select the correct answer using the codes given below.
    (a) (1) and (2)          (b) (2), (3) and (4)
    (c) (1) and (4)          (d) (1), (2), (3) and (4)

61. In the context of Indian economy, Open Market Operation refers to
    (a) Borrowing by scheduled banks from the RBI.
    (b) Lending by commercial banks to industry and trade.
    (c) Purchase and sale of government securities by the RBI.
    (d) None of the above.

62. Radiation Particles can be of types Alpha, Beta or Gamma particles. In this context consider the following statements:
    1. Alpha particles can be blocked by a piece of paper and human skin.
    2. Beta particles can penetrate through skin.
    3. Gamma rays can not be blocked from penetrating.
    Select the correct statement/statements using the codes given below:
    (a) 1 and 2 only
    (b) 2 and 3 only
    (c) 1 and 3 only
    (d) 1, 2 and 3

63. Consider the following statements :
    1. Constitution declares Delhi as the seat of the Supreme court.
    2. The president can appoint other place or places as seat of the Supreme court.
    Which of the following are correct –
    (a) 1 only          (b) 2 only
    (c) Both 1 and 2    (d) None

64. Which of the following is the objective of "Laqshya" initiative?
    (a) To reduce-maternal and new-born mortality, morbidity and still births
    (b) To reduce power transmission losses
    (c) To provide employment to youth of Jammu and Kashmir.
    (d) To increase the enrollment of girl-child at primary level.

65. Which among the following is/are man-made sources of radiation?
1. Transportation of Nuclear Material
2. Uranium Mining
3. Radiation Therapy
4. Terrestrial Radiations
Select the correct answer using the codes given below:
(a) 1, 2 and 4 only     (b) 1, 2 and 3 only
(c) 1, 2, 3 and 4        (d) 2, 3 and 4 only

66. Priority Sector Lending by banks in India constitutes the lending to:
1. Agriculture
2. Export credit
3. Social Infrastructure
4. Renewable Energy
Select the correct answer using the codes given below:
(a) 1, 2 and 3          (b) 1, 3 and 4
(c) 2, 3 and 4          (d) 1, 2, 3 and 4

67. Consider the following statements with reference to Project "MAUSAM."
1. It will Showcase a Transnational Mixed Route (including Natural and Cultural Heritage) on the world Heritage list.
2. Archaeological Society of India (ASI) is the nodal agency of this project
Which of the above statement/statements is/are correct?
(a) Only (1)            (b) Only (2)
(c) Both (1) and (2)    (d) Neither (1) nor (2)

68. Choose the correct statements:
1. Supreme court can transfer a case pending in one high Court to another hight court.
2. Supreme court exercise power of superitendence over sub-ordinate courts and tribunals.
(a) 1 only              (b) 2 only
(c) Both 1 and 2        (d) None of the Above

69. With reference to the 18$^{th}$ century political events of India Consider the following statements:
1. The Durrani dynasty was founded by Nadir Shah.
2. The consequences of the war with Ahmad Shah Abdali were politically advantageous for the Marathas.
Select the correct answer from the codes given below:
(a) 1 only              (b) 2 only
(c) Both 1 and 2        (d) Neither 1 nor 2

70. Select the correct statement about Free Space Optical Communication technology,
(a) Data is transmitted by propagation of different electromagnetic waves in vacuum.
(b) Data is transmitted by propagation of light waves in free space.
(c) Data is transmitted by propagation of light waves in free space using optical fibers.
(d) Data is transmitted by propagation of light waves in vacuum using free space optical fibers.

71. If tax rate decreases with the increase in the tax base then it is called.
(a) Progressive taxation
(b) Regressive taxation
(c) Impact of tax
(d) Incidence of tax

72. Consider the following statements with respect to Wildlife Institute of India (WII)
1. It works under the Ministry of Environment, forests and climate change.
2. It generates quality information and knowledge products in wildlife science through research and capacity building.
3. It is involved in Tiger Conservation Projects.
Which of the above statements is/are correct?
(a) (1) and (3)         (b) (1) and (2)
(c) all are correct     (d) (2) and (3)

73. Recently, it was found that the rapid warming of Arabian sea is the cause of increase in erratic rainfall in central India. which of the following is/are true in this context?
1. Increased El Nino events have raised the temperature of Arabian sea thus increasing the number of cyclones originating in Arabian sea.
2. Increase in the temperature of Arabian sea is due to its land locked nature which causes the heat to be trapped in its basin area.
Select the correct answer using the codes given below.
(a) Only (1)            (b) Only (2)
(c) Both (1) and (2)    (d) Neither (1) nor (2)

74. Which of the following is/are not the socialist directive principle as enshrined in part-IV of the constitution:
1. Organise Village Panchayats.
2. Equal pay for equal work for men and women.
3. To prohibit the consumption of intoxicating drinks and drugs.
4. Maternity relief and humane conditions of work.
(a) 1, 2 and 3 only     (b) 1 and 3 only
(c) 2 and 4 only        (d) All the above

75. The Gangetic gharial has been re-introduced in 3 states where it had become extinct. Which of the following is not among such 3 states?
(a) Uttar Pradesh       (b) West Bengal
(c) Madhya Pradesh      (d) Rajasthan

76. Who among the following was/were associated with 'Social Reform Movements in South India' ?
1. Mahadev Govind Ranade.
2. Ram Krishna Bhandarkar.
3. Sree Narayan Guru.
Select the correct answer using the code given below :
(a) 1 only              (b) 1 and 2 only
(c) 3 only              (d) 1, 2 and 3

77. Consider the following statements:
1. Roads constructed in India prior to the advent of the British rule were not fit for modern transport.
2. Railways introduced by Britishers adversely affected the self-sufficiency of the village economics in India.
Choose the correct statement/statements the statements given below:
(a) 1 only              (b) 2 only
(c) 1 and 2 only        (d) Neither 1 nor 2

78. With reference to the Samkhya School of philosophy, consider the following statements:
1. It is strongly dualist.
2. Samkhya acknowledges the final cause of Ishvara (God).
Select the correct statement/statements using the codes given below:

(a)  1 only          (b)  2 only
(c)  Both 1 and 2    (d)  Neither 1 nor 2

79.  Consider the following statements:
1.  CAG is responsible only to the parliament.
2.  CAG has no control over the issue of money from the consolidated fund of India.
3.  CAG submits audit reports to parliament.
Choose the correct statments:
(a)  All 1, 2 and 3    (b)  Only 1 and 2
(c)  Only 2 and 3      (d)  Only 1 and 3

80.  Consider the following pairs:
1.  Tropical dry deciduous : Madhya Pradesh, Gujarat
2.  Tropical moist deciduous : Punjab
3.  Montane wet temperate : Arunachal Pradesh.
Which among the following pairs represent the dominant vegetation type of the paired state/states.
(a)  1 and 2 only    (b)  2 and 3 only
(c)  1 and 3 only    (d)  1, 2 and 3 all

81.  A situation in which people change from one job to another and remain unemployed during this interval period is known as–
(a)  Structural Unemployment
(b)  Frictional Unemployment
(c)  Cyclical Unemployment
(d)  Voluntary Unemployment

82.  Which of the following best describes 'SOHUM?
(a)  Indigenously developed low-cost micro-hearing device for hearing-impaired adults.
(b)  Micro-hearing device for persons with impaired hearing.
(c)  Micro-hearing device for children above 2 years of age.
(d)  Indigenously developed low-cost hearing device for hearing-impaired newborns.

83.  Which of the following is/are among the steps taken for conservation of vultures in India?
1.  Prohibition on usage of anti-inflammatory diclonefac.
2.  Creation of vulture safe zones.
3.  India Bird Conservation Network.
4.  National Action Plan on Vulture Conservation.
Select the correct answer using the codes given below
(a)  (1), (2) and (3)
(b)  (2), (3) and (4)
(c)  (1), (2) and (4)
(d)  (1) and (2)

84.  Read the following statements with reference to Geographical Indication (GI) status of tag:
1.  Gobindobhog rice from Puri district of Odisha has recently got the GI status.
2.  The GI tag is an indication that the product is originating from a definite geographical territory.
3.  GI tag is limited only to any agricultural product originated from a definite geographical region.
Select the incorrect statement/statements using the codes given below:

(a)  1 and 2 only    (b)  2 and 3 only
(c)  1 and 3 only    (d)  1, 2 and 3

85.  In context of the Khilafat Movements' which among the following were basic tenants of the movement.
1.  The Turkish Sultan or Khalifa must retain control over the Muslim sacred places in the erst while ottoman empire.
2.  The jazirat-ul-Arab (Arabia, Syria, Iraq, Palestine) must remain under Muslim sovereignity.
3   The Khalifa must be left with sufficient territory to enable him to defend the Islamic faith.
Select the correct answer using the code given below :
(a)  1 only          (b)  2 and 3 only
(c)  1 and 3 only    (d)  1, 2 and 3

86.  Consider the following statements:
1.  In a recent research, 90 % of boys and girls have found a deficiency in vitamin D in India.
2.  To meet the shortage of vitamin D in schoolchildren, assembly time shift from 11:00 to 1:00 pm
3.  Union Health Ministry has launched a nationwide campaign to spread awareness about availing Vitamin D through natural sunlight.
Select the correct answer using the code given below
(a)  1 and 2         (b)  2 and 3
(c)  1 and 3         (d)  All of the above

87.  With reference to ARPIT Scheme, Consider the following statements:
1.  It was launched by Ministry of Human Resource Development (MHRD)
2.  It is a Leadership development training programme for second level academic functionaries in public funded higher education institutions.
Which of the statement(s) given above is/are correct?
(a)  1 only          (b)  2 only
(c)  Both 1 and 2 (d)   Neither 1 nor 2

88.  Consider the following statements with respect to LEAP Scheme
1.  It is an initiative of online professional development of 15 lakh higher education faculty using the MOOCs platform SWAYAM.
2.  It was launched by Ministry of Human Resource Development (MHRD)
3.  The implementation of LEAP Programme will be through 15 NIRF top ranked Indian Institutions
Which of the statement(s) given above is/are correct?
(a)  1 only.         (b)  1 and 3 only
(c)  2 and 3 only    (d)  1, 2 and 3

89.  Consider the following about sovereign gold bond scheme:
1.  Investments in such bonds by banks will be counted in calculation in SLR
2.  Bonds cannot be used as collateral for loans.
3.  It is issued by the RBI on behalf of the Government of India.
Select the correct answer using the code given below
(a)  1 and 2         (b)  2 and 3
(c)  1 and 3         (d)  1, 2 and 3

90. With reference to "otulipenia" which was recently in news, which of the following statements is/are correct?
    1. It is a new rare auto-inflammatory disease discovered recently in young children.
    2. A patient with otulipenia will develop symptoms including hypertension, insomnia and whooping cough.
    3. It is caused by a malfunction of a single gene on chromosome 5, Otulin.
    Select the correct answer using the code given below
    (a) 1 and 2 only      (b) 2 and 3 only
    (c) 1 and 3 only      (d) 1, 2 and 3

91. Regarding "Middle East respiratory syndrome coronavirus (MERS-CoV)" which of the following statements are correct?
    I. It is a viral respiratory disease caused by a novel coronavirus.
    2. It was first identified in Saudi Arabia in 2012.
    3. Some laboratory-confirmed cases of MERS-CoV infection are reported as asymptomatic but generally MERS symptoms include fever, cough and shortness of breath.
    Select the correct answer using the code given below
    (a) 1 and 2 only      (b) 2 and 3 only
    (c) 1 and 3 only      (d) 1, 2 and 3

92. Consider the following pairs
    Folk Dance----------State
    1. Dumhal---------- Jammu & Kashmir
    2. Dhamyal------ Haryana
    3. Mayur Nritya----- Himanchal Pradesh
    Which of the pair given above is/are correct?
    (a) 1 only            (b) 1 and 2 only
    (c) 3 only            (d) 2 and 3 only

93. India was re-elected on the executive board of which UN body on Nov 2017?
    (a) UNESCO           (b) UNAID
    (c) UNDP             (d) UNICEF

94. Direction: In the following question, there are two statements in which one is statement A and the other is Reason R. Choose your answer from the four options given below:
    (a) If A and R are true and R is the correct explanation of A
    (b) If A and R are true and R is not a correct explanation of A
    (c) A is true but R is False
    (d) A is false and R is true
    **Statement (A):** Qiran-us-Saadain was written by Amir Khusrau in 1289 AD.
    **Reason (R):** Qiran-us-Saadain contains the events of meeting of Bughra Khan, the Subedar of Bengal with his son and the Sultan of Delhi Kaikubad

95. Consider the following Statements about Reserve Bank of India (RBI)
    1. On 26$^{th}$ January, 1952, Reserve Bank of India (RBI) was formed.
    2. RBI was nationalized in 1949
    3. The first Headquarters of Reserve Bank of India (RBI) was formed in Kolkata.

Which of the statement given above is/are correct?
(a) 1 and 2 only      (b) 2 and 3 only
(c) 1 and 3 only      (d) 1, 2 and 3

96. With respect to Red Fort of Agra, Consider the following statements:
    1. It is situated on the bank of river Yamuna.
    2. It was constructed by the Mughal emperor Akbar in 1565.
    3. It is tagged as world heritage site by UNESCO in 1989
    Select the correct answer using the code given below
    (a) 1 and 2 only      (b) 2 and 3 only
    (c) 1 and 3 only      (d) 1, 2 and 3

97. Consider the following statements about cVIGIL App that Election commission of India recently launched?
    1. Citizens can use the app to confidentially report violation of election code of conduct.
    2. The app works on Android OS Jellybean and later versions
    Which of the statements given above is/are correct?
    (a) 1 only            (b) 2 only
    (c) Both 1 and 2      (d) Neither 1 nor 2

98. Consider the following Pairs:

| Crafts | | Heritage of |
|---|---|---|
| 1. Pashmina Shawls | – | Kashmir |
| 2. Brass Handicrafts | – | Rajasthan |
| 3. Phulkari embroidery | – | Jharkhgand |

    Which of the pair given above is/are correct?
    (a) 1 only            (b) 1 and 2 only
    (c) 3 only            (d) 2 and 3 only

99. **Direction:** In the following question, there are two statements in which one is statement A and the other is Reason R. Choose your answer from the four options given below:
    (a) If A and R are true and R is the correct explanation of A
    (b) If A and R are true and R is not a correct explanation of A
    (c) A is true but R is False
    (d) A is false and R is true
    **Statement (A):** Rajatarangini, ("River of Kings") historical chronicle of early India, written in Sanskrit verse by the Kashmiri Brahman Kalhana in 1148, that is justifiably considered to be the best and most authentic work of its kind.
    **Reason (R):** It covers the entire span of history in the Kashmir region from the earliest times to the date of its composition. He is regarded as Kashmir's first historian. Like the Shahnamah is to Persia, the Rajataringini is to Kashmir.

100. With reference to Steel Plant of India, Consider the following Statements:
    1. Salem Steel Plant is a major producer of world-class stainless steel. Presently Salem steel plant export stainless steel to some of the advanced countries such as the USA.
    2. Rourkela steel plant was established during second five-year plan.
    3. Durgapur Iron and steel Plant (West Bengal) was developed by the help of British Companies
    Which of the statement given above is/are correct?
    (a) 1 and 2 only      (b) 2 and 3 only
    (c) 1 and 3 only      (d) 1, 2 and 3

# RESPONSE SHEET

| | | | | | | | | | |
|---|---|---|---|---|---|---|---|---|---|
| 1. | ⓐⓑⓒⓓ | 2. | ⓐⓑⓒⓓ | 3. | ⓐⓑⓒⓓ | 4. | ⓐⓑⓒⓓ | 5. | ⓐⓑⓒⓓ |
| 6. | ⓐⓑⓒⓓ | 7. | ⓐⓑⓒⓓ | 8. | ⓐⓑⓒⓓ | 9. | ⓐⓑⓒⓓ | 10. | ⓐⓑⓒⓓ |
| 11. | ⓐⓑⓒⓓ | 12. | ⓐⓑⓒⓓ | 13. | ⓐⓑⓒⓓ | 14. | ⓐⓑⓒⓓ | 15. | ⓐⓑⓒⓓ |
| 16. | ⓐⓑⓒⓓ | 17. | ⓐⓑⓒⓓ | 18. | ⓐⓑⓒⓓ | 19. | ⓐⓑⓒⓓ | 20. | ⓐⓑⓒⓓ |
| 21. | ⓐⓑⓒⓓ | 22. | ⓐⓑⓒⓓ | 23. | ⓐⓑⓒⓓ | 24. | ⓐⓑⓒⓓ | 25. | ⓐⓑⓒⓓ |
| 26. | ⓐⓑⓒⓓ | 27. | ⓐⓑⓒⓓ | 28. | ⓐⓑⓒⓓ | 29. | ⓐⓑⓒⓓ | 30. | ⓐⓑⓒⓓ |
| 31. | ⓐⓑⓒⓓ | 32. | ⓐⓑⓒⓓ | 33. | ⓐⓑⓒⓓ | 34. | ⓐⓑⓒⓓ | 35. | ⓐⓑⓒⓓ |
| 36. | ⓐⓑⓒⓓ | 37. | ⓐⓑⓒⓓ | 38. | ⓐⓑⓒⓓ | 39. | ⓐⓑⓒⓓ | 40. | ⓐⓑⓒⓓ |
| 41. | ⓐⓑⓒⓓ | 42. | ⓐⓑⓒⓓ | 43. | ⓐⓑⓒⓓ | 44. | ⓐⓑⓒⓓ | 45. | ⓐⓑⓒⓓ |
| 46. | ⓐⓑⓒⓓ | 47. | ⓐⓑⓒⓓ | 48. | ⓐⓑⓒⓓ | 49. | ⓐⓑⓒⓓ | 50. | ⓐⓑⓒⓓ |
| 51. | ⓐⓑⓒⓓ | 52. | ⓐⓑⓒⓓ | 53. | ⓐⓑⓒⓓ | 54. | ⓐⓑⓒⓓ | 55. | ⓐⓑⓒⓓ |
| 56. | ⓐⓑⓒⓓ | 57. | ⓐⓑⓒⓓ | 58. | ⓐⓑⓒⓓ | 59. | ⓐⓑⓒⓓ | 60. | ⓐⓑⓒⓓ |
| 61. | ⓐⓑⓒⓓ | 62. | ⓐⓑⓒⓓ | 63. | ⓐⓑⓒⓓ | 64. | ⓐⓑⓒⓓ | 65. | ⓐⓑⓒⓓ |
| 66. | ⓐⓑⓒⓓ | 67. | ⓐⓑⓒⓓ | 68. | ⓐⓑⓒⓓ | 69. | ⓐⓑⓒⓓ | 70. | ⓐⓑⓒⓓ |
| 71. | ⓐⓑⓒⓓ | 72. | ⓐⓑⓒⓓ | 73. | ⓐⓑⓒⓓ | 74. | ⓐⓑⓒⓓ | 75. | ⓐⓑⓒⓓ |
| 76. | ⓐⓑⓒⓓ | 77. | ⓐⓑⓒⓓ | 78. | ⓐⓑⓒⓓ | 79. | ⓐⓑⓒⓓ | 80. | ⓐⓑⓒⓓ |
| 81. | ⓐⓑⓒⓓ | 82. | ⓐⓑⓒⓓ | 83. | ⓐⓑⓒⓓ | 84. | ⓐⓑⓒⓓ | 85. | ⓐⓑⓒⓓ |
| 86. | ⓐⓑⓒⓓ | 87. | ⓐⓑⓒⓓ | 88. | ⓐⓑⓒⓓ | 89. | ⓐⓑⓒⓓ | 90. | ⓐⓑⓒⓓ |
| 91. | ⓐⓑⓒⓓ | 92. | ⓐⓑⓒⓓ | 93. | ⓐⓑⓒⓓ | 94. | ⓐⓑⓒⓓ | 95. | ⓐⓑⓒⓓ |
| 96. | ⓐⓑⓒⓓ | 97. | ⓐⓑⓒⓓ | 98. | ⓐⓑⓒⓓ | 99. | ⓐⓑⓒⓓ | 100. | ⓐⓑⓒⓓ |

# HINTS & EXPLANATIONS

1. (a) When a Money Bill is presented to the governor, he may either give his assent, withhold his assent or reserve the bill for presedential asset but cannot return the bill for re-consideration of the state legislature.

   When such a Money Bill is reserved for the consideration of the president, the president may either give his assent to the bill or withhold his assent to the bill but cannot return the bill for reconsideration of the state legislature.

2. (c) Satavahana rulers were identified through metronymics but the succession to the throne was generally patrilineal. The satavahana rulers claim to have been Brahamans and they promoted Buddhism. Many Chaityas and monasteries were made during Satavahana reign.

3. (b) In a biodigester, the organic wastes are converted into methane and water with the help of different microorganisms under anaerobic conditions.

4. (b) Venture capital is a long term start-up capital provided to new entrepreneurs.

   – Venture capital is financing that investors provide to start up companies and small business that are believed to have long-term growth potential.

   – Venture capital generally comes from well-off investors, investment banks and any other financial institutions.

   – However it does not always take just a monetary form; it can be provided in the form of technical or managerial expertise.

   **Source:** The Hindu

5. (a) The concept and practice of raga, according to scholars, matured by the fifth century A.D. Raga is a series of five or more notes, upon which a melody is based. Ragas were recognised named on the basis of several factors, classified and defined.

   Talas are rhythmic cycles. They have a universal unity, besides being quite complicated.

6. (d) Sendai Framework for Disaster Risk Reduction (2015-2030) identifies investing in Disaster Risk Reduction (DRR) for resilience and to "build back better" in reconstruction as priorities. It recognizes that the state has the primary role to reduce disaster risk but that responsibility should be shared with other stakeholders including local government, the private sector and other stakeholders.

7. (a) Rivers affect salinity only at areas where they enter sea and not the whole of it.

8. (c) Both the Statements (1) and (2) given in the question are correct. The objective of the project is to improve livelihoods of the poor, especially that of women and the disadvantaged people in the project area. The identification of districts for the project was done, by the State Governments based on social and economic backwardness.

9. (c) River Indravati and Hasdeo flow through Chhattisgarh while river Barakar flows through Jharkhand. Rivers that flow through Chhattisgarh:

   – Mahanadi.

   – Godavari

   – Indravati

   – Hasdeo

   – Shivnath

   – Sabari

   – Rihand

10. (d) The legislature in parliamentary system ensures executive accountability at various stages: policy making, implementation of law or policy during and post-implementation stage.

    The legislature does this through the use of a variety of devices:

    – Deliberation and discussion

    – Approval or Refusal of laws

    – Financial Control

    – No Confidence Motion

    – Question Hour.

    – Zero Hour

    – Adjournment motion

    – The most powerful weapon that enables the parliament to ensure executive accountability is the no-confidence motion.

11. (c) In the Gupta period, like the shudras women were also allowed to listen to the epics and the Puranas, and advised to worship Krishna. Members of the higher order came to acquire more and more land which made them more polygamous and more property minded.

12. (d) Metals react with acids to produce salt and liberate hydrogen gas. Metals are electropositive because they lose electrons from their outermost shell and turned positively charged.

13. (a) Indian astronomers have identified the supercluster of galaxies and named it as 'Saraswati'. It spans over 650 million light years in its expanse and containing over 10,000 galaxies. The total mass of it equals to 20

million billion Suns.

14. (b) The control of inflation needs a multi-pronged strategy. Some of the Measures to Control inflation are

1.  **Monetary Measures:**
    – Credit control
    – Demonetisation of currency
    – Issue of new currency

2.  **Fiscal Measures:**
    – Reduction in unnecessary expenditure
    – Increase in direct taxes
    – Decrease in Indirect taxes
    – Surplus budget

3.  **Trade Measures:**

4.  **Administrative Measures:**
    – Rational Wage Policy
    – Price Control
    – Rationing

15. (a) Article-323(B) empowers the appropriate legislature (Parliament or state legislature) to establish a tribunal for the adjudication of election disputes.

The constitution declares that the validity of any law relating to the delimination of constituencies or the allotments of seats to such constituencies cannot be questioned in any court.

Consequently, the orders issued by the Delimination Commission become final and cannot be challenged in any court.

16. (c) The Himalayas surprisingly have no active volcano at all.

In Africa some volcanoes are found along the East African Rift valley e.g. Mt Kilimanjaro and Mt. Kenya both probably extinct. The only active volcano of west Africa is Mt. Cameroon.

Volcanoes are located in a fairly clearly defined pattern around the world, closely related to regions that have been intensely folded or faulted

Volcanoes occur along coastal mountain ranges as off-shore islands and in the midst of oceans, but there are few in the interiors of continents.

17. (c) India is not the signatory of the 1967 protocol relating to the status of refugees. So, Rohingya cannot claim the residence on legal ground and thus provision of non-refoulement does not extend to immigrants.

18. (c) A formal impeachment is not required for the removal of vice-president. He can be removed by a resolution of the Rajya sabha passed by an absolute majority. Notably no ground has been mentioned in the constitution for his removal.

The vice-president can hold office beyond his term of five years until his successor assumes charge. He is also eligible for re-election to that office. He may be elected for any number of times.

19. (c) In August 1858, the British parliament passed an act that set an end to the rule of the company. It ended the system of double government by abolishing the Board of control and court of Directors. This act established a 15-member council of India to assist the secretary of state for India. The council was an advisory body.

20. (c) Bats can emit sound frequency greater than 20,000 Hz.

21. (d) The head of invisibles record the receipts and payments regarding services exports and imports and other current account payments viz.

(1) Non-factor services

(2) Income

(3) Private Transfers

–  Non-factor services refer to all invisible receipts or payments not attributable to conventional factor of production, i.e. labour (remittances from overseas migrants).

–  Income includes transactions regarding income from investments in the form of dividends, profits and interest from loans, rent from house property and income generated through employment.

–  Private transfer include grants, gifts etc.

22. (d) Haws bill Turtle are highly migratory. They are found throughout tropical water, larger extent subtropical, Atlantic, Indian pacific ocean.

23. (d) To get Indian Cooperation in the war effort, the viceroy announced the August offer. The Congress rejected the August offer. Nehru said," Dominion status concept is dead as a door mail.

24. (a) Statement (1), (2) and (3) are correct with reference to Anthracite grade of coal.

In India, it is found only in Jammu and Kashmir and that too in small quantity. it ignites slowly and has very little volatile matter.

25. (c) The constitution does not specify the size of the council of ministers. They are determined by the prime minister.

26. (b) Gravitational force is a type of weak force. The force is proportional to the product of the masses of the objects and inversely proportional to the square of the distance between them.

27. (d) Credit plays a vital and very positive role in the economy. Government often plays a very vital role providing institutionalize credit.

Interest rate, collateral and documentation requirement and the mode of repayment together comprise what is called the terms of credit.

–   The terms of credit vary substantially from one credit arrangement to another. They may vary depending on the nature of the lender and the borrower.

–   Collateral is an asset that the borrower own and (such as land, building, vehicle) and uses this as a guarantee to a lender until the loan is rapaid.

    **Source:** N.C.E.R.T - 10th Economics

28. (a) Statements (1) and (3) are correct. Besides this, in March 2017, Kerala became the first state to declare internet as a basic right for every citizen. The search giants are also required to have 'in-house' experts to spot illegal content and pull them down.

29. (d) Lok Adalats have been given statutory status under the Legal Services Authorities Act, 1987. Under the Act, the award (decision) made by the Lok Adalats is deemed to be a decree of a civil court and is final and binding on all parties and no appeal against such an award lies before any court of law. But the parties are free to initiate litigation by approaching the court of appropriate jurisdiction by filing a case by following the required procedure, in exercise of their right to litigate.

30. (c) The Law and the Lawyers was written by Mahatma Gandhi.

31. (b) Maharashtra with 53 parts has highest number of ports in India. Maharashtra is followed by Gujarat (40) and Andhra Pradesh (12).

32. (a) Rajasthan was the first state of establish Panchayati Raj. The scheme was inaugurated by the Prime Minister on Oct. 2, 1959 in Nagaur district.

    After the enactment of 73rd Amendment Act of 1992, the state governments are under Constitutional obligation to adopt the new Panchayati Raj system in accordance with the provisions of the act.

    Consequently, neither the formation of panchayats nor the holding of elections at regular intervals depend on the will of the state government any more.

33. (d) Angel investors invest in small startups or entrepreneurs. These investors are often among an entrepreneur's family and friends. The capital provided by angel investors to these startups may be a one-time investment to help them to propel their business or it may ongoing injection of money to support and carry start-up through its difficult early stages.

    **Source:** The Hindu

34. (d) All the statements given in the question are correct.

35. (c)

36. (a) SHAKTI is a scheme approved by the Union Cabinet, It is a coal linkage policy to Harness and allocate Koyla (coal) transparently in India. The SWADHAR scheme was launched by the Union Ministry of Women and Child Development for rehabilitation of women in difficult circumstances.

37. (a) Corporate tax is levied on the company's profit income. There is not any separate tax called corporate tax. It is also an income tax. But the contribution of tax from corporate to the income tax is large. So it is shown under separate head.

38. (c) The Lepakshi paintings are characterised by the earth tones and the nearly complete absence of blue, in fact primary colours in general.

    Realism is the keynote of the Mughal School of painting. The subjects are largely drawn from incidents connected with the magnificient court life of the time.

39. (d) All the above are factors responsible for flourishing cotton textile industry in Tamil Nadu.

    Tamil Nadu has the largest number of cotton textile mills in the country. Tamil Nadu produces about 45% of mill spun cotton of the country.

40. (c) Olympic Task Force was formed with an aim to improve the performance of Indian Sportspersons in next three coming Olympics. Pullela Gopichand, Abhhinav Bindra, Viren Rasquinha and others are members of this Task force. One of the recommendations submitted by task force is for restructuring of Sports Authority of India.

41. (d) The protection of Human Rights Act of 1993 provides for the creation of not only the National Human Rights Commission but also a State Human Rights Commission.

    –   So far (2011) 20 states have constituted the State Human Rights Commissions through official Gazette Notifications.

    –   A State Human Rights Commission can also inquire into violation of Human Rights in respect of Subjects mentioned in the concurrent list.

    –   Therefore both statements are wrong.

42. (c) Mercury is the most common and most toxic in water bodies. It occurs in water as monomethyl mercury. Most industrial effluents have mercury. Methyl mercury vapours cause fatal poisoning.

    High level of mercury in fish stocks have been found, mainly in coastal areas. Toxicity of mercury is much greater than any other substance, about 1000 time more potent than colchicines.

43. (c) Circadian Rhythm is associated with Day and night cycle and it also influences various physiological processes inside body. It is not related with silence and noise phases.

44. (a) Shadow puppets are flat, leather puppets made translucent. When they are pressed against the screen with a strong source of light behind it, silhouettes are created on the screen.

Shadow puppets are popular in Andhra Pradesh, Maharashtra, Karnataka, Odisha and Kerla.

Glove puppets are manipulated by the puppeteer in full view of the audience.

Rod puppets are larger than glove puppets. They are manipulated by rods from below. It is found in West Bengal and Odisha.

**Source:** Spectrum : Indian Culture

45. (b) Article-324(4): The president may also appoint after consulation with the election commission such regional commissioners as he may consider necessary to assist the election commission.

Article-324(5): The conditions of service and tenure of office of the election commissioners and the regional commissioners shall be determined by the president.

46. (b) In 1955, the village and small-scale industry committee, also called the Karve Committee, noted the possibility of using small-scale industries for promoting rural development.

**Source:** N.C.E.R.T - 11th Economics

47. (d) Weathering is defined as mechanical disintegration and chemical decomposition of rocks through the actions of various elements of weather and climate.

The agents/ causes of weathering are

– Carbonation

– Hydration

– Oxidation & Reduction

– Unloading and Expansion

– Freezing, Thawing and Frost Wedging.

– Biological weathering (ie burrowing and wedging by organisms like earthworms, termites, rodents etc.)

48. (b) SUNREF housing project is a joint initiative of National Housing Bank (NHB), French Development Agency (FDA) and the European Union of India.

49. (d) The state election commissioner, though appointed by the governor of the state, can be removed by the president only.

State election commission is a constitutional body which is entrusted with the task of conducting elections for the Panchayati Raj institutions or local governments.

50. (b) Chiru has been placed under Endangered list of species in the wildlife protection Act:1972. Chiru is found in China, India (J & K). High altitude plain, hill plateau and Montane valley. Chiru is hunted for (Shahtosh) which is used for making "Shawls".

51. (b) Swadesh Bandhab Samiti was set up by Ashwin Kumar Dutt.

52. (c) Gothenburg Protocol aims to abate acidification, eutrophication and ground level ozone and is a part of the convention on long Range Transboundary Air Pollution.

Kyoto Protocol aims to reduce the emissions of the Green House Gases such as Methane, Nitrous Oxide, Hydrofluorocarbons, Perflurocarbons, Sulphur hexafluoride and carbon dioxide.

The Minamata Convention on Mercury is an international treaty designed to protect human health and the environment from anthropogenic emissions and releases mercury and mercury compounds.

53. (c) Auditory ossicles or ear ossicles present in the each ear as three small bony structures. These are helpful in increasing the efficiency of transmission of sound waves to the ear.

54. (d) Under Article-32: Supreme court can issue writs on all the above mentioned grounds i.e. the writ of Habeas Corpus, Mandamus, Prohibition, Quowarranto, Certiorari can be issued.

Article-226: High Court can issue writs for the restoration of Fundamental Rights.

The writ jurisdiction of high court is wider than supreme court, as it can issue writs not only for the restoration of Fundamental Rights but also on other grounds.

**Source:** N.C.E.R.T- XIth (Indian Constitutionat Work)

55. (b) Socio-Economic Caste Census-2011 (SECC-2011) is a survey of socio economic particulars of rural and urban Households comprising three components viz. census in Rural Areas has been conducted by the Ministry of Rural Development (MORD), census in urban areas under the administrative jurisdiction of the Ministry of Housing and Urban Poverty Alleviation (MoHUPA) and caste census under the administrative control of Ministry of Home Affairs, Registrar General and Census Commissioner of India (under the over all co-ordination of Ministry of Rural Development).

– SECC 2011 was the first paperless census in India conducted on hand-held electronic devices by the government in 640 districts.

– The rural development ministry has taken a decision to use the SECC data in all its programmers such as MGNREGA, National Food Security Act etc.

**Source:** The Hindu

56. (b) Reasons (1), (2) and (3) are correct. Besides these, competing use of land will put more pressure on forests in future. While India has done well in conserving some species like tiger, it needs to up its ante as far as Protected Area Network is concerned, where its neighbours like Bhutan and Nepal fare better.

57. (b) Cyclical unemployment is a situation where people are thrown out from job due to a recession in the economy. This is also known as demand deficiency unemployment. The root cause for this type of unemployment is lack of aggregate demand.

**Source:** Key concepts - Shankarganesh

58. (b) The Mahanadi rises in the highlands of Chhattisgarh. It flows through Odisha to reach the Bay of Bengal. The length of the river is about 860 km. Its drainage basin is shared by Maharashtra, Chhattisgarh, Jharkhand and Odisha.

59. (a) MARTIAL LAW
   – It affects only Fundamental Rights.
   – It suspends the government and ordinary law courts.
   – It is imposed to restore the breakdown of law and order due to any reason.
   – It is imposed in some specific areas of the country.
   – It has no specific provision in the constitution. It is implicit.

60. (d) Zero Budget Natural farming is a natural farming technique in which farming is done without use of chemicals and without using any credits or spending any money on purchased inputs. It has been developed by Subhash Palekar.

61. (c) Open Market Operations refer to the purchase and sale of the government Securities by RBI from/to market. The objectives of Open Market Operations is to adjust the rupee liquidity conditions in the economy on a durable basis. When RBI sells government security in the markets the banks purchase them.

62. (a) Gamma rays can penetrate easily to human skin and damage cells on its way through, reaching free and can only be blocked by a very thick, strong, massive piece of concrete.

63. (a) Chief Justice of India (Not President) has the power to appoint other seat of Supreme court. But he/she can do so only with the approval of president. Art – 130 deals with seat of the Supreme court.

64. (a) Government of India has recently launched Laqshya-Labour Room Quality Improvement Initiative. Its objective is to reduce preventable maternal and new-born mortality, morbidity and still births by improving the quality of care provided in the labour room. It will be implemented in Government medical colleges besides District Hospitals and Sub-District Hospitals and community Health Centres.

65. (b) **Natural Sources of Radiation:** They include cosmic rays from space and terrestrial radiations from radio-nuclides present in earth's crust such as radium-224, Uranium-238, thorium-232, potassium-40, carbon-14 etc.

   **Man-made Sources of Radiation:** (1) Nuclear power plants (2) Nuclear weapon (3) Transportation of nuclear material. (4) Disposal of nuclear waste (v) Uranium Mining (vi) Radiation therapy.

66. (d) **Current Priority Sector Categories**
   1. Agriculture
   2. MSME
   3. Export Credit
   4. Education
   5. Housing
   6. Social Infrastructure
   7. Renewable energy and others.

67. (c) Both the statements given in the question are correct. The project aims to understand how the knowledge and manipulation of the monsoon winds has shaped interactions across the Indian Ocean and led to the spread of shared knowledge systems, traditions, technologies and ideas along maritime routes.

68. (a)
   – Statement 1 is correct.
   – High court exercises power of supritendence over subordinate courts and tribunals. Supreme court has no such powers.
   – Article - 139 (A) deals with transfer of cases.

69. (d) Nadir Shah was murdered by his troops and his conquests in Afghanistan passed into the hands of one of his commanders Ahmad Shah Abdali. Abdali founded the Durrani dynasty.

   A decisive battle took place between Marathas and Ahmad Shah Abdali at Panipat in 1761. The consequences of the was with Ahmad Shah Abdali were disastrous for the Marathas. It dealt a severe blow to Maratha supremacy in India, particularly in the northern territories .Whatever unity existed among them ended after the war.

   **Source:** N.C.E.R.T - 8th (old): Modern India

70. (d) In Free Space Optical Communication technology, data is transmitted by propagation of light waves in free space allowing optical connectivity. The technology uses optical beams through free space/vacuum for transmission using an optical transceiver at both ends to provide bidirectional capability.

71. (b) If the tax rate decreases with the increase in the tax base, it is called regressive tax. Here those who receive income/spend/purchase worth of ₹ 100,000 pay lesser tax rate than those who receive ₹ 10,000.

72. (b) The National Tiger Conservation Authority was established in December 2005 following a recommendation of The Tiger Task Force Constituted by the Prime Minister of India for reorganised management of Project Tiger and many Tiger Reserves in India.

73. (c) Some of the other reasons behind the Rapid warming of Arabian sea which led to erratic rainfall in Central India are identified as:
   ⇒ Warming of Arabian Sea in India and Pakistan region has led to presence of large amount of moisture in atmosphere.

⇒ Increase in carbon emission in post industrialization period has led to global warming thus increasing the sea surface temperature of Arabian sea.

74. (b) To organise village panchayat (Art-40) and prohibition of consumption of intoxicating drugs (Art-47) are Gandhian directive principles (not the Liberal).

75. (b) The Gangetic gharial has been re-introduced in the rivers of Uttar Pradesh, Madhya Pradesh and Rajasthan where it had become extinct.

76. (c) Mahadev Govind Ranade and Ram Krishna Bhandarkar were associated with reform movements in western India.

77. (c) Under the colonial regime, basic infrastructure such as railways, ports, water transport, posts and telegraphs did develop. However the real motive behind this development was not to provide basic amenities to the people but to subserve various colonial interests.

Roads constructed in India prior to the advent of the British rule were not fit for modern transport. These roads were primarily build to mobilise the army within India and drawing out raw materials from the countryside to the nearest railway station or the part to send these to far away England.

The railways affected the structure of the Indian Economy in two ways. It enabled people to undertake long distance travel and thereby break geographical and cultural barriers. Secondly it fostered commercialisation of Indian agriculture which adversely affected the self-sufficiency of the village economics in India.

78. (a) The Samkhya School of Philosophy is founded by Sage Kapila. It is strongly dualist: Universe consist of two realities. Purusa (consciousness) and Prakriti (phenomenal realm of matter).

Samkhya denies the final cause of Ishvara (God).

79. (b) 1. CAG is an agent of the parliament and conducts audit of expenditure on behalf of the parliament. Therefore it is responsible only to the parliament.

2. The Constitution of India visualises the CAG to be comptroller as well as Auditor General. However in practice, the CAG is fulfilling the role of an Auditor-General only and not that of a comptroller.

3. The CAG submits audit reports to the president: The president lays these reports before both houses of parliament.

**Source:** M. Lakshmikant

80. (c) Moist deciduous forests are found throughout India except in the western and north-western regions.

– Dry deciduous forests are found throughout the northern part of the country except in the North-east. It is also found in Madhya Pradesh, Gujarat, Andhra Pradesh, Karnataka and Tamilnadu.

– Montane wet temperate forests are found in the region to the east of Nepal into Arunachal Pradesh, receiving a minimum rainfall of 2000 mm.

81. (b) Frictional unemployment occurs when people change from one job to another and remain unemployed during this interval period. This can happen even in a situation of full employment. In order to avoid this usually people resign the current job only after getting employment elsewhere.

**Source:** Key concepts - Shankarganesh

82. (d) 'SOHUM' is an indigenously developed low-cost hearing device for hearing impaired newborns. This innovative medical device uses brain-stem auditory evoked response technology.

83. (c) ⇒ **Conservation steps taken for vultures in India includes**

- Prohibition on usage of anti-inflammatory Diclonefac
- National Action Plan (2006) on Vulture Conservation
- Vulture Safe Zones (in-situ conservation initiative)
- Ramadevarabetta Vulture Sanctuary

The Indian Bird Conservation Network was established in 1998 by the Bombay Natural History Society (BNHS). It is a network of NGOs and individuals to monitor and safeguard important Bird Areas in Indian-Priority sites for conservation.

84. (c) Gobindobhog rice from Burdwan district of West Bengal has recently got the Geographical indication status. The GI tag is an indication that the agricultural, natural or manufactured product in originating from a definite geographical territory.

85. (d) It was a movement of Indian Muslims, led by Ali brothers. The congress supported the movement and Mahatma Gandhi sought to conjoin it to the non-cooperation Movement.

86. (a) To spread awareness about availing Vitamin D through natural sunlight and consuming fortified food among school-going children, The Food Safety and Standards Authority of India (FSSAI) has launched a nationwide campaign. The project was implemented in collaboration with the New Delhi Municipal Council (NDMC), North MCD and several private schools through a Joint Noon Assembly.

87. (a) Annual Refresher Programme in Teaching (ARPIT) is a major and unique initiative of online professional development of 15 lakh higher education faculty using the MOOCs platform SWAYAM.

88. (c) Leadership for Academicians Programme (LEAP) is a three weeks Flagship leadership development training programme (2 weeks domestic and one week foreign training) for second level academic functionaries in public funded higher education institutions. The implementation of LEAP Programme will be through 15 NIRF top ranked Indian Institutions.

89. (c) Sovereign Gold Bonds (SGB) are government securities denominated in grams of gold. It was first launched under the gold monetization scheme of 2015. It is issued by the RBI on behalf of the Government of India. These Bonds can be used as collateral for loans.

90. (c) National Institute of Health (NIH) researchers have discovered a new rare auto-inflammatory disease in young children, called otulipenia. A patient diagnosed with otulipenia will develop symptoms including fever, skin rashes, diarrhea, joint pain and overall failure to grow or thrive.

91. (d) At the end of October, 2018, a total of 2266 laboratory conformed cases of Middle East respiratory syndrome were reported globally. The maximum were reported from Saudi Arabia.

92. (b) Dumhal is a form of Dance performed by the Rauf tribe of Jammu & Kashmir. It is performed by men who wear long and colorful robes, accompanied by tall conical caps. 'Dhamyal' or 'Dhuph' is one of the most popular folk dances of Haryana. 'Dhuph' is a circular drum and is played by male dancers. The dance is performed as a part of celebration after a long day's work in the fields. Mayur Nritya, the dance form is prevalent in the state of Uttar Pradesh. 'Mayur Nritya' is performed by dancers who wear specially designed clothes so as to resemble a peacock. It is performed while worshipping Lord Krishna.

93. (a) In the election held at the 39th session of the general conference of UNESCO, in November, 2017 in Paris, India was re-elected on Friday as a member of the executive board of the UN educational, scientific and cultural organization (UNESCO).

94. (a)

95. (b) The Reserve Bank of India was set up on April 1, 1935.

96. (a) Red Fort of Agra is an exceptionally amazing masterpiece that represents the magnificent architecture of primeval epoch. It is tagged as world heritage site by UNESCO in 1983.

97. (c) The Election Commission of India has launched a mobile App, "cVigil" which Citizens can use to confidentially report violation of election code of conduct. The app works on Android OS Jellybean and later versions. The ECI hopes the app will ensure a free and fair conduct of 2019 Lok Sabha polls.

98. (b) Phulkari embroidery technique from the Punjab region and Haryana literally means flower work. It is a kind of embroidery that has complex designs made through vertical, horizontal and diagonal stitches, this whole work is done with white or yellow silk floss on cotton khaddarh and starts from the centre on the fabric called "chashm-e-bulbul" and spreads to the whole fabric.

99. (a)

100. (d) Salem Steel Plant, a special steels unit of Steel Authority of India Ltd, located at Tamil Nadu. Rourkela Steel Plant (RSP), the first integrated steel plant in the public sector in India, was set up with German collaboration with an installed capacity of 1 million tonnes. Durgapur steel plant was set up in the late fifties with the help of Britain.

# 5   MOCK TEST

1. With reference to the taxation policy of government of India consider the following statements:
   1. Since 1991, there has been a continuous reduction in the taxes on individual incomes.
   2. Moderate rates of income tax encourage savings and voluntary disclosure of income.

   Which of the statement/statements given above is/are correct?
   (a) 1 only     (b) 2 only
   (c) Both 1 and 2     (d) Neither 1 nor 2

2. Which among the following Ramsar Sites is/are located in Kerala.
   1. Ashtamudi     2. Nalsarovar
   3. Vemabanad     4. Sasthamkotta

   Select the correct answer from the codes given below:
   (a) 2, 3 and 4 only     (b) 1, 2 and 4 only
   (c) 1, 3 and 4 only     (d) 1, 2, 3 and 4

3. Consider the following statements:
   1. The preamble is a source of power to legislature.
   2. The preamble is a prohibition upon the powers of legislature.
   3. The preamble is non-justiciable.

   Which of the above statements is/are correct:
   (a) 1 and 2 only     (b) 2 and 3 only
   (c) 3 only     (d) 2 only

4. Which among the following can be considered as the consequences of the revolt of 1857?
   1. It transfered the powers of East India company to the British crown.
   2. Landlords and Zamindars were provided security of rights over their Lands.

   Select the correct answer using the codes given below.
   (a) 1 only     (b) 2 only
   (c) Both 1 and 2     (d) Neither 1 nor 2.

5. With reference to language and literature in India, consider the following statements:
   1. Tamil was the earliest of the dravidian language to be developed for literary purposes.
   2. India never really had a common language (used by the masses) in ancient period.

   Which of the statement/statements is given above is/are correct?
   (a) 1 only     (b) 2 only
   (c) Both 1 and 2     (d) Neither 1 nor 2

6. Which of the following is/are not example of Tectonic plateau:
   1. Harz of Germany
   2. Tibetan plateau
   3. Columbia Snake plateau
   4. Bolivian plateau

   Select the correct answer from the codes given below:
   (a) 2 and 3 only     (b) 3 and 4 only
   (c) 1 and 2 only     (d) 3 only

7. Read the following statements with reference to properties of Lithium-ion batteries and Lead acid batteries
   1. Lithium-Ion batteries are nearly 100% efficient while the efficiency of lead-acid batteries is 70%
   2. Lithium-ion batteries use a much cleaner technology as compared to lead-acid batteries
   3. Lithium-ion batteries are discharged only up to 50% while it is more than 80% for lead acid batteries

   Which of the statements given above is/are correct?
   (a) 1 and 2 only     (b) 2 and 3 only
   (c) 1 and 3 only     (d) 1, 2 and 3

8. The Dhola-Sadia Bridge in Assam has been put to the service of nation very recently. In this context consider the following statements.
   1. It has been built over river Lohit.
   2. It has been renamed as Bhupen Harzarika bridge.

   Select the correct answer using the codes given below:
   (a) 1 only     (b) 2 only
   (c) Both 1 and 2     (d) Neither 1 nor 2

9. Consider the following statements with reference to "Manipuri" dance forms.
   1. It is purely a religious dance form.
   2. Manipuri dancers wear ankle bells.

   Which of the statement/statements give above is/are correct?
   (a) 1 only     (b) 2 only
   (c) Both 1 and 2     (d) Neither 1 nor 2

10. Which among the following can be considered as a trade barrier:
    1. Duty on import and export
    2. Quota
    3. Production subsidies
    4. Packaging requirements
    5. Safety regulations

    Select the correct using the codes given below:
    (a) 1, 2, 3 and 5     (b) 2, 3, 4 and 5
    (c) 1, 3 and 4     (d) 1, 2, 3, 4 and 5

11. Consider the following statements with reference to Convention on Biological Diversity (CBD).

   1. It aims to develop national strategies for the conservation and sustainable use of biological diversity.

   2. CBD convention is not legally binding.

   3. CBD covers biodiversity at all levels: Ecosystem, Species and Genetic resources.

   Which of the statement/statements given above is/are correct?

   (a) 1 and 2 only      (b) 2 and 3 only

   (c) 1 and 3 only      (d) 1, 2 and 3

12. Which of the following statement/statements is/are correct with reference to GST?

   (1) GST has been defined as a tax on supply of goods or services or both, except supply of alcoholic liquor for human consumption.

   (2) Temporarily, five petroleum products viz. Petroleum crude, motor spirit, high speed diesel, natural gas and aviation turbine have been kept out of GST.

   (3) On inter-state supply of goods and services, an integrated GST (IGST) would be levied and will be collected by the centre.

   Select the correct answer using the codes given below:

   (a) Only (1)      (b) (1) and (2)

   (c) (1) and (3)      (d) All are correct

13. Consider the following statements.

   (1) All India tiger estimation is carried out once in every four years based on the Tiger Task Force approval.

   (2) The Tigers are monitored in tiger reserves through a special field protocol which is Phase-IV monitoring.

   Which of the above statements are correct in context of tiger conservation in India?

   (a) Only (1)      (b) Only (1)

   (c) Both (1) and (2)    (d) Neither (1) nor (2)

14. Consider the following statements:

   1. The metamorphosis of neutrino is due to radioactivity

   2. The neutrino changes its identity due to collision with heavier particles

   Select the correct answer using the codes given below:

   (a) 1 only      (b) 2 only

   (c) Both 1 and 2    (d) Neither 1 nor 2

15. 1. Stupa and Chaitya are part of Jaina Monastic Complexes.

   2. The great Stupa at Sanchi was made with bricks but later it was covered with stones.

   With reference to religious monuments of ancient India which of the statements/statements given above is/are true.

   (a) 1 only      (b) 2 only

   (c) Both 1 and 2    (d) Neither 1 nor 2

16. The term of the legislative assembly can be extended during the period of national emergency by a law of parliament for

   (a) One year at a time (for any length of time)

   (b) 6 months at a time (for any length of time)

   (c) 9 months at a time (for any length of time)

   (d) 3 months at a time (for any length of time)

17. Which of the following is/are correct with reference to Domestic Systematically Important Bank (DSIBs)?

   (1) Banks with assets over 1% of the GDP are considered DSIBs.

   (2) DSIBs are categorised under five buckets.

   (3) Recently, RBI has listed HDFC bank as DSIB.

   Select the correct answer using the codes given below:

   (a) (1) and (2)      (b) Only (3)

   (c) (2) and (3)      (d) All are correct

18. Which of the following is/are duties and functions of the CAG as laid down by the parliament:

   1. He audits the account related to expenditure from consolidated fund of each state and each union territory

   2. He audits all expenditure from public account of India as well as the public account of each state.

   3. He audits all bodies and authorities substantially financed from the state revenue.

   4. He compiles and maintains the accounts of state government.

   (a) 1, 2 and 3 only    (b) 2, 3 and 4 only

   (c) 1, 3 and 4 only    (d) All 1, 2, 3 and 4

19. Consider the following statements.

   1. Chromoplasts and leucoplasts are types of plastids.

   2. Chromoplasts and leucoplasts contain genetic material.

   Select the correct answer using the codes given below:

   (a) 1 only      (b) 2 only

   (c) Both 1 and 2    (d) Neither 1 nor 2

20. Consider the following statements:

   1. Sehjdharis are those who follow Sikhism but without being Amritdharis or baptised.

   2. They do not perform ceremonies according to Sikh rites.

   With reference to Sehjdhari Sikhs which of the above statement stands true?

   (a) 1 only      (b) 2 only

   (c) Both 1 and 2    (d) Neither 1 nor 2

21. With reference to the World Trade Organisation (WTO) consider the following statements:

   1. WTO is expected to establish a rule-based trading regime.

   2. The WTO agreements cover trade in goods as well as services.

   Which of the statements given above is/are correct?

   (a) 1 only      (b) 2 only

   (c) Both 1 and 2    (d) Neither 1 nor 2

22. Which among the following stands true with reference to tropical rain forests:

   1. Rainfall is distributed throughout the year.

   2. Soil is virtually useless for agricultural purposes.

   3. Vegetation is virtually stratified.

   Select the correct answer using the codes given below:

   (a) 1 only      (b) 2 and 3 only

   (c) 1 and 3 only      (d) 1, 2 and 3

23. Which of the following is not among the initiatives taken for the conservation of birds:
    (1) Bonn Convention (2) IUCN red data list
    (3) Indian Wildlife Act 1972
    Select the correct answer using the codes given below:
    (a) (2) and (3) only (b) (1) and (3) only
    (c) (1), (2) and (3) all (d) (1) and (2) only

24. Consider the following statements:
    1. A speaker protem is appointed by president.
    2. The chairman of Rajya sabha is a member of Rajya sabha.
    Select the correct statement/statements from the codes given below:
    (a) 1 only (b) 2 only
    (c) Both 1 and 2 (d) Neither 1 nor 2

25. Read the following statements with reference to Mitochondria,
    1. The Inner membrane is porous and the outer membrane is folded.
    2. It contains DNA
    3. It contains Ribosomes
    Which of the statements given above is/are correct?
    (a) 1 only (b) 2 and 3 only
    (c) 1 and 3 only (d) 1, 2 and 3

26. Arrange the following mountain ranges in the chronological order (beginning with the oldest mountains).
    1. Mountains of Scandinavia.
    2. Rockies and the Alps.
    3. Ural mountains.
    Select the correct answer using the codes given below:
    (a) 1, 2, 3 (b) 3, 2, 1
    (c) 1, 3, 2 (d) 3, 1, 2

27. With reference to Open Prisons in India which among the following statements stands false?
    (a) Open Prisons involve minimum security and is mainly depend on the self-discipline of the inmates.
    (b) Uttar Pradesh has maximum number of open prisons.
    (c) These are open only for the convicts and not for the prisoners of trial.
    (d) None of these

28. With reference to the constitution of India which of the following statements is/are correct.
    1. The government can interfere in religious matters for rooting out certain social evils.
    2. One can persuade people to convert from one religion to another.
    (a) 1 only (b) 2 only
    (c) Both 1 and 2 (d) None of the above

29. In case of electromagnetic induction, the maximum current is produced when
    (a) The angle between magnetic field and direction of motion of coil is 45°
    (b) The angle between magnetic field and direction of motion of coil is 30°
    (c) The angle between magnetic field and direction of motion of coil is 180°
    (d) The angle between magnetic field and direction of motion of coil is 90°

30. Which among the following is/are among the legislative protection given to Judges?
    (a) Judges are exempted from the criminal proceedings for something said or done in the course of their judicial duties.
    (b) The government cannot initiate criminal proceedings against a sitting or former judge of a superior court.
    (c) Both (a) and (b)
    (d) None of the these.

31. In which of the following documents we find evidences that India would be a mixed economy with elements of both capitalism and socialism:
    1. The Industrial Policy Resolution of 1948.
    2. The Directive Principles of State Policy.
    Select the correct answer using the codes given below:
    (a) 1 only (b) 2 only
    (c) Both 1 and 2 (d) Neither 1 nor 2

32. Short-lived Climate Pollutants (SLCP) include a variety of gases that have short-term warming effects often in excess of $CO_2$, but don't stay in the atmosphere for long.
    Which among the following is not a SLCP?
    (a) Black carbon (Soot) (b) Methane
    (c) HFCs (d) Carbon Monoxide

33. Certain elements make up 97% of the mass of our bodies and are more than 95% of the mass of all living organisms. Which among the following are counted among such elements.
    1. Carbon 2. Hydrogen
    3. Potassium 4. Oxygen
    Select the correct answer from the codes given below:
    (a) 1, 2 and 3 only (b) 2, 3 and 4 only
    (c) 1, 2 and 4 only (d) All the above

34. Which of the following statements regarding Green Bonds is/are correct?
    1. It is an equity instrument to support green projects like renewable energy, emission reductions etc.
    2. First ever green bonds have been issued by world bank.
    Select the correct answer using the code given below:
    (a) 1 only (b) 2 only
    (c) Both 1 and 2 (d) Neither 1 nor 2

35. The compound known as 'Mahanine', isolated by Indian scientists from curry leaves has been found to inhibit the growth of which of the following parasites in laboratory mouse,
    1. Kala-azar 2. Malaria
    3. Chikungunya
    Select the correct answer using the codes given below:
    (a) 1 only (b) 2 only
    (c) 2 and 3 only (d) 1 and 3 only

36. With reference to the Lahore session of 1929, consider the following statements:
    1. It decided that 26 January would be observed as the Poorna Swarajya Day.
    2. It declared the attainment of Poorna Swaraj as the goal of the Indians people.
    3. It passed a resolution demanding Dominion status for India.

    Select the correct statement/statements using the codes given below.
    (a) 1 only　　　　　(b) 2 and 3 only
    (c) 1 and 3 only　　(d) 1, 2 and 3

37. Consider the following statements with reference to Special Drawing Rights (SDR):
    1. SDR is an exchange rate system.
    2. SDR is a loan arrangement.

    Select the incorrect answer using the codes given below.
    (a) 1 only　　　　　(b) 2 only
    (c) Both 1 and 2　　(d) Neither 1 nor 2

38. Consider the following statements regarding the second Indian Factories Act: 1891
    1. It provided for a weekly holiday for all workers.
    2. Working hours for women were fixed and daily hours of work for children were reduced to 7.

    Which of the above statements is/are correct.
    (a) 1 only　　　　　(b) 2 only
    (c) Both 1 and 2　　(d) Neither 1 nor 2

39. Chennai receives moderate temperature in summer as well as winter. While in case of Delhi, it receives extremes of temperature, both in summer and winter. What could be the reason behind this phenomenon.
    (a) Level of pollution
    (b) Distance from the Sea
    (c) Average height from sea level
    (d) None of the above

40. Consider the following statements:
    1. Constitution provides for reservation of seats for SCs/STs in Lok Sabha and State Assemblies.
    2. Constitution provides for reservation of seats for SCs/STs in Rajya Sabha.

    Which of the above statements are correct.
    (a) 1 only　　　　　(b) 2 only
    (c) Both 1 and 2　　(d) None of the above

41. Interface used to connect supercomputers at short distances and high speeds is known as
    (a) HIPPI　　　　　(b) HDMI
    (c) PCI　　　　　　(d) PCI-X

42. Which of the following missiles was/were developed under the Integrated Guided Missile Development Programme of DRDO?
    1. BrahMos　　　　2. Trishul
    3. Prahaar　　　　　4. Nag

    Select the correct answer using the codes given below:
    (a) 1 and 3 only　　(b) 2 and 4 only
    (c) 1, 2 and 3 only　(d) 2, 3 and 4 only

43. In which of the following types of biotic interaction, one species is harmed while the other is unaffected:
    (a) Commensalism　(b) Mutualism
    (c) Amensalism　　(d) Parasitism

44. The electoral college for the election of vice-president consist of
    1. Elected members of both houses of parliament.
    2. Nominated members of both the houses of parliament.
    3. Elected members of the state legislative assemblies.

    Select the correct answer using the codes given below:
    (a) 1 and 2 only　　(b) 2 and 3 only
    (c) 1 and 3 only　　(d) 1, 2 and 3

45. With reference to the First Round Table Conference held in London, consider the following statements:
    1. It was organised to consider the reforms proposed by Simon commission.
    2. The Hindu Mahasabha and the Muslim league both attended this conference.
    3. Indian National Congress attended the first Round table conference.

    Select the correct answer using the code given below:
    (a) 1 only　　　　　(b) 2 and 3 only
    (c) 1 and 3 only　　(d) 1, 2 only

46. Consider the following statements with reference to different schemes of the government
    1. The Swachh Bharat Abhiyan aims to achieve the vision of a 'Clean India' by October, 2nd 2019.
    2. The New Manufacturing Policy raises the output target form 16% of GDP to 25% by 2020.

    Select the correct answer using the codes given below:
    (a) 1 only　　　　　(b) 2 only
    (c) Both 1 and 2　　(d) Neither 1 nor 2

47. In which of the following types of biotic interaction one species benefits while the other is harmed:
    (a) Predation　　　(b) Commensalism
    (c) Parasitism　　　(d) Both (a) and (c)

48. Which among the following was/were the causes of the failure of Revolt of 1857?
    1. The mutineers lacked a clear understanding of the exact nature of colonial rule.
    2. Mutineers did not have a forward looking programme.
    3. Modern Nationalism was yet unknown in India.

    Select the correct answer using the codes given below.
    (a) 1 only　　　　　(b) 2 and 3 only
    (c) 1 and 3 only　　(d) 1, 2 and 3.

49. Consider the following statements with reference to Dr. Ambedkar scheme for social integration through Inter-caste marriages:
    1. The scheme aims to counter the practice of marrying on traditional grounds of caste/sub-castes in any religion practiced within Indian Territory.
    2. The one-time incentive under the scheme is ₹ 2.5 lakh.

    Select the correct answer using the codes given below:
    (a) 1 only　　　　　(b) 2 only
    (c) Both 1 and 2　　(d) Neither 1 nor 2

50. 'Sibir', sometimes seen in the news, is related to which of the following?
    (a) Chinese Anti-torpedo combat ship
    (b) Nuclear submarine of Turkey
    (c) World's biggest icebreaker ship
    (d) 'Made in India' ship

51. Consider the following statements with reference to the Major River systems in India:
    1. The Godavari is the largest Peninsular river.
    2. River Kaveri and Mahanadi do not make deltas at their mouth.
    3. River Musi and Ghatprabha are tributaries of Godavari.
    Which of the statements given above is/are correct?
    (a) 1 only
    (b) 2 and 3 only
    (c) 1 and 3 only
    (d) 1 and 2 only

52. The 52$^{nd}$ Amendment Act pertains to the process by which legislators may be disqualified on grounds of defection:
    In this context consider the following statements.
    1. A legislator is to be disqualified if he/she voluntarily resigns from his/her party.
    2. If an independent member joins a political party, he/she is to be disqualified.
    Choose the correct statement/statements using the codes given below.
    (a) 1 only
    (b) 2 only
    (c) Both 1 and 2
    (d) None of the above

53. Which of the following is correct with respect to Hydroponics?
    (a) It is means of growing of plants in a soil less medium or in an aquatic based environment.
    (b) Hydroponic growing uses mineral nutrient solutions. to feed the plants in water without soil.
    (c) Both (a) and (b).
    (d) Neither (a) nor (b).

54. 1. National Income calculated at constant price is called nominal income.
    2. National Income calculated at current price is called real income.
    Which of the above given statement is/are true.
    (a) 1 only
    (b) 2 only
    (c) Both 1 and 2
    (d) Neither 1 nor 2

55. The writings of the Chinese traveller Hiuen Tsang who (visited India during 7th century) gives good account of Indian society of that time. In this context. Which of the following statements is/are correct?
    1. Patliputra was in a state of decline.
    2. Prayag and Kannauj in the doab had become Politically important.
    3. The tradesmen had to pay duties at ferry and barrier stations.
    Select the correct answer using the codes given below.
    (a) 1 only
    (b) 2 and 3 only
    (c) 1 and 3 only
    (d) 1, 2 and 3

56. The "Peace Clause" of WTO is related to
    (a) Doha Round
    (b) Bali Conference
    (c) Geneva Round
    (d) Buenos Aires Summit

57. Consider the following sectors.
    (1) Industry
    (2) Domestic consumption.
    (3) Agricultural consumption.
    (4) Commercial consumption.
    Select the correct order of consumption of electricity by different sectors.
    (a) (4), (3), (2), (1)
    (b) (3), (1), (2), (4)
    (c) (1), (2), (3), (4)
    (d) (4), (1), (3), (2)

58. Consider the following statements:
    1. The Minimum Support Price (MSP) was for the first time declared for rice.
    2. MSP is decided on the Recommendations of Commission for Agricultural Costs and Price.
    Which of the statement/statements given above is/are correct?
    (a) 1 only
    (b) 2 only
    (c) Both 1 and 2
    (d) Neither 1 nor 2

59. Which of the following statements is/are correct with reference to Brahmo Samaj?
    1. It advocated ploytheism and denounced idol worship.
    2. It discarded faith in divine avataras incarnations.
    3. It advocated abolition of Purdah System.
    Select the correct answer using the code given below.
    (a) 1 only
    (b) 1 and 2 only
    (c) 2 and 3 only
    (d) 1, 2 and 3 all

60. Governor can remove a minister (State Assembly) only on the advice of
    (a) Chief Minister
    (b) Prime Minister
    (c) President
    (d) His own discretion

61. With reference to the National Commission for Scheduled Castes, consider the following statements.
    1. It is appointed by the president.
    2. The commission presents an annual report to parliament.
    3. The commission while investigating any matter has all the powers of a civil court.
    Which of the above given statements is/are correct.
    (a) 1 and 2 only
    (b) 1 and 3 only
    (c) 2 and 3 only
    (d) 1, 2 and 3 all are correct

62. In the context of Mahalwari system consider the following statements:
    1. It had elements of both Zamindari and Ryotwari system.
    2. It introduced the concept of average rents for different soil classes.
    3. The state share of the revenue was one third of the rental value and it was agreed for 30 years.

Select the correct statement/statements using the codes given below:

(a)  1 only      (b)  1 and 2 only

(c)  3 only      (d)  2 and 3 only

63. Read the following statements with reference to Free Movement Regime between Indian and Myammarese citizens,

1. It is and arrangement for trans-boundary movement of tribal communities only.

2. The tribal communities along the border can stay for a week without Visa across the boundary for travel up to 100 km.

Select the correct answer using the codes given below:

(a)  1 only      (b)  2 only

(c)  Both 1 and 2      (d)  Neither 1 nor 2

64. 1. Expenses of the Supreme court are charged on the consolidated fund of India.

2. Parliament is authorised to curtail the jurisdiction of the Supreme court.

Choose the incorrect statements.

(a)  1 only      (b)  2 only

(c)  Both 1 and 2      (d)  None of the above

65. Read the following statements with reference to Indian Surrogacy (Regulation) Bill, 2016.

1. Surrogacy would be allowed only for Infertile Indian married heterosexual couples.

2. The age of female partner in case of heterosexual couples should be between 23-50 years.

3. The issueless women is ineligible to be a surrogate mother.

Select the correct answer using the codes given below:

(a)  1 only      (b)  3 only

(c)  2 and 3 only      (d)  1, 2 and 3

66. Consider the following:

1. Uttarakhand    2. Bihar

3. Madhya Pradesh    4. West Bengal

5. Chhattisgarh

Villages from which of the above states are participatig in Ganga Gram project,

(a)  1, 2, 3, and 4 only    (b)  1, 2 and 4 only

(c)  1, 3 and 4 only    (d)  1, 2, 3, 4 and 5

67. Which of the Schemes does not come under ministry of MSME?

(a)  Scheme of fund for regeneration of traditional industries (SFURTI)

(b)  PM Employment Generation Program (PMEGP)

(c)  Launchpad program

(d)  ASPIRE

68. Certain organism occur primarily and most abundantly in the Ecotone. These are known as

(a)  Niche      (b)  Phagotrophs

(c)  Edge species      (d)  None of the above

69. 1. The EVMs were used for the first time in 1998 in Assembly elections of Bihar and U.P.

2. The EVMs were used for the first time in General elections (entire state) to the Assembly of Goa in 1999.

Which of the statements given above is/are correct?

(a)  1 only      (b)  2 only

(c)  Both 1 and 2      (d)  None of the above

70. Which of the followingis not among the efforts to eradicate the "Elephantiasis" disease in India?

(1)  National Filaria Control Programme

(2)  National Vector Borne Disease Control Programme

(3)  Hathipaon Mukt Bharat Programme

Select the correct answer using the codes given below:

(a)  Only (1)

(b)  Only (2)

(c)  Only (3)

(d)  None of the (1), (2) and (3)

71. Consider the following statements.

(1)  Estuaries are sharp edged mouth of rivers, devoid of any deposits.

(2)  Usually Estuaries are not fertile.

(3)  Narmada, Tapi and Kaveri rivers form Estuaries

(4)  Rift valleys never witness Estuaries.

Which of the statements given above is/are correct?

(a)  (1) and (2)      (b)  (1) and (3)

(c)  (1), (3) and (4)      (d)  All are correct

72. In the "Index of Eight core industries", which one of the following is given the lowest weightage?

(a)  Coal(b)      Electricity

(c)  Fertilizer      (d)  Steel

73. With respect to Travel and Tourism Competitive Index released by World Economic Forum consider the following statements.

(1)  India ranked $40^{th}$ among 136 economies across the world.

(2)  The theme of the 2017 edition was, paving the way for a more sustainable and inclusive future.

Which of the above statement/statements is/are correct?

(a)  Only (1)      (b)  Only (2)

(c)  Both (1) and (2)      (d)  Neither (1) and (2)

74. With reference to "Ladakh Renewable Energy Initiative;" which of the following stands false?

(a)  It is being implemented by Ministry of Environment, forests and climate change.

(b)  It aims to set up small/micro hydel projects, solar thermal systems etc. in the Ladakh region.

(c)  The Biaras small Hydro Power Project is the first project to be commissioned under this initiative.

(d)  None of these

75. Consider the following statements with reference to the Vienna Convention : 1988.

1. It pertains to the protection of the Ozone layer.

2. It includes legally binding reduction goals for the use of CFCs.

Which of the statements/statements given above is/are correct?

(a)  1 only      (b)  2 only

(c)  Both 1 and 2      (d)  Neither 1 nor 2

76. Which of the following is not among recommendation of Balwant Rai Mehta Committee:
    (a) Establishment of a three-tier panchayat.
    (b) Village panchayat should be directly elected.
    (c) Zila parishad should be the executive body.
    (d) The district collector should be the chairman of the zila parishad.

77. Which of the following is not true about "Islamic Alliance to fight Terrorism"?
    (a) It is a Saudi Led Coalition of 40 countries.
    (b) It aims to delink Islam from terrorism.
    (c) Iran, Syria and Iraq are part of it.
    (d) None of these

78. Atmosphere is mainly heated by–
    (a) Radiation      (b) Conduction
    (c) Insolation      (d) Convection

79. Consider the following statements related to chit funds:
    1. It is regulated under the Central Act of chit funds Act, 1982.
    2. Chit funds are included in the definition of Non-Banking Financial Companies by RBI.
    Which of the statement/statements given above is/are correct?
    (a) 1 only      (b) 2 only
    (c) Both 1 and 2      (d) Neither 1 nor 2

80. Cold deserts are home to highly adaptive, rare endangered fauna. Which of the following species could be found in cold deserts.
    (1) Chiru
    (2) Brown Bear
    (3) Black Necked Crane
    (4) Asiatic Wild Cat
    Select the correct answer using the codes given below:
    (a) 1, 2 and 3 only      (b) 2, 3 and 4 only
    (c) 1, 3 and 4 only      (d) 1, 2, 3 and 4

81. Which of the following statements are correct regarding the Directive Principles of State Policy?
    1. They impose a moral obligation on the state authorities for their application.
    2. Public Opinion is the real force behind the application of D.P.S.P.
    (a) 1 only      (b) 2 only
    (c) Both 1 and 2      (d) None of the above

82. Which of the following factors affect demand in an economy:
    1. Increase in Money Supply
    2. Repayment of Public Debt
    3. Cheap Monetary Policy
    4. Increase in Public expenditure
    Select the correct answer from the codes given below:
    (a) 1, 2 and 3      (b) 2, 3 and 4
    (c) 1, 2 and 4      (d) 1, 2, 3 and 4

83. Consider the following statements with reference to white tigers.
    1. Bandhavgarh (MP) houses the world's first white tiger sanctuary.
    2. There are only around 200 white tigers left in the world.

Select the correct statement/statements from the codes given below:
    (a) 1 only      (b) 2 only
    (c) Both 1 and 2      (d) Neither 1 nor 2

84. Assam hills of the Indian sub-continent predominantly receives:
    (a) Convectional rainfall
    (b) Torrential downpour
    (c) Orographic rainfall
    (d) Cyclonic rainfall

85. Consider the following statements:
    1. TAPI pipeline is 1814 km long gas pipeline connecting Turkey-Afghanistan-Pakistan-India.
    2. India and Pakistan will equally share the supplied gas through TAPI gas pipeline.
    Which of the statements given above is/are correct?
    (a) 1 only      (b) 2 only
    (c) Both 1 and 2      (d) Neither 1 nor 2

86. Which of the following describes Agri-Udaan appropriately:
    (a) To support innovation and entrepreneurship in agriculture.
    (b) Steps taken to effectively double farmers income by 2022.
    (c) To support diversification of agriculture.
    (d) To develop agricultural exports to their optimum potential.

87. Consider the following statements with respect to Yuva Sahakar-Cooperative Enterprise Support and Innovation Scheme:
    1. The scheme is an initiative under Ministry of Youth Affairs and Sports.
    2. It is a youth-friendly scheme for attracting them to cooperative business ventures.
    Which of the given statements is/are correct?
    (a) Only 1      (b) Only 2
    (c) Both 1 and 2      (d) Neither 1 nor 2

88. With context to Muhafiz, a social security scheme, consider the following statements:
    1. It is a social scheme to provide institutionalized socio-economic security to workers in the unorganized sector in India.
    2. These schemes will cover accidental, life and disability insurance besides providing educational scholarships to the children of to workers in the unorganized sector in Jammu & Kashmir.
    Which of the statement(s) given above is/are correct?
    (a) 1 only      (b) 2 only
    (c) Both 1 and 2      (d) Neither 1 nor 2

89. Which one of the following statements about 'Niryat Bandhu Scheme' is correct?
    (a) It is a scheme for mentoring first generation entrepreneurs
    (b) It is a scheme for crop protection.
    (c) It is a scheme for the vulnerable section of the society.
    (d) It is a scheme for monitoring rural poor.

90. Consider the following statements:
    1. Hendra virus (HeV) infection is a rare emerging zoonosis that causes severe and often fatal disease in both infected horses and humans.
    2. The natural host of the virus has been identified as being fruit bats of the Pteropodidae Family, Pteropus genus.
    3. Symptoms of HeV infection in humans range from mild influenza-like illness to fatal respiratory or neurological disease.
    Select the correct answer using the code given below
    (a) 1 and 2 only      (b) 2 and 3 only
    (c) 1 and 3 only      (d) 1, 2 and 3

91. Consider the following statements:
    1. Lassa fever is an acute viral haemorrhagic illness caused by *Lassa virus*.
    2. It is transmitted to humans from contacts with food or household items contaminated with rodent excreta.
    3. The disease is endemic in the rodent population in parts of West Africa.
    Select the correct answer using the code given below
    (a) 1 and 2 only      (b) 2 and 3 only
    (c) 1 and 3 only      (d) 1, 2 and 3

92. Consider the following statements
    1. Recently the RBI has constituted an Expert Committee on Micro, Small and Medium Enterprises under the chairmanship of Shri U.K. Sinha
    2. UK Sinha committee was set up to review the existing MSME focused policies and its impact on the sector
    Which of the pair given above is/are correct?
    (a) 1 only            (b) 2 only
    (c) Both 1 and 2      (d) Neither 1 nor 2

93. Consider the following pairs
    Name of the Satellites  Types of Satellite
    1. HysIS              Earth Observation
    2. GSAT-6A            Communication Satellites
    Which of the pair given above is/are correct?
    (a) 1 only            (b) 2 only
    (c) Both 1 and 2      (d) Neither 1 nor 2

94. Consider the following statement about the prominent characteristics of Monsoonal Rainfall in India.
    1. Rainfall is seasonal in character
    2. It has a declining trend with increasing distance from the sea.
    3. The monsoon rains occur in wet spells of few days duration at a time.
    Select the correct answer using the code given below
    (a) 1 and 2 only      (b) 2 and 3 only
    (c) 1 and 3 only      (d) 1, 2 and 3

95. **Direction:** In the following question, there are two statements in which one is statement A and the other is Reason R. Choose your answer from the four options given below:
    (a) If A and R are true and R is the correct explanation of A
    (b) If A and R are true and R is not a correct explanation of A
    (c) A is true but R is False
    (d) A is false and R is true

    **Statement (A):** Khawaja Nizamuddin Ahmed Harvi wrote Tabkat-i-Akbari in the time of Akbar and completed in 1593 AD.
    **Reason (R):** It is a significant book for the history of Saiyyad and Lodhi rulers.

96. Which of the following statement is true about Ajanta caves?
    1. Ajanta caves were tagged as the UNESCO World Heritage Sites in 1983.
    2. Currently these caves are taken care by the Archeological Survey of India.
    3. The general style of paintings at The Ajanta caves seems to have influenced paintings in Tibet and Srilanka.
    Select the correct answer using the code given below
    (a) 1 and 2 only      (b) 2 and 3 only
    (c) 1 and 3 only      (d) 1, 2 and 3

97. Regarding the recommendation of Ashok Mehta Committee, Consider the following statements:
    1. The three-tier system of Panchayati-Raj should be replaced by the two-tier system.
    2. The state government should not supersede the Panchayati Raj institution.
    3. Seats for SCs and STs should be reserved on the basis of their population.
    Which of the statements given above is / are correct?
    (a) 1 and 2 only      (b) 2 and 3 only
    (c) 1 and 3 only      (d) 1, 2 and 3

98. Consider the following pairs
    | Terms | Context Field |
    | --- | --- |
    | 1. Close Rate/Ratio | Sales |
    | 2. 'Libor' | Banking |
    | 3. Banana republic | Marketing |
    Which of the pair given above is/are correct?
    (a) 1 only            (b) 1 and 2 only
    (c) 3 only            (d) 2 and 3 only

99. **Direction:** In the following question, there are two statements in which one is statement A and the other is Reason R. Choose your answer from the four options given below:
    (a) If A and R are true and R is the correct explanation of A
    (b) If A and R are true and R is not a correct explanation of A
    (c) A is true but R is False
    (d) A is false and R is true

    **Statement (A):** Amir Khursrau's Khaliq-e-bari, which is known as oldest printed dictionary of the world deals with Hindi and Persian words.
    **Reason (R):** Amir Khursrau is regarded as the "father of qawwali".

100. Consider the following Statements:
    1. Madhya Pradesh is the only Diamond producing state in India
    2. Bauxite is the ore which is used in manufacturing of Aluminium.
    3. POSCO steel plant in Orissa was developed by Korea
    Which of the statement given above is/are correct?
    (a) 1 and 2 only      (b) 2 and 3 only
    (c) 1 and 3 only      (d) 1, 2 and 3

## RESPONSE SHEET

| | | | | |
|---|---|---|---|---|
| 1. ⓐⓑⓒⓓ | 2. ⓐⓑⓒⓓ | 3. ⓐⓑⓒⓓ | 4. ⓐⓑⓒⓓ | 5. ⓐⓑⓒⓓ |
| 6. ⓐⓑⓒⓓ | 7. ⓐⓑⓒⓓ | 8. ⓐⓑⓒⓓ | 9. ⓐⓑⓒⓓ | 10. ⓐⓑⓒⓓ |
| 11. ⓐⓑⓒⓓ | 12. ⓐⓑⓒⓓ | 13. ⓐⓑⓒⓓ | 14. ⓐⓑⓒⓓ | 15. ⓐⓑⓒⓓ |
| 16. ⓐⓑⓒⓓ | 17. ⓐⓑⓒⓓ | 18. ⓐⓑⓒⓓ | 19. ⓐⓑⓒⓓ | 20. ⓐⓑⓒⓓ |
| 21. ⓐⓑⓒⓓ | 22. ⓐⓑⓒⓓ | 23. ⓐⓑⓒⓓ | 24. ⓐⓑⓒⓓ | 25. ⓐⓑⓒⓓ |
| 26. ⓐⓑⓒⓓ | 27. ⓐⓑⓒⓓ | 28. ⓐⓑⓒⓓ | 29. ⓐⓑⓒⓓ | 30. ⓐⓑⓒⓓ |
| 31. ⓐⓑⓒⓓ | 32. ⓐⓑⓒⓓ | 33. ⓐⓑⓒⓓ | 34. ⓐⓑⓒⓓ | 35. ⓐⓑⓒⓓ |
| 36. ⓐⓑⓒⓓ | 37. ⓐⓑⓒⓓ | 38. ⓐⓑⓒⓓ | 39. ⓐⓑⓒⓓ | 40. ⓐⓑⓒⓓ |
| 41. ⓐⓑⓒⓓ | 42. ⓐⓑⓒⓓ | 43. ⓐⓑⓒⓓ | 44. ⓐⓑⓒⓓ | 45. ⓐⓑⓒⓓ |
| 46. ⓐⓑⓒⓓ | 47. ⓐⓑⓒⓓ | 48. ⓐⓑⓒⓓ | 49. ⓐⓑⓒⓓ | 50. ⓐⓑⓒⓓ |
| 51. ⓐⓑⓒⓓ | 52. ⓐⓑⓒⓓ | 53. ⓐⓑⓒⓓ | 54. ⓐⓑⓒⓓ | 55. ⓐⓑⓒⓓ |
| 56. ⓐⓑⓒⓓ | 57. ⓐⓑⓒⓓ | 58. ⓐⓑⓒⓓ | 59. ⓐⓑⓒⓓ | 60. ⓐⓑⓒⓓ |
| 61. ⓐⓑⓒⓓ | 62. ⓐⓑⓒⓓ | 63. ⓐⓑⓒⓓ | 64. ⓐⓑⓒⓓ | 65. ⓐⓑⓒⓓ |
| 66. ⓐⓑⓒⓓ | 67. ⓐⓑⓒⓓ | 68. ⓐⓑⓒⓓ | 69. ⓐⓑⓒⓓ | 70. ⓐⓑⓒⓓ |
| 71. ⓐⓑⓒⓓ | 72. ⓐⓑⓒⓓ | 73. ⓐⓑⓒⓓ | 74. ⓐⓑⓒⓓ | 75. ⓐⓑⓒⓓ |
| 76. ⓐⓑⓒⓓ | 77. ⓐⓑⓒⓓ | 78. ⓐⓑⓒⓓ | 79. ⓐⓑⓒⓓ | 80. ⓐⓑⓒⓓ |
| 81. ⓐⓑⓒⓓ | 82. ⓐⓑⓒⓓ | 83. ⓐⓑⓒⓓ | 84. ⓐⓑⓒⓓ | 85. ⓐⓑⓒⓓ |
| 86. ⓐⓑⓒⓓ | 87. ⓐⓑⓒⓓ | 88. ⓐⓑⓒⓓ | 89. ⓐⓑⓒⓓ | 90. ⓐⓑⓒⓓ |
| 91. ⓐⓑⓒⓓ | 92. ⓐⓑⓒⓓ | 93. ⓐⓑⓒⓓ | 94. ⓐⓑⓒⓓ | 95. ⓐⓑⓒⓓ |
| 96. ⓐⓑⓒⓓ | 97. ⓐⓑⓒⓓ | 98. ⓐⓑⓒⓓ | 99. ⓐⓑⓒⓓ | 100. ⓐⓑⓒⓓ |

# HINTS & EXPLANATIONS

1. **(c)** Tax reforms are concerned with the reforms in government's taxation and public expenditure policies which are collectively known as its fiscal policy.

   Since 1991, there has been a continuous reduction in the taxes on individual incomes as it was felt that high rates of income tax were an important reason for tax evasion.

   It is now widely accepted that moderate rates of income tax encourage savings and voluntary disclosure of income.

   **Source:** N.C.E.R.T – 11th – Economics

2. **(c)** Nalsarovar bird sanctuary is a Ramsar Site and is located in Gujarat.

3. **(c)** The current opinion held by the supreme court that the preamble is a part of the constitution and is in consonance with the opinion of the founding fathers of the constitution.

   However, two things should be noted:

   1. The preamble is neither a source of power to legislature nor a prohibition upon the powers of legislature.

   2. It is non-justiciable, that is, its provisions are not enforceable in courts of law.

4. **(c)** The Britishers introduced in some crucial changes after 1857 revolt in order to avoid such uprising in future. The British Parliament passed a new Act in 1858 and transfered the powers of the East India company to the British crown in order to ensure a more responsible management of Indian Affairs. Policies were made to protect landlords and Zamindars and gave them security of rights over their lands.

5. **(c)** The Dravidian languages are Tamil,Telugu, Kannada and Malayalam of which Tamil was the earliest to be developed for literary purposes.

   India never really had a common language used by the masses. Even when sanskrit grew to prominence and was widely used, it was still the language of the learned sections of the population.

   **Source:** Spectrum's : Indian Culture

6. **(d)** Tectonic plateaux are formed by earth movements which cause uplift and are normally of a considerable size and fairly uniform altitude. They include continental blocks like the Deccan plateau in India examples of tectonic plateaux are Harz of Germany, Tibetan plateau and the Bolivian plateau.

7. **(a)** Lithium-Ion batteries are nearly 100% efficient while the efficiency of lead-acid batteries is 70%. Lithium-ion batteries use a much cleaner technology as compared to lead-acid batteries. Lithium-ion batteries are discharged 100% while it is less than 80% for lead acid batteries.

8. **(c)** Dhola-Sadia Bridge is a three-lane bridge stretching 9.15 kilometre built over river Lohit, which is a tributary of the Brahmaputra river.

9. **(a)** Manipuri dance is a purely religious dance form and it aims for spiritual experience, also in socio-cultural events. It has its own specific aesthetics, values, conventions and ethics.

   Manipuri dancers do not wear ankle bells to accentuate the beats tapped out by the feet and the dancers feet never strike the ground hard.

10. **(d)** The policy instruments which obstruct trade are called barriers to trade. It can be Tariff Barriers or Non-Tariff Barriers.

    Tariff means the duty on import and export of a goods.

    The major non-tariff barriers are:

    – Quota

    – Production Subsidies

    – Export Subsidies

    – Health, Sanitary and Safety regulations

    – Packaging requirements

11. **(c)** Convention on Biological Diversity (CBD) Biodiversity Convention is a key document regarding sustainable development.

    – Its objective is to develop national strategies for the conservation and sustainable use of biological diversity.

    – CBD covers biodiversity at all levels: Ecosystem, Species and Genetic resources.

    – CBD is legally binding: Countries that join it (parties) are obliged to implement its provisions.

12. **(d)** All the statements (1), (2) and (3) given in the question are correct . Five petroleum products viz. Petroleum crude, motor spirit (petrol), high speed diesel, natural gas and aviation turbine fuel have temporarily been kept out and GST council can decide the date from which they shall be included in GST.

13. **(c)** Both the statements given in the question are correct. The tigers are monitored in tiger reserves through a special field protocol (Phase-IV monitoring) which involves recording day to day field evidence collating camera trap pictures of tigers.

    It also uses information technology for improved surveillance (e-Eye System) using thermal cameras.

14. **(d)** The metamorphosis of neutrino is not due to radioactivity or collision with heavier particles. The change is only due to its mass.

15. (c) Stupa, Vihara and Chaitya are part of Buddhist and Jaina Monastic Complexes but the largest number belongs to the Buddhist religion.

    The great Stupa at Sanchi was built with bricks during the time of Ashoka and later it was covered with stone and many new additions were made.

16. (a) During the proclamation of national emergency, the team of the assembly can be extended by a law of parliament for one year at a time (for any length of time).

    However, this extension cannot continue beyond a period of six months after the emergency has ceased to operate.

17. (c) Recently RBI listed HDFC as Domestic-systematically Important Bank (DSIB). Banks whose assets cross 2% of the GDP are considered DSIBs. DSIBs are categorized under five buckets. According to these buckets the banks have to keep aside the Additional Common Equity Tier 1 as a percentage of Risk Weighted Assets (RWAs).

18. (b) CAG has the mandate to audit accounts related to expenditure from consolidated fund of India, that of states and consolidated fund of only those union territories that have a Legislative Assembly (that is Delhi and Pondicherry).

    – All other statements are correct.

    – Besides CAG also audits other corporations and bodies when so required by related laws.

    **Source:** M. Lakshmikant.

19. (c) Chromoplasts and leucoplasts are types of plastids and contain DNA.

20. (a) Sehjdharis are those who follow Sikhism but without being Amritdharis or baptised. They do not adopt baptismal vows of the Khalsa Panth initiated by Guru Gobind Singh. They might be born in Hindu, Sikh or other families but follow the Sri Guru Granth Sahib. They perform ceremonies according to Sikh rites.

21. (c) The WTO was founded in 1995 as the successor organisation to the General Agreement on Trade and Tariff (GATT).

    – WTO is expected to establish a rule-based trading regime in which nations cannot place arbitrary restrictions on trade.

    – WTO's purpose is also to enlarge production and trade of services to ensure optimum utilisation of world resources and to protect the environment.

    – The WTO agreements cover trade in goods as well as services to facilitate international trade (bilateral and multilateral) through removal of tariff as well as non-tariff barriers and providing greater market access to all member countries.

    **Source:** N.C.E.R.T – 11<sup>th</sup> Economics

22. (d) Tropical rainforests occur near the equator. Tropical rainforests are among the most diverse and rich communities on the earth. The flora is highly diversified.

    The extreme dense vegetation of the tropical rainforests remains vertically stratified with tall trees often covered with vines, creepers, lianas.

    The lowest layer is an under-story of trees, shrubs, herbs, like ferns and palms.

    Soil of tropical rain forest becomes virtually useless for agricultural purposes because of high rate of leaching.

    Under growth is restricted in many areas by the lack of sunlight at ground level.

23. (c) IUCN red data list highlights the endangered and threatened species of Birds.

    – Bonn Convention aims to conserve/protect the migratory species of wild animals.

24. (a) As provided by the constitution, the speaker of the last Lok Sabha vacates his office immediately before the first meeting of the newly elected Lok Sabha.

    Therefore, the president appoints a member of the Lok sabha as the speaker protem. He presides over the first sitting of the newly-elected Lok-sabha. His main duty is to administer oaths to the new members. He also enables the house to elect the new speaker.

    The vice-president of India is the ex-officio chairman of the Rajya sabha.

    Unlike the speaker (who is a member of the house), the chairman is not a member of the House. But like the speaker, the chairman also cannot vote in the first instance.

25. (b) Mitochondria is a double membranous cellular organelle with inner folded membrane and outer porous membrane. In addition to various constituents, it also contains its own DNA and ribosomes.

26. (c) The three most recent mountain building movements are

    1. **Caledonian:** It raised mountains of Scandinavia and Scotland and is represented in North America.

    2. **Hercynian:** It raised mountain ranges of the Ural Mountains, the Pennines and Welsh High lands in Britain, the Harg Mountains in Germany, the Appalachians in America as well as the high plateaux of Siberia and China.

    3. **Alpine:** Young fold mountains ranges were buckled up and overthrust on a gigantic scale. Being the most recently formed these ranges such as the Alps, Himalayas, Andes and Rockies. These are the loftiest and the most imposing.

27. (b) Open prisons refer to the prisons that involve minimum security and are mainly dependent on the self discipline of the inmates. The rules of these prisons are less stringent as compared to the rules the other prisons. Rajasthan has as many as 29 open prisons, the highest in the country. The prisons at times become self governed by a method commonly known as Bandi

Panchayat. Under this, 5 prisons are selected who become members of the panchayat and look into the administrative functioning of the prison.

28. (c) Freedom of religion becomes a matter of political controversy for many reasons.

    The constitution has guaranteed the right to propagate one's religion (Art-25). This includes persuading people to convert from one religion to another. However the constitution does not allow forcible conversions. It only gives us the right to spread information about over religion and thus attracts others to it.

    Rights provided under Article-19(1) are not absolute. The govt. can impose restrictions on the practice of freedom of religion in order to protect public order, morality and health. The government can interfere in religious matters for rooting out certain social evils.

    **Source:** N.C.E.R.T (XI$^{th}$); Indian constitution at work.

29. (d) The maximum current is produced when the angle between magnetic field and direction of motion of coil is 90°.

30. (a) The government can initiate criminal proceedings against a sitting or former judge of a superior court under sub-section (2) of section (3) of the Judges (Protection) Act,1985 if it can produce material evidence to show that a judgement or a judicial decision was passed after taking a bribe.

31. (c) Nehru and many other leaders were firm that India would be a socialist society with a strong public sector but also with private property and democracy; the government would plan for the economy with the private sector being encouraged to be part of the plan effort.

    – The Industrial Policy Resolution of 1948 and Directive Principles of The Indian Constitution reflected this outlook.

    – The Industrial Policy 1948 ushered India in to the system of mixed economy.

    **Source:** N.C.E.R.T – 11$^{th}$ – Economics

32. (d) It has been estimated that SLCP mitigation has the potential to avoid upto 0.6°C of warming by mid century while aggressive $CO_2$ mitigation in a comparable scenario leads to less than half as much near term reduction in warming.

    The SLCP includes methane, HFCs, black carbon (Soot), tropospheric ozone etc.

33. (c) Carbon, hydrogen, oxygen, nitrogen and phosphorus as elements and compounds make up 97% of the mass of our bodies and are more than 95% of the mass of all living organisms.

34. (d) Bonds basically are debt instruments which help issues to get capital while the investors receive fixed income in the form of interest.

In case of Green Bonds, the issuer gets capital from the investors only if the investment (capital) is being raised to fund green projects relating to renewable energy or emission reductions etc.

35. (a) The compound known as 'Mahanine' which was isolated from curry leaves has been found to inhibit the growth of kala-azar parasite in laboratory mouse.

36. (a) The congress session of Lahore in 1926 passed the resolution declaring Poorna Swaraj to be the congress objective and it also decided that 26 January would be observed as the independence day. The Madras session of congress headed by M.A. Ansari passed a resolution which declared the attainment of complete independence as the goal of Indian people. In the session of 1928 at Calcutta it passed a resolution demanding Dominion status.

37. (c) SDR is a reserve created by International Monetary Fund (IMF) to help countries that have Balance of Payment Problem.

    SDR has two dimensions, one it is an exchange rate system and another it is a loan arrangement.

    As an exchange rate system, the SDR is an average exchange rate derived from a basket of five currencies viz., US $, Euro, UK Sterling Pound and Japanese Yen and Chinese renminbi (RMB).

    As a loan arrangement, the member countries are entitled to get loan from IMF's Special Drawing Account. It is also known as Paper Gold.

    **Source:** Key Concepts – Sankarganesh

38. (c) The second Indian Factories Act was passed in 1891. It provided weekly holiday for all workers. Working hours of women and children were changed but hours of work for men were still left unregulated.

39. (b) There are six major factors that control the climate of any place. They are latitude, altitude, pressure and wind system, distance from the sea (continentality), ocean currents and relief features. Oceans and seas play moderating effect on air temperature. The varying land breeze and sea breeze help the coastal areas to maintain moderate range of climate. Delhi is far away from the oceans/sea. Therefore Delhi witness continental climate.

    Coastal areas witness Maritime climate while interiors witness continental climate.

40. (a) 1. Constitution provides for reservation of seats in the Lok Sabha and State Legislative Assemblies for the Scheduled Castes and Schedule Tribes. This provision of reservation has been extended upto 2020.

    2. There is no constitutional provision for reservation of any kind in the council of states or the upper house, which has members elected by the State Assemblies as distinct from the directly elected Lok Sabha.

3. Art-330 provides for reservation of SC/STs in Lok Sabha but no mention of reservation in Rajya Sabha.

41. (a) HIPPI is a parallel interface designed to connect supercomputers at higher speeds.

42. (b) Missiles developed under the Integrated Guided Missile Development Programme of DRDO are Nag, Agni, Trishul, Prithvi and Akash.

43. (c) In Amensalism one species is harmed, the other is unaffected. For example. A large tree shades a small plant, retarding the growth of the small plant. The small plant has no effect on the large tree.

44. (a) The electoral college for the election of the vice-president is different from that of president in two respects.

1. It consists of both elected and nominated members of the parliament.

2. It does not include the members of the state legislative assemblies.

45. (d) In November 1930, the British government convened the First Round Table conference in London to consider the reforms proposed by Simon Commission. The congress boycotted it. But it was attended by the representatives of Indian Princess, Muslim League, Hindu Mahasabha and some others.

46. (a) The Swachh Bharat Abhiyan aims to achieve the vision of a 'Clean India' by October, 2$^{nd}$ 2019. The new Manufacturing Policy raises the output target from 16% of GDP to 25% by 2025.

47. (d) Types of biotic interaction:

**Mutualism** – Both species benefit.

**Commensalism** – One species benefits, the other is unaffected.

**Competition** – Both species are harmed by the interaction.

**Predation** and **Parasitism** – One species benefits, the other is harmed.

**Amensalism** – One species is harmed, the other is unaffected.

**Neutralism** – There is no net benefit or harm to either species.

48. (d) Lack of coherent ideology, under standing of colonial rule and absence of the feelings of modern nationalism were some important causes of the failure of the revolt of 1857.

49. (b) Dr. Ambedkar scheme for social integration through Inter-caste marriages aims to counter the Hindu practice of marrying on traditional grounds of caste/sub-castes. The selected couples are eligible for one-time incentive of ₹ 2.5 lakh.

50. (c) Word's biggest icebreaker ship 'Sibir' was launched by Russia which can break through ice up to 3 m thick. 'Sibir' is powered by nuclear reactor.

51. (a) Most of the major rivers of the Peninsula such as the Mahanadi the Godavari, the Krishna and the Kaveri flow eastwards and drain into the Bay of Bengal. These rivers make deltas at their Mouths.

– The Tungabhadra, the Koyana, the Ghatprabha, the Musi and the Bhima are some of the tributaries of the Krishna River. Its drainage basin is shared by Maharashtra, Karnataka and Andhra Pradesh.

52. (c) Through 52 Amendment Act: Articles-101, 102, 190 and 191 were changed. It laid down the process by which legislators may be disqualified on grounds of defection. A member of parliament may be disqualified if:

– He/She voluntarily resigns from the party on whose ticket he/she has been elected.

– Does not vote/abstain as per party's whip.

– If an independent member joins a political party.

A nominated member who was not member of a party could join a party within 6 months, after that period.

53. (c) Hydroponics is a subset of hydroculture, which means growing of plants in a soil less medium or in an aquatic based environment. It also uses minerals and nutrients present in the solution of water to feed the plants in water without soil besides Sunlight and Water.

54. (d) The national income at constant price means the total quantity of all final goods and services produced in a particular year, multiplied by the price of base year (constant price). The national income calculated by this method is called the real income.

The National Income at current price means the total quantity of all final goods and services produced in a particular year (current price). The national income calculated by this method is called the nominal Income.

55. (d) Hiuen Tsang had come to study in the Buddhist university of Nalanda. He spent many years in Harsha's court and widely travelled in India. His account shows that Patliputra was in a state of decline. Prayag and Kannauj had become more important. The tradesmen had to pay at barrier stations.

56. (b) India wants to implement its food security scheme by providing food entitlements at subsidised rates to 2/3$^{rd}$ of its population. To realize this, the government will have to procure a huge quantity of grains from farmers. The government procures grains at certain MSPs.

However, WTO norms under the Agreement on Agriculture may hamper the plan as the rules set a subsidy cap of 10% of the value of production for developing countries.

If India breaches that limit it would create dispute and may be dragged to the WTO Disputes Settlement Body. The 'Peace clause' proposed by the WTO general secretary offers an interim solution by allowing the developing countries to offer subsidies to farmers that are currently prohibited under WTO norms.

The clause will restrict other WTO members from seeking penalties and facilitating the government to procure grains at MSPs and sell them at subsidised rates through public distribution system (PDS).

**Source:** The Hindu

57. (c) Consumption of Electricity (in %) in India (2008–09):

| | | |
|---|---|---|
| Industrial consumption | – | 37.1% |
| Domestic consumption | – | 24.7% |
| Agricultural consumption | – | 20.4% |
| Commercial consumption | – | 10.2% |
| Railways | – | 2.2% |
| Others | – | 5.4% |

58. (b)– The minimum support price was announced by the government of India for the first time in 1966-67 for wheat in the wake of the Green Revolution and Extended harvest, to save the farmers from depleting profits.

   – MSP is the price at which government purchases crops from the farmers, whatever may be the price for the crops.

   – The government decides the support price for various agricultural commodities after taking into account the following:
   1. Recommendations of commission for agricultural costs and prices
   2. Views of state governments
   3. Views of ministers
   4. Other relevant factors

59. (b) In its pursuit of social reform, the Brahmo Samaj attacked many dogmas and superstitions Prevelant during that time. It worked for a respectable status for women in society, condemned sati , worked for abolition of purdah system discouraged child marriages and polygamy. It denounced polytheism and idol worship. It also discarded faith in divine avataras.

60. (a)

61. (b) The National Commission for Scheduled Castes is appointed by the president by warrant under his hand and seal. Their conditions of service and tenure of office are also determined by president.

   The commission presents an annual report to the president.

   The president places all such reports before the parliament.

   The commission, while investigating any matter or inquiring into any complaint, has all the powers of a civil court trying a suit.

62. (b) In the Mahalwari system, the state share of the revenue was two- third of the rental value.

63. (a) The Free Movement Regime between India and Myanmar is an arrangement for movement of tribal communities residing along the border to move 16 km across the border without Visa restrictions.

64. (b) The salaries, allowances and pensions of judges and all the administrative expenses of Supreme court are charged on consolidated fund of India. Thus they are non-votable by the parliament.

   The constitution has guaranteed to the Supreme court, jurisdiction of various kinds and therefore parliament is not authorised to curtail the jurisdiction and powers of the Supreme court.

   **Source:** M. Lakshmikant.

65. (d) As per Indian Surrogacy Bill surrogacy would be allowed only for infertile Indian married heterosexual couples where the woman is between 23 to 50 years. The age of male partner in case of heterosexual couples should be between 26 to 55 years. Issue less of unmarried women are prohibited under the Bill to be surrogate mothers.

66. (b) Villages from Uttarakhand, Bihar, Uttar Pradesh, Jharkhand and West Bengal are participating in Ganga Gram Project. Ganga Gram Project is an integrated approach for holistic development of villages situated on the banks of the holy river Ganga with active participation of villagers.

67. (c) E-commerce giant Amazon has launched its global start up program 'launchpad' in India. The program will enable Indian startups to sell their products overseas.

68. (c) Sometimes the number of species and the population density of some of the species is much greater in zone of ecotones, than either of the adjoining communities. This is called edge effect.

   The organisms which occur primarily or most abundantly in this zone are known as edge species. In the terrestrial ecosystems edge effect is especially applicable to birds.

69. (b) – In 1989 a provision was made to facilitate the use of Electronic Voting Machine (EVMs) in elections.
   – The EVMs were used for the first time in 1998 on experimental basis in selected constituencies in the elections to the Assemblies of Rajasthan, Madhya Pradesh and Delhi.
   – The EVMs were used for the first time in the general elections (entire state) to the Assembly of Goa in 1999.

   **Source:** M. Lakshmikant

70. (b) The National Vector Borne Disease Control Programme is a programme for Prevention and control of Vector Borne diseases like Malaria, Filariasis, Kala azar, Japenese encephalitis, Dengue and Chikungunya.

71. (a) Estuaries are sharp edged mouth of rivers, devoid of any deposits. Usually Estuaries do not have fertile lands. Narmada and Tapi rivers form Estuaries. They are in the regions of high tides. Rift valleys witness Estuaries.

72. (c) Fertilizer production has been given the lowest weight are in the Index of eight core industries.

73. (c) Both the statements (1) and (2) are correct. The Index measures factors and policies that enable the sustainable development of Travel and Tourism sector.

74. (a) "Ladakh Renewable Energy Initiative" is being implemented by the Ministry of New and Renewable Energy.

75. (a) The Vienna Convention came into effect in 1988, for the protection of the ozone layer. It does not include legally binding reduction goals for the use of CFCs, the main chemical agents causing ozone depletion. These are laid out in the accompanying Montreal Protocol.

76. (c) Balwant Rai Mehta Committee recommended that zila parishad should be the advisory, co-ordinating and supervisory body. While Ashok Mehta Committee recommended that zila parishad should be the executive body and made responsible for planning at the district level.

77. (c) Iran, Syria and Iraq are not the part of "Islamic Alliance to fight Terrorism." Doha though part of the group did not participate in it in the wake of boycott led by Saudi Arabia.

78. (b) Conduction the atmosphere is mainly heated by conduction from the earth. Therefore it can be expected that places nearer to the earth's surface are warmer than those higher-up. Thus temperature decreases with increasing height above sea level. This rate of decrease with altitude (lapse rate) is never constant, varying from place to place and from season to season.

79. (c) According to the definition given in the chit fund Act, 1982, a chit fund company is a company which acts/conducts/supervises chits. The scheme of the chit fund companies can be organised or unorganised.

Reserve Bank of India has allowed non-resident Indians (NRIs) to invest in chit fund to encourage flow of capital into the country.

80. (a) Cold desert is the home for highly adaptive, rare endangered fauna, such as Asiatic Ibex, Tibetan Argali, Ladakh Uriyal, Bharal, Tibetan Antelope (Chiru), Tibetan Gazelle, Wild Yak, Snow Leopard, Brown Bear, Tibetan Wolf, Wild Dog and Tibetan Wild Ass, Woolly hare, Black Necked Crane etc.

White-footed fox and Asiatic Wildcat are found in tha desert, which is a hot desert.

81. (c) Article-37 makes it clear that Directive Principles are fundamental in the governance of the country and it shall be the duty of the state to apply these principles in making laws.

Alladi Krishna Swamy Ayyar observed in the constituent Assembly that "No minister responsible to people can afford to overlook directive principles.

82. (d) **Factors Affecting Demand:**
1. Increase in money supply leads to price rise and increased consumption.
2. The increase in the disposable income leads to higher spending on the part of households.

3. Cheap monetary policy means loan availability at very low interest rate and at easy terms.
4. The Repayment of public debt borrowed by government to public leaves people with more money.

83. (c) Both the statements mentioned in the question are true with respect to white tigers.

Recently a rare 'White Tiger' has been spotted for the first time in the Nilgiris.

White tigers have been put in schedule 1 of Wild Life (Protection) Act 1972.

84. (c) Unlike convectional rain which is caused by convection currents, orographic/relief rainfall is formed wherever moist air is forced to ascend a mountain barrier. It is best developed on the windward slopes of mountains where the prevailing moisture- laden winds come from the sea.

85. (b) Turkmenistan-Afghanistan-Pakistan-India (TAPI) gas pipeline is 1,814 Km long gas pipeline. India and Pakistan will equally share the 38 million standard cubic metres a day (mmscmd) each of supplied gas through TAPI pipeline.

86. (a) the government has launched a new AGRI-UDAAN programme to promote innovation and entrepreneurship in agriculture, will mentor startups and help them connect with potential investors. The programme will help convert innovative ideas from India's rural youth into viable businesses.

87. (c) Union Minister of Agriculture and Farmers' Welfare has launched Yuva Sahakar-Cooperative Enterprise Support and Innovation Scheme of National Cooperative Development Corporation (NCDC). It is youth-friendly scheme aimed at attracting youth to cooperative business ventures.

88. (b) The J&K Government has launched a major welfare scheme named "Muhafiz" (Guardian), for the workers in the unorganized sector to provide them institutionalized socio-economic security. Under the scheme around 3 lakh workers registered with Jammu and Kashmir Building and Other Construction Workers Welfare Board (JKBOCWWB), will be covered under accidental, life and disability insurance besides providing educational scholarships to their children.

89. (a) Niryat Bandhu Scheme was first introduced in Oct.2011 by the Director General of foreign trade for international business mentoring first generation entrepreneurs in International Business enterprises.

90. (d) Hendra virus (HeV) is a member of the family *Paramyxoviridae* and one of two virus species in the genus *Henipavirus* (the other being *Nipah virus*). HeV was first isolated in 1994 from specimens obtained during an outbreak of respiratory and neurologic disease in horses and humans in Hendra, a suburb of Brisbane, Australia.

91. (d) Lassa fever is a viral infection, primarily transmitted to humans through contact with food or household items contaminated with rodent urine, faeces, or blood. Person-to-person transmission is through direct or indirect contact with body fluids of an infected person. Prevention of Lassa fever relies on promoting good community hygiene to keep rats out of the house and prevent contamination of food supplies.

92. (c) Govt. has announced in December, 2018 that the RBI will constitute an 8 members Expert Committee under the chairmanship of Shri U.K. Sinha on Micro, Small and Medium Enterprises. The Expert Committee will submit its report by the end of June, 2019.

93. (c) HysIS is earth observation satellites launched on 29th November, 2018. GSAT-6A is a Communication Satellites launched on 29th March 2018.

94. (d) The Indian summer monsoon typically lasts from June-September with large areas of western and central India receiving more than 90% of their total annual precipitation during the period, and southern and northwestern India receiving 50%-75% of their total annual rainfall. Overall, monthly totals average 200-300 mm over the country as a whole, with the largest values observed during the heart of the monsoon season in July and August.

95. (a)

96. (d) Ajanta caves are the set of 29 Buddhist cave temples. The Caves shaped into the face of a mountain, appear as a horseshoe around the Wangorah River. The paintings and sculptures of Ajanta, considered masterpieces of Buddhist religious art, have had a considerable artistic influence.

97 (d) In December 1977, the Janta Government appointed a committee on Panchayati Raj institutions under the chairmanship of Ashok Mehta. It submitted its report in August 1978 and made 132 recommendations to revive and strengthen the declining Panchayati Raj System in the country.

98. (b) LIBOR, the acronym for London Interbank Offer Rate, is the global reference rate for unsecured short-term borrowing in the interbank market. The term "Banana Republic", Popularly is referred to small Latin American Caribbean or African countries , that economically depends upon the exports of a limited resources (usually fruits, crops), which is dominated by a rich.

99. (b)

100. (d) Madhya Pradesh is the only state with a diamond mine in the country as well as in Asia. During the year 2017-18, Madhya Pradesh has produced 28,424 carats of diamonds (up to December 2017). The Majhgawan mine at Panna in the Madhya Pradesh is the only source of diamonds in Asia producing 30,000 carats every year. POSCO India Private Limited (commonly POSCO India or Posco-India) is an Indian subsidiary of Korean conglomerate POSCO. Its parent company POSCO signed a memorandum of understanding in June 2005 with the state government of Odisha to construct a $12 billion steel plant

**Max. Marks : 200**       **Time : 2 hrs.**

1. In the following number series only one number is wrong. Find out the wrong number.

   8, 11, 17, 47, 128, 371, 1100

   (a) 11      (b) 47
   (c) 17      (d) 371

2. If 'A × D' means 'A is the sister of D', 'A + D' means 'D is the daughter of A' and 'A ÷ D' means 'A is the mother of D', then how will 'N is the aunt of M' be denoted?

   (a) M + L × N      (b) M ÷ L + N
   (c) L × N ÷ M      (d) N × L ÷ M

3. Maya starts at point T, walks straight to point U which is 4 ft away. She turns left at 90° and walks to W which is 4 ft away, turns 90° right and goes 3 ft to P, turns 90° right and walks 1 ft to Q, turns left at 90° and goes to V, which is 1 ft away and once again turns 90° right and goes to R, 3 ft away. What is the distance between T and R ?

   (a) 4 ft      (b) 5 ft
   (c) 7 ft      (d) 8 ft

4. A dice is thrown four times and its four different positions are shown below. Find the number on the face opposite the face showing 2.

   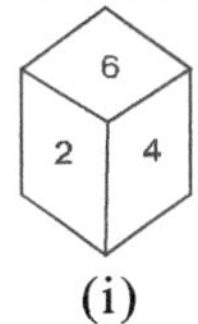 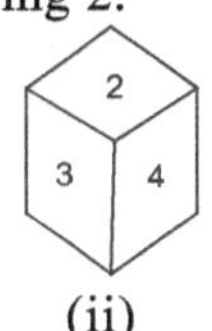 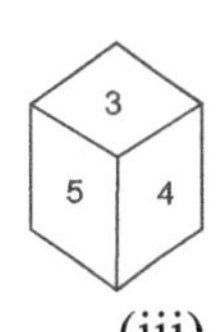 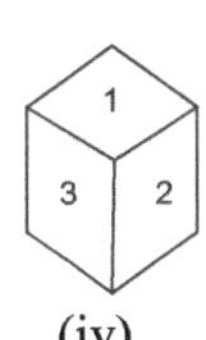

      (i)        (ii)        (iii)        (iv)

   (a) 3      (b) 4
   (c) 5      (d) 6

5. Among the four alternatives choose which one can be the similar box as the question figure.

   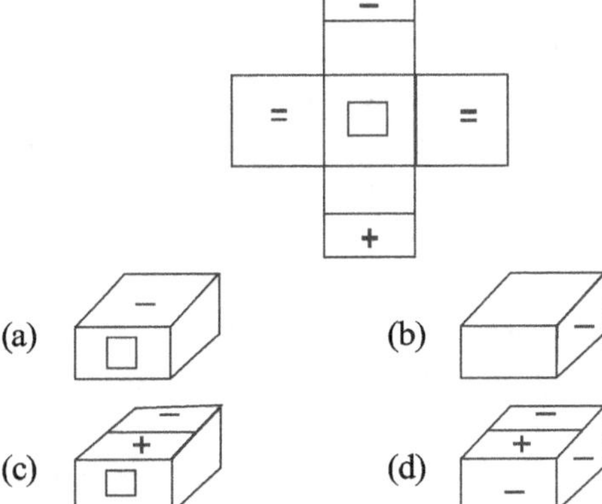

6. Study the following question figures and select the option that completes the given series.

   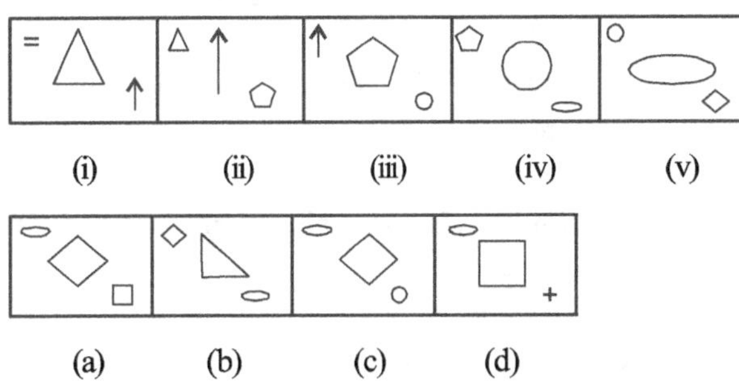

   (i)      (ii)      (iii)      (iv)      (v)

   (a)      (b)      (c)      (d)

7. Study the following information carefully and answer the question given below.

   A, B, C, D, E, F, G, H and K are sitting around a circle facing the centre. B is fourth to the left of G who is second to the right of C. F is fourth to the right of C and is second to the left of K. A is fourth to the right of K. D is not an immediate neighbour of either K or B. H is third to the right of E.

   In which of the following combinations is the third person sitting between the first and the second persons?

   (a) EKB      (b) CHB
   (c) AGC      (d) FGD

**Directions** (Qs. 8-15) : *Read the following passages and answer the questions that follow them.*

### PASSAGE-1

The doctrinal teachings of Protestant and Catholic reformers were inimical and anathema to one another. But their broader aims and aspirations could at times look remarkably similar. Both hoped to create a more spiritual Church, and a godlier, disciplined, and ordered society. And both confronted similar obstacles, in the ignorance, apathy, or sheer bloody-mindedness of local communities who might see little reason to change their ways at the behest of high-minded idealists. It makes little sense to consider the Catholic and Protestant Reformations separately from each other, and their contrasting, and sometimes converging, trajectories need to be treated side-by-side.

8. Which of the following statements are not implied by the passage ?

   I. the Protestant and Catholic reformers both agreed upon common goals and aspirations.

   II. communities responded with reason and tolerance to the idealism of the reformers.

III. the Catholic and Protestant Reformations should be studied simultaneously.

IV. the doctrines of the two Reformations did not suit each other.

(a) I and IV  (b) I and II

(c) IV and III  (d) II and III

9. Which of the following created obstacles in the process of reformation?

(a) the high-minded idealism of the local communities.

(b) the ignorance of the reformers.

(c) the apathy of the local communities

(d) the similarity of the goals of Protestant and Catholic reformations.

10. The trajectory of the two reformations

(a) converge occasionally and diverge rarely.

(b) should be studied separately.

(c) are results of dissimilar histories.

(d) help in understanding each other.

11. Which of the following statements is closest to the main argument of the passage?

(a) the Catholic and Protestant Reformations were popular movements.

(b) the Reformations were brought out by a common reaction against social ignorance.

(c) the Protestant and the Catholic Reformations cannot be studied separately.

(d) the doctrines of the Protestants and the Catholics are very different from each other.

12. Which word is same as **hostile** in the paragraph?

(a) inimical  (b) anathema

(c) apathy  (d) trajectories

### PASSAGE-2

In the last decade, the banking sector has been restructured with a high degree of automation and products that mainly serve middle-class and upper middle-class society. Today there is need for a new agenda for the banking and non-banking financial services that does not exclude the common man.

13. Which one of the following is the message that is essentially implied in the above passage?

(a) Need for more automation and more products of bank

(b) Need for a radical restructuring of our entire public finance system

(c) Need to integrate banking and non-banking institutions

(d) Need to promote financial inclusion

### PASSAGE-3

Despite the economic crunch world-wide that saw pulverization of some of the largest banking and finance giants, Indian banking houses have managed to show positive growth this quarter. Some of India's leading national banks have posted a net profit rise of more than 40% over the last quarter amid global turmoil. This would come as a big shot in the arm for the investors and consumers of these banks even though apprehension is mounting on other banking and broking firms worldwide. One of the main reasons behind the success of these banks this quarter, would be their direct backing by the Government of India. People take solace in their investments in public sector watching the bailout packages being cashed out by governments all over the world to save big business houses.

Other private banks in India have also reported a substantial net profit over the last quarter given the international and domestic scenario one cannot put this down as a mundane achievement. While others are on a cost cutting sphere and firing employees, Indian companies are actually working on boosting staffing in banking and broking sectors. This can be seen as a big boon in a days to come when the current recession eases and the economy gradually comes back on to the fast track. The finance minister has assured Indian public about the sound health of all Indian banks. This could also be evident from the fact that there have been no mergers and takeovers in Indian banking sector in a contrast to word scenario where finance houses are looking for mergers to cut costs on operations. We definitely are not looking to thrive; rather few dare looking for growth. It is just that the pace of growth is a little slow now as compared to a year or two before. These are hard times to test the hard. The weak in business and career will be weeded out and it is sometimes very beneficial for business on the long run.

14. What, according to the author, is the reason for the success of Indian national banks in this quarter?

(a) Indian national banks do not have any commitments in troubled foreign markets

(b) These banks can never face financial crisis because of their sheer size

(c) These banks are ready to give loans at a very low rate of interest

(d) The public is ready to invest in these banks because of the knowledge that these banks get strong support from the Government

15. Which of the following statements is definitely true in the context of the passage?

(A) India has not been affected by the economic slowdown

(B) Indian banks are showing growth in this quarter despite the recession

(C) While banking industry in the West are severely affected by recession in the past, it is now gradually recovering and showing a positive growth.

(a) Only (A)  (b) Only (B)

(c) Only (C)  (d) Only (A) and (B)

16. The graph below shows the distribution according to height of a group of jockeys at a south Florida horse track. Select the statement that correctly describes a relationship between measures of central tendency for this distribution.

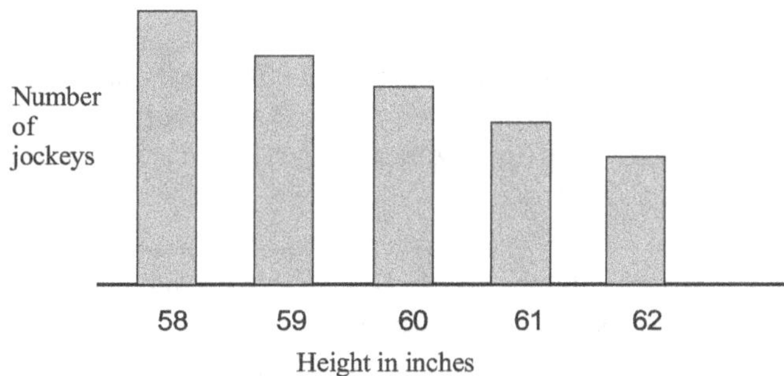



(a)    The mean is less than the mode.

(b)    The mode and the mean are the same.

(c)    The median is greater than the mode.

(d)    The median and the mean are the same.

17. The yield versus fertiliser input is shown in the graph.

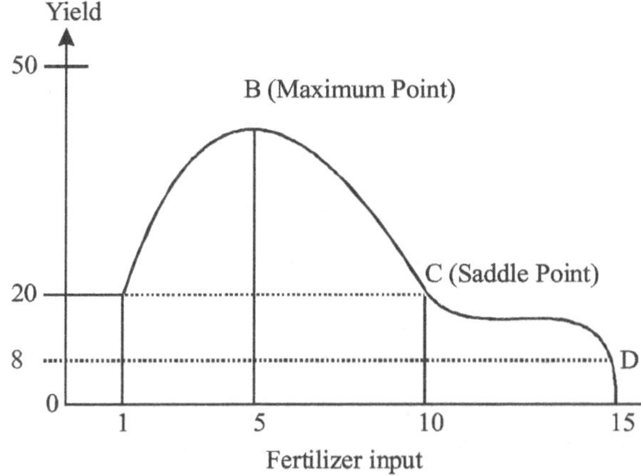



Consider the following statements based on this graph.

I.    Yield is zero at $B$ and $C$.

II.    There is no yield with no fertiliser input.

III.    The yield is minimum at D.

IV.    The yield is neither minimum nor maximum at C.

Which of the above statements are correct?

(a)    I, II and IV       (b)    III and IV

(c)    II and III        (d)    I, III and IV

18. $55^3 + 17^3 - 72^3$ is divisible by

(a)  both 3 and 13     (b) both 7 and 17

(c)  both 3 and 17     (d) both 7 and 13

19. Which digits should come in place of * and $ if the number 62684*$ is divisible by both 8 and 5?

(a)  4, 0     (b) 0, 4     (c) 0, 0     (d) 4, 4

20. There are two integers 34041 and 32506, when divided by a three-digit integer $n$, leave the same remainder. What is the value of $n$?

(a)  298           (b) 307

(c)  461           (d) can't be determined

21. In a housing society, 30 per cent of the residents are men over the age of 18 and 40 per cent are women over the age of 18. If there are 24 children living in the housing society, then how many total residents live ?

(a)  32     (b) 80     (c) 94     (d) 112

22. Two equal sums were lent, one at the rate of 11% p.a. for five years and the other at the rate of 8% p.a. for six years, both under simple interest. If the difference in interest accrued in the two cases is ₹ 1008. find the sum.

(a) ₹ 11,200        (b) ₹ 5,600

(c) ₹ 12,600        (d) ₹ 14,400

23. ₹ 1220 is divided, among $A$, $B$, $C$ and $D$, such that $B$'s share is $\frac{5}{9}$ th of $A$'s; $C$'s share is $\frac{7}{10}$ th of $B$'s and $D$ has $\frac{1}{3}$ as much as $B$ and $C$ together. Find $A$'s share.

(a) ₹ 540    (b) ₹ 802    (c) ₹ 100    (d) ₹ 650

24. In what ratio should freely available water be mixed with the wine worth ₹ 60 per litre so that after selling the mixture at ₹ 50 per litre, the profit will be 25%?

(a) 1 : 2    (b) 2 : 3    (c) 3 : 4    (d) 4 : 5

 (Qs.25–27): *Study the following information to answer the questions given below:*

A building has seven floors numbered one to seven, in such a way that the ground floor is numbered one, the floor above it number two, and so on, such that the topmost floor is numbered seven. One out of seven people viz, A, B, C, D, E, F and G, lives on each floor. A lives on fourth floor. E lives on the floor immediately below F's floor. F does not live on the second or the seventh floor. C does not live on an odd-numbered floor. B does not live on a floor immediately above or below C's floor. D does not live on the topmost floor. G does not live on any floor below E's floor.

25. Who lives on the topmost floor?

(a)  B                 (b)  C

(c)  E                 (d)  G

26. Who lives immediately above D's floor?

(a)  A                 (b)  B

(c)  C                 (d)  F

27. Four of the following five are alike in a certain way and so form a group. Which is the one that does not belong to that group?

(a)  F                 (b)  D

(c)  B                 (d)  C

 (Qs.28–29): *Study the following information carefully and answer the questions, which follow:*

Five plays A, B, C, D and E were organized in a week from Monday to Saturday with one play each day and no play was organized on one of these days. Play D was organized before Thursday but after Monday. Play E was organized on Saturday. Play C was not organized on the first day. Play B was organized on the next day on which play C was organized. Play A was organized on Tuesday.

28. On which day was play B was organized?
    - (a) Thursday
    - (b) Friday
    - (c) Wednesday
    - (d) data inadequate

29. On which day was no play organized?
    - (a) Monday
    - (b) Wednesday
    - (c) Thursday
    - (d) Data inadequate

30. In the question below is given a statement followed by two assumptions number I and II. An assumption is something supposed or taken for granted. You have to consider the statement and the following assumption and decide which of the assumptions is implicit in the statement.

    Give answer:
    - (a) if only assumption I is implicit.
    - (b) if only assumption II is implicit.
    - (c) if either assumption I or II is implicit.
    - (d) if neither assumption I nor II is implicit.

    **Statement:** The local citizens group submitted a memorandum to the civic authority for allowing them to convert the vacant plot in the locality into a garden at their own cost.

    **Assumptions:**
    **I.** The local citizen group may be able to gather enough funds to develop the garden
    **II.** The civic authority may not accede to the request of the local citizen group.

31. Select the answer figure in which the question figure is hidden.

    **Question figure**

    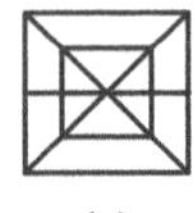  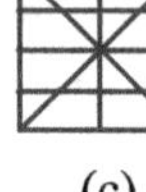 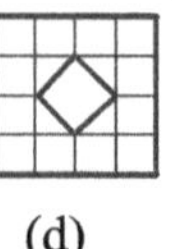

      (a)      (b)      (c)      (d)

**Directions** (Qs. 32–33): *Study the following information carefully and answer the questions given below:*

Following are the conditions for selecting Manager – Finance in an organization:

The candidate must
- I. be at least 30 years and not more than 35 years as on 1. 11. 2017
- II. be a graduate in any discipline with at least 55% marks
- III. be a post graduate degree/diploma holder in Management with Finance specialization with at least 60% marks.
- IV. have post – qualification work experience of at least six years in the finance department of an organization
- V. have secured at least 50% marks in the preliminary interview
- VI. have secured at least 40% marks in the final interview.

In the case of a candidate who satisfies all the above conditions EXCEPT
- (i) at (IV) above, but has post-qualification work experience of at least three years as Deputy Finance Manager in an organization, his/her case is to be referred to VP – Finance
- (ii) at (VI) above, but has obtained atleast 60% marks in the preliminary interview, his/her candidature is to be considered under 'wait list' .

In each question below, details of one candidate are given. You have to take one of the following courses of action based on the information provided and the conditions and sub – conditions given above and mark the number of that course of action as your answer. You are not to assume anything other than the information provided in each question. All these cases are given to you as on 1. 1. 2017.

**Mark answer (a)** if the candidate is to be selected

**Mark answer (b)** if the candidate is not to be selected

**Mark answer (c)** if the candidate is to be kept on waiting list

**Mark answer (d)** if the case is to be referred to VP - Finance

32. Neelam Johri has secured 38% marks in the final interview. She has also secured 65% marks in both B.Com and postgraduate degree in Finance department of an organization for the past six years after completing her postgraduate degree. She was born on 16th August 1986. She has secured 63% marks in the preliminary interview.

33. Anirban Chowdhury was born on 8th March 1986. He has secured 65% marks in B.Sc and 62% marks in postgraduate degree in Finance Management. He has working in the Finance department of a company for the past seven years after completing her post-graduation. He has secured 50% marks in the final interview and 40% marks in the preliminary interview.

34. Among five friends, P, Q, R, S and T, each scored different marks in the examination. P scored more than Q but less than R. S scored more than only T. Who amongst the following scored the second highest marks?
    - (a) P
    - (b) Q
    - (c) R
    - (d) S

**Directions** (Qs. 35-36): *Study the following information to answer the given questions:*

In a certain code, 'she sat on chair' is written as 'ik ma ja de', 'he sat on table' is written as 'de da ik phi', 'chair is on cart' is written as 'ik pa ma ki', and 'he is looking smart' is written as 'jo va ki phi'.

35. Which is the code for 'chair'?
    - (a) ma
    - (b) ik
    - (c) pa
    - (d) ja

36. 'she cart smart' is written as what in the code language?
    - (a) va pa ja
    - (b) pa je ik
    - (c) ja jo pa
    - (d) Either (a) or (c)

37. Select the missing number from the given responses:

| 6 | 5 | 26 |
|---|---|----|
| 4 | 7 | 32 |
| ? | 9 | 44 |

   (a)  8      (b)  31      (c)  32      (d)  36

38. A man climbing up a wall of 24 metres high, climbs 16 m on one day but slipped back by 3m 40cms in the evening. How far had the man reached on that day?

   (a)  12.6 m         (b)  19 m 40 cm

   (c)  12 m 40 cm     (d)  11.4 m

39. A Woman has only 25 p and 50 p coins in her bag. If in all she has 40 coins which total rupees 12.75, then the number of 50 p coins is

   (a)  15         (b)  17

   (c)  11         (d)  13

40. How many triangles are there in the given figure?

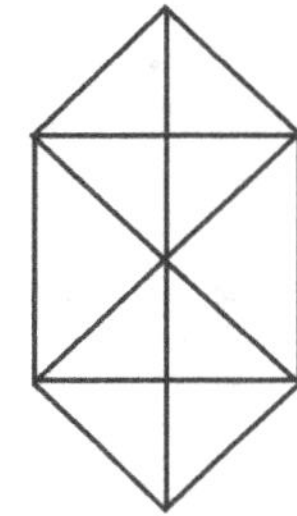

   (a)  20         (b)  22

   (c)  28         (d)  32

**Directions** (Qs. 41-42): *Read the following passages and answer the questions that follow them.*

### PASSAGE-1

Why do people prefer open defecation and not want toilets or, if they have them, only use them sometimes? Recent research has shown two critical elements : ideas of purity and pollution, and not wanting pits or septic tanks to fill because they have to be emptied. These are the issues that nobody wants to talk about, but if we want to eradicate the practice of open defecation, they have to be confronted and dealt properly.

41. Which among the following is the **most crucial message** conveyed by the above passage?

   (a)  The ideas of purity and pollution are so deep-rooted that they cannot be removed from the minds of the people.

   (b)  People have to perceive toilet use and pit-emptying as clean and not polluting.

   (c)  People cannot change their old habits.

   (d)  People have neither civic sense nor sense of privacy.

### PASSAGE-2

The very first lesson that should be taught to us when we are sensible enough to understand it, is that complete freedom from the obligation to work is unnatural, and ought to be illegal, as we can escape our share of the burden of work only by throwing it on someone else's shoulders. Nature ordains that the human race shall perish of famine if it stops working. We cannot escape from this tyranny. The question we have to settle is how much leisure we can afford to allow ourselves.

42. The **main idea** of the passage is that

   (a)  it is essential for human beings to work

   (b)  there should be a balance between work and leisure

   (c)  working is a tyranny which we have to face

   (d)  human's understanding of the nature of work is essential

**Directions** (Qs. 43-47): *Read the following passages and answer the questions that follow them.*

From apparel to aerospace, steel to software, the pace of technological innovation is quickening. No longer can companies afford to miss a generation of technology and expect to remain competitive. Adding to the pressure, innovations are increasingly crossing industry boundaries: a new fibre developed by the textile industry has potential for building materials and medical equipment. Some companies are adept at using a diversity of technologies to create new products that transform markets. But many others art floundering because they rely on a technology strategy that no longer works in such a fast changing environment. The difference between success and failure is not how much a company spends on research and development, but how it approaches it.

There are two possible approaches. Either a company can invest in R & D that replaces an older generation of technology - the "break through" approach - or it can focus on combining existing technologies into hybrid technologies - the "technology fusion" approach. It blends incremental technical improvements from several previously separate fields of technology to create products that revolutionise markets.

In a world where the old maxim "one technology one industry" no longer applies a singular breakthrough strategy is inadequate; companies need to include both the breakthrough and fusion approaches in their technology strategy. Relying on breakthroughs alone fails because it focuses the R & D efforts too narrowly ignoring the possibilities of combining technologies. Yet many Western companies still rely almost exclusively on the breakthrough approach. The reasons are complex : a distrust of outside innovations, a not-invented-here engineering arrogance, an aversion to sharing research results.

43. Which of the following is false, according to the passage?

   (a)  Technological innovation is happening at a fast pace.

   (b)  All technological innovations have applicability in other industries.

   (c)  Companies failing to adopt new technology may fail.

   (d)  Companies which adopt technologies of other industries have an advantage.

   (d)  Technology becomes obsolete in a fast changing environment.

44. Which of the following would correctly reflect the position regarding the two approaches to technology adoption ?
    (a) Both approaches are to be used at the same time
    (b) "Breakthrough" approach is only to be used
    (c) "Technology fusion" approach is only to be used
    (d) "Breakthrough approach" is preferable for many companies

45. Which of the following features of technology has been highlighted most prominently by the author of the passage?
    (a) Its improper utilisation by some companies
    (b) The speed at which innovations are happening
    (c) The expenses involved in developing technology
    (d) The two approaches to adopting technology

46. What does the author want to highlight by using the example "apparel to aerospace" and "steel to software"?
    (a) Many industries are trying to improve technology
    (b) His knowledge about the various industries
    (c) The widespread applicability of technological innovation
    (d) The speed of the technological innovation

47. What, according to the author, is "adding to the pressure" on the companies?
    (a) Applicability of technologies of other industries to them
    (b) Increasing speed of technological innovations
    (c) Work load on their R & D departments
    (d) Finding funds for increased R & D activities

48. A can do a piece of work in 25 days and $B$ in 20 days. They work together for 5 days and then $A$ goes away. In how many days will $B$ finish the remaining work ?
    (a) 17 days         (b) 11 days
    (c) 10 days         (d) 15 days

49. If a man travels at 30 km/h, he reaches his destination late by 10 minutes but if he travels at 42 km/h then he reaches 10 minutes earlier. The distance travelled by him is
    (a) 30 km    (b) 35 km    (c) 45 km    (d) 36 km

50. What will be the acute angle between hands of a clock at 2 : 30?
    (a) 105°     (b) 115°     (c) 95°     (d) 135°

51. The area of a square field is 576 km². How long will it take for a horse to run around at the speed of 12 km/h ?
    (a) 12 h     (b) 10 h     (c) 8 h     (d) 6 h

52. 250 men took a dip in a water tank at a time, which is 80 m × 50 m. What is the rise in the water level if the average displacement of 1 man is 4 m³?
    (a) 22 cm    (b) 25 cm    (c) 18 cm    (d) 30 cm

53. What is the sum of all the two-digit numbers which when divided by 7 gives a remainder of 3?
    (a) 94                (b) 676
    (c) 696             (d) None of these

54. In a certain office, 72% of the workers prefer tea and 44% prefer coffee. If each of them prefers tea or coffee and 40 like both, the total number of workers in the office is :
    (a) 200    (b) 240    (c) 250    (d) 320

55. 4 boys and 2 girls are to be seated in a row in such a way that the two girls are always together. In how many different ways can they be seated?
    (a) 1200     (b) 7200     (c) 148     (d) 240

56. In a company, each employee gives a gift to every other employee. If the number of gifts is 61, then the number of employees in the company is :
    (a) 11       (b) 13       (c) 12       (d) 8

57. A pair of dice is thrown thrice. The probability of throwing doublets at least once is
    (a) $\dfrac{1}{36}$                  (b) $\dfrac{25}{216}$
    (c) $\dfrac{125}{216}$             (d) None of these

**Directions** (Qs. 58-61) : *Study the following pie-chart and table carefully and answer the questions given below :*

Percentage wise distribution of the number of mobile phones sold by a shopkeeper during six months

**Total number of mobile phones sold = 45,000**

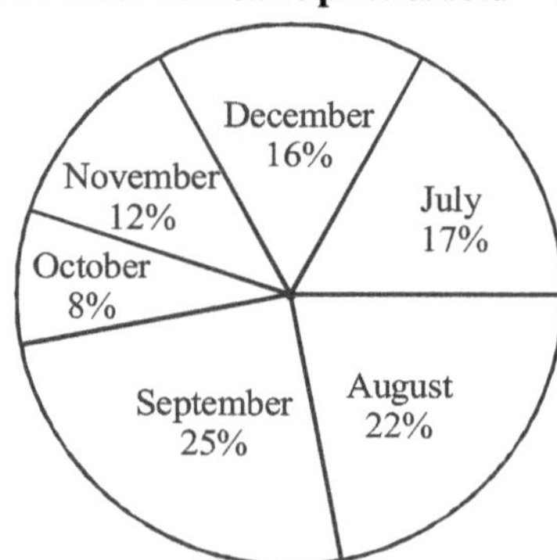


The respective ratio between the number of mobile phones sold of company A and company B during six months

| Month | Ratio |
|---|---|
| July | 8:7 |
| August | 4:5 |
| September | 3:2 |
| October | 7:5 |
| November | 7:8 |
| December | 7:9 |

58. What is the respective ratio between the number of mobile phones sold of company B during July and those sold during December of the same company?
    (a) 119:145                (b) 116:135
    (c) 119:135                (d) 119:130

59. If 35% of the mobile phones sold by company A during November were sold at a discount, how many mobile phones of company A during that month were sold without a discount?
    (a) 882          (b) 1635       (c) 1638       (d) 885

60. If the shopkeeper earned a profit of ₹433/- on each mobile phone sold of company B during October, what was his total profit earned on the mobile phones of that company during the same month?

    (a) ₹6,49,900/-          (b) ₹6,45,900/-
    (c) ₹6,49,400/-          (d) ₹6,49,500/-

61. The number of mobile phones sold of company A during July is approximately what percent of the number of mobile phones sold of company A during December ?

    (a) 110      (b) 140      (c) 150      (d) 130

62. After distributing the sweets equally among 25 children, 8 sweets remain. Had the number of children been 28, 22 sweets would have been left after equally distributing. What was the total number of sweets ?

    (a)  328                 (b)  348
    (c)  358                 (d)  Data inadequate

63. If $0 < x < 5$ and $1 < y < 2$, then which of the following is true?

    (a)  $x + y < 0$          (b)  $-3 < 2x - 3y < 4$
    (c)  $-6 < 2x - 3y < 7$   (d)  $-3 < 3x - y < 2$

64. A library has an average of 510 visitors of Sunday and 240 on other days. The average number of visitors per day in a month of 30 days beginning with a Sunday is

    (a)  250                 (b)  276
    (c)  280                 (d)  285

65. Samant bought a microwave oven and paid 10% less than the original price. He sold it with 30% profit on the price he had paid. What percentage of profit did Samant earn on the original price?

    (a)  17%                 (b)  20%
    (c)  27%                 (d)  32%

**Directions** (Qs. 66 - 67) : *In the questions below a statement is given followed by two conclusions I & II. Take the statement to be true and then decide which of the conclusions logically follows. Mark your answer as*

    (a)  if the conclusion I follows,
    (b)  if the conclusion II follows,
    (c)  if either conclusion I or II is follow,
    (d)  if neither conclusion I nor II follows.

66. **Statements :**   A study of planning commission reveals boom in revenues. However, this has been of little avail owing to soaring expenditure. In the event, there has been a high dose of deficit financing, leading to marked rise in prices. Large financial outlays year after year had little impact on the standard of living.

    **Conclusions :**   I.  A boom in revenues leads to soar in prices.

    II. Large financial outlays should be avoided.

67. **Statements :**   The average number of students per teacher is 50 in the urban area whereas it is 60 in rural areas. The national average is 55.

    **Conclusions :**   I.  The student-teacher ratio in the rural areas is higher than in the urban areas.

    II. More students study with the same teacher in the rural areas as compared to those in the urban areas.

**Directions** (Qs. 68-71) : *In these questions, four alternative summaries are given below each text. Choose the option that captures essence of the text..*

68. Local communities have often come in conflict with agents trying to exploit resources, at a faster pace for an expanding commercial-industrial economy. More often than not, such agents of resource- intensification are given preferential treatment by the state, through the grant of generous long leases over mineral of fish stocks, for example, of the provision of raw material at an enormously subsidized price, With the injustice so compounded, local communities at the receiving end of this process, have no resource except direct action, resisting both' the state and outside exploiters through a variety of protest techniques. These struggles might perhaps be seen as a manifestation of a new kind of class conflict.

    (a)  Preferential treatment given by the state to agents of resource-intensification for an expanding commercial-industrial economy exacerbates injustice to local communities and leads to direct protests from them, resulting in a new type of class conflict.

    (b)  The grant of long leases to agents of resource intensification for an expanding commercial industrial economy leads to direct protests from the local community, which sees it as unfair.

    (c)  A new kind of class conflict arises from preferential treatment given to agents of resource intensification by the state , which the local community sees as unfair.

    (d)  Local communities have no option but to protest against agents of resource- intensification and create a new type of class conflict when they are given raw material at subsidized prices for an expanding commercial-industrial economy.

69. The human race is spread all over the world, from the polar regions to the tropics. The people of whom it is made up eat different kinds of food, partly according to the climate in which they live, and partly according to the kind of food which their country produces. In hot climates, meat and fat are not much needed; but in the Arctic regions they seem to be very necessary for keeping up the heat of the body. Thus, in India, people live chiefly on different kinds of grains, eggs, milk, or sometimes fish and meat. In Europe, people eat more meat and less grain. In the Arctic region; where no grains and fruits are produced, the Eskimo and other races live almost entirely on meat and fish.

(a) In hot countries, people eat mainly grains while in the Arctic, they eat meat and fish because they cannot grow grains.

(b) Hot climates require people to eat grains while cold regions require people to eat meat and fish.

(c) Food eaten by people in different regions of the world depends on the climate and produce of the region, and varies from meat and fish in the Arctic to predominantly grains in the tropics.

(d) While people in Arctic regions like meat and fish and those in hot regions like Indian prefer mainly grains, they have to change what they eat depending on the local climate and the local produce.

70. You seemed at first to take no notice of your school fellows, or rather to set yourself against them because they were strangers to you, they knew as little of you as you did of them; this would have been the reason for their keeping aloof from you as well, which you would have felt as a hardship. Learn never to conceive a prejudice against others because you know nothing of them. It is bad reasoning, and makes enemies of half the world. Do not think ill of them till they behave ill to you; and then strive to avoid the faults which you see in them. This will disarm their hostility sooner than pique of resentment or complaint.

(a) You encountered hardship amongst your school-fellows because you did not know them well. You should learn to not make enemies because of your prejudices irrespective of their behaviour towards you.

(b) The discomfort you felt with your school-fellows was because both sides knew little of each other. Avoid prejudice bad behaviour from others, and then win them over by shunning the faults you have observed.

(c) The discomfort you felt with your school-fellows was because both sides knew little of each other. You should not complain unless you find others prejudiced against you and have attempted to carefully analyse the faults you have observed in them.

(d) You encountered hardship amongst your school- fellow because you did not know them well. You should learn to not make enemies because of your prejudices unless they behave badly with you.

71. Although, almost all climate scientists agree that the Earth is gradually warming, they have long been of two minds about the process of rapid climate shifts within larger periods of change. Some have speculated that the process works like a giant oven or freezer, warming or cooling the whole planet at the same time. Others think that shifts occur on opposing schedules in the Northern and Southern Hemispheres, like exaggerated seasons. Recent research in Germany examining climate patterns in the Southern Hemisphere at the end of the last Ice Age strengthens the idea that warming and cooling occurs at alternate times in the two hemispheres. A more definitive answer to this debate will allow scientists to better predict when and how quickly the next climate shift will happen.

(a) Research in Germany will help scientists find a definitive answer about warming and cooling of the Earth and predict climate shifts in the future in a better manner.

(b) Scientists have been unsure whether rapid shifts in the Earth's climate happen all at once or on opposing schedules in different hemispheres; finding a definitive answer will help them better predict climate shift in future.

(c) Scientists have been unsure whether rapid shifts in the Earth's climate happen all at once or on opposing schedules in different hemispheres; research will help find a definitive answer and better predict climate shift in future.

(d) More research rather than debates on warming or cooling of the Earth and exaggerated seasons in its hemispheres, will help scientists in Germany predict climate changes better in future.

**Directions** (Qs. 72-77) : *Read the following passages and answer the questions given below.*

### PASSAGE-1

Whenever a major airplane accident occurs, there is a dramatic increase in the number of airplane mishaps reported in the media, a phenomenon that may last for as long as a few months after the accident. Airline officials assert that the publicity given the gruesomeness of major airplane accidents focuses media attention on the airline industry, and the increase in the number of reported accidents is caused by an increase in the number of news sources covering airline accidents, not by an increase in the number of accidents.

72. Which of the following if true, would seriously weaken the assertions of the airline officials?

(a) Airline accidents tend to occur far more often during certain peak travel months

(b) The publicity surrounding airline accidents is largely limited to the country in which the crash occurred

(c) News organisations do not have any guidelines to help them decide how severe an accident is

(d) Airplane accidents receive coverage by news sources only when the news sources find it advantageous to do so

### PASSAGE-2

The cost of housing in many urban parts of India has become so excessive that many young couples, with above–average salaries, can only afford small apartments. EMI and rent commitments are so huge that they cannot consider the possibility of starting a family since a new baby would probably mean either the mother or father giving up a well–paid position – something they can ill afford. The lack of or great cost of child-care facilities further precludes the return of both parents to work.

73. Which of the following adjustments could practically be made to the situation described above which would allow young couples to improve their housing prospects?
    (a) Encourage couples to have one child only.
    (b) Encourage couples to remain childless.
    (c) Encourage young couples to move to cheaper areas for living.
    (d) None of these is likely to have an impact on the current situation.

### PASSAGE-3

A famous singer recently won a lawsuit against an advertising firm for using another singer in a commercial to evoke the famous singer's well known rendition of a certain song. As a result of the lawsuit, advertising firms will stop using imitators in commercials. Therefore, advertising costs will rise, since famous singers' services cost more than those of their imitators.

74. The conclusion above is based on which of the following assumptions?
    (a) Commercials using famous singers are usually more effective than commercials using imitators of famous singers
    (b) Most people are unable to distinguish a famous singer's rendition of a song from a good imitator's rendition of the same song
    (c) The original versions of some well-known songs are unavailable for use in commercials
    (d) The advertising industry will use well-known renditions of songs in commercials

### PASSAGE-4

Some observers have taken the position that the recently elected judge is biased against men in divorce cases that involve child custody. But the statistics reveal that in 40% of such cases, the recently elected judge awards custody to the fathers. Most other judges award custody to fathers in only 20%–30% of their cases. This record demonstrates that the recently elected judge has not discriminated against men in cases of child custody.

75. The argument above is flawed in that if it ignores the possibility that
    (a) A large number of the recently elected judge's cases involve child custody disputes.
    (b) The recently elected judge is prejudiced against men in divorce cases that do not involve child custody issues.
    (c) The majority of the child custody cases that have reached the recently elected judge's court have been appealed from a lower court.
    (d) The evidence shows that men should have won custody in more than 40% of the recently elected judge's cases involving divorcing fathers.

### PASSAGE-5

Three years after the Bhakra Nangal Dam was built, none of the six fish species native to the area was still reproducing adequately in the river below the dam. Because the dam reduced the average temperature range of the water from approximately 40° to approximately 10°, biologists have hypothesized that sharp increases in water temperature must be involved in signaling the affected species to begin their reproduction activities.

76. Which of the following statements, if true, would most strengthen the scientists' hypothesis?
    (a) The native fish species were still able to reproduce in nearby streams where the annual temperature range remains approximately 40°.
    (b) Before the dam was built, the river annually overflowed its banks, creating temporary backwaters that were used as breeding areas for the local fish population.
    (c) The lowest temperature ever recorded in the river prior to dam construction was 30°; whereas the lowest recorded river temperature after construction was completed has been 40°.
    (d) Non-native fish species, introduced after the dam was completed, have begun competing with the native species for food.

### PASSAGE-6

In the sport of maxiball, in which the objective is to score more goals than the opposing team, each team member faces off against one member of the other team. The coach for the Panthers predicts victory over the Cougars in an upcoming match between these two maxiball teams. The chief reason for the coach's prediction is that the Cougars' best defensive player will not be defending against Fonsica, who is the Panthers' highest scoring player.

77. Which of the following, if true, would cast most doubt on the accuracy of the prediction made by the Panthers' coach above?
    (a) The Panthers have defeated fewer opponents than the Cougars this year.
    (b) The Cougars' highest scoring player will not be defending against Fonsica.
    (c) The Panthers' best defensive player will not be defending against the Cougars' highest scoring player.
    (d) Fonsica is not the Panthers' best defensive player.

**Directions** *(Qs. 78-80 ) : Read the following passage and answer the questions that follow them.*

The idea of dead scientists engaging in an experiment in eugenics is incredible enough. Yet the most striking feature in this episode is the power that is ascribed to science itself. While spiritualism evolved into a popular religion, complete with a heavenly "Summerland" where the dead lived free from care and sorrow, the intellectual elite of psychical researchers thought of their quest as a rigorously scientific inquiry. But if these Victorian seekers turned to science, it was to look for an exit from the world that science had revealed. Darwinism had disclosed a purposeless universe without human meaning; but purpose and meaning could be restored, if only science could show that the human mind carried on evolving after the death of the body. All of these seekers had abandoned any belief in traditional religion. Still, the human need for a meaning in life that religion once satisfied could not be denied, and fuelled the faith that scientific investigation would show that the human story continues after death. In effect, science was used against science, and became a channel for belief in magic.

Much of what the psychical researchers viewed as science we would now call pseudo-science. But the boundaries of scientific knowledge are smudged and shifting, and seem clear only in hindsight. There is no pristine science untouched by the vagaries of faith. The psychical researchers used science not only to deal with private anguish but also to bolster their weakening belief in progress. Especially after the catastrophe of the First World War, the gradual improvement that most people expected would continue indefinitely appeared to be faltering. If the scripts were to be believed, however, there was no cause for anxiety or despair. The world might be sliding into anarchy, but progress continued on the other side. Many of the psychical researchers believed they were doing no more than showing that evolution continues in a post-mortem world. Like many others, then and now, they confused two wholly different things. Progress assumes some goal or direction. But evolution has neither of these attributes, and if natural selection continued in another world it would feature the same random death and wasted lives we find here below.

Darwinism is impossible to reconcile with the notion that humans have any special exemption from mortality. In Darwin's scheme of things species are not fixed or everlasting. How then could only humans go on to a life beyond the grave? Surely, in terms of the prospect of immortality, all sentient beings stand or fall together. Then again, how could anyone imagine all the legions of the dead – not only the human generations that have come and gone but the countless animal species that are now extinct – living on in the ether, forever?

Science could not give these seekers what they were looking for. Yet at the same time that sections of the English elite were looking for a scientific version of immortality, a similar quest was under way in Russia among the "God-builders" – a section of the Bolshevik intelligentsia that believed science could someday, perhaps quite soon, be used to defeat death.

78. How was "science used against science" according to the author?

(a) People sought science to seek an exit from the world created by science.

(b) Science was used to spread the belief of life after death or eternal life.

(c) Science was used to destroy the very essence of science.

(d) Scientists used the scientific techniques to spread unscientific ideas.

79. What is the confusion of past and present day psychical researchers?

(a) They confuse progress with immortality.

(b) They confuse evolution with progress.

(c) They think progress in evolution leads to development.

(d) They confuse evolution with progress in life in another world.

80. One is constantly hearing of passwords being lacked on the internet. Suppose that you are the manager of a famous bank. And your site has been hacked. What immediate steps would you take?

(a) Close the site down for a few days

(b) Change the passwords

(c) Install more efficient security software

(d) All of the above

# SOLUTIONS

1. (c) The series is $\times 3 - 13$

2. (d) $\begin{matrix} \bar{N} - \bar{L} \\ | \\ M^{+} \end{matrix}$ Hence, N is the aunt of M.

3. (d) The movements of Maya from T to R are as shown in Figure

Distance between T and R

$= TR = TU + UR$

$= TU + PW + QV$

$= (4 + 3 + 1)\text{ft} = 8 \text{ ft.}$

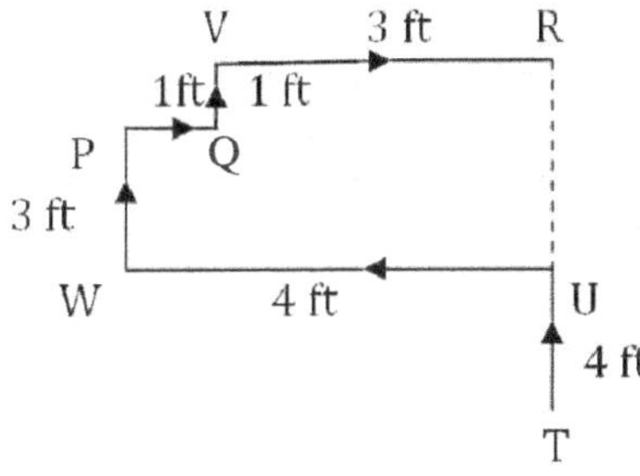


4. (c) From figure i, ii and iv we conclude that 6, 4, 3 and 1 lie adjacent to 2. Hence, 5 be opposite of 2.

5. (a) From the alternatives it is very easy to recognize option (a) as it satisfies all the conditions of a dice formation.

6. (a) In each step, the upper element is lost, the middle element reduces in size and becomes the upper element, the lower element enlarges and become the middle element and every time a new element appears at the bottom of the figure.

7. (d)

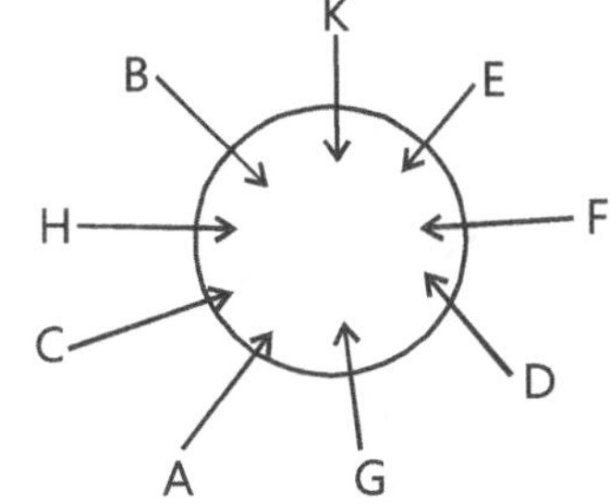


8. (b) Both the options i and ii are totally opposite to what is given in the passage. Hence b is the correct answer.

9. (c) As mentioned in the passage, ignorance, apathy and bloody mindedness on the part of local communities were the obstructions for the reformers.

10. (d) None of the above three options match the content of the passage. The last sentence indicates that d is the appropriate answer.

11. (c) The first sentence of the passage indicates that despite disparities and differences, the broader aims and aspirations of the two are similar. Also, the concluding sentence mentions that it makes little sense to study the two differently.

12. (a) The synonym of 'inimical' is unfavourable, opposite or hostile.

13. (d) The biggest problem in our country is the disparity in the financial status of the citizens. For instance, all the wealth is mostly accumulated by the elite class and the upper - middle class. However, the poor continues to be deprived and exploited. The banking sector should look forward to promote financial inclusion, for equal distribution of financial services.

14. (d)    15. (b)

16. (c) This is an example of data **skewed to the right.** In this distribution we know that the mode is 58, because 58 is the value under the tallest column. But 58 is also the smallest value in this distribution. This indicates that both the mean an median should be greater than 58 .

Hence the choice (c) is correct.

17. (b) Yield rate is not zero at $B$ and $C$. Despite of no fertilisers input the yield is 20. So, both I and II statements are wrong while III and IV are correct because yield is minimum at $D$ and the yield is neither minimum nor maximum at point $C$.

18. (c) $55^3 + 17^3 - 72^3 = (55)^3 + (17)^3 - (55 + 17)^3$

$= 55^3 + 17^3 - [(55)^3 + (17)^3 + 3 \times 55 \times 17 \times 72]$

$= -3 \times 55 \times 17 \times 72$

19. (a) Since the given number is divisible by 5, so 0 or 5 must come in place of \$. But, a number ending with 5 is never divisible by 8. So, 0 will replace \$.

Now, the number formed by the last three digits is 4*0, which becomes divisible by 8, if * is replaced by 4. Hence, digits in place of * and \$ are 4 and 0 respectively.

20. (b) Let the common remainder be $x$. Then numbers $(34041 - x)$ and $(32506 - x)$ would be completely divisible by $n$.

Hence the difference of the numbers $(34041 - x)$ and $(32506 - x)$ will also be divisible by $n$ or $(34041 - x - 32506 + x) = 1535$ will also be divisible by $n$.

Now, using options we find that 1535 is divisible by 307.

21. (b) 30% of the residents are children.

$\therefore$ 30% of the total residents $= 24$

$\therefore$ Total number of residents in the society

$= \dfrac{24}{30} \times 100 = 80$

**22.** (d) Let the sum be ₹ $x$.

$$\therefore \frac{x \times 11 \times 5}{100} - \frac{x \times 8 \times 6}{100} = 1008$$

$$\Rightarrow \frac{7x}{100} = 1008 \Rightarrow x = ₹14400$$

**23.** (a) If $A$'s share is 1, $B$'s share $= \dfrac{5}{9} \times 1 = \dfrac{5}{9}$

$C$'s share $= \dfrac{7}{10} \times \dfrac{5}{9} = \dfrac{7}{18}$;

$D$'s share $= \dfrac{1}{3}\left(\dfrac{5}{9} + \dfrac{7}{18}\right) = \dfrac{17}{54}$

$$\therefore A : B : C : D = 1 : \frac{5}{9} : \frac{7}{18} : \frac{17}{54}$$

$$= 54 : 30 : 21 : 17.$$

$$\therefore A\text{'s share} = \frac{54}{122} \times 1220 = ₹540.$$

**24.** (a) Selling price $= ₹\,50$
Therefore, the cost price
$= ₹\,40$, which is the average price.
It means the wine, worth ₹ 60 becomes worth ₹ 40 when the water was mixed in it. So we can conclude that in the mixture of ₹ 60, there is wine worth ₹ 40 and the rest is water. Therefore, the ratio of water and wine is 20 : 40 i.e., 1 : 2 :

**Alternatively :**

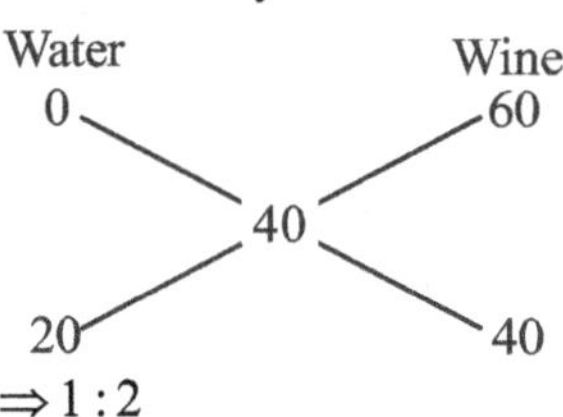


$$\Rightarrow 1 : 2$$

**Solution for 25–27:**

| 7 | G |
|---|---|
| 6 | C |
| 5 | D |
| 4 | A |
| 3 | F |
| 2 | E |
| 1 | B |

**25.** (d) is the correct answer

**26.** (c) is the correct answer

**27.** (d) is the correct answer; All others live on odd numbered floors

**Solution for 28–29 :**

| Day | Play |
|---|---|
| Monday | No play |
| Tuesday | A |
| Wednesday | D |
| Thursday | C |
| Friday | B |
| Saturday | E |

**28.** (b) is the correct answer.

**29.** (a) is the correct answer.

**30.** (a) Assumption I is implicit in "at their own cost". Assumption II is contrary to what the citizens may have assumed.

**31.** (c) 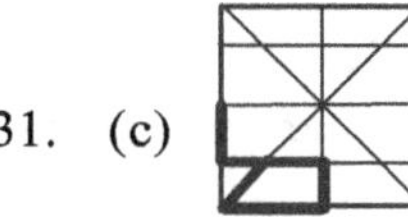

**Solution for 32-33:**

| Candidate | I | II | III | IV/i | V | VI/(ii) |
|---|---|---|---|---|---|---|
| Neelam | ✓ | ✓ | ✓ | ✓ | ✓ | (✓) |
| Anirban | ✓ | ✓ | ✓ | ✓ | x | ✓ |

**32.** (c) **33.** (b)

**34.** (a) $R > P > Q > S > T$
P scored the second highest marks.

**35.** (a) 'on' is 'ik', so from 1st and 3rd code, chair - ma

**36.** (d) 'she' is 'ja' as from 1st code. 'cart' is 'pa'. 'smart' only present in last and also 'looking' only in last, so for smart - 'jo' or 'va'.

**37.** (a)

| 6 | 5 | 26 |
|---|---|---|
| 4 | 7 | 32 |
| ? | 9 | 44 |

$5 \times 4 + 6 = 26$
$7 \times 4 + 4 = 32$
$9 \times 4 + x = 44$
$x = 44 - 36$
$x = \boxed{8}$

**38.** (a) 

So net height climbed in one day
$= 16 - 3.40$
$= 12.6$ m

**39.** (c) Let woman has number of 25 p coins $= x$
Number of 50 p coins $= y$

Then, value of 25 p coins $= ₹\dfrac{x}{4}$

value of 50 p coins $= ₹\dfrac{y}{2}$

Now, $\dfrac{x}{4} + \dfrac{y}{2} = 12.75$ ...(1)

and $x + y = 40$ ...(2)

On solving question. (1) and (2), $y = 11$
Hence, the number of 50 p coins is 11.

40. (b) 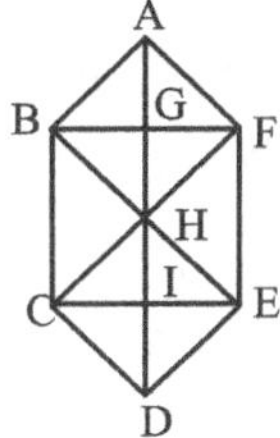

The Triangles are :

$\triangle ABG, \triangle AGF, \triangle ABF, \triangle ABH, \triangle AFH, \triangle BGH, \triangle BFH, \triangle BFE,$
$\triangle BFC, \triangle BHC, \triangle BEC, \triangle CHI, \triangle CHE, \triangle CFE, \triangle CID, \triangle CED, \triangle DIE,$
$\triangle DHE, \triangle FHE, \triangle EIH, \triangle FGH$ and $\triangle DHC = 22$ triangles.

41. (d) The third sentence of the passage confirms statements II and III are correct. Statement I is not mentioned in the passage.

42. (d) None of the options is mentioned or implied in the passage.

43. (b) Refer to the first sentence of para 3... In a world —— single breakthrough strategy is in adequate.

44. (a) Refer to para 2 which clearly says that either of the two approaches can be used.

45. (b) The very first line of the passage emphasises that the pace of technological innovation forces one to stay on one's toes, and this sets the tone of the whole passage.

46. (e) The widespread applicability of technological innovations ranging from the simplest to the most hi-tech and the earliest to the latest is highlighted by these examples.

47. (a) The 3rd sentence of para 1 says that innovations causing industry boundaries are adding to the pressure.

48. (b) $(A + B)$'s 5 days' work

$$= 5\left(\frac{1}{25} + \frac{1}{20}\right) = \frac{45}{100} = \frac{9}{20}$$

Remaining work $= \left(1 - \frac{9}{20}\right) = \frac{11}{20}$

$\frac{11}{20}$ of the work would be finished by $B$ in

$$\frac{\frac{11}{20}}{\frac{1}{20}} = 11 \text{ days.}$$

49. (b) Let the distance travelled be $x$ km.
Then, the correct time at a speed of 30 km/h

$$= \frac{x}{30} - \frac{10}{60}$$ and the correct time at a speed of 42 km/h =

$$\frac{x}{42} + \frac{10}{60}$$

Now, $\dfrac{x}{30} - \dfrac{10}{60} = \dfrac{x}{42} + \dfrac{10}{60}$

or $\dfrac{x}{30} - \dfrac{x}{42} = \dfrac{2}{6}$ or $\dfrac{12x}{1260} = \dfrac{2}{6}$ or $x = 35$ km

50. (a) At 2'O Clock, Minute Hand will be $10 \times 6 = 60°$ behind the Hour Hand.

In 30 minutes, Minute Hand will gain $\left(5\dfrac{1}{2}\right)^{\circ} \times 30$

$= 150 + 15 = 165°$

∴ Angle between Hour Hand and Minute Hand $= 165 - 60 = 105°$

51. (c) Area of field $= 576 \text{ km}^2$. Then,

each side of field $= \sqrt{576} = 24$ km

Distance covered by the horse
$=$ Perimeter of square field $= 24 \times 4 = 96$ km

∴ Time taken by horse $= \dfrac{\text{distance}}{\text{speed}} = \dfrac{96}{12} = 8$ h

52. (b) Total volume of water displaced by 250 men
$= 250 \times 4 = 1000 \text{ m}^3$

∴ Rise in water level (h) $= \dfrac{\text{Volume}}{\text{Base area}}$

$= \dfrac{1000}{80 \times 50} = 25$ cm

53. (b) This series is like $\rightarrow 10, 17, 24, .....94.$
Here $n = 13, d = 7$ and $a = 10$
Using the formula for the sum

$$S_n = \frac{n}{2}\Big[2a + (n-1\ d)\Big], \text{sum} = 676$$

**Alternatively,** Using the average method,
Average $= (1\text{st number} + \text{last number})/2$

$= \dfrac{10 + 94}{2} = 52$

So, the sum $=$ average $\times$ number of numbers
$= 52 \times 13 = 676$

54. (c) Let total number be $x$. Then

$$n(A) = \frac{72}{100}x = \frac{18x}{25}, \quad n(B) = \frac{44}{100}x = \frac{11x}{25}$$

and $n(A \cap B) = 40$

$n(A \cap B) = n(A) + n(B) - n(A \cup B)$

$\Rightarrow x = \dfrac{18x}{25} + \dfrac{11x}{25} - 40 \Rightarrow x = 250$

55. (d) Assume the 2 given students to be together (i.e. one). Now these are five students.
Possible ways of arranging them are $= 5! = 120$
Now they (two girls) can arrange themselves in 2! ways.
Hence total ways $= 120 \times 2 = 240$

**56.** **(c)** Let the total number of employees in the company be $n$.
Total number of gifts

$$= {}^nC_2 = \frac{n(n-1)}{2} = 66 \Rightarrow n^2 - n - 132 = 0$$

or $(n+11)(n-12) = 0$ or $n = 12$
[$-11$ is rejected]

**57.** **(d)** Doublets occur when the numbers thrown are $(1, 1), (2, 2), \ldots\ldots, (6, 6)$. Therefore the probability of a doublet

occurring in single throw $= \dfrac{6}{36} = \dfrac{1}{6}$.

The probability of a doublet not occurring at all in three

throws $= \left(\dfrac{5}{6}\right)^3 = \dfrac{125}{216}$.

Required probability $= 1 - \dfrac{125}{216} = \dfrac{91}{216}$.

**Solutions (58-61):**

| | Total number of Mobiles Sold | Total Number of Mobiles Sold of Company A | Total Number of Mobiles Sold of Company B |
|---|---|---|---|
| July | 7650 | 4080 | 3570 |
| August | 9900 | 4400 | 5500 |
| September | 11250 | 6750 | 4500 |
| October | 3600 | 2100 | 1500 |
| November | 5400 | 2520 | 2880 |
| December | 7200 | 3150 | 4050 |

**58.** **(c)** Number of mobiles sold of company B in July $= 3570$
Number of mobiles sold of company B in December $= 4050$
Required Ratio $= 3570 : 4050 = 119 : 135$

**59.** **(c)** Total mobiles sold by company A during November $= 2520$
Total mobiles sold by this company at discount $= 35\%$ of $2520 = 882$
Total mobiles sold by company A without discount $= 2520 - 882 = 1638$

**60.** **(d)** Mobile phones sold of company B during October $= 1500$
Total profit earned on the mobile phones
$= ₹(433 \times 1500) = ₹ 6,49,500$

**61.** **(d)** Number of mobile phones sold of company
A during July $= 4080$
Number of mobile phones sold by company A during December $= 3150$
Required percentage

$$= \frac{4080}{3150} \times 100 = 129.5 \approx 130\%$$

**62.** **(c)** Let the total number of sweets be $(25x + 8)$.
Then, $(25x + 8) - 22$ is divisible by 28
$\Leftrightarrow$ $(25x - 14)$ is divisible by $28 \Leftrightarrow 28x - (3x + 14)$ is divisible by 28
$\Leftrightarrow$ $(3x + 14)$ is divisible by $28 \Leftrightarrow x = 14$.
$\therefore$ Total number of sweets $= (25 \times 14 + 8) = 358$.

**63.** **(c)** $0 < x < 5$ ...(1)
$0 < 2x < 10$ ...(2) (multiply (1) by 2)
$1 < y < 2$ ...(3)
$-6 < -3y < -3$ ...(4) (multiply (3) by $-3$)
adding (4) and (2)
$0 - 6 < 2x - 3y < 10 - 3$ *i.e.*, $-6 < 2x - 3y < 7$.

**64.** **(d)** Since the month begins with Sunday, so there will be five Sundays in the month

$\therefore$ Required average $= \left(\dfrac{510 \times 5 + 240 \times 25}{30}\right)$

$$= \frac{8550}{30} = 285$$

**65.** **(a)** Let original price $= ₹ 100$.

Then C.P. $= ₹ 90$, S.P. $= 130\%$ of $₹ 90 = ₹\left(\dfrac{130}{100} \times 90\right)$

$= ₹ 117$.

$\therefore$ Required percentage $= (117 - 100)\% = 17\%$.

**66.** **(d)** Both of the conclusion are invalid.

**67.** **(b)** Unless absolute figures are given, no conclusion of the type I can be made. Since average no. of students per teacher (60) in rural areas is higher than the average no. of students per teacher (50) in urban areas, we can conclude that more students study with the same teacher in the rural areas as compared to those in the urban areas.

**68.** **(c)** (c) is the most appropriate option. Option (a) doesn't talk about the expanding commercial-industrial economy. (b) does not explain the effect of the struggles i.e. 'a new conflict', (d) is not correct as it talks specifically only of raw materials for expanding economy. Further it says local communities are creating new type of conflicts, which is untrue.

**69.** **(a)** (a) is clearly the correct option. (b), (c) and (d) are only inferences. (a) covers the complete scope of the passage. It offers the explanation of the passage while others merely offer citations.

**70.** **(b)** It is the correct choice. It best summarises the points made in the passage and the advice given. The other options state one or the other thing incorrectly. In (a) the second statement is clearly wrong. In (c) & (d) statement 1 covers only one aspect of the passage. In second statement, 'learn to not make enemies' is not talked about in the passage.

71. (b) Option (b) is the answer because it talks about scientists being unsure about rapid shifts in earth's climate and how finding a definitive answer will help them to predict the future climatic changes. Option (a) cannot be the answer as it talks about research in general and the paragraph gives more emphasis on finding a "definitive answer" in terms of climate change. Option (c) is not considered as it gives emphasis only on research done in Germany. Option (d) is also ruled out because it specifically gives more importance to scientists of Germany.

72. (a) The airline officials asserts that the increase of the number of reported accidents is caused by an increase in the number of new sources covering airline accidents and not by an increase number of accidents. The above assertion weakens if (a) is true. There might be a situation when in some peak travel months lot of accidents have occured and the media has reported the same because of which the number of reported accidents have increased.

73. (d) None of the options (a), (b) and (c) can improve the housing prospects of young couples. (a) is not correct as even bearing one child could lead the mother or father giving up her/his job. Further it might be difficult to get back the similar job. (b) is not correct as it offers no solution but puts an end to their family plans. (c) is not correct as shifting to cheaper areas for living will lead to poor standard of living which they would not like to maintain.

74. (b) A lot of advertisement firms use imitators in commercials to evoke some famous singer's renditions of certain songs. The firms do so because they believe that people are unable to distinguish a famous singer's rendition of a song from a good imitator's rendition of the same song.

75. (d) The correct answer (d), points out the flaw in the argument. Specifically, it points out that the author of the argument was comparing the recently elected judge to other judges, not to the evidence presented in the recently elected judge's cases. In other words, the author of the argument made an unwarranted assumption that the recently elected judge did not rule against many men in custody battles where the evidence clearly favoured the men. As with strengthening and weakening questions, the correct answer in flaw questions often involves unwarranted assumptions.

76. (a) (a) most strengthens the conclusion that the scientists reached. It does so by showing that there is a control group. In other words, a similar population, not subjected to the same change as the population near the dam, did not experience the same type of result. Here the basic assumption about the conclusion that scientists reached is that 'because of the reduction of average temperature range of the water, the reproduction of the native fish species has reduced drastically'. Option (a) clearly strengthens the assumption.

77. (c) If (c) is true, then the Cougars are likely to score more goals than if (c) is not true. The more goals the Cougars score the less likely the coach's prediction will come true. (a) tends to weaken the argument. However, we are not informed whether the Panthers and Cougars have played the same teams or the same number of teams this year. Without this additional information, the effect of (a) on the coach's argument is dubious. Moreover, (a) does not address the coach's *chief reason* for his prediction. (b) fails to provide sufficient information to assess its effect on the coach's argument. We must also be informed how Fonsica's effectiveness as a defender.

(d) fails to provide sufficient information to assess its effect on the coach's argument. (d) would weaken the argument if Fonsica will be defending against the Cougars' highest scoring player. However, we are not informed whether this is the case.

78. (b) The author states that the most striking feature of this discussion was the power ascribed to science. Science and Darwin's theory of evolution had revealed a world that looked meaningless and in order to satisfy the human need of 'meaning in life', the researchers were now trying to use science to confirm the existence of life after death. The author says that science became a channel for belief in magic (life after death) and this is how science was used against science. This means that science was used to propagate the believe in life after death. Hence correct option is (b).

79. (b) Refer to last three sentences of para 2.

80. (d) All of the above

# MOCK TEST - 7

**Max. Marks : 200**                                      **Time : 2 hrs.**

1. If $653xy$ is divisible by 80 then the value of $x + y$ is
   (a) 2    (b) 3    (c) 4    (d) 6

2. A number N is divisible by 3 and 4 but not by 9 then which one of the following cannot be an integer?
   (a) N/6    (b) N/42    (c) N/18    (d) N/21

3. A hall is 13 metres 53 cm long and 8 metres 61 cm broad is to be paved with minimum number of square tiles. The number of tiles required is:
   (a) 123    (b) 77    (c) 99    (d) 57

4. The sum of third, fourth and fifth part of a number exceeds half of the number by 34. Find the number.
   (a) 60    (b) 120
   (c) 30    (d) None of these

5. A's income is 60% of B's income, and A's expenditure is 70% of B's expenditure. If A's income is 75% of B's expenditure, find the ratio of A's saving to B's saving.
   (a) 5 : 1    (b) 1 : 5    (c) 3.5 : 1    (d) 2 : 7

6. A sum of money invested at simple interest triples itself in 8 years. How many times will it become in 20 years time?
   (a) 8 times    (b) 7 times    (c) 6 times    (d) 9 times

7. A certain sum of money was divided among $A$, $B$ and $C$ in a certain way. $C$ got half as much as $A$ and $B$ together got. $A$ got one third of what $B$ and $C$ together got. What is the ratio of $A$'s share to that of $C$'s share?
   (a) 1 : 4    (b) 3 : 4    (c) 4 : 1    (d) 3 : 5

8. A milkman sells the milk at the cost price but he mixes the water (freely available) in it and thus he gains 9.09%. The quantity of water in the mixture of 1 litres is :
   (a) 83.33 mL    (b) 90.90 mL
   (c) 99.09 mL    (d) Can't be determined

9. A man can do a piece of work in 10 days but with the assistance of his son, the work is done in 8 days. In how many days, his son alone can do the same piece of work?
   (a) 15 days    (b) 22 days
   (c) 30 days    (d) 40 days

10. A train 300 m long is running at a speed of 90 km/hr. How many seconds will it take to cross a 200 m long train running in the opposite direction at a speed of 60 km/hr?
    (a) $7\dfrac{1}{5}$    (b) 60    (c) 12    (d) 20

11. A clock gains 15 minutes per day. It is set right at 12 noon. What time will it show at 4.00 am, the next day?
    (a) 4 : 10 am    (b) 4 : 45 am
    (c) 4 : 20 am    (d) 5 : 00 am

12. A drawing room is 7.5 m long, 6.5 m broad and 6 m high. Find the length of paper 2.5 dm wide to cover its walls allowing 8 sq. m for doors:
    (a) 368 m    (b) 640 m    (c) 625 m    (d) 888 m

13. Three equal cubes are placed adjacently in a row. Find the ratio of the total surface area of the resulting cuboid to that of the sum of the total surface areas of the three cubes :
    (a) 5 : 7    (b) 7 : 9
    (c) 9 : 7    (d) None of these

14. How many terms of an AP must be taken for their sum to be equal to 120 if its third term is 9 and the difference between the seventh and the second term is 20?
    (a) 6    (b) 9    (c) 7    (d) 8

15. From 125 metre high towers, the angle of depression of a car is 45°. Then how far the car is from the tower ?
    (a) 125 metre
    (b) 60 metre
    (c) 75 metre
    (d) 95 metre

16. How many new words are possible from the letters of the word PERMUTATION?
    (a) 11!/2!
    (b) (11!/2!) − 1
    (c) 11! − 1
    (d) None of these

17. The number of ways in which a couple can sit around a table with 6 guests if the couple take consecutive seat is
    (a) 1440    (b) 720
    (c) 5040    (d) None of these

18. The probability that the two digit number formed by digits 1, 2, 3, 4, 5 is divisible by 4 is
    (a) $\dfrac{1}{30}$    (b) $\dfrac{1}{20}$
    (c) $\dfrac{1}{5}$    (d) None of these

**Directions** (Qs. 19–22): *Study the following graph and answer these questions given below it.*

### Tea in India (In Million kg)

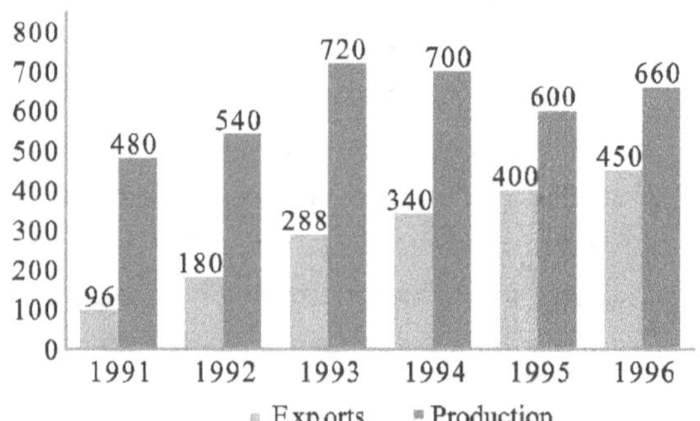

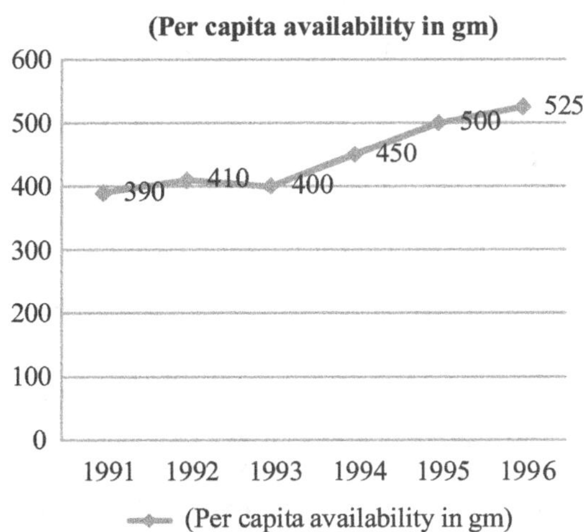



**19.** Which year shows the maximum percentage of export with respect to production?

(a) 1992    (b) 1993    (c) 1996    (d) 1995

**20.** The population of India in 1993 was:

(a) 800 million      (b) 1080 million

(c) 985 million      (d) 900 million

**21.** If the area under tea production was less by 10% in 1994 than in 1993, then the approximate rate of increase in productivity of tea in 1994 was:

(a) 97.22      (b) 3

(c) 35      (d) Cannot be determined

**22.** The average proportion of tea exported to the tea produced over the period is:

(a) 0.87    (b) 0.47    (c) 0.48    (d) 0.66

**23.** The graph below depicts the expenditure of two family P and Q over a period 1990 to 2010.

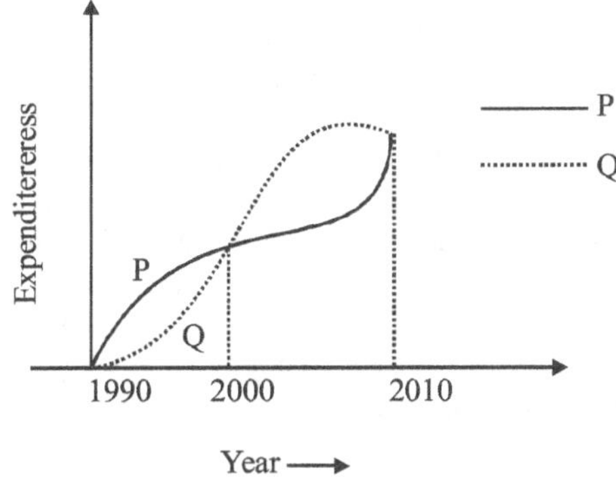



From the graph, which one of the following can be concluded?

(a) On the average P expenditeres more than Q during this period.

(b) On The average P expenditures less than Q during this period

(c) The expenditures of P and Q were equal during this period.

(d) The expenditures of P less than Q during 1990 to 2000.

**24.** The median of a set of 9 distinct observations is 20.5. If each of the largest 4 observation of the set is increased by 2, then the median of the new set

(a) is increased by 2

(b) is decreased by 2

(c) is two times the original median

(d) Remains the same as that of the original set

**25.** Which of the following is the solution set of $|2x - 3| < 7$ ?

(a) $\{x : -5 < x < 2\}$      (b) $\{x : -5 < x < 5\}$

(c) $\{x : -2 < x < 5\}$      (d) $\{x : x < -5 \text{ or } x > 2\}$

**26.** The average salary of all the workers in a workshop is ₹8,000. The average salary of 7 technicians is ₹12,000 and the average salary of the rest is ₹6,000. The total number of workers in the workshop is :

(a) 21      (b) 20

(c) 23      (d) 22

**27.** A space research company wants to sell its two products A and B. If the product A is sold at 20% loss and the product B at 30% gain, the company will not lose anything. If the product A is sold at 15% loss and the product B at 15% gain, the company will lose ₹ 6 million in the deal. What is the cost of product B ?

(a) ₹140 million      (b) ₹120 million

(c) ₹100 million      (d) ₹80 million

**Directions** (Qs. 28-31): *Read the following passages and answer the questions based on them.*

### PASSAGE-1

A species that exerts an influence out of proportion to its abundance in an ecosystem is called a keystone species. The keystone species may influence both the species richness of communities and the flow of energy and materials through ecosystems. The sea star Pisaster ochraceus, which lives in rocky intertidal ecosystems on the Pacific coast of North America, is also an example of a keystone species. Its preferred prey is the mussel Mytilus californianus. In the absence of sea stars, these mussels crowd out other competitors in a broad belt of the intertidal zone. By consuming mussels, sea star creates bare spaces that are taken over by a variety of other species.

A study at the University of Washington demonstrated the influence of Pisaster on species richness by removing sea stars from selected parts of the intertidal zone repeatedly over a period of five years. Two major changes occurred in the areas from which sea stars were removed. First, the lower edge of the mussel bed extended farther down into the intertidal zone, showing that sea stars are able to eliminate mussels completely where they are covered with water most of the time. Second, and more dramatically, 28 species of animals and algae disappeared from the sea star removal zone. Eventually only Mytilus, the dominant competitor, occupied the entire substratum. Through its effect on competitive relationships, predation by Pisaster largely determines which species live in these rocky intertidal ecosystems.

28. What is the crux of the passage ?
    (a) Sea star has a preferred prey.
    (b) A preferred prey determines the survival of a keystone species.
    (c) Keystone species ensures species diversity.
    (d) Sea star is the only keystone species on the Pacific coast of North America.

29. With reference to the passage, consider the following statements :
    1. Mussels are generally the dominant species in intertidal ecosystems.
    2. The survival of sea stars is generally determined by the abundance of mussels.
    Which of the statements given above is/are correct ?
    (a) 1 only            (b) 2 only
    (c) Both 1 and 2      (d) Neither 1 nor 2

30. Which of the following is/are implied by the passage?
    1. Mussels are always hard competitors for sea stars.
    2. Sea stars of the Pacific coast have reached the climax of their evolution.
    3. Sea stars constitute an important component in the energy flow in intertidal ecosystem.
    Which of the statements given above is/are correct?
    (a) 1 and 2           (b) 2 only
    (c) 1 and 3           (d) 3 only

31. Consider the following assumptions:
    1. The food chains/food web in an ecosystem are influenced by keystone species.
    2. The presence of keystone species is a specific characteristic of aquatic ecosystems.
    3. If the keystone species is completely removed from an ecosystem, it will lead to the collapse of the ecosystem.
    With reference to the passage, which of the above assumptions is/are valid ?
    (a) 1 only            (b) 2 and 3 only
    (c) 1 and 3 only      (d) 1, 2 and 3

### PASSAGE-2

We have hard work ahead. There is no resting for any of us till we redeem our pledge in full, till we make all the people of India what destiny intends them to be. We are citizens of a great country, on the verge of bold advance, and we have to live up to that high standard. All of us, to whatever religion we may belong are equally the children of India with equal rights, privileges and obligations. We cannot encourage communalism or narrowmindedness, for no nation can be great whose people are narrow in thought or action.

32. The challenge the author of the above passage throws to the public is to achieve.
    (a) a high standard of living, progress and privileges
    (b) equal privileges, fulfilment of destiny and political tolerance
    (c) spirit of adventure and economic parity
    (d) hard work, brotherhood and national unity

### PASSAGE-3

"The individual, according to Rousseau, parts his person and all his power in common under the supreme direction of the General will and in our corporate capacity we receive each member as an indivisible part of the whole."

33. In the light of the above passage, the nature of General Will is best described as
    (a) the sum total of the private wills of the individuals
    (b) what is articulated by the elected representatives of the individuals
    (c) the collective good as distinct from private wills of the individuals
    (d) the material interests of the community

34. Most citizens are very conscientious about observing a law when they can see the reason behind it. For instance, there has been very little need to actively enforce the recently implemented law that increased the penalty for godmen duping people of their money by playing with their emotions. This is because citizens are very conscientious about duping someone in the name of religion, as it leaves their religious gurus with a bad name.
    Which of the following statements would the author of this passage be most likely to believe?
    (a) The increased penalty alone is a significant motivation for most citizens to obey the law.
    (b) There are still too many inconsiderate citizens in the society.
    (c) Godmen should not be allowed to play with the emotions of the people.
    (d) Society should make an effort to teach citizens the reasons for its laws.

### PASSAGE-4

The concept of 'creative society' refers to a phase of development of a society in which a large number of potential contradictions become articulate and active. This is most evident when oppressed social groups get politically mobilised and demand their rights. The upsurge of the peasants and tribals, the movements for regional autonomy and self-determination, the environmental movements, and the women's movements in the developing countries are signs of emergence of creative society in contemporary times. The forms of social movements and their intensity may vary from country to country and place to place within a country. But the very presence of movements for social transformation in various spheres of a society indicates the emergence of a creative society in a country.

35. What does the author imply by "creative society" ?
    1. A society where diverse art forms and literary writings seek incentive.
    2. A society where social inequalities are accepted as the norm.
    3. A society where a large number of contradictions are recognised.
    4. A society where the exploited and the oppressed groups grow conscious of their human rights and upliftment.
    Select the correct answer using the codes given below :
    (a) 1, 2 and 3        (b) 4 only
    (c) 3 and 4           (d) 2 and 4

36. What according to the passage are the manifestations of social movements ?
    1. Aggressiveness and being incendiary.
    2. Instigation by external forces.
    3. Quest for social equality and individual freedom.
    4. Urge for granting privileges and self-respect to disparaged sections of the society.
    Select the correct answer using the codes given below :
    (a) 1 and 3      (b) 2 and 4
    (c) 3 and 4      (d) 1, 2, 3 and 4

37. With reference to the passage, consider the following statements :
    1. To be a creative society, it is essential to have a variety of social movements.
    2. To be a creative society, it is imperative to have potential contradictions and conflicts.
    Which of the statements given above is/are correct ?
    (a) 1 only      (b) 2 only
    (c) Both 1 and 2      (d) Neither 1 nor 2

**Directions : (Qs. 38-39) :** *The following questions are based on three passages in English to test the comprehension of English language. Read each passage and answer the questions that follow.*

### PASSAGE-5

The nature of the legal imperatives in any given state corresponds to the effective demands that state encounters, and that these, in their turn, depend, in a general way, upon the manner in which economic power is distributed in the society which the state controls.

38. The statement refers to:
    (a) the antithesis of Politics and Economics
    (b) the interrelationship of Politics and Economics
    (c) the predominance of Economics over Politics
    (d) the predominance of Politics over Economics

### PASSAGE-6

"The conceptual difficulties in National Income comparisons between underdeveloped and industrialised countries are particularly serious because a part of the national output in various underdeveloped countries is produced without passing through the commercial channels."

39. In the above statement, the author implies that:
    (a) the entire national output produced and consumed in industrialized countries passes through commercial channels
    (b) the existence of a non-commercialized sector in different underdeveloped countries renders the national income comparisons over countries difficult
    (c) no part of national output should be produced and consumed without passing through commercial channels
    (d) a part of the national output being produced and consumed without passing through commercial channels is a sign of underdevelopment

### PASSAGE-7

Patriotism is a very complex feeling, built up out of primitive instinct and highly intellectual convictions. There is love of home and family and friends, making us peculiarly anxious to preserve our own country from invasion. There is the mild instinctive liking for compatriots against foreigners. There is pride, which is bound up with the success of the community to which we feel we belong. There is a belief, suggested by pride, but reinforced by history, that one's own nation represents a great tradition and stands for ideals that are important to the human race. But besides all these, there is another element, at once nobler and more open to attack, an element of worship, of willing sacrifice, of joyful merging of the individual life in the life of the nation. This religious element in patriotism is essential to the strength of the State, since it enlists the best that is in most men on the side of national sacrifice.

40. Which of the following is the central theme of the given passage?
    (a) Component elements of patriotism
    (b) Historical Development of patriotism
    (c) The role of religion and history in Patriotism
    (d) Need for patriotism in nation building

41. What does the author imply by using the phrase "open to attack" for the element of worship in patriotism?
    (a) This element is unnecessary in some instances of patriotic behaviour.
    (b) This element will call for various acts of national sacrifice.
    (c) This element has no historical basis, yet it is important.
    (d) This element cannot be justified on rational grounds.

### PASSAGE-8

We are not only afraid of being in the dark; we are also suspicious of being kept in the dark. We often feel that the universe has a hidden order that we cannot quite comprehend. In ancient times, this order was attributed to the gods — omnipotent beings who controlled human fate. Greek myths in particular portrayed humans as pawns in the great games played by the gods. More recently, there are suspicions of global conspiracies. These conspiracies are cited for events that are too important to be random. We no longer describe them as "Acts of God," so they must be the work of other people — people who are hiding their influence over us and covering their involvement. They are keeping the rest of us in the dark. Among the events attributed to these people an political assassinations and UFO sightings. Examining these events in minute detail results in a long list of "coincidences," which in the minds of the conspiracy buffs, are too numerous to be truly random. There must be a central planner who is at the hub of a sinister form of order. No one admits to the conspiracy so there must be a cover-up . Better to think that we are all being kept in the dark by sinister forces than to admit that there is no order.

42. Which of the following statements, if true, would weaken the underlying logic of the above passage ?

    i.   The human need for order is a highly exaggerated notion. It more often than not leads to creation of theories about the universe. The more sensational the theory, the more prevalent it becomes.

    ii.  The universe is less guided by pure randomness than by well-defined natural processes which are subject to randomness at varying intervals of time and space.

    iii. To strengthen their case for a variety of conspiracies, the conspiracy buffs are extrapolating from a very small set of observed "coincidences".

    iv.  The persons propounding the different conspiracy theories are usually novelists who use these theories as backdrop during the construction of the plots of the novels.

    v.   The human fear of being kept in the dark is much stronger than the fear of lack of lack of order in the workings of the universe.

    (a) i, ii and iii        (b) i, ii and iv
    (c) i, iii and iv        (d) i, iv and v

43. Which of the following statements, if true, would strengthen the case for belief in sinister forces and conspiracies being at work in the above paragraph ?

    i.   Though science has progressed a lot in the last two centuries or so, it is still unable to explain/account to more than 80% of the phenomena in the universe.

    ii.  There is now the existence of photographic evidence of presence of UFOs and a growing number of parallel studies showing that the human mind can easily be manipulated to do someone else's will through various events that manipulate the 'perceived reality'.

    iii. The fear of our actions and thoughts being controlled by someone else has intensified with the widespread popularity of the depiction of its gory outcomes by different novelists and movie makers.

    iv.  There is a strong movement to reintroduce the teachings of the biblical evolutionary process and the presence of God in schools around the world.

    v.   The Darwinian study of evolution of species, the cornerstone of beliefs in fathomable randomness of the workings of the universe has come under a scathing attack for its inaccurate depiction of the causes and process of evolution.

    (a) i and iv            (b) i and v
    (c) ii, iii and v       (d) i, ii and v

**PASSAGE-9**

It was found by a Newsweek weekly poll that for the first time, a majority of Indian youths now believe that gay and lesbian couples deserve legal recognition. 55% of the poll's respondents stated they support legally sanctioned unions. The poll also indicated that there was increased backing for inheritance and other property rights and that 39% support legalising gay marriage.

44. Which one of the following if true, most weakens the assertion of increased support for gay unions among the Indian people?

    (a) The poll firm used by Newsweek to conduct the survey is owned and operated by a company not aligned with any political organisations.

    (b) All polling was conducted through random telephone calls to people across the nation.

    (c) Respondents queried by Newsweek choose which poll questions to answer.

    (d) Other news magazines were conducting a similar poll during the same period that Newsweek was.

45. The statements above most strongly support which of the following assertions?

    (a) The gay population of India is higher than it was.

    (b) Acceptance of gays and lesbians is higher in India than it was.

    (c) Marriage proponents have persuaded a larger set of the population to take part in the poll.

    (d) The gay population of India is lower than it was.

46. What should come in place of the question mark (?) in the following number series?

    16.  6, 9, 15, 27, 51, ?

    (a) 84                 (b) 99
    (c) 123                (d) 75

47. A + B means A is the brother of B; A – B means A is the wife of B; and A * B means A is the mother of B. Which of the following means M is the brother-in-law of P?

    (a) M – N + P          (b) M + N – P
    (c) M * N + P          (d) M – P * N

48. A school bus driver starts from the school, drives 2 km. towards North, takes a left turn and drives for 5 km. He then takes a left turn and drives for 8 km, before taking a left turn again and driving for further 5 km. The driver finally takes a left turn and drives 1 km before stopping. How far and towards which direction should the driver drive to reach the school again?

    (a) 3 km towards North    (b) 7 km towards East
    (c) 6 km towards South    (d) 5 km towards North

49. Among the four alternatives choose which one can be the similar box as the question figure.

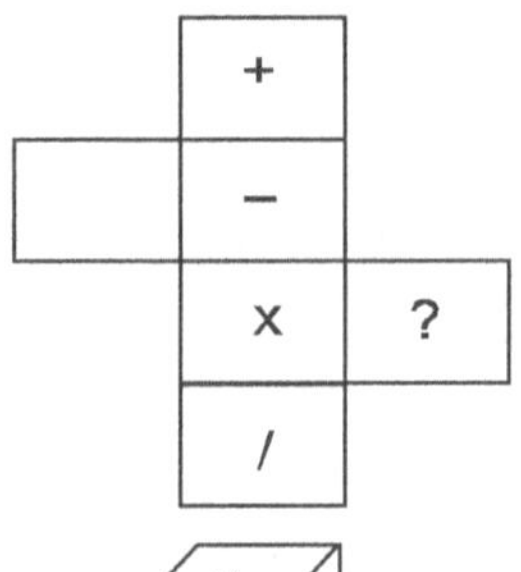


(a) 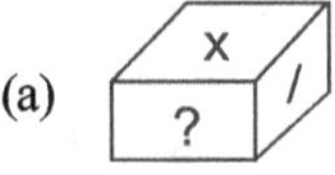


(b) 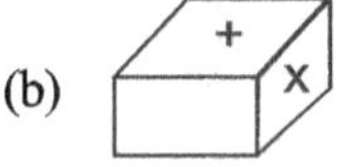


(c) 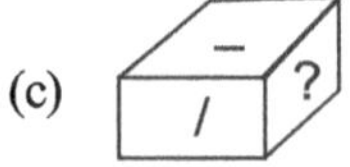


(d) 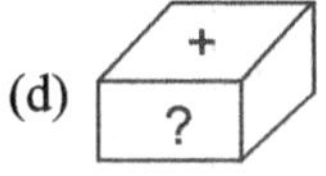

50. Below there are three different positions of a dice. Find the number of dots on the face opposite to the face with one dot.

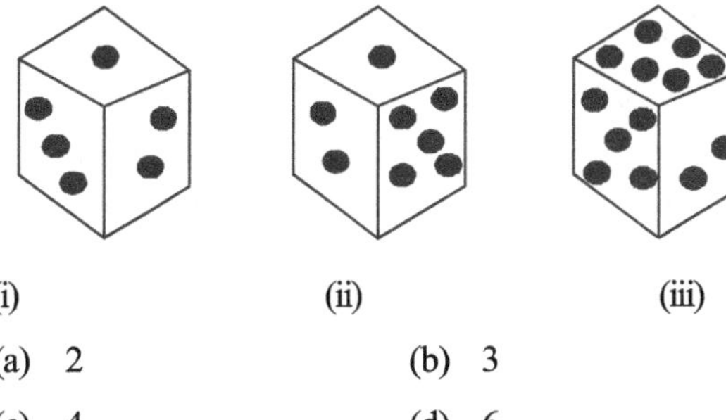

(i)   (ii)   (iii)

(a)  2  (b)  3

(c)  4  (d)  6

51. In the following question you are given four series of questions with a question mark you have to find out the answer for the question mark that completes the series from the answer figures.

**Problem Figures**

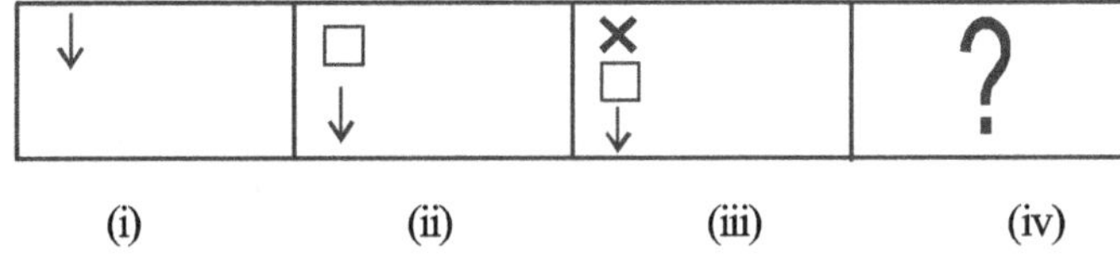

(i)   (ii)   (iii)   (iv)

**Answer Figures**

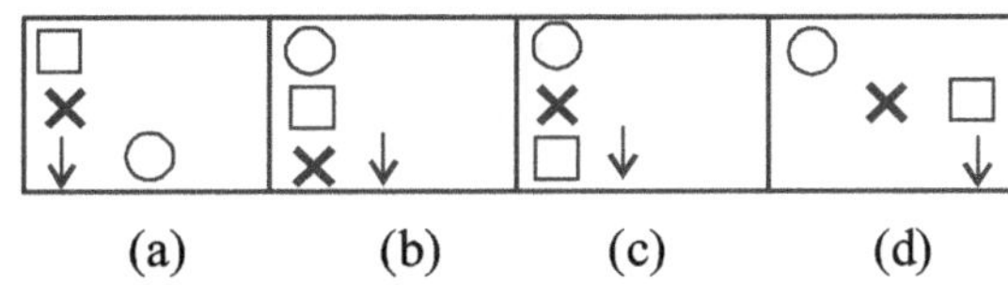

(a)   (b)   (c)   (d)

52. Study the following information carefully and answer the question given below.

Eight friends, A, B, C, D, E, F, G and H , are sitting around a rectangular table in a such a way that two persons sit on each of the four sides of the table facing the centre. Persons sitting on the opposite sides are exactly opposite each other. D faces North and sits exactly opposite. of H. E is on the immediate left of H. A and G sits on the same side. G is exactly opposite B, who is on immediate right of C. A is left of D.

Which of the following pairs of persons has both the persons sitting on the same side with first person sitting to the right of second person?

(a)  DF  (b)  CB

(c)  FC  (d)  AG

**Directions** (Qs. 53–57): *Study the following information to answer the given questions:*

Twelve people are sitting in two parallel rows containing six people each, in such a way that there is an equal distance between adjacent persons. In row 1, P, Q, R, S, T and V are seated and all of them are facing south. In row 2, A, B, C, D, E and F are seated and all of them are facing north. Therefore, in the given seating arrangement each member seated in a row faces another member of the other row. A sits third to right of D. Neither A nor D sits at extreme ends. T faces D. V does not face A and V does not sit at any of the extreme ends. V is not an immediate

neighbour of T. B sits at one of the extreme ends. Only two people sit between B and E. E does not face V. Two persons sit between R and Q. R is not an immediate neighbour of T. C does not face V. P is not an immediate neighbour of R.

53. Who amongst the following sit at extreme ends of the rows?
    (a)  B, E  (b)  S, T
    (c)  P, R  (d)  B, F

54. Who amongst the following faces A?
    (a)  R  (b)  T
    (c)  P  (d)  S

55. How many persons are seated between T and S?
    (a)  One  (b)  Two
    (c)  Three  (d)  Four

56. P is related to V in the same way as C is related to F. Which of the following is E related to, following the same pattern?
    (a)  B  (b)  D
    (c)  C  (d)  A

57. Which of the following is true regarding F?
    (a)  F sits second to right of C
    (b)  F is not an immediate neighbour of A.
    (c)  F sits third to left of D
    (d)  F faces V.

58. The question given below consists of a statement, followed by two arguments numbered I and II. You have to decide which of the arguments is a 'strong' argument.

    **Give answer:**
    (a)  if only argument I is strong
    (b)  if only argument II is strong
    (c)  if either I or II is strong
    (d)  if neither I nor II is strong

    **Statement:** Should there be a maximum limit for the number of ministers in the Central government ?

    **Arguments:** I. No. The political party in power should have the freedom to decide the number of ministers to be appointed.

    II. Yes. The number of ministers should be restricted to a certain percentage of the total number of seats in the parliament to avoid unnecessary expenditure.

59. In the following question, there are four answer figures which can be formed from the cut out pieces given in

    **Question figure:**

    Choose the correct answer.

    **Answer figures:**

     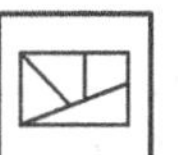  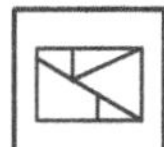

    (a)   (b)   (c)   (d)

 **(Qs.60–61):** *Study the following information carefully and answer the questions which follow:*

A research institute is recruiting a librarian to digitize its information resources, among other duties. Candidates must possess, the following criteria. The candidate must

(I)   Be not less than 35 years and not exceed 40 years as on 01. 11. 2017

(II)   Have a Bachelor's Degree in Library and Information Science with 65% marks

(III)   Have a Ph.D in Library Science

(IV)   Have post qualification experience of at least 4 years in a University Library

However, if the candidate fulfills the above mentioned criteria except

(i)   at (II) above, but has a UGC NET certification with all the other above criteria fulfilled, he/she may be referred to the Dean.

(ii)   at (IV) above but all the eligibility criteria are met and the candidate has at least one year experience in a research institute, he/she may be offered contractual appointment for a year.

Based on the above criteria, study carefully whether the following candidates are eligible for the recruitment process and mark your answer as follows. You are not to assume anything other than the information provided in each question.

All cases are given to you as on 1. 11. 2017

**Mark answer** (a) if he/she is to be short listed

**Mark answer** (b) if he/she should be referred to the Dean.

**Mark answer** (c) if he/she may be offered contractual appointment if required

**Mark answer** (d) if the data provided are inadequate to take a decision.

60.   Kirit Shukla obtained her doctorate and Bachelor's degree from Patna University. She obtained 63% in graduation. She obtained her UGC NET qualification in 2005 when she was 26.

61.   Dr. Samir Bali has a Ph.D Library Science and has been with the Institute of Fundamental Research as Assistant Librarian since October 2016. He graduated with a degree in Library and Information Science in 2002 at the age of 22. He obtained 70% in his graduation.

62.   There are five statues - L, M, N, O and P - each of them having different height. Statue L is smaller than only statue M. Statue O is smaller than statue N. Statue O is longer than statue P. The height of the tallest statue is 20 feet. The height of the second smallest statue is 11 feet.

What will be the height of the third tallest statue?

(a)   13 feet  (b)   10 feet

(c)   19 feet  (d)   9 feet

63.   In a certain code 'TEAM WORK' is written as 'NBFUJQNV' and 'SOME' is written as 'PTDL'. How is 'PERSON' written in that code ?

(a)   QDOOPT  (b)   QDOMNR

(c)   SFQMNR  (d)   SFQOPT

64.   In a certain code language 'how many are there' is written as 'ka na ta da' and 'many are welcome here' is written as 'na pa ni ka'. How is 'how' written in that code language?

(a)   ta  (b)   da

(c)   ta or da  (d)   Data inadequate

65.   Find the missing number.

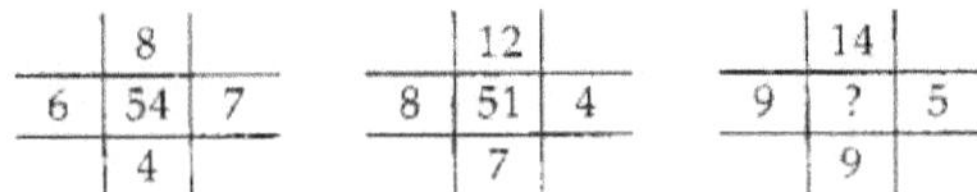

(a)   53  (b)   71

(c)   76  (d)   68

66.   Little wooden cubes each with a side of one inch are put together to form a solid cube with a side of three inches. This big cube is then painted red all over on the outside. When the big cube is broken up into the original little ones, how many cubes will have paint on two sides ?

(a)   4  (b)   8

(c)   12  (d)   0

67.   A bus leaves Delhi with half the number of women as men. At Meerut, ten men get down and five women get in. Now there are equal number of men and women. How many passengers boarded the bus initially at Delhi ?

(a)   36  (b)   45

(c)   15  (d)   30

68.   How many triangles are there in the question figure?

(a)   18  (b)   24

(c)   28  (d)   30

 **(Qs. 69–70):** *In each of the following questions, a statement is given followed by two conclusions I and II. Give answer:*

**(a)   if only conclusion I follows;**

**(b)   if only conclusion II follows;**

**(c)   if either I or II follows;**

**(d)   if neither I nor II follows;**

69. **Statement :** "The Government will review the present policy of the diesel price in view of further spurt in the international oil prices" — A spokesman of the Government.

    **Conclusions :** I. The Government will increase the price of the diesel after the imminent spurt in the international oil prices.

    II. The Government will not increase the price of the diesel even after the imminent spurt in the international oil prices.

70. **Statement :** Being from a business family, Chandan was apparently convinced by his parents and other family members to join the family trade.

    **Conclusions :** I. People should take up their family profession so that family prosper.

    II. It is necessary to keep family members happy by choosing family business.

**Directions** (Qs. 71–80): *Read the following passages and answer the questions based on it.*

### PASSAGE-1

71. Various studies have shown that our forested and hilly regions, in general, where biodiversity as reflected in the variety of flora is high, are places where poverty appears to be high. And these same areas are also the ones where educational performance seems to be poor. Therefore, it may be surmised that, even disregarding poverty status, richness in biodiversity goes hand in hand with educational backwardness.

    Which one of the following statements, if true, can be said to best provide supporting evidence for the surmise mentioned in the passage

    (a) In regions where there is little variety in flora, educational performance is seen to be as good as in regions with high variety in flora, when poverty levels are high.

    (b) Regions which show high biodiversity also exhibit poor educational performance, at low levels of poverty.

    (c) Regions which show high biodiversity reveal high levels of poverty and poor educational performance.

    (d) In regions where there is low biodiversity, at all levels of poverty, educational performance is seen to be good.

### PASSAGE-2

72. From Cochin to Shimla, the new culture vultures are tearing down acres of India's architectural treasures. Ancestral owners often fobbed off with a few hundred rupees for an exquisitely carved door or window, which fetches fifty times that much from foreign dealers, and yet more from the drawing room sophisticates of Europe and the US. The reason for such shameless rape of the Indian architectural wealth can perhaps, not wrongly, be attributed to the unfortunate blend of activist disunity and local indifference.

    It can be inferred from the above passage that

    (a) The environment created by the meeting between activist disunity and local difference is ideal for antique dealers to thrive in India.

    (b) Only Indians are not proud of their cultural heritage and are hungry for the foreign currency that is easily available in return of artefacts.

    (c) Most Indian families have heirlooms which can be sold at high prices to Europeans and Americans.

    (d) India provides a rich market for unscrupulous antique dealers.

### PASSAGE-3

73. In a recent report, the gross enrolment ratios at the primary level, that is the number of children enrolled in classes one to five as a proportion of all children aged 6 to 10, were shown to be very high for most states; in many cases they were way above 100 percent. These figures are not worth anything, since they are based on the official enrolment data complied from school records. They might as well stand for 'gross exaggeration ratios'.

    Which one of the following options best supports the claim that the ratios are exaggerated?

    (a) The definition of gross enrolment ratio does not exclude, in its numerator, children below 6 years or above 10 years enrolled in classes one to five .

    (b) A school attendance study found that many children enrolled in the school records were not meeting a minimum attendance requirement of 80 percent.

    (c) A study estimated that close to 22 children enrolled in the class one records were below 6 years of age and still to start going to school.

    (d) Demographic surveys show shifts in the population profile which indicate that the number of children in the age group 6 to 10 years is declining.

## PASSAGE-4

74. Some decisions will be fairly obvious - "no-brainers." Your bank account is low, but you have a two week vacation coming up and you want to get away to some place warm to relax with your family. Will you accept your in-laws' offer of free use of their Florida beachfront condo ? Sure. You like your employer and feel ready to move forward in your career. Will you step in for your boss for three weeks while she attends a professional development course? Of course

Choose the option that best captures the essence of the text given above :

A.   Some decisions are obvious under certain circumstances. You may, for example, readily accept a relative's offer of free holiday accommodation. Or step in for your boss when she is away.

B.   Some decisions are no brainers. You need not think when making them. Examples are condo offers from in-laws and job offers from bosses when your bank account is low or boss is away.

C.   Easy decisions are called "no-brainers" because they do not require any cerebral activity. Examples such as accepting free holiday accommodation abound in our lives.

D.   Accepting an offer from in-laws when you are short on funds and want a holiday is a no-brainer. Another no-brainer is taking the boss's job when she is away.

(a)   A                           (b)   B

(c)   C                           (d)   D

## PASSAGE-5

75. The theory of games is suggested to some extent by parlour games such as chess and bridge. Friedman illustrates two distinct features of these games. First in a parlour game played for money, if one wins the other (others )loses (lose), Second, these games are games involving a strategy. In a game of chess, while choosing what action is to be taken a player tries to guess how his/her opponent will react to the various actions he or she might take. In contrast, the card pastime, 'patience ' or 'solitaire' is played only against chance.

Which one of the following can best be described as a 'game?"

(a)   The team of Tenzing Norgay and Edmund Hillary climbing Mt. Everest for the first time in human history.

(b)   A national level essay writing competition.

(c)   A decisive war between the armed forces of India and Pakistan over Kashmir.

(d)   Oil Exporter's Union deciding on world oil prices, completely disregarding the countries which have at most minimal oil production.

## PASSAGE-6

76. Try before you buy; We use this memorable saying to urge you to experience the consequences of an alternative before you choose it, whenever this is feasible. If you are considering buying a van after having  always owned sedans, rent one for a week or borrow a friend's. By experiencing the consequences first hand, they become more meaningful. In addition, you are likely to identify consequences you had not even thought of before. May be you will discover that it is difficult to park the van in your small parking space at work, but that, on the other hand , your elderly father has a much easier time getting in and out of it

Choose the option that best captures the essence of the text given above :

A.   If you are planning to buy a van after being used to sedans, borrow a van or rent it and try it before deciding to buy it. Then you may realize that parking a van is difficult while it is easier for your elderly father to get in and out of it.

B.   Before choosing an alternative,  experience its consequences if feasible. If, for example, you want to change from sedans to a van, try one before buying it. You will discover aspects you may never have thought of.

C.   Always try before you buy anything. You are bound to discover many consequences. One of the consequences of going in for a van is that it is more difficult to park than sedans at the office car park.

D.   We urge you to try products such as vans before buying them. Then you can experience consequences you have not thought of such as parking problems. But your father may find vans more comfortable than cars.

(a)   A                           (b)   B

(c)   C                           (d)   D

## PASSAGE-7

77. Some scientists believe that, in certain species of birds, actual particles of metal within the brain react to the Earth's magnetic field in the same way as the needle in a compass. It is this mechanism that is thought to underlie the birds' amazing ability to navigate accurately over distances of thousands of miles by day and night during migration. To test this theory, researchers surgically removed the metal particles from the heads of some birds and then released them, alongwith a number of untreated birds, at the usual time and place of their annual winter migration.

Which of the following results would most seriously weaken the theory being tested?

(a) The untreated birds were confused by the erratic flight patterns of the surgically treated birds and failed to migrate successfully.

(b) The surgically treated birds were able to follow their usual flight patterns successfully by day, but not by night.

(c) The surgically treated birds were able to migrate about as accurately as the untreated birds.

(d) The surgically treated birds were able to migrate successfully only when closely following a group of untreated birds.

### PASSAGE-8

78. For our nation to compete successfully in the high technology enterprises of the future, workers with skills in maths and science will be needed. But it is doubtful that they will be available, since there is a shortage of high school maths and science teachers that shows no signs of improving. Industry can help alleviate this problem by funding scholarship grants and aid to college students who graduate in maths and science with the hope of pursuing teaching careers.

Which of the following, if true, would most probably prevent the proposed plan from achieving its intended effect?

(a) After graduation from college, most maths and science graduates opt for jobs in industry rather than in teaching.

(b) Many high schools have been forced to lower their standards in hiring maths and science teachers.

(c) More scholarship money is already available for students of maths and science than is available for those in any other field.

(d) Population statistics show that the number of high school students is expected to decline over the next ten years.

### PASSAGE-9

79. Although dentures produced through a new computer-aided design process will cost more than twice as much as ordinary dentures, they should still be cost effective. Not only will fitting time and X-ray expense be reduced, but the new dentures should fit better, diminishing the need for frequent refitting visits to the dentist's office.

Which of the following must be studied in order to evaluate the argument presented above?

(a) The amount of time a patient spends in the fitting process versus the amount of money spent on X-rays

(b) The amount by which the cost of producing dentures has declined with the introduction of the new technique for producing them

(c) The degree to which the use of the new dentures is likely to reduce the need for refitting visits when compared to the use of ordinary dentures

(d) The amount by which the new dentures will drop in cost as the production procedures become standardized and applicable on a larger scale

### PASSAGE-10

80. Traditionally, decision making by doctors that is carefully, deductively reasoned has been considered preferable to intuitive decision making. However, a recent study found that senior surgeons used intuition significantly more than did most residents or mid-level doctors. This confirms the alternative view that intuition is actually more effective than careful, methodical reasoning.

The conclusion above is based on which of the following assumptions?

(a) Senior surgeons are more effective at decision making than are mid-level doctors.

(b) Senior surgeons have the ability to use either intuitive reasoning or deductive, methodical reasoning in making decisions.

(c) The decisions that are made by mid-level and entry-level doctors can be made as easily by using methodical reasoning as by using intuitive reasoning.

(d) Senior surgeons use intuitive reasoning in making the majority of their decisions.

# SOLUTIONS

1. (d) Since $80 = 8 \times 10$   or   $80 = 16 \times 5$

   Thus y (i.e., unit digit) must be zero.

   $\therefore$   $653xy = 653x0$, where $653x0$ must be divisible by 16 or $653x$ is divisible by 8.

   Thus the last 3-digit number $53x$ will be divisible by 8.

   Hence, at $x = 6$, we get the required result.

   $\therefore$   $x + y = 6 + 0 = 6$

2. (c) As per the given condition N must be divisible by 12, so N must be in the form of 12k where k is not divisible by 3 (As N is not divisible by 9). Hence N/18 cannot be an integer.

3. (b) $13\,m\,53\,cm = 1353\,cm$ and $8\,m\,61\,cm = 861\,cm$.

   H.C.F. of 1353 and 861 is 123.

   Now since minimum tiles are required for having the floor so area of the tile has to be the greatest so its size is greatest which is 123 cm.

   $\therefore$ the number of square tiles

   $$= \frac{\text{Area of the floor}}{\text{Area of the tile}} = \frac{1353 \times 861}{123 \times 123} = 77$$

4. (b) Let X be the given number. Then

   $X/3 + X/4 + X/5 - X/2 = 34$.

   Solving this, we get $X = 120$.

5. (b) Let 100 units be B's income and X units be B's expenditure

   $\Rightarrow$ A's income $= 60$ units.

   A's expenditure $= 70X/100$ units.

   But $60 = (75/100)\,X \Rightarrow X = 80$.

   i.e., B's saving $= (100 - 80)$ units $= 20$ units.

   Hence A's saving $= 60 - \dfrac{70}{100} \times 80 = 4$ units.

   i.e., A's saving : B's saving $= 4 : 20 = 1 : 5$.

6. (c) Tripling in 8 years means that the interest earned in 8 years is equal to 200% of the capital value. Thus, interest per year (simple interest) is 25% of the capital. In 20 years, total interest earned = 500% of the capital and hence the capital would become 6 times it's original value.

7. (b) Let us represent their shares by the corresponding letter of their names.

   $A + B = 2C$ and $B + C = 3A$.

   $\Rightarrow A + 3A - C = 2C$ (since $B = 3A - C$)

   $4A = 3C \Rightarrow A : C = 3 : 4$

8. (a) Profit (%) $= 9.09\% = \dfrac{1}{11}$

   Since the ratio of water and milk is $1 : 11$,

   Therefore the ratio of water is to mixture $= 1 : 12$

   Thus the quantity of water in mixture of 1 litre

   $$= 1000 \times \frac{1}{12} = 83.33\,ml$$

9. (d) (Man + Son)'s one day's work $= \dfrac{1}{8}$

   Man's one day's work $= \dfrac{1}{10}$

   $\Rightarrow$ Son's one day's work $= \dfrac{1}{8} - \dfrac{1}{10} = \dfrac{1}{40}$

   $\therefore$ Son can do it in 40 days.

10. (c) Relative speed $= 90 + 60 = 150$ km/hr.

    Total distance to be covered $= 300 + 200 = 500\,m$

    $$\text{Time required} = \frac{500}{150 \times 1000} \times 3600 = 12\,\text{sec.}$$

11. (a) The clock gains 15 min in 24 hours.

    Therefore, in 16 hours, it will gain 10 minutes.

    Hence, the time shown by the clock will be 4:10 am.

12. (b) Net area = Total area of 4 walls $- 8m^2$

    and Area of 4 walls $= 2\,(1 + b) \times h = 168m^2$

    $$\text{Length of paper} = \frac{160}{0.25} = 640m$$

13. (b) Let us consider that surface area of each face of the cube 1 cm$^2$.

    $\therefore$   Total surface area of the cuboid $= 14\,cm^2$

    and Total surface area of the 3 cubes $= 18\,cm^2$

    Hence, required ratio $= 14 : 18 = 7 : 9$

14. (d) $T_3 = a + 2d = 9$

    $T_7 = a + 6d$

    $T_2 = a + d$

    According to question,

    $a + 6d - (a + d) = 20 \Rightarrow 5d = 20$

    $d = 4$

    $T_3 = a + 2 \times 4 = 9$

    $a = 1$

$\Rightarrow\quad 120 = \dfrac{n}{2}[2a + (n-1)d]$

$\Rightarrow\quad 240 = n[2a + (n-1)d]$

$\Rightarrow\quad 240 = n[2 + (n-1)4]$

$\Rightarrow\quad 120 = n[1 + (n-1)2]$

$\Rightarrow\quad 120 = n + 2n^2 - 2n$

$\Rightarrow\quad n = 8$

Hence, 8 terms.

15. (a)

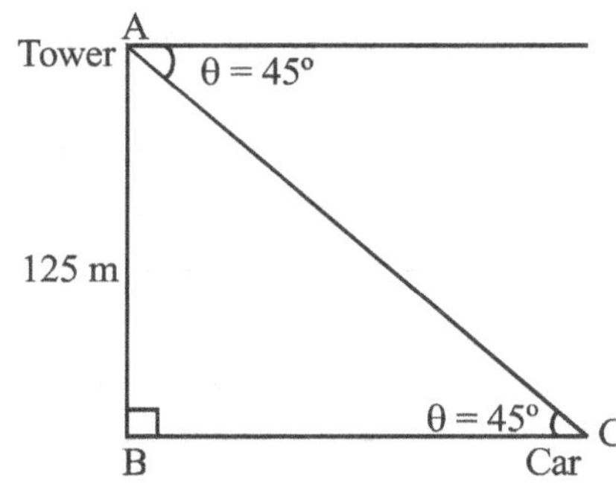


In $\triangle ABC$

$\tan\theta = \dfrac{AB}{BC} \Rightarrow \tan 45° = \dfrac{125}{BC} \Rightarrow 1 = \dfrac{125}{BC}$

$BC = 125\,m$

Hence, car is 125 m far from the tower.

16. (b) Number of 11 letter words formed from the letter P, E, R, M, U, T, A, I, O, N = 11!/2!.

Number of new words formed = total words – 1 = (11!/2!) – 1.

17. (a) A couple and 6 guests can be arranged in $(7-1)!$ ways. But in two people forming the couple can be arranged among themselves in 2! ways.

$\therefore$ the required number of ways $= 6! \times 2! = 1440$

18. (c) Given digits are 1, 2, 3, 4, 5

Total no. of 2 digits numbers formed

$= (5)^2 = 25$

Favourable cases are 12, 24, 32, 44, 52

No. of favourable cases = 5

$\therefore\quad$ Required probability $= \dfrac{5}{25} = \dfrac{1}{5}$

19. (c) 1996 shows maximum percentage of 68.18% export with respect to production.

20. (b) Tea available in India 1993 = 720 – 288 = 432 and per capita availability in 1993 = 0.4kg. therefore, the

population in India is $\dfrac{432}{0.4} = 1080$ million

21. (d) Cannot be determined since there is no data given about area.

22. (b) Tea exported over the period = 96 + 180 + 288 + 340 + 400 + 450 = 1754 million kg and tea produced over the period

= 480 + 540 + 720 + 700 + 600 + 660 = 3700 million kg. The average proportion

$= \dfrac{1754}{3700} = 0.47$

23. (a) From the graph we cna see that area of P is greater then Q. Hence, on the average P expenditures more than Q during this period.

24. (d) Since n = 9, then median $= \left(\dfrac{9+1}{2}\right)^{th} = 5^{th}$ observation

Now, last four observations are increased by 2.

$\because$ The median is 5th observation, which remains unchanged.

$\square$ There will be no change in median.

25. (c) If the expression between the absolute value bars is positive. It's less than +7 or, if the expression between the bars is negative, it's greater than –7. In other words,

$2x - 3$ is between –7 and +7

$-7 < 2x - 3 < 7$

$-4 < 2x < 10$

$-2 < x < 5$

26. (a) Let the total no. of workers be x.

Now, $8000\,x = 7 \times 12000 + (x-7) \times 6000$

$\Rightarrow\quad x = \dfrac{42000}{2000} = 21$

27. (d) Since, selling price of both the products is same

$\therefore$ % loss = % gain

$\Rightarrow 20\%$ of A = 30% of B $\Rightarrow A/B = 3/2$

Let cost of product A = 3x and cost of product B = 2x.

According to the question,

$$3x \times \dfrac{15}{100} - 2x \times \dfrac{15}{100} = 6$$

$\Rightarrow\quad 45x - 30x = 600 \Rightarrow x = \dfrac{600}{15} = 40$

Hence, cost of product B $= 2 \times 40 = ₹\,80$ million

28. (c) Option (c) is correct answer as the author shows that not only mussels are affected but other 28 species also disappeared.

29. (d) Neither 1 nor 2 is correct as the dominant species is the keystone species and that is sea star. The sea stars do not live exclusively on mussels as their removal resulted in the disappearance of 28 species more.

30. (c) Only 1 and 3 are correct statements as the 'sea stars' are the keystone species which influences both richness of communities and flow of energy.

31. (c) Assumption 1 is correct as disappearance of 28 species along with mussels. Assumption 3 is also correct according to the passage.

32. (b) The challenge the author throws to the public is to achieve equal privileges, fulfilment of destiny and political tolerance.

33. (c) The nature of General Will, in the passage, is best described as the collective good as distinct from Private Wills of the individuals.

34. (d) The opening sentence provides the cue to solving this problem, which clearly says that the citizens will definitely obey a law if they understand the reason behind its imposition. So the society should make an effort to teach citizens the reasons for its laws.

35. (c) 1 is eliminated as " art form" is not mentioned in the passage. Social inequalities are not accepted. Only 3 and 4 are mentioned.

36. (b) According to passage Instigation by external forces (social group get politically .... ) and "urge for granting privileges and self respect to disparaged section of the society" are manifestations of social movements.

37. (c) Statement 1 is correct as stated in the passage "The forms of .... in a country". Statement 2 is correct as "phase of development ..... active".

38. (b) The word 'corresponds' indicates a strong bond or the interrelationship between politics and economics, for effective formulation of state policies.

39. (d) According to the author, the national output has to pass through the commercial channels, before consumption, lacking which would lead to loss of income, leading to underdevelopment and economic disparity.

40. (b) From the second sentence onwards, the passage lists the elements of patriotism one and by one. Thus, this option is the correct one.

41. (d) Using the phrase "open attack", the author implies that this element is not justifiable and nobody would like to sacrifice his life rationally. In fact, the last sentence calls it as "religious element", implying that being rational is not behind it.

42. (a) The underlying logic of the passage is that we, and the conspiracy theorists within us, think more about what we do not know; and do not give importance to "order" in which these are happening.

So, statement (i) weaken the logic by indicating that too much importance is given to "order" and (ii) weakens it by citing lack of order, as the para states that there is a long list of "coincidences." Statement (iii) weakens it by stating 'small set of observed coincidences' because the passage says they are 'more 'numerous'. (iv) statement is irrelevent. Statement (v) strengthens the logic by providing the reason for such thought.

43. (c) Since, the undelying logic of the passage supports the existence of "order" whereas (i) negates it so it is ruled out. (ii) and (iii) support the logic that there is some force or directing agent behind everything.

Statement (iv) speaks about "reintroducing" as if we are not concerned about the order anymore, so it is ruled out.

Statement (v) is indicating that Darwin's explanations of randomness in evolution are under 'scathing' attack for 'inaccuracy' and supports the logic.

44. (c) In order to assure a statistically valid result, the sample size must be statistically valid and free of bias. Having a politically neutral organization in charge of polling is standard practice and avoids influencing the questions or the pollers, so such a condition would not weaken the central assertion, which eliminates choice (a).

Random phone calling avoids selecting respondents from specific demographics and geographic areas, which also minimizes bias, so option (b) is also unsuitable. The fact of other polls being conducted in the same period has no effect on the poll in question, as they are independent events; thus, choice (d) is invalid as well. Only choice (c). where the respondents' bias affects the questions answered, could provide a valid argument against the poll's objectivity; thus, option (c) is correct.

45. (b) Based on the statements in the paragraph above, the poll was specifically focused on the question of legal unions and/or marriages for the gay and lesbian population. Since the statements reflect no information or speculation about the percentage of gays and lesbians among the general population, both options (a) and (b) can be rejected, as there is no information or inference to draw on.

Also, since the statements specifically reflect respondents' opinion on a specific population with regards to marriage, there is no general information from which to draw an overall opinion of marriage itself, which eliminates option (c) from consideration. Only the assertion in option (b) can reasonably be drawn from the statements in the question; thus, it is the correct answer.

46. (b) The series is $+3, +6, +12, +24, +48, ....$

47. (b) $M^+ - N^- = P$ Hence, M is the brother-in law of P.

**48.** (d)

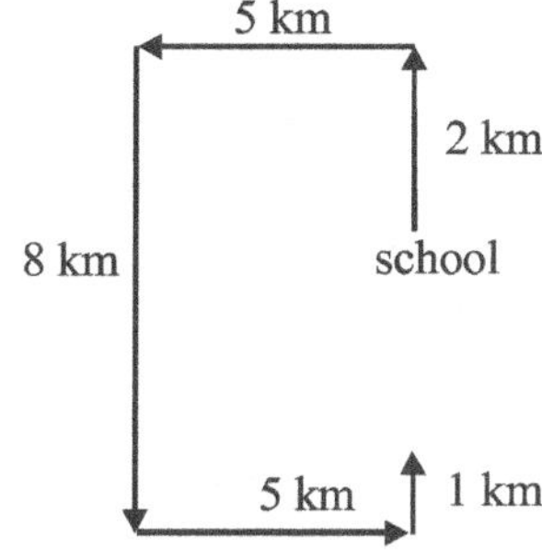


Remaining distance $= 8 - (2+1) = 5$ km

Hence the driver requires to drive 5 km more.

**49.** (a) Option (a), it is clear from the alternatives.

**50.** (d) As 1, 3, 5, and 6 are adjacent to 2 in all the three positions, if 3 is opposite to 5 that we came across from the figures. So, it is obvious that one will be opposite to 6.

**51.** (c) Every time a new figure is introduced the previous figure moves one unit in anti-clock wise direction.

**52.** (d)

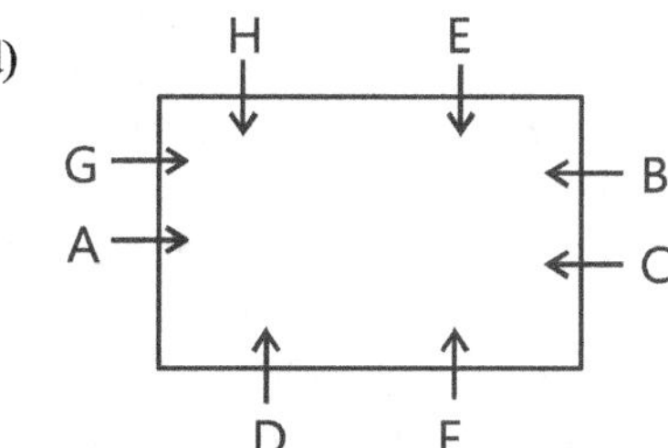


**Solution for 53– 57:**

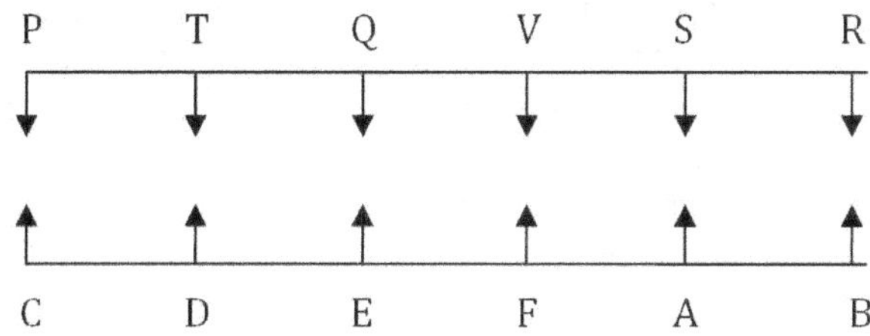


**53.** (c) is the correct answer

**54.** (d) is the correct answer

**55.** (b) is the correct answer

**56.** (a) is the correct answer

**57.** (d) is the correct answer

**58.** (b) Clearly, there should be some norms regarding the number of ministers in the Government, as more number of ministers would unnecessarily add to the Government expenditure. So, argument II holds strong. Also, giving liberty to the party in power could promote extension of unreasonable favour to some people at the cost of government funds. So, argument I does not hold.

**59.** (b)

**Solution for 60-61:**

| I | II/(i) | III | IV/(ii) Ans. |
|---|---|---|---|
| ✓ | – | – | – |
| ✓ | ✓ | ✓ | ✓ |

**60.** (d)

**61.** (c)

**62.** (a) Statue L is smaller than only statue M. Therefore, M is the tallest statue.

$N > O > P$

Now, $\qquad M > L > N > O > P$

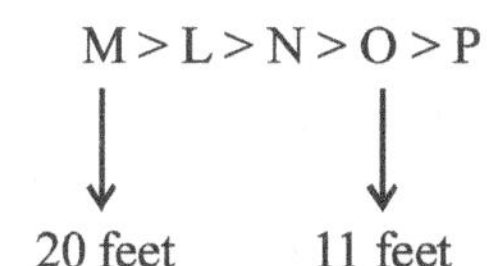


The tallest statue is 20 feet high. Therefore, the second tallest statue may be 19 feet, 18 feet ..... high.

Therefore, the third tallest statue will be less than 19 feet and more than 11 feet high.

**63.** (c)

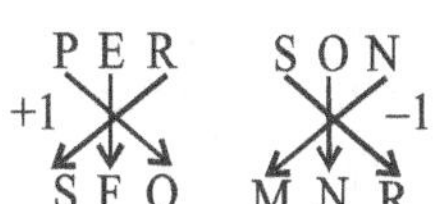


**64.** (c) how many are there → ka na ta da ... (i)

many are welcome here → na pa ni ka ... (ii)

From equations (i) and (ii) many are → na ka

how → ta or da

**65.** (d) The pattern is:

$(6 \times 7) + 8 + 4 = 54$

$(8 \times 4) + 12 + 7 = 51$

$(9 \times 5) + 14 + 9 = 68$

**66.** (b)

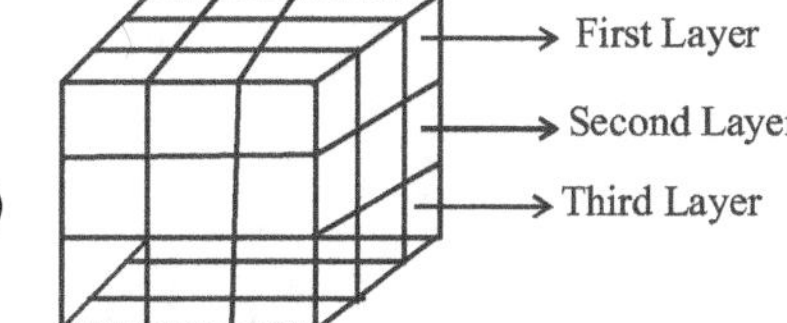


4 cubes each of the first and third layers will have paint on two sides only.

Therefore, total number of cubes having paint on two sides.

$= 4 \times 2 = \boxed{8}$

67. (b) Suppose the number of women boarded the bus at Delhi is x.

Therefore, the number of men = 2x

According to question,

$2x - 10 = x + 5$

$\Rightarrow 2x - x = 10 + 5$

$\therefore x = 15$

Total number of passengers boarded the bus initially = 3x

$= 3 \times 15 = 45$

68. (c)

69. (c) Either I or II can follow. As the government would be reviewing the diesel prices in light of the spurt in the international oil prices, the government can either decide to increase or keep the price stagnant (increasing subsidy.)

70. (d) I and II are assumptions and not conclusions.

71. (c) (c) is the only correct choice, which can be inferred from the passage that high biodiversity goes hand in hand with poverty and poor educational performance.

72. (a) The passage refers to disunity of activists and local indifference to India's architectural treasures. Thus, (a) comes across as a best choice as the situation it created in which antique dealers can thrive. Other options are clearly not suggested may appear correct but is not as apt as (a).

73. (c) (c) is the best option as it shows that children below 6 years of age were enrolled in class I, the age interval does not fit into this level, thus the ratio is exaggerated.

74. (a) (a) comes across as the only reasonable option as the decisions to be taken in the passage are fairly obvious i.e. with a low bank account a free holiday offer may be taken up or if we are ready to move forward in our career then we can step in for the boss, when she is away. (a) is the most appropriate choice as its mentions that some decision are obvious under certain circumstances while other options, are not.

75. (b) According to the passage only (b) can be described as a game because, it is fulfilling both the features illustrated by Friedman i.e. in the competition one will win and the other lose and writing an essay involves a strategy.

76. (b) (b) is the only option as the passage clearly means to say that one should experience the consequences before choosing an alternative as then they become more meaningful. Also one can discover aspects one may not have ever thought of. Other options are more specifically about the van, whereas the point of the passage is to make a general statement about trying alternatives with van as an example.

77. (c) Since the metal component in the birds' brain help them navigate, surgically removing them would render them, ineffective in their flight. This option weakens the concept.

78. (a) If after graduation, most maths and science graduates take up jobs in the industry or corporate MNCs, then there would be an acute shortage of manpower for teaching, and would hamper the proposed plan.

79. (c) The correct answer (c), highlights an assumption in the passage argument. It shows that the author must be assuming that the reduction in refitting with the new dentures compared to ordinary dentures is significant in order to conclude that that difference will help offset an initial outlay that is twice as much. In other words, if you answer the question posed by answer choice (c) with "not much," the argument is weakened. If you answer it with "a tremendous amount," the argument is strengthened. The other answer choices are all irrelevant because no matter what the answers are, there is no impact on the relationship between the evidence presented in the stimulus argument and its conclusion.

80. (a) The correct answer is (a), which provides a missing link in the author's reasoning by making a connection from the evidence: that intuition is used more by senior surgeons than other, less-experienced doctors, and the conclusion: that, therefore, intuition is more effective. None of the other choices help bridge this gap in the chain of reasoning. Although some of the other statements may be true, they are not responsive to the question. In fact, they mostly focus on irrelevant factors such as appropriateness, ease of application, ability, etc.

# MOCK TEST - 8

**Max. Marks : 200**  **Time : 2 hrs.**

1. J2Z, K4X, I7V, ?, H16R which one of the following can replace the question mark?
   (a) I11T
   (b) L11S
   (c) L12T
   (d) J11T

2. P's father Q is B's paternal uncle and A's husband M is P's paternal uncle. How is A related to B?
   (a) Cousin
   (b) Aunt
   (c) Mother
   (d) data inadequate

3. I am facing West. I turn 45° in the clockwise direction and then 180° in the same direction and then 270° anti-clockwise. Which direction am I facing now ?
   (a) South-west
   (b) South
   (c) West
   (d) North-west

4. Among the four alternatives which one cannot be the similar box as the question figure.

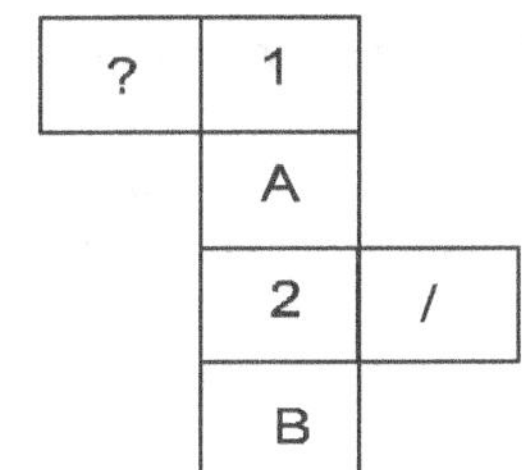

   (a) 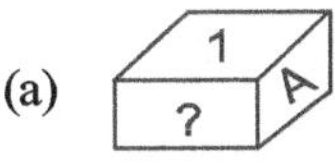
   (b) 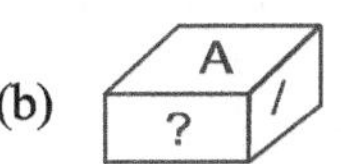
   (c) 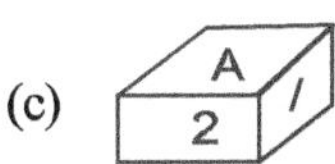
   (d) 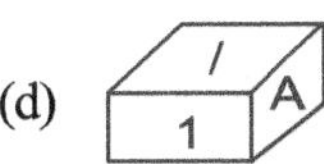

5. Two positions of a block are shown below. When 2 is at the bottom which number will be at the top?

   (a) 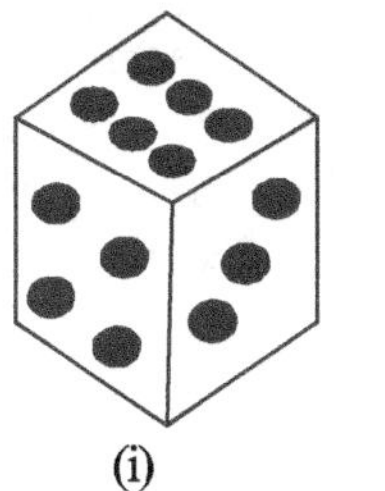  (b) 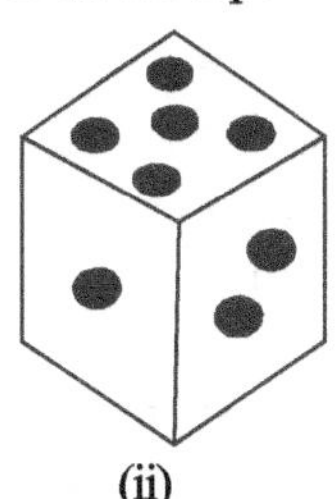

   (i)   (ii)
   (a) 1
   (b) 4
   (c) 6
   (d) cannot be determine

6. When a number is divided by 387, the ramainder obtained is 48. If the same number is divided by 43, the remainder obtained will be:
   (a) 0   (b) 3   (c) 5   (d) 35

7. If the number 2304ab is completely divisible by 80, then what will be the value of a + b?
   (a) 4   (b) 9   (c) 6   (d) 8

8. HCF and LCM of four numbers a, b, c and d are 12 and 48. Which of the following can be value of a ?
   (a) 4   (b) 16   (c) 24   (d) 60

9. If three numbers are added in pairs, the sums equal 10, 19 and 21. The numbers are
   (a) 4, 6, 10
   (b) 6, 4, 15
   (c) 3, 5, 10
   (d) 2, 5, 15

10. In some quantity of ghee, 60% is pure ghee and 40% is vanaspati. If 10 kg of pure ghee is added, then the strength of vanaspati ghee becomes 20%. The original quantity was :
    (a) 10 kg   (b) 15 kg   (c) 20 kg   (d) 25 kg

11. A lent ₹ 5000 to B for 2 years and ₹ 3000 to C for 4 years on simple interest at the same rate of interest and received ₹ 2200 in all from both of them as interest. The rate of interest per annum is:
    (a) 5%   (b) 7%   (c) $7\frac{1}{8}\%$   (d) 10%

12. Incomes of two companies A and B are in the ratio of 5 : 8. Had the income of company A been more by ₹ 25 lakh, the ratio of their incomes would have been 5 : 4. What is the income of company B?
    (a) ₹ 80 lakh
    (b) ₹ 50 lakh
    (c) ₹ 40 lakh
    (d) ₹ 60 lakh

**Directions** (Qs. 13-18) : *The following passages and answer the questions based on them.*

### PASSAGE-1

Television might be abused and then it may warp the minds of its viewers, especially those young ones who are susceptible and sensitive to every kind of impression. But if it is properly used, it may lead to the enhancement of human life itself. We should try, by means of this great mode of communication, which has such an instant impact on the minds of the people who view it, to enable them to cast off superstition, to emancipate their minds from any kind of narrowness; and combat every kind of false idea which may have become lodged in their minds.

It is, therefore, a great means of education. We should use it for that purpose and it is my earnest hope that it will be employed for the good purpose of improving the quality of our men and women and not for making them shoddy and couch-potatoes.

We should show documentaries, short plays, films and abridgement of classics, so that what the students do not get in school and college might be provided to them when they watch television. Under proper management, television may be regarded as one of the most efficacious modes of mass communication. In it you have sight, hearing, pictures and music all mixed together.

13. The writer calls television as a great means of education because
    (a) it performs the function of a teacher
    (b) it offers lessons as in a classroom
    (c) it teaches viewers to fight many social and personal evils
    (d) it displays various educational programmes

14. Consider the following statements regarding the proper use of television by people
    I. It enhances their life.
    II. It entertains them.
    III. It makes them busy.
    IV. It enables them to rise above archaic prejudices.
    Which of the above statements is/are brought out in the passage?
    (a) Only II        (b) I and IV
    (c) I, II and IV        (d) All of these

15. Consider the following statements regarding the abuse of television
    I. It probably has a detrimental effect on national pride.
    II. It might not have any impact on the minds of viewers.
    III. It may change the eating habits of people.
    IV. It might disturb the minds of the viewers.
    Which of the above statements is/are borne out in the passage?
    (a) Only IV        (b) I, III and IV
    (c) I, II and III        (d) All of these

### PASSAGE-2

Researches suggest that there are creatures that do not know what light means at the bottom of the sea. They do not have either eyes or ears; they can only feel. There is no day or night for them. There are no winters, no summers, no sun, no moon and no stars. It is as if a child spent its life in darkness in bed, with nothing to see or hear. How different our own life is! Sight shows us the ground beneath our feet and the heavens above us-the sun, moon, stars, shooting stars, lightning and the sunset. It shows us day and night. We are able to hear voices, the sound of the sea and music. We feel, we taste, we smell. How fortunate we are!

16. The passage is mainly about.
    (a) life of sea creatures at the bottom of the sea
    (b) the differences among creatures of the earth and those of the sea
    (c) how wonderful our lives were and will be
    (d) the superiority of human beings over some creatures in terms of senses

17. We discover that the sea creatures
    (a) have the same senses that we do
    (b) have no sense of hearing as well as sight
    (c) live in darkness because no light reaches to the bottom
    (d) do not hear the sound of sea as they are accustomed to it

18. In the passage a child in darkness is likened to
    (a) someone who lives where there are no seasons
    (b) an animal without the sense of touch
    (c) a sea creature with no seeing or hearing ability
    (d) deaf child unaffected by the environment

19. In the following question there are four answer figures which can be formed from the cut out pieces given in question figure. Select the correct option.
    **Question Figure :**

**Answer Figures :**

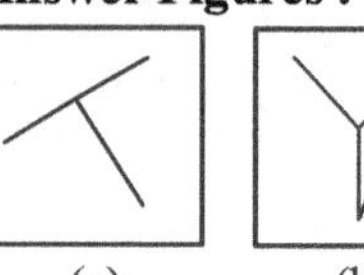  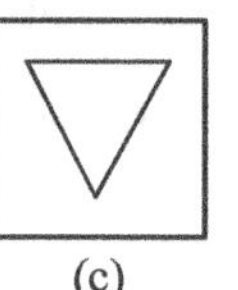 

    (a)       (b)       (c)       (d)

20. Which of the following options would replace the question mark.

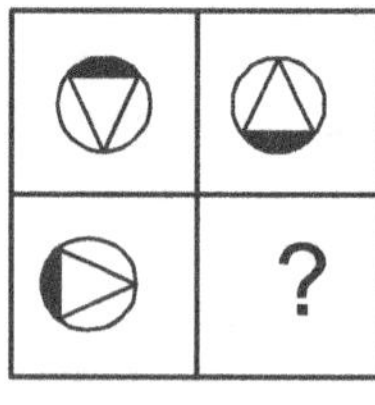 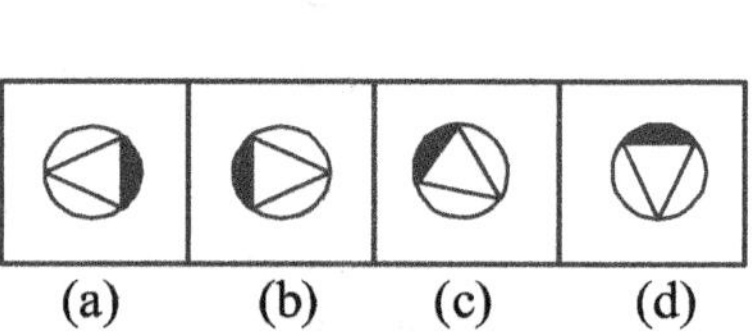

    (a)       (b)       (c)       (d)

21. Study the following information carefully and answer the given question.
    Eight friends P, Q, R, S, T, V, W, and Y are sitting around a square table in such a way that four of them sit at four corners of the square while four sit in the middle of each of the four sides. The ones who sit at the four corners face the centre while those who sits in the middle of the sides face outsides.
    P, who face the centre, sits third to the right of V. T who face the centre, is not an immediate neighbour of V. Only one person sits between V and W . S sits second to the right of Q. Q faces the centre. R is not an immediate neighbour of P.
    Four of the following five are alike in a certain way and so form a group. Which is the one that does not belong to that group?
    (a) R        (b) W
    (c) V        (d) S

**Directions** (Qs.22 – 24): *Read the following information carefully and answer the questions which follow.*

P, Q, R, S, T and V live on different floors of the same building having six floors numbered one to six (the ground floor is numbered 1, the floor above it is numbered 2, and so on, and the topmost floor is numbered 6). There are two floors between on which Q and V live. Q lives on a floor below V's floor. Neither P nor T lives on a floor immediately above or immediately below the floor on which Q lives. P does not live on an odd-numbered floor. There is only one floor between the floors on which S and T live. T does not live on a floor immediately above or immediately below the floor on which R lives.

22. On which of the following floors does V live?
    (a) 4th        (b) 3rd
    (c) 6th        (d) 5th

23. Who among the following lives on the topmost floor, i.e. floor number 6?
    (a) T        (b) S
    (c) R        (d) P

24. How many floors are there between the floors on which R and T live?
    (a) None      (b) One
    (c) Two      (d) Three

25. The wheat sold by a grocer contained 10% low quality wheat. What quantity of good quantity wheat should be added to 250kg of wheat so that the percentage of low quality wheat becomes 5%?
    (a) 285 kg   (b) 250 kg   (c) 135 kg   (d) 150 kg

26. A can do 50% more work as B can do in the same time. B alone can do a piece of work in 20 hours. A, with help of B, can finish the same work in how many hours ?
    (a) 12     (b) 8     (c) $13\frac{1}{3}$     (d) $5\frac{1}{2}$

27. A constable is 114 meters behind a thief. The constable runs 21 meters per minute and the thief runs 15 meters in a minute. In what time will the constable catch the thief ?
    (a) 19 minutes      (b) 18 minutes
    (c) 17 minutes      (d) 16 minutes

28. On January 12, 1980, it was Saturday. The day of the week on January 12, 1979 was –
    (a) Saturday      (b) Friday
    (c) Sunday      (d) Thursday

29. There are two concentric circles whose areas are in the ratio of 9 : 16 and the difference between their diameters is 4 cm. What is the area of the outer circle?
    (a) $32 \text{cm}^2$      (b) $64\pi \text{ cm}^2$
    (c) $36 \text{ cm}^2$      (d) $48 \text{ cm}^2$

30. If *P, R, T* are the area of a parallelogram, a rhombus and a triangle standing on the same base and between the same parallels, which of the following is true?
    (a) $R < P < T$      (b) $P > R > T$
    (c) $R = P = T$      (d) $R = P = 2T$

31. Find the number of terms of the A.P. 98, 91, 84, ...... must be taken to give a sum of zero :
    (a) 14     (b) 15     (c) 31     (d) 29

**Directions** *(Qs. 32-36) : Read the following passages and answer the items that follow them. Your answers to these items should be based on the passages only.*

### PASSAGE-1

What climate change will undeniably do is cause or amplify events that hasten the reduction of resources. Competition over these diminishing resources would ensue in the form of political or even violent conflict. Resource- based conflicts have rarely been overt and are thus difficult to isolate. Instead they take on veneers that appear more politically palatable. Conflicts over resources like water are often cloaked in the guise of identity or ideology.

32. What does the above passage imply?
    (a) Resource-based conflicts are always politically motivated.
    (b) There are no political solutions to resolve environmental and resource based conflicts.
    (c) Environmental issues contribute to resource stresses and political conflicts.
    (d) Political conflicts based on identity or ideology cannot be resolved.

### PASSAGE-2

The man who is perpetually hesitating about which of the two things he should do first, will do neither. The man who resolves, but suffers a change of his resolution by the first counter-suggestion of a friend, who fluctuates from opinion to opinion and veers from plan to plan, can never accomplish anything. He will at best be stationary and probably retrograde in all. It is only the man who first consults wisely, then resolves firmly and then executes his purpose with inflexible perseverance, undismayed by those petty difficulties which daunt a weaker spirit, that can advance to eminence in any line.

33. The keynote that seems to be emerging from the passage is that
    (a) we should first consult wisely and then resolve firmly
    (b) we should reject suggestions of friends and remain unchanged
    (c) we should always remain broad-minded
    (d) we should be resolute and achievement-oriented

### PASSAGE-3

A moral act must be our own act; must spring from our own will. If we act mechanically, there is no moral content in our act. Such action would be moral, if we think it proper to act like a machine and do so. For, in doing so, we use our discrimination. We should bear in mind the distinction between acting mechanically and acting intentionally. It may be moral of a king to pardon a culprit. But the messenger carrying out the order of pardon plays only a mechanical part in the king's moral act. But if the messenger were to carry out the king's order considering it to be his duty, his action would be a moral one. How can a man understand morality who does not use his own intelligence and power of thought, but lets himself be swept along like a log of wood by a current ? Sometimes a man defies convention and acts on his own with a view to absolute good.

34. Which of the following statements best describe/describes the thought of the writer ?
    1. A moral act calls for using our discretion.
    2. Man should react to a situation immediately
    3. Man must do his duty.
    4. Man should be able to defy convention in order to be moral.

    Select the correct answer from the codes given below :
    (a) 1 only      (b) 1 and 3
    (c) 2 and 3      (d) 1 and 4

35. Which of the following statements is the nearest definition of moral action, according to the writer ?
    (a) It is a mechanical action based on official orders from superiors.
    (b) It is an action based on our sense of discretion.
    (c) It is a clever action based on the clarity of purpose.
    (d) It is a religious action based on understanding.

36. The passage contains a statement "lets himself be swept along like a log of wood by a current." Among the following statements, which is/are nearest in meaning to this ?

    1. A person does not use his own reason.

    2. He is susceptible to influence/pressure.

    3. He cannot withstand difficulties/ challenges.

    4. He is like a log of wood.

    Select the correct answer using the codes given below :

    (a) 1 only            (b) 1 and 2

    (c) 2 and 3          (d) 1 and 4

**Directions** (Qs.37–39): *Read the following information and answer the questions given below:*

(i) P, Q, R, S and T finished the work, working from Monday to Saturday, one of the days being a holiday, each working overtime only on one of the days.

(ii) R and T did not work overtime on the first day

(iii) Q worked overtime the next day after the holiday

(iv) The overtime work done on the previous day of the holiday was by R.

(v) There was two days gap between the days on which P and Q worked overtime.

(vi) P worked overtime the next day of the overtime day of S.

37. When did T work overtime?

    (a) On the day previous of that on which S worked overtime

    (b) On the next day of the day on which Q worked overtime

    (c) Two days after the day on which S worked overtime

    (d) Cannot be determined

38. Which of the following is a correct statement?

    (a) P worked overtime, last among them.

    (b) P worked overtime earlier than S

    (c) The holiday was on Friday

    (d) S worked overtime earlier than Q

39. On what day did R work overtime?

    (a) Monday          (b) Tuesday

    (c) Thursday         (d) Wednesday

40. Study the following information carefully and answer the question given below:

(i) A, B, C, D, E, F, G and H are eight students, each having a different height.

(ii) D is shorter than A but taller than G

(iii) E is taller than H but shorter than C

(iv) B is shorter than D but taller than F

(v) C is shorter than G

(v) G is not as tall as F

    Which of the following is definitely false?

    (a) G is shorter than F     (b) C is shorter than F

    (c) F is taller than C      (d) All are true

**Directions** (Qs.41–42): *Study the following information carefully and answer the questions given below:*

Following are the conditions for selecting Chief Manager Sales in an organization. The candidate must

(I) be a graduate in any discipline with at least 60% marks.

(II) have secured at least 55% marks in the selection process.

(III) be at least 30 years and not more than 40 years as on 1. 5. 2017

(IV) be a postgraduate degree/diploma holder in Marketing/Sales Management

(V) have post – qualification work experience of at least eight years in the Sales/Marketing division of an organization.

In the case of a candidate who satisfies all the conditions EXCEPT

(i) at (II) above, but has secured more than 65% marks in graduation, the case is to be referred to GM – sales.

(ii) at (V) above, but has post – qualification work experience of at least five years as Manager – Sales in an organization, the case is to be referred to VP Sales.

In each question below details of one candidate are given. You are to take one of the following courses of action based on the information and the conditions and sub-conditions given above and mark the number of that course of action as the answer. You are not to assume anything other than the information provided in each case. All these cases are given to you as on 01. 05. 2017

**Mark answer** (a) if the candidate is to be selected

**Mark answer** (b) if the data provided are inadequate to take a decision

**Mark answer** (c) if the case is to be referred to the GM – Sales

**Mark answer** (d) If the case is to be referred to the VP - Sales

41. Mohan Das was born on 25th March 1984. He has secured 60% marks in both graduation and 55% marks in the selection process. He is a first-class post graduate degree holder in Management. He has been working for the last eight years in the sales division of an organization.

42. Pravin Vohra was born on 2nd July 1980. He has working in the sales division of an organization for the past ten years after completing his post- graduate degree in Sales Management with 50% marks. He has secured 68% marks in graduation and 50% marks in the selection process.

43. In an examination out of 100 students, 75 passed in English 60 passed in Mathematics and 45 passed in both English and Mathematics. What is the number of students passed in exactly one of the two subjects?

    (a) 45    (b) 60    (c) 75    (d) 90

44. The alphabets of word ALLAHABAD are arranged at random. The probability that in the words so formed, all identical alphabets are found together, is

    (a) 1/63           (b) 16/17

    (c) 5!/9!          (d) None of these

45. On a railway route there are 20 stations. What is the number of different tickets required in order that it may be possible to travel from every station to every other station?

    (a) 40     (b) 380    (c) 400    (d) 420

46. In tossing three coins at a time, what is the probability of getting at most one head?

 (a) $\dfrac{3}{8}$  (b) $\dfrac{7}{8}$  (c) $\dfrac{1}{2}$  (d) $\dfrac{1}{8}$

**Directions** (Qs. 47-49) : *Read the given passage and answer the questions that follow.*

Don't shoot the messenger is usually a good rule to live by. But it is hard when it comes to Bernie Madoff, the former billionaire serving a 150-year jail term for running history's biggest Ponzi scheme.

Yet, in jailhouse interviews, Madoff has given a valuable insight into causes of the Great Recession, whose awful impact has blighted millions of lives across America and around the world.

No one can deny Madoff's activities were an appalling fraud, but, he insists, what about the involvement of everyone else in the global financial system.

"They had to know," Madoff told the New York Times, referring to the banks and hedge funds that greedily reaped millions in fees from his operations. He pointed out to New York magazine that he refused to give the banks any information as to how he got such high returns and would not let them do due diligence. Yet they never complained. "These banks and these funds had to know there were problems," he said.

No wonder that Irving Picard, the trustee representing Madoff's victims, has filed a civil suit seeking damages from banks who did business with Madoff. They include big Wall Street names like HSBC, Citigroup, JP Morgan and Merrill Lynch. Just because Madoff is a crook sitting in jail does not mean he isn't right when he tells us to look elsewhere, too.

Yet, unfortunately, Madoff is the only one behind bars. That is the worst thing about the whole sorry saga. Madoff and his scheme have become a useful foil for the entire finance industry – and a distraction from its venality. It's always Madoff that the tabloids put on the front pages. It's Madoff who is the ultimate banking bogey man. It's Madoff who spurs public outrage and whose jailing has satiated a quest for justice. It is the classic "one bad apple" defence of the kind banks and Wall Street specialise in. It is not the system's or the bosses' fault, they say, it is just a few rogue operators and they have been dealt with.

But we should not be fooled. We should listen to Madoff when he fingers the whole financial sector and the giant firms within it as part of the problem, too. He told New York magazine:

"It's unbelievable … no one has had any criminal convictions. The whole new regulatory reform is a joke."

He's not alone in being amazed that, despite the astonishing frauds and manipulations by Wall Street during the boom years, not one top banking or hedge fund executive sits in jail. It is indeed jaw-dropping.

47. Which of these can be inferred as the 'insight' given by Madoff?
 (a) The Recession was caused by a few rogue operators.
 (b) The Recession was caused by the failure of the banks and financial organizations.
 (c) The Recession was caused by the venality of the finance industry.
 (d) The Recession was caused, in part, by the actions of the banking and financial industry.

48. Why does the author call Madoff the ultimate banking bogeyman?
 (a) Madoff has come to represent the wrongs committed by the banking industry.
 (b) Madoff has come to represent the type of agent that caused the recession.
 (c) Madoff's actions were like those of a bogeyman.
 (d) Madoff was to blame for the banking industry losing millions.

49. Which one of these would be the best title for the passage?
 (a) Bernie Madoff – The new banking poster boy
 (b) Beyond Madoff - Who else is to blame for the Recession?
 (c) How did Bernie Madoff cause the Recession?
 (d) How did the financial sector contribute to the Recession?

50. In a certain code language **"who are you"** is written as **"432"**, **"they is you"** is written as **"485"** and **"they are dangerous"** is written as **"295"**. How is **"dangerous"** written in that code language?
 (a) 2  (b) 4
 (c) 5  (d) 9

51. Ravi has spent a quarter $\left(\dfrac{1}{4}\right)$ of his life as a boy, one–fifth $\left(\dfrac{1}{5}\right)$ as a youth, one-third $\left(\dfrac{1}{3}\right)$ as man and thirteen (13) years in old age. What is his present age?
 (a) 70 years  (b) 80 years
 (c) 60 years  (d) 65 years

52. Find the missing number from the given responses.

 6  18  9
 12  36  18
 24  ?  36

 (a) 18  (b) 72  (c) 54  (d) 60

53. Shan is 55 years old, Sathian is 5 years junior to Shan and 6 years senior to Balan. The youngest brother of Balan is Devan and he is 7 years junior to him. So what is the age difference between Devan and Shan?
 (a) 18 years  (b) 15 years
 (c) 13 years  (d) 7 years

54. How many triangles can be found out from the following figure:

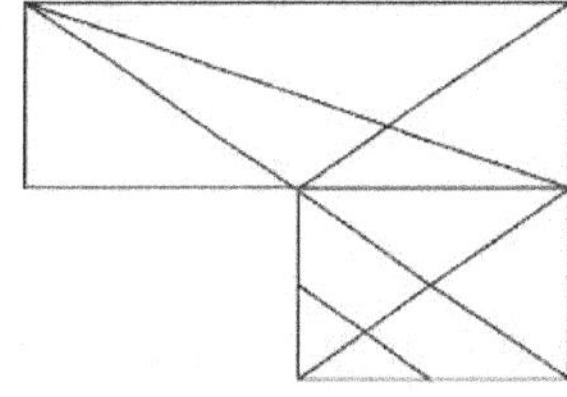

 (a) 17  (b) 21
 (c) 24  (d) 25

(a)    **if only conclusion I follows;**

(b)    **if only conclusion II follows;**

(c)    **if either I or II follows;**

(d)    **if neither I nor II follows;**

55.    **Statement :**    'We follow some of the best and effective teaching and learning practices used by leading institutes all over the world'. — A statement of professor of MN Institute.

**Conclusions :**    I.    The MN Institute is one of the leading institutes of the world.

II.    Whatever is being followed by world's leading institutes will definitely be good and useful.

56.    **Statement :**    In the absence of national health insurance or social security cover, a person with limited resources has to depend on government hospitals, which are crowded, overburdened and understaffed.

**Conclusions :**    I.    National health insurance is meant only for the affluent sections of society.

II.    The government hospitals provide treatment on nominal charges or free.



| Years | Place | | | | |
| --- | --- | --- | --- | --- | --- |
| | Churchgate | Dadar | Kandivali | Borivali | Virar |
| 2005 | 5.3 | 3.8 | 1.5 | 2.7 | 1.1 |
| 2006 | 12.5 | 8.3 | 3.4 | 4.8 | 2.1 |
| 2007 | 16.7 | 11.7 | 5.5 | 6.6 | 1.8 |
| 2008 | 20.9 | 13.6 | 9.8 | 12.7 | 3.6 |
| 2009 | 25.8 | 14.5 | 11.5 | 14.1 | 5.5 |
| 2010 | 30.3 | 20.9 | 15.6 | 15.9 | 7.8 |

57.    In which place did the monthly rent not increase consistently from year 2005 to 2010?

(a) Churchgate          (b) Dadar

(c) Kandivali          (d) Virar

58.    In which year at Churchgate, the monthly rent increased more than 100 per cent from the previous year ?

(a) 2006      (b) 2007      (c) 2008      (d) 2009

59.    What is the difference between the monthly rent at Dadar in the year 2009 and Borivali in the year 2007?

(a) ₹ 7,600

(b) ₹ 7,900

(c) ₹ 8,100

(d) ₹ 8,600

60.    Monthly rent at Kandivali in the year 2008 was approximately what per cent of the total monthly rent at Virar over all the years together ?

(a) 30          (b) 38          (c) 42          (d) 45



### PASSAGE-1

Some people have questioned the judges objectivity in cases of sex discrimination against women. But the record shows that in sixty percent of such cases, the judges have decided in favour of the women. This record demonstrates that the judges have not discriminated against women in cases of sex discrimination against women.

61.    The argument above is flawed if it ignores the possibility that

(a)    Many judges find it difficult to be objective in cases of sex discrimination against women

(b)    A large number of the judges' cases arose out of allegations of sex discrimination against women

(c)    The judges are biased towards women defendants or plaintiffs in cases that do not involve sex discrimination

(d)    The majority of the cases of sex discrimination against women that have reached the judges' courts have been appealed from a lower court

### PASSAGE-2

In a famous experiment at the IISC campus, when a cat smelled milk, it salivated. In the experiment, a bell was rung whenever food was placed near the cat. After a number of trials, only the bell was rung, whereupon the cat would salivate even though no food was present. Such behaviour has been observed in other animals such as dogs, monkeys, etc. and is a vital input for training domesticated animals.

62.    Which of the following conclusions may be drawn from the above experiment?

(a)    The ringing of a bell was associated with food in the mind of the cat.

(b)    Cats and other animals can be easily tricked.

(c)    A conclusion cannot be reached on the basis of one experiment.

(d)    Two stimuli are stronger than one.

## PASSAGE-3

Poverty measurement is an unsettled issue, both conceptually and methodologically. Since poverty is a process as well as an outcome; many come out of it while others may be falling into it. The net effect of these two parallel processes is a proportion commonly identified as the 'head count ratio', but these ratios hide the fundamental dynamism that characterises poverty in practice. The most recent poverty reestimates by an expert group has also missed the crucial dynamism. In a study conducted on 13,000 households which represented the entire country in 1993-94 and again on 2004-05, it was found that in the ten-year period 18.2% rural population moved out of poverty whereas another 22.1% fell into it over this period. This net increase of about four percentage points was seen to have a considerable variation across states and regions.

63. Which of the following is a **conclusion** which can be drawn from the facts stated in the above paragraph ?
    (a) Accurate estimates of number of people living below poverty line in India is possible to be made.
    (b) Many expert groups in India are not interested to measure poverty objectively.
    (c) Process of poverty measurement needs to take into account various factors to tackle its dynamic nature.
    (d) People living below poverty line remain in that position for a very long time.
    (e) None of these

## PASSAGE-4

Argentina's beef cattle herd has dropped to under 50 million from 57 million ten years ago in 1990. The animals are worth less, too: prices fell by over a third last year, before recovering slightly . Most local meat packers and processors are in financial trouble, and recent years has seen a string of plant closures. The Beef producer's Association has now come up with a massive advertisement campaign calling upon Argentines to eat more beef-their "juicy, healthy, routed, plate-filling steaks."

64. Which one of the following , if true, would contribute most to a failure of the campaign?
    (a) There has been a change in consumer preference towards eating leaner meats like chicken and fish.
    (b) Prices of imported beef have been increasing, thus making locally grown beef more competitive in terms of policy.
    (c) The inability to cross breed native cattle with improved varieties has not increased production to adequate levels.
    (d) Animal rights pressure groups have come up rapidly, demanding better and humane treatment of farmyard animals like beef cattle

## PASSAGE-5

Although in the limited sense of freedom regarding appointment and internal working, the independence of the Central Bank is unequivocally ensured, the same cannot be said of its right to pursue monetary policy without co-ordination with the central government. The role of the Central Bank has turned out to be subordinate and advisory in nature.

65. Which one of the following best supports the conclusion drawn in the passage?
    (a) The decision of the chairman of the Central Bank to increase the bank rate by two percentage points sent shock waves in industry, academic and government circles alike.
    (b) Government has repeatedly resorted to monetisation of the debt despite the reservations of the Central Bank.
    (c) The Central Bank does not need the central government's nod for replacing soiled currency notes.
    (d) The inability to remove coin shortage was a major shortcoming of this government.

## PASSAGE-6

Most citizens are very conscientious about observing a law when they can see the reason behind it. For instance, there has been very little need to actively enforce the recently implemented law that increased the penalty for godmen duping people of their money by playing with their emotions. This is because citizens are very conscientious about duping someone in the name of religion, as it leaves their religious gurus with a bad name.

66. Which of the following statements would the author of this passage be most likely to believe?
    (a) The increased penalty alone is a significant motivation for most citizens to obey the law.
    (b) There are still too many inconsiderate citizens in the society.
    (c) Godmen should not be allowed to play with the emotions of the people.
    (d) Society should make an effort to teach citizens the reasons for its laws.

## PASSAGE-7

The burning of coal, oil and other combustible energy sources produces carbon dioxide, a natural constituent of the atmosphere. Elevated levels of carbon dioxide are thought to be responsible for half the greenhouse effect. Enough carbon dioxide has been sent into the atmosphere already to cause a significant temperature increase. Growth in industrial production must be slowed, or production processes must be changed.

67. Which of the following, if true, would tend to weaken the strength of the above conclusion?
    (a) Many areas of the world are cold anyway, so a small rise in temperature would be welcome.
    (b) Carbon dioxide is bad for health
    (c) Most carbon dioxide is emitted by automobiles.
    (d) Industry is switching over to synthetic liquid fuel extracted from coal.

## PASSAGE-8

The purpose of the proposed law requiring a doctor's prescription for obtaining hypodermic needles is to lower the incidence of drug-related deaths, both accidental and intentional, involving hypodermic needles. But even knitting needles can be lethal if they fall into the wrong hands; yet everyone would agree that imposing legal restrictions on obtaining knitting needles would be preposterous. Hence the proposed law involving hypodermic makes no sense and should not be enacted.

68. Which of the following, it true, would provide most support for the argument above?
    (a) Knitting needles have been known to cause injury and death.
    (b) The benefits of hypodermic needles outweigh those of knitting needles.
    (c) The proposed law would not deter the sort of activity known to result in drug-related deaths.
    (d) Knitting needles are not readily available to anybody who wants to obtain them.

## PASSAGE-9

Newspaper publishers earn their profits primarily from advertising revenue, and potential advertisers are more likely to advertise in newspapers with a wide circulation—a large number of subscribers and other readers—than with other newspapers. But the circulation of the newspaper that is currently the most profitable one in this city has steadily declined during the last two years, while the circulation of one of its competitors has steadily increased.

69. Any of the following, if true, would help explain the apparent discrepancy between the two statements above EXCEPT:

    (a) Advertisers generally switch from the most widely circulated newspaper to another one only when the other one becomes the most widely circulated newspaper instead.
    (b) Advertising rates charged by the most profitable newspaper in the city are significantly higher than those charged by its competitors.
    (c) The most profitable newspaper in the city receives revenue from its subscribers as well from advertisers.
    (d) The number of newspapers competing viably with the most profitable newspaper in the city has increased during the last two years.

## PASSAGE-10

The company encourages its managers to interact regularly, without a pre-set agenda, to discuss issues concerning the company and society. This idea has been borrowed from the ancient Indian concept of religious congregation, called *satsang*. Designations are forgotten during these meetings; hence, it is not uncommon in these meetings to find a sales engineer questioning the CEO on some corporate policy or on his knowledge of customers

70. Based on the information provided in the above passage, it can be inferred that
    (a) The company is concerned about its reputation with its employees.
    (b) The company believes in fostering the spirit of dialogue without degenerating it into a position-based debate.
    (c) The company has some inter-personnel problems in the past due to which it felt the need for these corporate satsangs.
    (d) All of the above

71. The following graph shows the total revenues and total costs of QN Corporation, a publicly traded company, over the span 2007-2015. Recall that, for any year, profit = (revenue) - (cost).

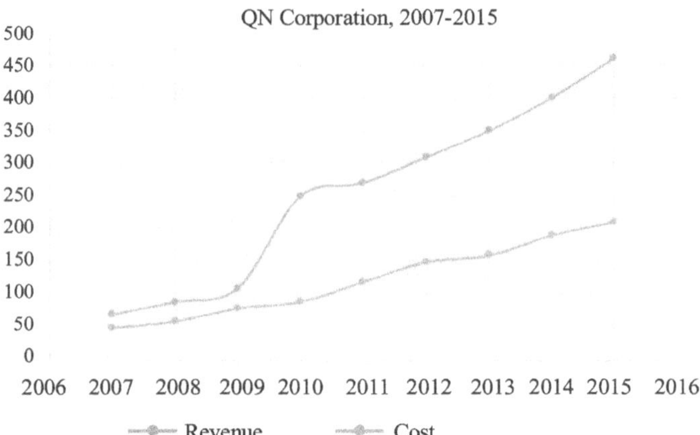


From 2009 to 2010, profit at QN Corporation increased by approximately what percent?
    (a) 81%          (b) 165%
    (c) 300%         (d) 433%

72. The graph below shows the distribution of a group of garages according to the number of junk cars in their garages. Select the statement that correctly gives a relationship between measures of central tendency for this distribution.

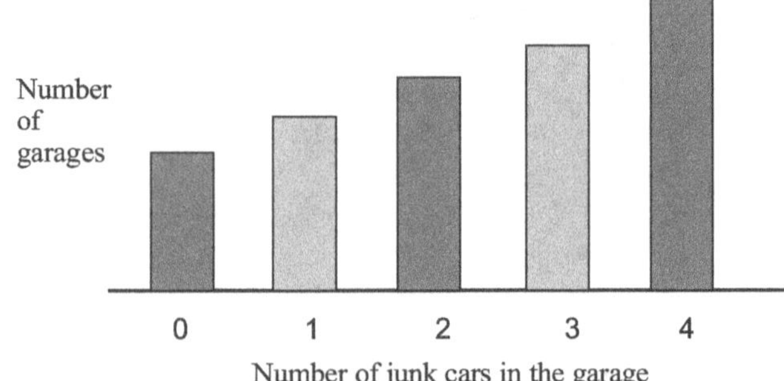


    (a) The mean is the same as the median.
    (b) The mean is less than the mode.
    (c) The mode is less than the mean.
    (d) The median is less than the mean.

73. If $x+y>5$ and $x-y>3$, then which of the following gives all possible values of $x$?
    (a) $x>3$    (b) $x>4$
    (c) $x>5$    (d) $x<5$

74. On an average 300 people watch the movie in Sahu cinema hall on Monday, Tuesday and Wednesday and the average number of visitors on Thursday and Friday is 250. If the average number of visitors per day in the week be 400, then the average number of people who watch the movie in weekends (*i.e.,* on Saturday and Sunday) is
    (a) 500    (b) 600
    (c) 700    (d) None of these

75. The profit earned when an article is sold for ₹ 800 is 20 times the loss incurred when it is sold for ₹ 275. At what price should the article be sold if it is desired to make a profit of 25%
    (a) ₹ 300    (b) ₹ 350
    (c) ₹ 375    (d) ₹ 400

76. In the question below is given a statement followed by two assumptions number I and II.

    An assumption is something supposed or taken for granted. You have to consider the statement and the following assumption and decide which of the assumptions is implicit in the statement.

    Give answer:

    (a) if only assumption I is implicit.

    (b) if only assumption II is implicit.

    (c) if either assumption I or II is implicit.

    (d) if neither assumption I nor II is implicit.

    **Statement:** Give adequate job-related training to the employees before assigning them full-fledged work

    **Assumption:** I. Training helps in boosting the performance of employees

    **II.** Employees have no skill sets before training is provided to them

**Directions** (Qs. 77-79) : *Read the passage below and answer the questions that follow.*

The government cannot afford to compartmentalize education. It has to be emphasized that any country which does not have a good university education will never be listed as an independent country and will never be able to progress. Only countries prepared to tolerate a second rate and subjugate status in the world would neglect higher education. If India has had any position in the comity of nations in the past, it was only because it had a better higher education than many of its Asian counterparts. This clearly lays emphasis on higher education, however, does not imply that it should be supported and developed at the cost of primary and secondary education.

77. Which of the following best explains the main idea of the passage?
    (a) Higher education is important for the growth of a country
    (b) To emphasize more on primary education rather than higher education
    (c) The government has made a wrong move in compartmentalizing education
    (d) To highlight the superiority of India in higher education as compared to the rest of the world

78. Which of the following is the most likely title of the passage?
    (a) Lack of higher education opportunities in India.
    (b) A comparison of higher education in India with that of the West
    (c) Importance of higher education in the growth of a country
    (d) Basic education versus higher education

79. The passage answers which of the followings
    I.   Why primary and secondary education is important?
    II.  How higher education is related to the growth of the country?
    III. Why higher education is important for the country?
    (a) Only I    (d) Both II and III
    (c) Only III    (d) All of these

80. While your opinions/arguments matter a lot, it is also extremely necessary to listen to others' opinions/views. What is the most important principle of active listening?
    (a) Asking a lot of questions
    (b) Acknowledging the speaker
    (c) Keep an eye on what everyone else is doing
    (d) Referring to FAQ's and asking questions accordingly.

# SOLUTIONS

1. (d) J2Z, K4X, I7V, ___, H16R

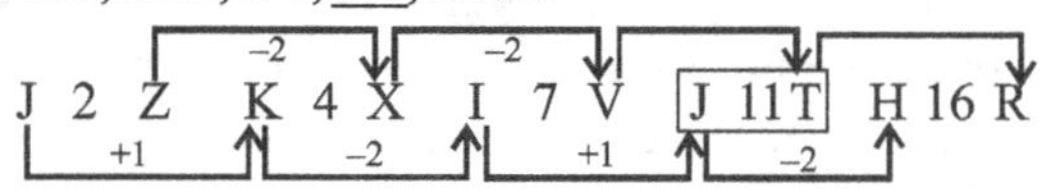

The numbers are increasing in the sequence: $+2, +3, +4, +5$.

2. (c) mother

3. (a) $45° + 180° - 270° = -45°$ ie, 45° anticlockwise from initial position. Hence, the required direction is south – west.

4. (b) In option (b) "?" and "/" are adjacent to each other, which cannot be possible.

5. (c) We assume number three is common in both the figures when the block in figure (ii) to be rotated so that three appears at the same position as in figure (i) and the numbers 5 and 2 move to the faces hidden behind the numbers 4 and 6 respectively. Thus, the combined figure will have 3 on right hand side face, 4 on the front face, 6 on the top face, 5 on the rear face and 2 on the bottom face. Clearly, when 2 is at the bottom, then 6 is at the top.

6. (c) $N = 387\,Q + 48$
$N = (43 \times 9)\,Q + (43 \times 1) + 5$
Hence, remainder obtained when N is divided by 43 = 5.

7. (d) It is clear that b will be zero. The last three digit 4a0 will be divisible by 8 if a = 0 or 8. So, a + b = 0 or 8.

8. (c) Here two concepts are asked Concept 1- The numbers must be more than or equal to HCF and less than or equal to LCM, and numbers must be a multiple of HCF and factor of LCM. Only option (c) satisfies these conditions.

9. (b) Let the numbers be x, y and z. Then,
$x + y = 10$ ..... (1)   $y + z = 19$ ..... (2)
$x + z = 21$ ..... (3)
Adding (1), (2) and (3), we get :
$2(x + y + z) = 50$
or $x + y + z = 25$.
Thus, $x = 25 - 19 = 6$; $y = 25 - 21 = 4$;
$z = 25 - 10 = 15$.
Hence, the required numbers are 6, 4 and 15.

10. (a) Let the original quantity be $x$ kg. Vanaspati ghee in
$$x \text{ kg} = \left(\frac{40}{100}x\right) \text{kg} = \left(\frac{2x}{5}\right) \text{kg}.$$
Now, $\dfrac{\frac{2x}{5}}{x+10} = \dfrac{20}{100} \Leftrightarrow \dfrac{2x}{5x+50} = \dfrac{1}{5}$
$\Leftrightarrow 5x = 50 \Leftrightarrow x = 10$ kg.

11. (d) Let the rate be R% p.a. Then,
$$\left(\frac{5000 \times R \times 2}{100}\right) + \left(\frac{3000 \times R \times 4}{100}\right) = 2200$$
$$\Rightarrow 100R + 120R = 2200 \Rightarrow R = \left(\frac{2200}{220}\right) = 10\%.$$

12. (c) Let the incomes of two companies $A$ and $B$ be $5x$ and $8x$ respectively.
From the question,
$$\frac{5x + 25}{8x} = \frac{5}{4} \Rightarrow 20x + 100 = 40x \; \therefore \; x = 5$$
$\therefore$ Income of company $B = 8x = ₹\,40$ lakh

13. (c) This answer choice paraphrases the last sentence of the first paragraph. The other choices do not answer the 'means of education' phrase in the question.

14. (b) Both statements I and IV are given in the first paragraph. The other statements are not mentioned in the passage.

15. (a) Statement IV paraphrases 'it may warp the minds of its viewers', which is mentioned in the first sentence of the passage. Statement II is contrary to this and statements I and III are not mentioned in the passage.

16. (d) The passage focuses mainly on the superiority of human beings over some creatures due to senses that we have.

17. (b) It is clearly stated in the passage that the sea creatures in the story have no sense of hearing as well as sight.

18. (c) In the passage, a child in darkness is compared with small sea creatures with no sense of seeing or hearing.

19. (b) The figure in option (b) is one of the part of the question figure.

20. (a)

21. (d)

Other sits in the middle of the sides

**Solution for(22-24)**

| Floor | Person |
|-------|--------|
| 6 | P |
| 5 | T |
| 4 | V |
| 3 | S |
| 2 | R |
| 1 | Q |

22. (a) is the correct answer

23. (d) is the correct answer

24. (c) is the correct answer

25. (b) Here, 10% of 250 kg = 25 kg
So good quality of wheat is 225.
To become the 5% low quality of wheat, we add 250 kg of more wheat.

**26. (b)** B alone can do a work in 20 hours.

$\therefore$ A alone can do $\dfrac{3}{2}$ of the work in 20 hours.

i.e., A alone can do the same work in $\dfrac{40}{3}$ hours

$\therefore$ (A + B)'s one hour's work $= \dfrac{3}{40} + \dfrac{1}{20} = \dfrac{5}{40} = \dfrac{1}{8}$

$\Rightarrow$ A and B together can finish the whole work in 8 hours.

**27. (a)** $V_{relative} = (21 - 15)\,\text{m/min} = 6\,\text{m/min}$
Time taken to catch the thief

$= \dfrac{114}{6}\,\text{min} = 19\,\text{minutes}$

**28. (b)** The year 1979 being an ordinary year, it has 1 odd day.

So, the day on 12th January 1980 is one day beyond on the day on 12th January, 1979.

But, January 12, 1980 being Saturday.

$\therefore$ January 12, 1979 was Friday.

**29. (b)** $\dfrac{r}{R} = \dfrac{3x}{4x}$

$\because$ $4x - 3x = 2$

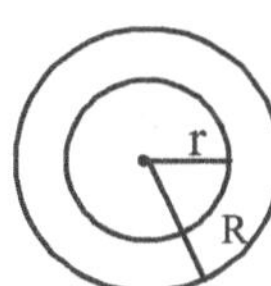

$\Rightarrow$ $x = 2$
$\therefore$ Outer radius $= 8$ cm
$\therefore$ Area of outer circle $= \pi \times (8)^2 = 64\,\pi\,\text{cm}^2$

**30. (d)** Parallelogram Area $= 1 \times b$
Rhombus area $= 1 \times b$

Triangle area $= \dfrac{l \times b}{2}$

Therefore R = P = 2T.

**31. (d)** $S_n = \dfrac{n}{2}\big[2a + (n-1)\,d\big]$

$0 = \dfrac{n}{2}\big[196 + (n-1)\times(-7)\big]$

$\Rightarrow$ $0 = n\,(203 - 7n)$
$\Rightarrow$ $7n = 203$ or $n = 0$
$\Rightarrow$ $n = 29$
Since $n = 0$ is not acceptable.
The A.P. is 98, 91, 84, .......... 0, ......., $-91, -98$

**32. (c)** The passage elucidates the environmental issues contributing to resource stresses and political conflict.

**33. (a)** The essence of the passage is that one should first consult wisely and then resolve firmly.

**34. (d)** Statement 1 is correct as the writer talks of 'moral act that should be done by our own will'. Statement 4 is also correct as it involves personal thinking and in order to be moral, one may have to defy convention.

**35. (b)** According to the writer moral action is neither mechanical nor based on clarity of purpose and religious action.

**36. (b)** Only statements 1 and 2 are correct as 'lets himself be swept away' means he does not hold his own ground.

**Solution for (37-39) :**

| Person | Overtime |
|---|---|
| S | Monday |
| P | Tuesday |
| R | Wednesday |
| Holiday | Thursday |
| Q | Friday |
| T | Saturday |

**37. (b)**    **38. (d)**    **39. (d)**

**40. (d)**
$A > D > G$   ....(ii)
$C > E > H$   ....(iii)
$D > B > F$   ....(iv)
$G > C$   ....(v)
$F > G$   ....(vii)
Combining these, we get $A > D > B > F > G > C > E > H$
(d) is the correct answer.

**Solution for 41-42:**

| Q .No. | I | II/(i) | III | IV | V/(ii) |
|---|---|---|---|---|---|
| 41. (c) | √ | √ | √ | √ | √ |
| 42. (d) | √ | √ | √ | √ | √ |

**43. (a)** Total number of students $= 100$
Let $E$ denote the students who have passed in English.
Let $M$ denote the students who have passed in Maths.
$\therefore$ $n(E) = 75$, $n(M) = 60$ and $n(E \cap M) = 45$
we know $n(E \cup M) = n(E) + n(M) - n(E \cap M) = 75 + 60 - 45 = 90$
Required number of students $= 90 - 45 = 45$

**44. (a)** (AAAA), (LL), HBD

$P = \dfrac{\dfrac{5!}{9!}}{\dfrac{9!}{4!\,2!}} = \dfrac{5! \times 4! \times 2!}{9!} = \dfrac{24 \times 2}{9 \times 8 \times 7 \times 6} = \dfrac{1}{63}$

**45. (b)** From each railway station, there are 19 different tickets to be issued. There are 20 railway station

So, total number of tickets $= 20 \times 19 = 380$.

**46. (c)** Possible samples are as follows
{HHH, HTH, HHT, THH, TTH, THT, HTT, TTT}
Let A be the event of getting one head.
Let B be the event of getting no head.
Favourable outcome for

$A = \{TTH, THT, HTT\}$

Favourable outcome for $B = \{TTT\}$

Total no. of outcomes $= 8$

$\therefore$ $P(A) = \dfrac{3}{8}$, $P(B) = \dfrac{1}{8}$

$\therefore$ Required probability = Probability of getting one head + Probability of getting no head, $= P(A) + P(B)$

$= \dfrac{3}{8} + \dfrac{1}{8} = \dfrac{4}{8} = \dfrac{1}{2}$

47. (d) Throughout the passage the author has argued that the banks and the financial sector had an important role in causing the Great Recession. Bernie Madoff is guilty but he is hardly the only person who deserves to go to prison. Refer to the lines "Just because Madoff is a crook sitting in jail does not mean he isn't right when he tells us to look elsewhere, too." Option (a) cannot be the answer as it cannot be the insight given by Madoff. Also, option (a) is contradictory to the author's opinion-"It is the classic "one bad apple" defence of the kind banks and Wall Street specialise in. It is not the system's or the bosses' fault, they say, it is just a few rogue operators and they have been dealt with...". Option (b) states that the recession was caused by the failure of banking organizations , which is incorrect. The option does not state what exactly this failure was. Option (c) is not the answer as the author merely mentions the venality of the finance industry. He/she does not attribute the Recession to it.

48. (b) The answer can be inferred from the lines "Madoff and his scheme have become a useful foil for the entire finance industry... ... It's Madoff who spurs public outrage and whose jailing has satiated a quest for justice". The author says that it is Madoff who is ultimately cast as the villain and the cause of the recession by the entire finance industry. Option (b) comes closest to expressing this. Option (a) is incorrect as it does not specifically discuss the role of banking industry in causing recession .

49. (b) This reflects the topic of the passage.

50. (d)

$$\text{Who } \overset{\triangle}{(are)} \quad \text{you} \quad = \quad 4 \quad 3 \quad \textcircled{2}$$
$$\overset{\triangle}{they} \quad \text{is} \quad \text{you} \quad = \quad 4 \quad 8 \quad \overset{\triangle}{5}$$
$$\overset{\triangle}{they} \quad (are) \quad \boxed{\text{dangerous}} \quad = \quad \textcircled{2} \quad \boxed{9} \quad \overset{\triangle}{5}$$

51. (c) Suppose his present age is x years.
According to question

$$\frac{x}{4} + \frac{x}{5} + \frac{x}{3} = x - 13$$

$$\Rightarrow \frac{15x + 12x + 20x}{60} = x - 13$$

$$\Rightarrow 47x = 60x - 780$$
$$\Rightarrow 60x - 47x = 780$$
$$\Rightarrow 13x = 780$$

$$\therefore x = \frac{780}{13} = 60 \text{ years}$$

52. (b) $6 \times 2 = 12 \times 2 = 24$
$9 \times 2 = 18 \times 2 = 36$
$18 \times 2 = 36 \times 2 = \boxed{72}$

53. (a) Age of Shan = 55 years
Age of Sathian = 55 − 5 = 50 years
Age of Balan = 50 − 6 = 44 years
Age of Devan = 44 − 7 = 37 years
Difference between the ages of Shan and Devan = 55 − 37 = 18 years.

54. (d)

55. (d) II may be an assumption which the professor is assuming before passing his statement but it definitely cannot be a conclusion. Hence, II does not follow. I may or may not be possible. Hence I, does not follow.

56. (b) It is clear that either there is no facility for health insurance available or it is available for only affluent sections. Hence, I cannot be definitely concluded. II follows from the given statement, as 'limited resources' of the person suggests that he will go to a hospital which provides treatment on nominal charges or free.

57. (d) As we follow the table, we can observe that the rent of all the cities gradually increases except virar, whose rent fluctuates from 2005 to 2010.

58. (a) If we observe that the Churchgate, monthly rent increases more than 100% in 2006.

59. (b)

66. (d) In 2008 Kandiwali was 9.8. Virar = 21.9, required % = [9.8/21.9] × 100 = 44.7% or 45%

61. (a) The record that 60% of judges have decided in favour of the women doesn't prove that the judges have not discriminated against women in cases of sex discrimination against women. There might be a possibility that there is a set of judges who are not objective in cases of sex discrimination against women, thus making the record equivalent to 60%. Hence we can say that there are some judges who have discriminated against women in cases of sex discrimination against women

62. (b) This passage is a typical example of Response to Stimuli. Clearly the cat starts salivating when the bell rungs because she has related the ringing of bell with food in the back of her mind.

63. (c) According to passage, the most recent poverty restumates by an expert group has missed the crucial dynamism so we can conclude procers of poverty measurement needs to take into account various factors to tackle its dynamic nature.

64. (c) (c) contributes most to the failure of the campaign because if production is not raised to adequate levels, and if cross bred varieties are not successfully brought about, there would be a lesser number of people eating beef. The passage mentions the drop in the cattle herd as the reason for this trouble. So, if the drop continues the campaign will fail.

65. (a) (a) is the only option that makes sense as the passage catagorically mentions that the Central Bank does not have the right to pursue monetary policy without coordination with the central government.

66. (d) The opening sentence provides the cue to solving this problem, which clearly says that the citizens will definitely obey a law if they understand the reason behind its imposition. So, the society should make an effort to teach citizens the reasons for its laws.

67. (a) In the third and fourth lines of the passage it is clearly mentioned that huge amount of carbon dioxide has already been sent into the atmosphere to cause global warming. So, option (a), if true would mean that there is no need to be concerned regarding this situation.

68. (a) The argument is essentially that the proposed law makes no sense because knitting needles are dangerous as well. The argument relies explicitly on an analogy between hypodermic and knitting needles. Thus, the two must be similar in all respects relevant to the argument. Otherwise, the argument is unconvincing. option (a) affirms that knitting needles are in fact dangerous, thereby affirming the analogy between the two types of needles. Options (b) and (c) each in its own way supports the bare assertion that the proposed law might not be effective. However, none of these answer choices affirms the argument's essential reasoning.

Option (d) actually *weakens* the argument, by providing a reason why hypodermic needles and knitting needles are *not* relevantly similar.

69. (d) Assuming that the number of viable competitors has increased during the last two years, the likely result would be to draw circulation away from already viable newspapers, including the most profitable ones. Given that profitability depends primarily on advertising revenues and therefore on circulation, (d) actually exacerbates the discrepancy between the two statements.

(a) help explain why the most profitable newspaper remains most profitable even though its circulation is declining: Advertisers have not yet begun to switch because the most profitable newspaper is still the most widely circulated.

(b) helps explain the discrepancy. Although the argument provides that advertisers are more likely to advertise with widely circulated newspapers than with others, it is entirely possible that other factors, such as advertising rates that a newspaper charges, also affect which newspapers advertisers choose.

(c) helps explain the discrepancy, by identifying another source of revenue and therefore another means of enhancing profitability. Simply stated, the more sources of revenue the more profitable a newspaper is likely to be. This in turn helps explain why the most profitable newspaper in the city remains the most profitable one, despite declining circulation.Obviously, as circulation decreases so does subscriber revenue, and thus overall profitability. Yet the newspaper's profitability is still greater than it would be without revenue, from its subscribers.

70. (b) (b) is the only option as according to the passage designations can be forgotten and even a subordinate like a sales engineer can question the CEO.

71. (d) We have a few different calculations to do here, but fortunately, the answers are spread out, so we can estimate. In 2009, revenue was about $110M and cost was about $80M, so profit was about $30M. In 2010,

revenue was $250M and cost ws abut $90M, So profit was about $160M. That's more than 5 times.

This is tricky. If something doubles, that's a 100% increase. If it triples, that's a 200% increase. Following this pattern, if something is multiplied by five, that's a 400% increase, because four identical parts were added to the original part.

In this problem, $160M is more than five times, but less than six times, $30M. Thus, the percent increase has to be between 400% and 500%. The only possibility is 433%.

72. (b) This is an example of data **skewed to the left.**

It is easy to identify the mode: the mode is 4, since 4 is the value under the tallest column.

Notice also that 4 is greatest number in this distribution. This indicates that the mean and the median should both be less than 4 (because in a collection of numbers that are not all identical the average number must be larger than the smallest number and smaller than the largest number).

We see that choice (b) is correct.

73. (b) $x + y > 5$ ...(1)

$x - y > 3$ ...(2)

Adding inequations (1) and (2), we get

$2x > 8$ i.e. $x > 4$

74. (c) $400 \times 7 = (300 \times 3) + (250 \times 2) + (n \times 2) \Rightarrow = 700.$

75. (c) The interpretation of the first statement is that if the loss at 275 is 1L, the profit at 800 is 20L.

Thus, $21L = 800 - 275 = 525 \rightarrow L = 25.$

Thus, the cost price of the item is ₹ 300.

To get a profit of 25%, the selling price should be $1.25 \times 300 = 375.$

76. (a) I is implicit in the need for training. But II takes things to an extreme with the phrase "no skill sets".

77. (a) The author has laid emphasis on the importance of higher education by stating that, any country which is devoid of having higher education will never be able to progress.

78. (c) The passage starts with the importance of higher education and this is the also the main idea of the passage. Option (a) is not mentioned in the passage. Options (b) and (d) are either distorted or partial reading of the passage.

79. (c) Primary and secondary education are important but why they are important is not mentioned in the passage. So, I is not right. Higher education is important but how it is related to the growth of the country is not mentioned in the passage. So, only III is right.

80. (b) It is extremely important to acknowledge the speaker and his views. It is not important to ask questions if you do not have a relevant point to make. Option c is also frivolous as it is not at all relevant to keep an eye on what everyone is doing. Option d cannot be the answer as referring to FAQ's is not a part of active listening.

# MOCK TEST - 9

**Max. Marks : 200**                                                    **Time : 2 hrs.**

**Directions** (Qs. 1-6) : *Read the following passages and answer the questions based on them.*

### PASSAGE - 1

The British monarch, Elizabeth II, in a green dress and leprechaun hat daintily sipping a glass of Guinness through a straw would have been a most fantastic depiction anytime in her past 59-year reign. But on Wednesday a cartoon in London's Independent came close to reality, excepting perhaps the frothy beer mug dancing in the air. For the first time in a century, ever since her grandfather, George V, crossed the Irish Sea, a reigning British monarch has set foot on Ireland. That absence of a hundred years puts into relief the bloodshed, bitter enmity and mistrust that have marked Anglo-Irish relations and cleaved the two nations all along. As a foil, her presence has been invested, not very surprising for Dublin, by a high degree of symbolism — some real, some exaggerated. The real: the queen's laying of the wreath at the Garden of Remembrance to honour the Irish patriots who fought against the British. The exaggerated: her green cloak to go with the Emerald Isle.

The queen's visit is meant to symbolise more than anything else an acknowledgment that history should not be allowed to stand in the way of the future; that the two nations have come a long way since the Easter Rising and the Irish War of Independence and the many fraught years since. While Sinn Fein's black balloons, the largely deserted streets and the heavy security presence reminded that history could not be too easily wished away, the queen took the first step towards a new rapprochement between the old adversaries. A year ago, British Prime Minister David Cameron had already apologised for the Bloody Sunday of 1972.

As Stephen said in Ulysses, "History is a nightmare from which I am trying to awake." That is quite like what the British and the Irish are trying to do.

1. Which of the following can be inferred from the passage?
   I. Relations between England and Ireland are cordial now.
   II. Both Irish and British have been making efforts to ease the tension between the two nations.
   III. The queen had chosen her attire to match Irish colours.
   (a) Only I           (b) II and III
   (c) I and II         (d) None of these

2. How is the quote from Ulysses relevant to Britain and Ireland?
   (a) After years of conflict between Britain and Ireland, efforts are being made to resolve issues.
   (b) After years of shared misfortune, Britain and Ireland are trying to make amends.
   (c) Both Britain and Ireland have a tragic past that they are trying to recover from.
   (d) Britain and Ireland have had bitter enmity and mistrust toward each other but that is now a thing of the past.

### PASSAGE-2

The Indian pharma industry is flourishing overseas, touching almost every part of the world. With low cost, speed and high-quality advantage, India is gearing up to become the hub for contract research and manufacturing. Having a competitive edge is one thing and maintaining it is another. Canada provides tax benefits of up to 46 per cent for research carried out within India. Others like Korea and China without a pool of scientists make up by facilitating foreign research in every conceivable way. India does not do any of this and faces many hurdles like diseases that it has been inflicted with since independence like malaria and Tuberculosis. While Indian companies have focused only on reverse engineering blockbuster drugs from MNCs, overseas scientists have displayed little interest in researching subcontinent specific diseases as there are more benefits and public interests in lifestyle drugs such as obesity.

3. According to the passage, the disadvantage of holding clinical trials abroad is
   (a) Research facilities in India are far more sophisticated
   (b) Delayed processing of test data
   (c) The laws abroad are more stringent
   (d) Higher cost resulting in the drain of financial resources

4. Which of the following measures has Korea taken to be competitive in the pharma industry?
   (a) It enacts relaxed tax laws
   (b) It collaborates with foreign research firms
   (c) It provides speedy regulatory approvals
   (d) It offers blockbuster drugs at highly subsidized rates

5. Which of the following is/are India's strength(s) in drug discovery and research?
   I. Relaxed patent laws.
   II. Reverse engineering of foreign blockbuster drugs.
   III. Incentives to foreign companies researching subcontinent diseases.
   (a) Only III        (b) I and III
   (c) Only I          (d) None of these

6. The Indian pharma industry
   (a) trails in research on health threats like obesity
   (b) is the largest growing in the world
   (c) only has the expertise to reverse-engineer drugs
   (d) provides quality research at low cost

7. $7^{12} - 4^{12}$ is exactly divisible by which of the following number?
   (a) 34    (b) 33    (c) 36    (d) 35

8. A red light flashes 3 times per minute and a green light flashes 5 times in two minutes at a regular intervals. If both lights start flashing at the same time, how many times do they flash together in each hour?
   (a) 30    (b) 24    (c) 20    (d) 60

9. A two digit number is such that the product of its digits is 12. When 9 is added to the number, the digits interchange their places, find the number :
   (a) 62    (b) 34    (c) 26    (d) 43

10. The average age of Mr. and Mrs Sinha at the time of their marriage in 1972 was 23 years. On the occasion of their anniversary in 1976, they observed that the average age of their family had come down by 4 years compared to their average age at the time of their marriage. This was due to the fact that their son Vicky was born during that period. What was the age of Vicky in 1980?
    (a) 6      (b) 7      (c) 8      (d) 5

11. 10% of the inhabitants of a village having died of cholera, a panic set in, during which 25% of the remaining inhabitants left the village. The population is then reduced to 4050. Find the number of original inhabitants.
    (a) 5000      (b) 6000      (c) 7000      (d) 8000

12. The ratio of the amount for two years under C.I. annually and for one year under S.I. is $6 : 5$. When the rate of interest is same, then the value of rate of interest is
    (a) 12.5%      (b) 18%      (c) 20%      (d) 16.66%

**Directions** *(Qs. 13 – 17): Study the following information to answer the given questions.*

Eight people, viz A, B, C, D, E, F, G and H are sitting in a straight line facing North. Each of them has passed a recruitment exam and must join the office in different months, viz January, February, March, April, May, June, July and August but not necessarily in the same order.

G sits third to the right of the person who joins in May. The person who joins in August sits second to the right of G. A and E are immediate neighbours of each other. Neither A nor E has joining dates in either May or August. Neither A nor E is an immediate neighbour of G.

H sits third to the right of the person whose joining date is in January. Neither A nor E has joining dates in January. H's joining date is not in August

Only two people sit between E and the person whose joining date is in July. The person whose joining date is in February sits on the immediate left of D.

Only one person sits between E and B. C joins before July. E joins after April. G joins after A.

13. In which of the following months does H join the office?
    (a) April             (b) June
    (c) July              (d) February

14. Who among the following sits exactly between E and B?
    (a) The person whose joining date is in May
    (b) The person whose joining is in January
    (c) D
    (d) A

15. 'H' is related to 'July' in a certain way based on the above arrangement. 'B' is related to 'June' following the same pattern. '________' is related to 'May' following the same pattern.
    (a) F             (b) G
    (c) A             (d) D

16. Which of the following is true regarding D?
    (a) Only two people sit to the left of D
    (b) D is sitting second to the right of the person whose joining date is in July.
    (c) E and B are immediate neighbours of D
    (d) None is true

17. Who among the following has joining date in June?
    (a) F                    (b) E
    (c) G                    (d) D

18. In a partnership, $A$ invests $\frac{1}{6}$ of the capital for $\frac{1}{6}$ of the time, $B$ invests $\frac{1}{3}$ of the capital for $\frac{1}{3}$ of the time and $C$, the rest of the capital for whole time. Find $A$'s share of the total profit of ₹2,300.
    (a) ₹100      (b) ₹200      (c) ₹300      (d) ₹400

19. Find the ratio in which rice at ₹7.20 a kg be mixed with rice at ₹5.70 a kg to produce a mixture worth ₹6.30 a kg.
    (a) $4 : 3$      (b) $3 : 4$      (c) $2 : 3$      (d) $3 : 2$

20. Two fill pipes A and B can fill a cistern in 12 and 16 minutes respectively. Both fill pipes are opened together, but 4 minutes before the cistern is full, one pipe A is closed. How much time will the cistern take to fill ?
    (a) $9\frac{1}{7}$ min.           (b) $3\frac{1}{3}$ min.
    (c) 5 min.            (d) 3 min.

21. A 200 m long train passes a 350 m long platform in 5s. If a man is walking at a speed of 4 m/s along the track and the train is 100 m away from him, how much time will it take to reach the man?
    (a) Less than 1 s      (b) 1.04 s
    (c) More than 2 s      (d) Data insufficient

22. The calendar for the year 2005 is the same as for the year :
    (a) 2010      (b) 2011      (c) 2012      (d) 2013

23. **Statement:** Should all those who are convicted for heinous crimes like murder or rape, beyond all reasonable doubts be given capital punishment or death penalty?

    **Arguments:** I. No. the death penalty should be given only in very rare and exceptional cases.

    II. Yes. This is the only way to punish such people who take others' lives or indulge in inhuman activities.

    III. Yes. Such severe punishments only will make people refrain from such heinous acts and the society will be safer.

    IV. No. Those who are repentant for the crime they committed should be given a chance to improve and lead a normal life.

    Which of the argument is/ase stsong argument (s) of the given statement.
    (a) Only II and IV are strong
    (b) All are strong
    (c) Only III is strong
    (d) Only II and III are strong

**Directions** **(Qs. 24 – 25)** : *Study the following information carefully and answer these questions given below:*

Following are the conditions for selecting Chief Manager – Marketing in an organization:

The candidate must

I.    be at least 35 years old as on 1–2–2017

II.   have secured at least 55% marks in graduation

III.  have secured at least 60% marks in post – graduate degree/diploma in Marketing Management.

IV.   have post – qualification work experience of at least 10 years in the marketing Division of an organization

V.    have secured at least 50% marks in the selection process.

In the case of a candidate who satisfies all the above conditions EXCEPT

(i)   at (IV) above, but has post – qualification work experience of at least six years as Manager – Marketing, the case is to b referred to Head – Marketing Division

(ii)  at (II) above, but has secured at least 65% marks in post graduate degree/diploma in Marketing Management, the case is to be referred to GM – Marketing.

In each question below, details of one candidate are given. You have to take one of the following courses of action based on the information provided and the conditions and sub – conditions given above and mark the number of that course of action as your answer. You are not to assume anything other than the information provided in each question. All these cases are given to you as on 01. 04. 2017.

Mark answer (a) if the case is to be selected.

Mark answer (b) if the case is to be referred to the Head – Marketing Division

Mark answer (c) if case is to be referred to GM – Marketing

Mark answer (d) if the data provided are inadequate to take a decision.

24.   Nayan Dastur was born on 8$^{th}$ October 1975. He has secured 55% marks in graduation and the selection process. He has been working in the Marketing Division of an Organization for the past ten years after completing her post graduate diploma in Marketing Management with 65% marks.

25.   Md. Yusuf was born on 29$^{th}$ January 1982. He has secured 55% marks in graduation and 52% marks in the selection process. He has also secured 68% marks in post graduate diploma Marketing Management. He has been working for the Marketing Division of an Organization.

**Directions** **(Qs. 26-27)** : *216 cubes of similar size are arranged in the form of a bigger cube (6 cubes on each side, i. e. , 6 × 6 × 6) all the exposed surfaces are painted.*

26.   How many of the cubes have no face painted?

    (a)  64    (b) 125    (c) 27    (d) None of these

27.   How many of the cubes have at least 2 faces painted?

    (a)  104    (b) 144    (c) 120    (d) None of these

**Directions** **(Qs. 28-30):** *Read the following passages and answer the questions based on them.*

### PASSAGE-1

The ability of an organism to adapt to environmental change is strictly controlled by how well it fits into the environment prior to change, which is directly related to time spent in that ecology. If an environment is stable over long periods of time, as was seen during the lengthy period between the Triassic and Cretaceous eras, the life forms that appear and flourish in that environment are so specialized to the climate and ecological system that any sudden change, even if relatively insignificant, can result in species extinction. The rise of mammals after the Cretaceous-Tertiary extinction event and the subsequent fall of dinosaurs is simply the best known example.

28.   What assumption is made in the argument as stated that, if incorrect, could weaken the argument's logic ?

    (a)  The extinction event was a geological phenomenon.

    (b)  Mammals developed some time after dinosaurs appeared.

    (c)  The Earth's climate stabilized into a subtropical system.

    (d)  Dinosaurs first appeared in the pre-triassic era.

29.   The reasoning behind this argument is flawed for what reason?

    (a)  It fails to recognize the superior flexibility of mammals in a variable environment.

    (b)  It relies on a sudden change for proof of its thesis.

    (c)  It correlated unrelated branches of science in an attempt to make an argument.

    (d)  It fails to account for other potential factors that could generate the result.

### PASSAGE-2

During the summer in the Arctic Ocean, sea ice has been melting earlier and faster. and the Winter freeze has been coming later. In the last three decades, the extent of summer ice has declined by about 30 per cent. The lengthening period of summer melt threatens to undermine the whole Arctic food web, atop which stand polar bears.

30.   Which among the following is the most crucial message conveyed by the above passage?

    (a)  Climate change has caused Arctic summer to be short but temperature to be high.

    (b)  Polar bears can be shifted to South Pole to ensure their survival.

    (c)  Without the presence of polar bears, the food chains in Arctic region will disappear.

    (d)  Climate change poses a threat to the survival of polar bears.

31.   Complete the given series:

    a, d, c, f, ?, h, g, ?, i

    (a) e, j              (b) e, k

    (c) f, j              (d) j, e

32. Study the following information to answer the given questions:

    (i) In a family of 6 persons, there are two couples.

    (ii) The lawyer is the head of the family and has only two sons – Mukesh and Rakesh – both teachers.

    (iii) Mrs. Reena and her mother-in-law both are lawyers

    (iv) Mukesh's wife is a doctor and they have a son, Ajay.

    What is the profession of Rakesh's wife?
    (a) Teacher
    (b) Doctor
    (c) lawyer
    (d) cannot be determine

33. Seven students Priya, Ankit, Raman, Sunil, Tony, Deepak and Vicky take a series of tests. No two students get similar marks. Vicky always scores more than Priya. Priya always scores more than Ankit. Each time either Raman scores the highest and Tony gets the least, or alternatively Sunil scores the highest and Deepak or Ankit scores the least. If Sunil is ranked sixth and Ankit is ranked fifth, which of the following can be true?

    (a) Vicky is ranked first or fourth

    (b) Raman is ranked second or third

    (c) Tony is ranked fourth or fifth

    (d) Deepak is ranked third or fourth

34. In each of the following questions you are given five series of questions, you have to find out the next series from the answer figures that follows the sequence of the question figures.

 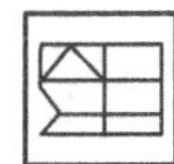  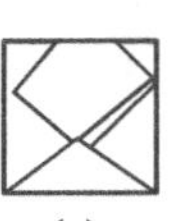 

    (1)    (2)    (3)    (4)    (5)

    (a)    (b)    (c)    (d)

35. Find in which among the following options, question figure is embedded.

    Question figure    (a)    (b)    (c)    (d)

36. The length of the two sides forming the right angle of a right-angled triangle are 6 cm and 8 cm. The length of its circumradius is :
    (a) 5 cm    (b) 7 cm    (c) 6 cm    (d) 10 cm

37. A rectangular piece of paper of dimensions 22 cm by 12 cm is rolled along its length to form a cylinder. The volume (in cm$^3$) of the cylinder so formed is (use $\pi = \dfrac{22}{7}$)

    (a) 562    (b) 412
    (c) 462    (d) 362

38. How many terms are there in A.P. whose first and fifth terms are $-14$ and 2 respectively and the sum is 40 :
    (a) 12    (b) 10    (c) 16    (d) 8

39. The top of two poles of height 20 m and 14 m are connected by a wire. If the wire makes an angle of 30° with the horizontal, then the length of the wire is
    (a) 12 m    (b) 10 m    (c) 8 m    (d) 6 m

40. How many different letter arrangements can be made from the letter of the word EXTRA in such a way that the vowels are always together?
    (a) 48    (b) 60    (c) 40    (d) 30

41. The number of different ways in which 8 persons can stand in a row so that between two particular person $A$ and $B$ are there always two person, is
    (a) $60(5!)$    (b) $15(4!) \times (5!)$
    (c) $4! \times 5!$    (d) None of these

42. A positive integer N is selected such that $100 < N < 200$. The probability that it is divisible by either 4 or 7 is :
    (a) $\dfrac{38}{99}$    (b) $\dfrac{24}{99}$
    (c) $\dfrac{34}{99}$    (d) $\dfrac{14}{99}$

43. The mean of six numbers is 30. If one number is excluded, the mean of the remaining numbers is 29. The excluded number is
    (a) 29    (b) 30
    (c) 35    (d) 45

44. The sum of the two numbers is 12 and their product is 35. What is the sum of the reciprocals of these numbers ?
    (a) $\dfrac{12}{35}$    (b) $\dfrac{1}{35}$
    (c) $\dfrac{35}{8}$    (d) $\dfrac{7}{32}$

45. Study the following information carefully and answer the questions given below.
    A, B, C, D, E, F, G and H are sitting around a circle facing the centre. B is third to the right of F and third to the left of H. C is fourth to the left of A. Who is not immediate neighbour of F or B. E is not immediate neighbour of B. G is second to the right of D.

    Who is third to the left of E?
    (a) A    (b) C
    (c) G    (d) Data inadequate

46. Dinesh and Ramesh start together from a certain point in the opposite direction on motorcycles. The speed of Dinesh is 60 km per hour and Ramesh 44 km per hour. What will be the distance between them after 15 minutes ?
    (a) 20 km.    (b) 24 km    (c) 26 km    (d) 30 km

47. Some equations have been solved on the basis of certain system. Find the correct answer for the unsolved equation on that basis.
    If $94 + 16 = 42$, $89 + 23 = 78$, then $63 + 45 = ?$
    (a) 18    (b) 28    (c) 38    (d) 48

48. Select the missing number from the given responses.

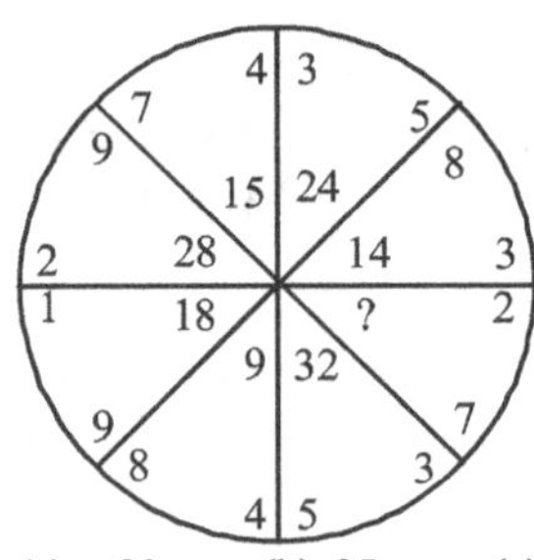

(a) 20     (b) 25     (c) 10     (d) 15

49. At present, the ratio between the ages of Arun and Deepak is 4 : 3. After 6 years, Arun's age will be 26 years. What is the age of Deepak at present?

(a) 15 years          (b) 19 years
(c) 24 years          (d) 12 years

50. How many triangles are there in the figure ?

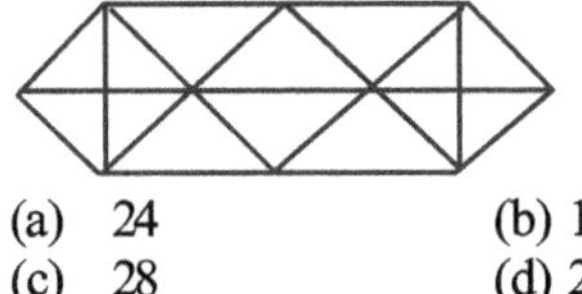

(a) 24                (b) 14
(c) 28                (d) 20

**Directions** (Qs. 51-52): *Study the following letters and their corresponding digit codes followed by certain conditions of coding and answer the questions given below them by finding out which of the digit combinations given in (a), (b), (c) and (d) is the coded form of the letter groups given in each question and mark your answers accordingly.*

| Letter : | P | N | A | J | I | R | E | B | U | K |
|----------|---|---|---|---|---|---|---|---|---|---|
| Digit :  | 5 | 3 | 9 | 1 | 4 | 6 | 2 | 7 | 0 | 8 |

**Conditions :**

(1) If both the first and the last letters in the group are vowels both should be coded as∗.

(2) If both the first and the last letters in the group are consonants both should be coded as #.

51. NAPKJI
    (a) ∗95814           (b) 395814
    (c) ∗9581∗           (d) 359814

52. KUNAJB
    (a) #0391#           (b) 803917
    (c) #0391∗           (d) ∗0391∗

**Directions** (Qs. 53 - 54) : *In each of the following questions, a statement is given followed by two conclusions I and II. Give answer :*

(a) if only conclusion I follows;
(b) if only conclusion II follows;
(c) if either I or II follows;
(d) if both I and II follow.

53. **Statement :** Research has proved that people eating high fat diets coupled with decreased level of exercises are prone to heart diseases.

**Conclusions :**

I. People should reduce their high-fat diet as a preventive method.

II. People must have sufficient level of exercise to reduce their chances of having heart disease.

54. **Statement :** From the next academic year, students will have the option of dropping Mathematics and Science for their school leaving certificate examination.

**Conclusions :**

I. Students who are weak in Science and Mathematics will be admitted.

II. Earlier students did not have the choice of continuing their education without taking these subjects.

55. In a certain party, there was a bowl of rice for every two guests, a bowl of broth for every three of them and a bowl of meat for every four of them. If in all there were 65 bowls of food, then how many guests were there in the party ?

(a) 65                (b) 24
(c) 60                (d) 48

56. A shopkeeper marks up his goods by 40% and gives a discount of 10%. Apart from this, he uses a faulty balance also, which reads 1000 gm for 800 gm. What is his net profit percentage?

(a) 57.5%             (b) 63.5%
(c) 42.5%             (d) 36.5%

**Directions** (Qs. 57-62): *Read the following passages and answer the question based on them.*

### PASSAGE-1

Developed countries have made adequate provisions for social security for senior citizens. State insurers (as well as private ones) offer medicare and pension benefits to people who can no longer earn. In India, with the collapse of the joint family system, the traditional shelter of the elderly has disappeared. And a state faced with a financial crunch is not in a position to provide financial security, So, it is advisable that the working population give serious thought to building a financial base for itself.

57. Which one of the following, if it were to happen, weakens the conclusion drawn in the above passage the most?

(a) The insurance sector is under developed and trends indicate that it will be extensively privatized in the future.

(b) The insurance sector is under developed and trends indicate that it will be extensively privatized in the future.

(c) India is on a path of development that will take it to a developed country status, with all its positive and negative implications.

(d) If the working population builds a stronger financial base, there will be a revival of the joint family system.

### PASSAGE-2

From Cochin to Shimla, the new culture vultures are tearing down acres of India's architectural treasures. Ancestral owners often fobbed off with a few hundred rupees for an exquisitely carved door or window, which fetches fifty times that much from foreign dealers, and yet more from the drawing room sophisticates of Europe and the US. The reason for such shameless rape of the

Indian architectural wealth can perhaps, not wrongly, be attributed to the unfortunate blend of activist disunity and local indifference.

58. It can be logically inferred from the above passage that
    (a) The environment created by the meeting between activist disunity and local difference is ideal for antique dealers to thrive in India.
    (b) Only Indians are not proud of their cultural heritage and are hungry for the foreign currency that is easily available in return of artefacts.
    (c) Most Indian families have heirlooms which can be sold at high prices to Europeans and Americans.
    (d) India provides a rich market for unscrupulous antique dealers.

### PASSAGE-3

During the past week, 120 PureTech Corporation employees have reported symptoms of a strain of food poisoning known as disporella, but only eight of these employees have tested positive for the strain. A PureTech spokesperson claims that the apparent outbreak of disporella can be attributed to contaminated food served two weeks ago at the company's annual employee picnic.

59. Which of the following, if true, would most support the claim made by the PureTech spokesperson above?
    (a) Disporella symptoms generally last only a few days.
    (b) PureTech's cafeteria facilities provide lunch to PureTech employees during every workday.
    (c) People with disporella do not generally test positive for disporella until at least one week after disporella symptoms begin to occur.
    (d) People with disporella often do not exhibit disporella symptoms until more than a week after contracting disporella.

### PASSAGE-4

Most citizens are very conscientious about observing a law when they can see the reason behind it. For instance, there has been very little need to actively enforce the recently-implemented law that increased the penalty for motorists caught leaving a gas station without paying for gas they had pumped into their vehicles. This is because citizens are very conscientious of the high cost of gasoline and they know that stealing gas will only further increase the price of gasoline for everyone.

60. Which of the following statements would the author of this passage be most likely to believe?
    (a) The increased penalty alone is a significant motivation for most citizens to obey the law.
    (a) There are still too many inconsiderate citizens in the local community.
    (c) High gasoline prices can be brought down if everyone does his or her part and pays for the gasoline they use at the pumps.
    (d) Society should make an effort to teach citizens the reasons for its laws.

### PASSAGE-5

Inflation can only be fundamentally caused by two factors—supply side factors and demand side factors. These factors are either reductions in the supply of goods and services or increase in demand due to either the increased availability of money or the reallocation of demand. Unless other compensating changes also occur, inflation is bound to result if either of this occurs. In economies prior to the introduction of banks (a pre-banking economy) the quantity of money available, and hence, the level of demand, was equivalent to the quantity of gold available.

61. If the statements above are true, then it is also true that in a pre-banking economy:
    (a) any inflation would be the result of reductions in the supply of goods and services.
    (b) if other factors in the economy are unchanged, increasing the quantity of gold available would lead to inflation.
    (c) if there is a reduction in the quantity of gold available, then, other things being equal, inflation would result.
    (d) whatever changes in demand occur, there would be compensating changes in the supply of goods and services.

**Directions** (Qs. 62-65): *Study the following graph to answer these questions.*

**Per cent profit earned by two Companies A & B over the years**

Profit = Income – Expenditure

$$\%\text{Profit} = \frac{\text{Profit}}{\text{Expenditure}} \times 100$$

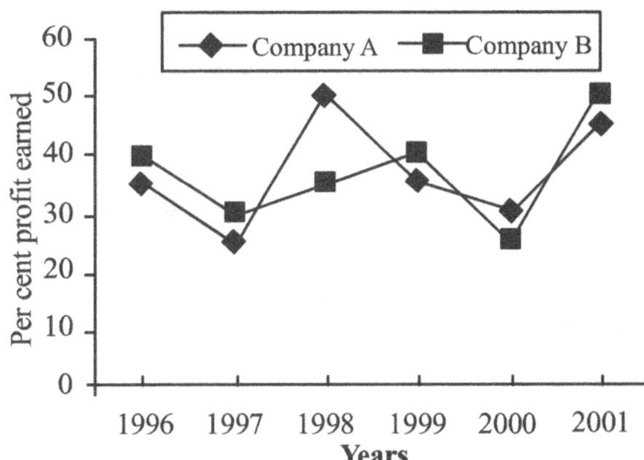


62. If the income of Company '*A*' in 1998 was ₹ 1,42,500 what was its expenditure in that year?
    (a) ₹1,05,000    (b) ₹95,000
    (c) ₹99,500    (d) ₹1,05,555

63. Expenditure of Company '*B*' in 1999 was 90% of its expenditure in 1998. Income of Company '*B*' in 1999 was what per cent of its income in 1998?
    (a) 130.5%    (b) $96\frac{2}{3}\%$
    (c) 121.5%    (d) $93\frac{1}{3}\%$

64. If the expenditure of Company '*A*' in 1997 was ₹ 70 lakhs and income of Company *A* in 1997 was equal to its expenditure in 1998, what was the total income (in ₹ lakh) of the Company *A* in 1997 & 1998 together?

    (a)  ₹175  (b)  ₹131.25
    (c)  ₹218.75  (d)  Cannot be determined

65. Expenditure of Company '*B*' in years 1996 and 1997 were in the ratio of 5 : 7 respectively. What was the respective ratio of their incomes?

    (a)  10 : 13  (b)  8 : 13
    (c)  13 : 14  (d)  11 : 14

66. The graph shows Distribution of 1,412,393 Examinees from Sept. 2007 to Aug. 2010

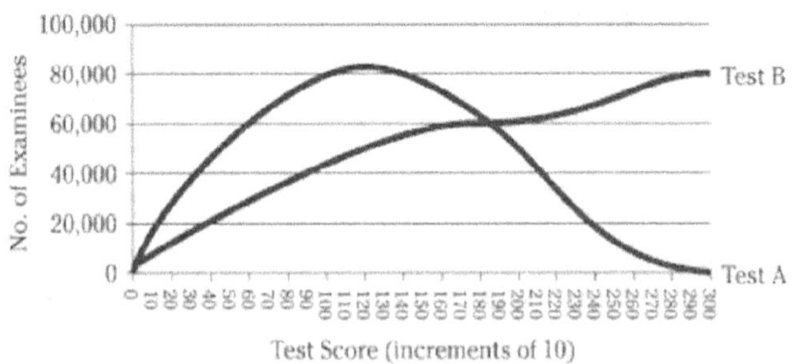


    If a Test A examinee is among a group of 40,000 examinees with the same score, what could be the examinee's score?

    (a)  20  (b)  40
    (c)  90  (d)  210

**Directions** (Qs. 67-71): *Read the following passages and answer the questions based on each.*

### PASSAGE-1

The pressure on Italy's 257 jails has been increasing rapidly. Those jails are old and overcrowded. They are supposed to hold up to 43,000 people -----9, 000 fewer than now. San Vittore in Milan, which has 1, 800 inmates, is designed for 800. The number of foreigners inside jails has also been increasing. The minister in charge of prisons fears that tensions may snap, and so has recommended to government an amnesty policy ?

67. Which one of the following, if true, would have most influenced the recommendation of the minister?

    (a)  Opinion polls have indicated that many Italians favour a general pardon.

    (b)  The opposition may be persuaded to help since amnesties must be approved by a two-thirds majority in parliament.

    (c)  During a recent visit to a large prison, the Pope whose pronouncements are taken seriously, appealed for 'a gesture of clemency'

    (d)  Shortly before the recommendation was made, 58 prisons reported disturbances in a period of two weeks.

### PASSAGE-2

Most large retail stores of all goods and brands hold discount sales in the month of November. The original idea of price reduction campaigns in November became popular when it was realized that the sales of products would generally slow down following the Diwali rush. The lack of demand could be solved by the simple solution of reducing prices. There is now an increasing tendency among major chains of stores across the country to have their "November sales" begin before Diwali. The idea behind this trend is to endeavour to sell the maximum amount of stock at a profit, even if that may not be at the maximum profit.

68. Which of the following conclusions *cannot* be drawn from the above?

    (a)  The incidence of "early" November sales results in lower holdings of stocks with the corollary of lower stock holding costs.

    (b)  Demand is a function of price; as you lower price, demand increases.

    (c)  Major stores seem to think it makes sense to have the November sales campaigns pre-Diwali.

    (d)  The major department stores do not worry as much about profit maximization as they do about sales maximization.

### PASSAGE-3

Szymanski suggests that the problem of racism in football may be present even today. He begins by verifying an earlier hypothesis tha clubs' wage bills explain 90% of their performance. Thus, if players' salaries were to be only based on their abilities, clubs that spend more should finish higher. If there is pay discrimination against some group of players-fewer teams bidding for black players thus lowering the salaries for blacks with the same ability as whites-that neat relation may no longer hold. He concludes that certain clubs seem to have achieved much less than what they could have, by not recruiting black players.

69. Which one of the following findings would best support Szymanski's conclusion?

    (a)  Certain clubs took advantage of the situational hiring above-average shares of black players.

    (b)  Clubs hiered white players at relatively high wages and did not show proportionately good performance.

    (c)  During the study period, clubs in towns with a history of discrimination against blacks, under performed relative to their wage bills

    (d)  Clubs in one region, which had higher proportions of black players, had significantly lower wage bills than their counterparts in another region which had predominantly white players.

### PASSAGE-4

The offer of the government to make iodised salt available at a low price of one rupee per kilo is welcome, especially since the government seems to be so concerned about the ill effects of noniodised salt. But it is doubtful whether the offer will actually be implemented. Way back in 1994, the governmental methods for reducing the costs of iodisation to about five paise per kilo. But these reports have remained just those-reports on paper.

70. Which one of the following, if true most weakens the author's contention that it is doubtful whether the offer will be actually implemented?
    (a) The government proposes to save on costs by using the three methods it has already devised for iodisation.
    (b) The chain of fair-price distribution outlets now covers all the districts of the state.
    (c) Many small-scale and joint sector units have completed trials to use the three iodisation methods for regular production.
    (d) The government which initiated the earlier effort is in place even today and has more information on the effects of no-iodised salt

The Shvets-chattra or the "White Umbrella" was a symbol of sovereign political authority placed over the monarch's head at the time of the coronation. The ruler so inaugurated was regarded not as a temporal autocrat but as the instrument of protective and sheltering firmament of supreme law. The white umbrella symbol is of great antiquity and its varied use illustrates the ultimate common basis of non-theocratic nature of states in the Indian traditions As such, the umbrella is found, although not necessarily a white one, over the head of Lord Ram, the Mohammedan sultans and Chatrapati Shivaji.

71. Which of the following best summarizes the above passage?
    (a) The placing of an umbrella over the ruler's head was a common practice in the Indian subcontinent.
    (b) The white umbrella represented the instrument of firmament of the supreme law and non-theocratic nature of Indian states.
    (c) The umbrella, not necessarily a white one, was a symbol of sovereign political authority.
    (d) The varied use of the umbrella symbolized the common basis of the non-theocratic nature of states in the Indiana tradition.

**Directions** (Qs. 72-80) : *Read the three passages given below and answer the questions based on them.*

### PASSAGE-1

Sea ice has a bright surface; so much of the sunlight that strikes it is reflected back into space. As a result, areas covered by sea ice do not absorb much solar energy. Sea ice also affects the movement of ocean waters.

Water below sea ice has a higher concentration of salt and is denser than surrounding ocean water and so it sinks. In this way, sea ice contributes to the ocean's global 'conveyor-belt' circulation. Cold, dense, polar water sinks and moves along the ocean bottom towards the equator, while warm water from mid-depth to the surface travels from the equator towards the poles. Changes in the amount of sea ice can disrupt normal ocean circulation, thereby leading to changes in global climate.

'Satellites can provide detailed measures of how much ice is covering the pole right now, but sediment cores are like fossils of the ocean's history', said Mr. Gregory. Sediment cores are essentially a record of sediments that settled at the sea floor, layer by layer, and they record the conditions of the ocean system during the time they settled. Scientists can search for a bio-chemical marker that is tied to certain species of algae that live only in ice. Polar bears, whales, walrus and seals are changing their feeding and migration patterns. Both the atmospheric currents and the ocean currents can be expected to change.

72. According to the passage, Sea ice formation contributes to
    (a) reflection of sunlight
    (b) global warming
    (c) movement of ocean waters
    (d) movement of atmospheric current

73. According to the passage, what helps Mr. Gregory study the ocean's history?
    (a) Sediment cores
    (b) Bio – chemical markers
    (c) Satellites
    (d) Fossils

74. Which of the following statement is supported by the author about the usage of bio-chemical markers?
    (a) To find the history of ocean structure
    (b) To find the existence of ice at that time
    (c) to find the changes in total volume of ice
    (d) To find the changes in surface area

75. The second paragraph in this passage explains
    (a) the formation of sea ice
    (b) rise of temperature on earth due to sea ice
    (c) water below the sea ice
    (d) how the ocean currents are formed

76. All of the following are possible side effects of sea ice melting except
    (a) change in ocean current
    (b) changes in migration patterns of polar bears
    (c) increase in temperature
    (d) increase in the density of Arctic sea water

### PASSAGE-2

The University Grants Commission's directive to college and university lecturers to spend a minimum of 22 hours a week in direct teaching is the product of budgetary cutbacks rather than pedagogic wisdom. It may seem odd, at first blush, that teachers should protest about teaching a mere 22 hours. However, if one considers the amount of time academics require to prepare lectures of good quality as well as the time they need to spend doing research, it is clear that most conscientious teachers work more than 40 hours a week. In university systems around the world lecturers rarely spend more than 12 to 15 hours in direct teaching activities a week. The average college lecturer in India does not have any office space. If computers are available, internet connectivity is unlikely. Libraries are poorly stocked. Now the UGC says universities must implement a complete freeze on all permanent recruitment, abolish all posts which have been vacant for more than a year, and cut staff strength by 10 per cent. And it is in order to ensure that these cutbacks do not affect the quantum of teaching that existing lecturers are being asked to work longer. Obviously, the quality of teaching and academic work in general will decline. While it is true that some college teachers do not take their classes regularly, the UGC and the institutions concerned must find a proper way to hold them accountable. An absentee teacher will continue to play truant even if the number of hours he/she is required to teach goes up.

All of us are well aware of the unsound state that the Indian higher education system is in today. Thanks to years of sustained financial neglect, most Indian universities and colleges do no research worth the name. Even as the number of students entering colleges has increased dramatically, public investment in higher education has actually declined in relative terms. Between 1985 and 1997, when public expenditure on higher education as percentage of outlays on all levels of education grew by more than 60 per cent in Malaysia and 20 per cent in Thailand, India showed a decline of more than 10 per cent. Throughout the world, the number of teachers in higher education per million population grew by more than 10 per cent in the same period; in India it fell by one per cent. Instead of transferring the burden of government apathy on to the backs of the teachers, the UGC should insist that the need of the country's university system be adequately catered to.

77. Which of the following is the reason for the sorry state of affairs of the Indian Universities as mentioned in the passage ?
    (a) The poor quality of teachers
    (b) Involvement of teachers in extra-curricular activities
    (c) Politics within and outside the departments
    (d) No getting enough financial assistance

78. Which of the following statements is/are TRUE in the context of the passage ?
    (A) Most colleges do not carry out research worth the name.
    (B) UGC wants lecturers to spend minimum 22 hours a week in direct teaching
    (C) Indian higher education system is in unsound state.
    (a) Only (A) and (C)    (b) All (A), (B) and (C)
    (c) Only (C)            (d) Only (B)

### PASSAGE-3

Leadership is often more persuasion and inspiration than coercion. It is an activity of persuading people to cooperate for achieving a common objective. The trait theory assumes that good leaders possess certain specific qualities. The theory purports that these common qualities and traits should be observed and studied carefully. The major shortcoming of this theory is that there seem to be very few traits which are common to all great leaders; rather, they all seem to have their own set of unique traits that define them. The contingency theory focuses on variables unique to the environment that determine which particular style of leadership is best suited for the situation. According to this theory, there are no universally accepted qualities that define great leadership. The behavioral theory of leadership focuses on the actions of leaders, not on the mental qualities or internal states that define them. According to this theory, poeple can learn to became leaders through teaching, observation and action. A leader should possess good communication skills and use new ways to carry out effective communication. The most valuable asset and quality of a leader is honesty. Once a leader compromises his or her integrity, his or her position is lost. The challenges and opportunities of the twenty-first century will require supreme organizational and institutional leadership.

79. Which of the flowering is mentioned in the text as a requirement of being a good leader?
    (a) Exuding self-confidence
    (b) Being a perfect motivator
    (c) Honesty
    (d) Attractiveness

80. The primary purpose of this passage is
    (a) explaining the theory of leadership
    (b) discussing the qualities of good leadership
    (c) providing tips for the success of an organization
    (d) understanding people and involving them to do their job

# SOLUTIONS

1. (d) None of the options are correct. Statement (I) cannot be inferred; refer to the lines "While Sinn Fein's black balloons, the largely deserted streets and the heavy security presence reminded that history could not be too easily wished away". They seem to suggest that there is still some tension between the two countries. (II) can be inferred from the passage. (III) cannot be inferred as the author writes, "The exaggerated: her green cloak to go with the Emerald Isle" indicating that looking for symbolism in the queen's choice of a cloak is an exaggeration.

2. (a) Option (a) best expresses how Britain and Ireland are trying to make things right. We cannot assume that everything has been resolved because there is evidence in the passage against this. Therefore, option (d) can be eliminated. Options (b) (shared misfortune) and (c) (tragic past) are too broad in scope and can be construed to mean anything.

3. (d) The second sentence of the passage brings out the fact that India is a low cost country, thus implying that holding clinical trials abroad is costlier.

4. (b) The fourth sentence of the passage is a generalised statement of option (b).

5. (d) Statement II is the only one mentioned in the passage and it is not given in any of the options.

6. (d) This is brought out in the second sentence of the passage.

7. (b) We know that, $(x^n - y^n)$ is divisible by $(x - y)$ for all n and is divisible by $(x^2 + y^2)$ for even n.
   $\therefore$ $(7^{12} - 4^{12})$ is divisible by $(7^2 - 4^2)$
   $\Rightarrow$ $(7^{12} - 4^{12})$ is divisible by 11 and 3
   $\therefore$ $(7^{12} - 4^{12})$ is divisible by 33.

8. (a) Interval of flashing for the red light $= \dfrac{60}{3}$
   $= 20$ sec
   Interval of flashing for the green light
   $= \dfrac{60 \times 2}{5} = 24$ sec
   So they will flash together at an interval of 120 sec (LCM of 20 & 24) $= 2$ min
   Hence in one hour they will flash together for $\dfrac{60}{2} = 30$ times.

9. (b) Let the tenth digit be x and unit digit be y. Then the two digit number $= 10x + y$
   but $x \times y = 12 \Rightarrow y = \dfrac{12}{x}$
   $\therefore$ the number is $\left(10x + \dfrac{12}{x}\right)$
   Again $10x + \dfrac{12}{x} + 9 = 10 \times \left(\dfrac{12}{x}\right) + x$

$\Rightarrow$ $10x^2 + 12 + 9x = 120 + x^2$
$\Rightarrow$ $9x^2 + 9x - 108 = 0 \Rightarrow x^2 + x - 12 = 0$
$\Rightarrow$ $(x + 4)(x - 3) = 0 \Rightarrow x = -4, 3$
but x cannot be negative
$\therefore$ $x = 3$ only
$\therefore$ $y = \dfrac{12}{x} = \dfrac{12}{3} = 4$
$\therefore$ the number $= 10x + y = 10 \times 3 + 4 = 34$

10. (b) Sum of ages of Mr. and Mrs. Sinha in 1972 = 46 years
    Sum of age of their family in 1976
    $= 19 \times 3 = 57$ years
    Sum of ages of Mr. and Mrs. Sinha in 1976 $= (46 + 8)$ years $= 54$ years
    $\therefore$ Age of Vicky in 1980
    $= 57 - 54 + 4 = 7$ years.

11. (b) Let the total number of original inhabitants be x. Then, $(100 - 25)\%$ of $(100 - 10)\%$ of $x = 4050$
    $\Rightarrow \left(\dfrac{75}{100} \times \dfrac{90}{100} \times x\right) = 4050 \Rightarrow \dfrac{27}{40}x = 4050$
    $\Rightarrow x = \left(\dfrac{4050 \times 40}{27}\right) = 6000.$
    $\therefore$ Number of original inhabitants $= 6000$.

12. (c) On the second year (in terms of C.I.) is
    $$\dfrac{P\left(1 + \dfrac{r}{100}\right)^2}{\left(P + \dfrac{Pr}{100}\right)} = \dfrac{6}{5} \quad \Rightarrow \left(1 + \dfrac{r}{100}\right) = \dfrac{6}{5}$$
    $\Rightarrow r = 20\%$

**Solution for (13 – 17):**

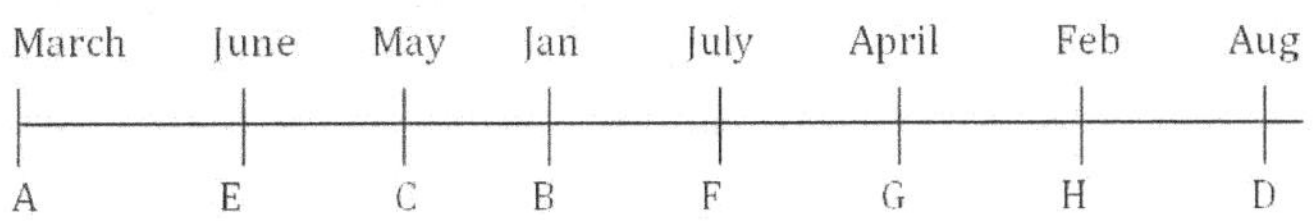


13. (d) is the correct answer
14. (a) is the correct answer
15. (a) is the correct answer
16. (d) is the correct answer
17. (b) is the correct answer

18. (a) Remaining capital $= 1 - \left(\dfrac{1}{6} + \dfrac{1}{3}\right) = \dfrac{1}{2}$
    Ratio of their profit
    $= \dfrac{1}{6} \times \left[\dfrac{1}{6} \times 12\right] : \dfrac{1}{3} \times \left[\dfrac{1}{3} \times 12\right] : \dfrac{1}{2} \times 12$
    $= \dfrac{1}{3} : \dfrac{4}{3} : 6 = 1 : 4 : 18$
    $\therefore$ $A$'s share $= \dfrac{1}{1 + 4 + 18} \times 2300 = ₹\,100$

**19.** **(c)** CP of 1kg 1st kind rice = ₹ 7.20
CP of 1kg 2nd kind rice = ₹ 5.70
CP of 1kg mixed rice = ₹ 6.30
By rule of alligation,

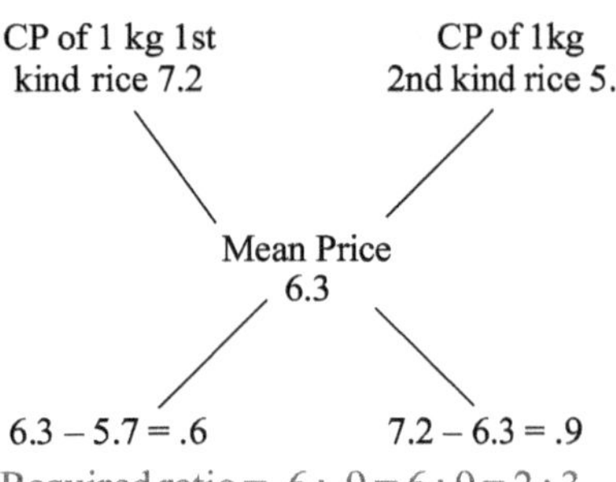


Required ratio = .6 : .9 = 6 : 9 = 2 : 3

**20.** **(a)** Let cistern will be full in x min. Then,
part filled by B in x min + part filled by A in (x – 4) min = 1

$$\Rightarrow \frac{x}{16} + \frac{x-4}{12} = 1 \Rightarrow x = \frac{64}{7} = 9\frac{1}{7} \text{ hours.}$$

**21.** **(a)** The train can cover (200 + 350) m distance in five seconds which means the speed of the train is 110 m/s. Relative speed of man and train is 114 m/s. To over the distance of 100 metre, it will take less than one second.

**22.** **(b)** Count the number of days from 2005 onwards to get 0 odd day.

| Year | 2005 | 2006 | 2007 | 2008 | 2009 | 2010 |
|---|---|---|---|---|---|---|
| Odd days | 1 | 1 | 1 | 2 | 1 | 1 |

= 7 or 0 odd day.

∴ Calendar for the year 2005 is the same as that for the year 2011.

**23.** **(c)** Clearly, a person committing a heinous crime like murder or rape should be so punished as to set an example for other not to attempt such acts in future. So, argument III holds strong. Argument I is vague while the use of the word 'only' in argument II makes it weak. Also, it cannot be assured whether a criminal is really repentant of his acts or not, he may also exhibit so just to get rid of punishment. So, argument IV also does not hold strong.

**Solution for 24-25 :**

| Q. No. | Name | I | I/(ii) | III | IV/(i) | V | Ans. |
|---|---|---|---|---|---|---|---|
| 24 | Nayan | ✓ | ✓ | ✓ | ✓ | ✓ | (a) |
| 25 | Yusuf | ✓ | ✓ | ✓ | ✓ | – | (d) |

**26.** **(a)** Number of the cubes with 0 faces painted is
$(6-2)^3 = 4^3 = 64$

**27.** **(b)** At least 2 faces painted means number of cubes with 2 face painted + number of cubes with 3 face painted =
$96 + 8 = 104$.

**28.** **(b)** Since, the thesis of the argument is that a direct relationship can be drawn between adaptability and time spent in an ecosystem, any assumption that would address them and/or adaptability could greatly affect the argument if wrong. Option (a) can be discarded immediately, because it addresses the possible cause of the extinction event; all that matters here is that there was an extinction event, not its cause. Similarly, option (c) can be rejected, as it only concerns climate, not adaptability or time.
While a weak connection is made with the idea of time in option (d), it is irrelevant because the extinction event, not time itself, was the agent of change; thus, option (d) can be rejected. Only option (b) addresses the unspoken assumption that mammals came along later and thus were less finely tuned to the environment, making them more adaptable; thus, it is the correct answer.

**29.** **(d)** In order for the reasoning to be flawed, there must be a structural defect in the logic, or a factor that was not considered when stating the original argument, such as poorly defined assumptions. For this argument, option (a) can be discarded right away, because the argument does not make any such claim, implied or direct, as outlined in the statement.
Option (b) can be discarded because it contradicts the thesis directly; adaptability is defined in part by sudden change, so sudden change would constitute valid proof. Since, the sciences referred to in the argument—climatology, ecology and (by inference) geology—are not unrelated, option (c) is patently false, and is thus not valid in this context. Only option (d), which accurately outlines that the argument fails to take into consideration other potential factors such as mutation, correctly addresses the question, making (d) correct.

**30.** **(d)** 'Climate change poses a threat to the survival of polar bears' is the most crucial message conveyed by the passage.

**31.** **(a)**

$$a \xrightarrow{+3} d \xrightarrow{-1} c \xrightarrow{+3} f \xrightarrow{-1} \boxed{e} \xrightarrow{+3} h \xrightarrow{-1} g \xrightarrow{+3} \boxed{j} \xrightarrow{-1} i$$

**32.** **(c)**

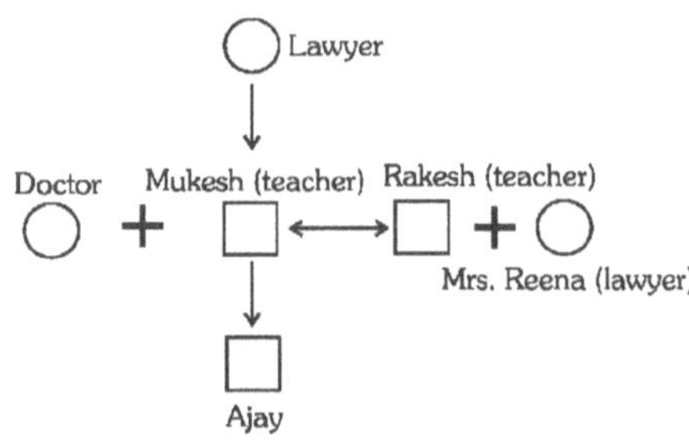


**33.** **(d)** Vicky > Priya
Priya > Ankit
One of them is true- Raman is highest or Tony is least or Sunil got highest and Deepak got least.
Since Sunil got the sixth and Ankit got the fifth rank, hence we can conclude that Raman must have got the highest and Tony must have got the least rank. And the order of ranks of Vicky, Priya and Ankit must be Vicky > Priya > Ankit. Vicky must have got the second or third rank and accordingly Priya must have got the third or fourth rank. Deepak must have got any rank among two, three and four.

**34.** **(c)**

**35.** (b) 

**36.** (a) In a right angled $\Delta$, the length of circumradius is half the length of hypotenuse.

$\therefore$ $H^2 = 6^2 + 8^2$

$H^2 = 36 + 64 \Rightarrow 100$

$H = 10\,cm$

Circumradius $= 5\,cm$

**37.** (c) $2\pi r = 22\,cm$

$r = \dfrac{22 \times 7}{2 \times 22} = \dfrac{7}{2}\,cm$

Height, $h = 12\,cm$

Volume of cylinder

$= \dfrac{22}{7} \times \dfrac{7}{2} \times \dfrac{7}{2} \times 12 = 462\,cm^3$

**38.** (b) $T_1 = a = -14$

$T_5 = a + 4d = 2$

$\Rightarrow$ $d = 4$

Now $S_n = \dfrac{n}{2}\big[2a + (n-1\;d)\big]$

$40 = \dfrac{n}{2}\big[-28 + (n-1\,4\,)\big]$

$\Rightarrow$ $n^2 - 8n - 20 = 0$

$\Rightarrow$ $n = 10$ or $n = -2$

Since number of terms can not be negative, hence $n = 10$

**Alternatively :** Since $S_n$ is very small, therefore we can solve it physically within seconds.

$T_1 = -14,\ T_5 = 2$

| $T_1$ | $T_2$ | $T_3$ | $T_4$ | $T_5$ | $T_6$ | $T_7$ | $T_8$ | $T_9$ | $T_{10}$ |
|---|---|---|---|---|---|---|---|---|---|
| $-14$ | $-10$ | $-6$ | $-2$ | $2$ | $6$ | $10$ | $14$ | $18$ | $22$ |
| | | | | | | | | | $40$ |

$\Rightarrow$ $T_1 + T_2 + \dots\dots + T_{10} = 18 + 22 = 40$

**39.** (a) Here, CD $= 20\,m$ [Height of big pole]

AB $= 14\,m$ [Height of small pole]

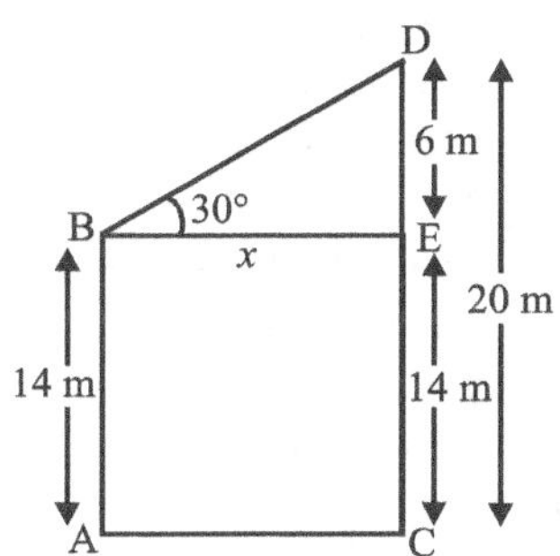

DE $=$ CD $-$ CE $\Rightarrow$ DE $=$ CD $-$ AB $[\because$ AB $=$ CE$]$

$\Rightarrow$ DE $= 20 - 14 = 6\,m$

In $\Delta BDE$, $\sin 30° = \dfrac{DE}{BD}$

$\Rightarrow$ $\dfrac{1}{2} = \dfrac{6}{BD} \Rightarrow BD = 12\,m$

$\therefore$ Length of wire $= 12\,m$

**40.** (a) Considering the two vowels $E$ and $A$ as one letter, the total no. of letters in the word 'EXTRA' is 4 which can be arranged in $^4P_4$, i.e. 4! ways and the two vowels can be arranged among themselves in 2! ways.

$\therefore$ reqd. no. $= 4! \times 2!$

$= 4 \times 3 \times 2 \times 1 \times 2 \times 1 = 48$

**41.** (a) The number of 4 persons including $A, B = {}^6C_2$

Considering these four as a group, number of arrangements with the other four $= 5!$

But in each group the number of arrangements $= 2! \times 2!$

$\therefore$ The required number of ways

$= {}^6C_2 \times 5! \times 2! \times 2! = 60\,(5!)$

**42.** (c) Numbers divisible by 4 are 104, 108.., 196; 24 in number. Numbers divisible by 7 are 105, 112, ....196; 14 in number. Numbers divisible by both, i.e. divisible by 28 are 112, 140, 168, 196; 4 in number. Hence, required probability

$= \dfrac{24}{99} + \dfrac{14}{99} - \dfrac{4}{99} = \dfrac{34}{99}$

**43.** (c) Sum of 6 numbers $= 30 \times 6 = 180$

Sum of remaining 5 numbers $= 29 \times 5 = 145$

$\square$ Excluded number $= 180 - 145 = 35$.

**44.** (a) Let the numbers be $a$ and $b$. Then, $a + b = 12$ and $ab = 35$.

$\therefore$ $\dfrac{a+b}{ab} = \dfrac{12}{35}$ $\Rightarrow$ $\left(\dfrac{1}{b} + \dfrac{1}{a}\right) = \dfrac{12}{35}$

$\therefore$ Sum of reciprocals of given numbers $= \dfrac{12}{35}$

**45.** (c) 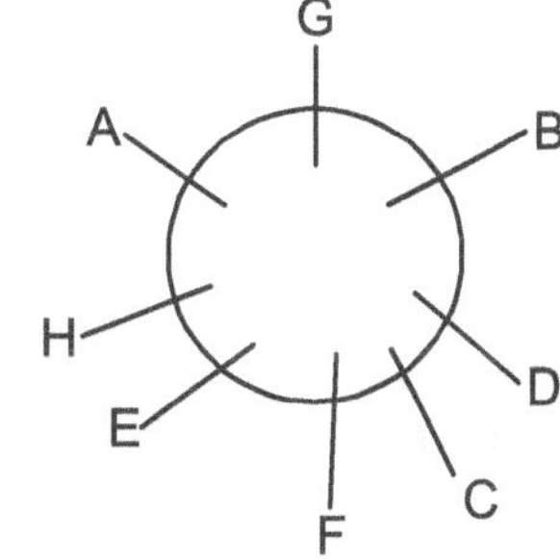

46. (c)   ← $\underline{60km/hr}$ ○ Dinesh

Ramesh○ $\xrightarrow{44km/hr}$

Relative speed of Dinesh and Ramesh's motorcycles = (60 + 44) = 10 4 km/hr

Distance travelled by them = Relative speed × Time covered,

$$104 \text{km/hr} \times \left(\frac{15}{60}\right) \text{hr} = \frac{104 \times 15}{60} = 26 \text{km}$$

47. (c)   $9 \times 4 + 1 \times 6 = 36 + 6 = 42$

$8 \times 9 + 2 \times 3 = 72 + 6 = 78$

Similarly

$6 \times 3 + 4 \times 5 = 18 + 20 = \boxed{38}$

48. (d)   The product of two numbers in a sector is equal to the central number in the previous sector.

$3 \times 5 = 15$

$8 \times 3 = 24$

$7 \times 2 = 14$

$5 \times 3 = \boxed{15}$

$8 \times 4 = 32$

$9 \times 1 = 9$

$9 \times 2 = 18$

$7 \times 4 = 28$

49. (a)   Suppose the present age of Arun is $4x$ years and that of Deepak is $3x$ years.

6 years hence,

Arun's age $= 4x + 6 = 26$

$\Rightarrow 4x = 26 - 6$

$$x = \frac{20}{4} = 5$$

∴   Present age of Deepak $= 3x = 15$ years

50. (c) 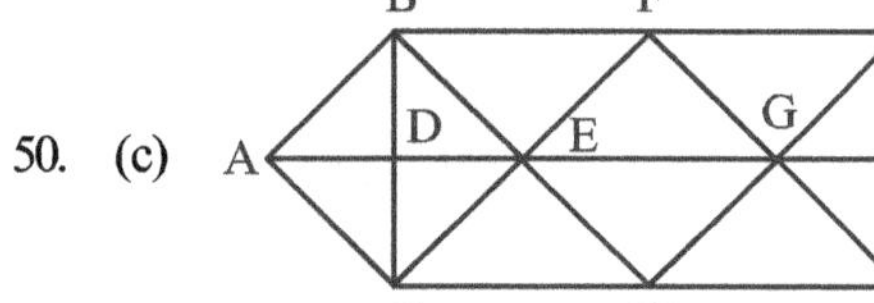

ΔABD, ΔADC, ΔBDE, ΔDEC,

ΔABC, ΔEBC, ΔACE, ΔABE,

ΔBEF, ΔFIG, ΔCEH, ΔHGK,

ΔFGE, ΔEGH, ΔGIL, ΔILJ,

ΔGLK, ΔLJK, ΔGIJ, ΔGKJ,

ΔGIK, ΔIJK, ΔBCH, ΔIHK,

ΔBFC, ΔFIK, ΔFCK, ΔHBI

Total Triangles = 28

51. (b)   NAPKJI   →   395814

52. (a)   KUNAJB   →   #0391#

53. (d)   Both follow because they together take care of the two problems leading to heart diseases.

54. (d)   Since the new system gives the students the option of dropping Science and Mathematics, so students weak in these subjects can also be admitted. So, I follows. Also, it is mentioned that the new system will come into effect from the next academic year. This means that it did not exist previously. So, II also follows.

55. (c)   Let the number of rice bowls be $x$,

the number of broth bowls be $y$

and the number of meat bowls be $z$.

Now, $x + y + z = 65$          …(1)

and   $2x = 3y = 4z$          …(2)

From (1) and (2), we have $x = 30$, $y = 20$, $z = 15$

Thus, the total number of guests $= 2x = 3y = 4z = 60$

56. (a)   Let us assume his CP/1000 gm = ₹ 100

So, his SP/kg (800 gm) = ₹ 126

So, his CP/800 gm = ₹ 80

So, profit = ₹ 46

So profit percentage = 46/80 × 100 = 57.5%

57. (d)   (d) comes across the right choice, as according to the passage, the working population needs a stronger financial base, since the joint family system is collapsing and thus, the elderly are not being given the traditional shelter and the state can't provided it as it faces a financial crunch. Thus, (d) is contrary to the conclusion drawn from the passage.

58. (a)   The passage refers to disunity of activists and local indifference to India's architectural treasures. Thus (a) comes across as a best choice as a situation it created in which antique dealers can thrive. Other options are clearly not suggested may appear correct but is not at apt as (a).

59. (d)   The argument relies on the unstated assumption that no other event since the picnic could have caused the outbreak instead. Statement (d) provides some evidence that the employees who have reported disporella symptoms in fact contracted disporella at least one week ago. Accordingly, (d) helps support the claim that it was the food served at the picnic two weeks ago that caused the outbreak. Admittedly, (d) would provide even stronger support if it indicated that symptoms never appear until one week after contamination. Nevertheless, (d) is the best of the five answer choices.

(a) has no effect on the argument. It is the time after contamination that symptoms begin to occur, *not* the duration of those symptoms, that is key to identifying the source of contamination.

(b) actually *weakens* the claim, by providing another possible explanation for the outbreak. Specifically, (b) provides for the possibility that the outbreak can be attributed to food served in the company's cafeteria rather than at the picnic.

(c) provides *some* support for the argument, in so far as it helps to explain why only a few of those reporting symptoms have tested positive so far. However, the spokesperson's claim is not just that the 120 employees have disporella but that it was the picnic food that caused the outbreak. (c) helps show that the 120 employees have disporella, but does not help explain how they contracted disporella. For this reason (d) is a better choice than (c).

60. (d) Choice (d) is correct because it neatly summarizes the main theme of the passage. We can instantly eliminate answer choice (a) because the passage never states how the increased penalty affects citizens. Choice (b) is too extreme, and overly negative. Besides, the overall theme of the passage is positive; the negative tone of choice (b) is controdicting it. Answer choice (c) is incorrect because the author stated only that adherence to the law would prevent the price of gasoline from rising further. He never said that this action would *lower* gas prices.

61. (b) As inflation is a result of increase in the availability of money (or gold in the pre-banking economy) so (c) is wrong and (b) is correct. (d) is wrong as it is out of context of the passage. (a) is wrong as it talks of 'any inflation' and leaves the inflation caused by increase in demand. This would have been correct if the option had mentioned that other factors remain unchanged.

62. (b) The percentage profit of company 'A' in 1998 = 50%
Income, = 142500 (given)

$$\text{Expenditure} = 142500\left(\frac{100}{100+50}\right) = ₹95000$$

63. (d) $E_{B99} = \dfrac{90}{100} \; E_{B98}$ (given)

$$I_{B99} = \frac{90}{100} \times \frac{140}{100} \times \frac{100}{135} (I_{B98})$$

$$I_{B99} = \frac{280}{300} \; I_{B98}$$

$$= \frac{280}{3} \% \text{ of } I_{B98} = 93\frac{1}{3}\% \text{ of } I_{B98}$$

64. (c) $E_{A97} = ₹70$ lakh

$$\Rightarrow I_{A97} = 70\left(\frac{125}{100}\right) = ₹87.5 \text{ lakh}$$

$$I_{A97} = E_{A98} = ₹87.5 \text{ lakh}$$

$$\therefore \quad I_{A98} = 87.5\left(\frac{150}{100}\right) = ₹131.25 \text{ lakh}$$

$$\therefore \quad \text{reqd value} = I_{A97} + I_{A98}$$
$$= 87.5 + 131.25 = ₹218.75 \text{ lakh}$$

65. (a) We have to find $I_{B96} : I_{B97}$
Given $E_{B96} = 5x$ and $F_{B97} = 7x$

$$I_{B96} = 5x\left(\frac{140}{100}\right) \text{ and } I_{B97} = 7x\left(\frac{130}{100}\right)$$

$$\therefore \quad I_{B96} : I_{B97} = \frac{5x}{7x}\left(\frac{140}{130}\right) = 10 : 13$$

66. (d) In the first graph, the line for Test A examinees crosses the 40,000 line at two points: 30 and 210. However, 30 isn't an answer choice, so if you chose Choice (A) or (B), you fell for the trap of not looking far enough on the chart. This examinee could also have a score of 210, which is an answer choice and the correct answer.

67. (d) (d) is the only choice which make sense since the Minister in charge of prisons would be influenced by incidence of disturbance as he had already fears of tensions snapping and have recommended an amnesty policy to his government.

68. (c) Statement (a) is true as the goods will be sold earlier so the cost of stocking will be reduced. (b) is clearly true as is directly mentioned in the passage. (d) is correct as it is clear from the last sentence of the passage that even a small profit is good enough for these stores. Only (c) conclusion can not be drawn from the passage.

69. (b) Infering from the passage, (b) supports Szymanski's conclusion because the passage suggests that clubs that had spend more on hiring white players should have finished higher. However, there is pay discrimination. So high pay may not mean good performance.

70. (c) (c) is the correct option as according to the passage the low price of one rupee per kilo can be brought about by small scale and joint sector units which have already completed trials for regular production. If the small scale sector can produce iodised salt at cheaper rate then selling the salt can be made practical through these sectors at a large scale.

71. (d) (d) best summarises the passage as can be inferred from the passage that the varied use of the Umberella symbol illustrates the common bases of non-theocratic nature of states and represents the instrument of firmament of supreme law as mentioned in the passage.

72. (c) According to passage, losing of sea salt causes dense water to move towards the equator and results in movement of ocean water. Option (c) is correct because the passage explains the process of movement of ocean water towards the equator.

Option (a) is wrong. The bright surface of the sea ice reflects the sunlight, but this is not caused by sea losing its salt. Option (b) is wrong. It is not the cause for the increase of earth's temperature. Option (d) is not true as global warming is not caused due to loss of salt.

73. (a) Deposits on a sea floor help Mr. Gregory to study ocean history. Option (a) is chosen because sediment cores are essentially a record of sediments that settled at the sea floor, layer by layer, and they record the conditions of the ocean system during the time they settled.

Option (b) is wrong. A bio-chemical marker is the study of the chemical process that occurs within living things. Option (c) is wrong. Although the satellites provide the information of the ocean structure, sediment cores are like fossils to the scientist to study the history of the ocean structure. Option (d) is wrong because fossils give clues of the prehistory of plants or animals.

74. (b) Existence of this marker in the sediment reveals the existence of the frozen land. Option (b) is correct since it agrees with the author's view that scientists can search for biochemical marker that is tied to certain species of algae that live only in ice. Therefore, this marker is used to find the existence of ice at that time.

Option (a) is wrong because history of ocean structures can be found by sediment core. Options (c) and (d) are wrong because these are not talked about in the passage.

75. (d) I explains how cold water moves towards the equator and the warm water at equator move towards the poles (Ocean currents). Option (d) is chosen because the whole paragraph explains how the ocean currents are formed. Option (a) is wrong because the lines give no explanation about the formation of sea ice. Option (b) is wrong because melting of sea ice cause the temperature to rise. This point is not mentioned in the given text. Option (c) is an irrelevant answer.

76. (d) Option (d) is chosen because sea ice melting does not increase the density of the Arctic sea. Also, nothing about it is mentioned in the passage. Options (a), (b) and (c) are the possible effects when the sea ice melts.

77. (d) Refer to para 2: 'years of sustained financial neglect'.

78. (b) All the statements are mentioned in the passage.

79. (c) In the passage, the author states that "the most valuable asset and quality of a leader is honesty." Therefore, Answer option (c) is the best answer.

80. (b) This passage is intended to convey the characteristics of leaders and what qualities they should possess to become a good leader. Therefore, (b) is the correct answer. Option (a) is a true statement. This passage highlights the qualities of leadership but that is only a part of what the passage discusses as a whole. Options (c) and (d) are completely wrong, as the main focus of the passage does not deal with the statements in these options.

**Max. Marks : 200**                                              **Time : 2 hrs.**

1. What should come in place of the question mark (?) in the following number series?

   71, 78, 99, 134, 183 ?

   (a) 253                 (b) 239
   (c) 246                 (d) 253

2. In a family of six persons A, B, C, D, E and F, there are two married couples. D is grandmother of A and mother of B. C is wife of B and mother of F. F is the granddaughter of E. How many male members are there in the family?

   (a) one                 (b) two
   (c) three               (d) cannot be determine

3. There are 6 volumes of books on a rack kept in order (such as, vol. 1, vol. 2 and so on). After some readers used them, their order got disturbed. The changes showed as follows: Vol. 5 was directly to the right of vol. 2. Vol. 4 has vol. 6 to its left and both were not at Vol. 3 splace. Vol. 1 has Vol. 3 on right and Vol. 5 on left. An even numbered volume is at Vol. 5's place.

   Find the order in which the books are kept now, from the 4 given alternatives:

   (a) 6, 3, 5, 1, 4, 2       (b) 4, 6, 3, 5, 1, 2
   (c) 3, 4, 1, 6, 5, 3       (d) 2, 5, 1, 3, 6, 4

**Directions (Qs. 4 – 8):** *Study the following information to answer the given questions:*

Twelve people are sitting in two parallel rows containing six people each such that they are equidistant from each other. In row 1 : P, Q, R, S, T and V are seated and all of them are facing South. In row 2 : A, B, C, D, E and F are seated and all of them are facing North. Therefore, in the given seating arrangement, each member seated in a row faces another member of the other row.

S sits third to the right of Q. Either S or Q sits at an extreme end of the line. The one who faces Q sits second to the right of E. Two people sit between B and F. Neither B nor F sits at an extreme end of the line. The immediate neighbour of B faces the person who sits third to the left of P. R and T are immediate neighbours. C sits second to the left of A. T does not face the immediate neighbour of D.

4. Who amongst the following sit at the extreme ends of the rows?

   (a) S, D              (b) Q, A
   (c) V, C              (d) P, D

5. Who amongst the following faces S?

   (a) A                (b) B
   (c) C                (d) D

6. How many persons are seated between V and R?

   (a) One             (b) Two
   (c) Three           (d) Four

7. P is related to A in the same way as S is related to B based on the given arrangement. Which of the following is T related to, following the same pattern?

   (a) C                (b) D
   (c) E                (d) F

8. Which of the following is true regarding T?

   (a) F faces T
   (b) V is an immediate neighbour of T
   (c) F faces the one who is second to the right of T
   (d) T sits at one of the extreme ends of the line

9. A, B, C, D, E, F, G and H are sitting along a circle facing the centre. F sits to the immediate right of D and third to the left of A. G sits third to the left of D who does not sit next to E, B sits next of G but not next to D. C does not sit next to either D or A.

   What is the position of H with respect to C?

   (a) Second to the left
   (b) First to the right
   (c) Third to the right
   (d) None of these

10. Three wheels can complete respectively 60, 36, 24 revolutions per minute. There is a red spot on each wheel that touches the ground at time zero. After how much time, all these spots will simultaneously touch the ground again?

    (a) 5/2 seconds       (b) 5/3 seconds
    (c) 5 seconds         (d) 7.5 seconds

11. A family consists of grandparents, parents and three grandchildren. The average age of the grandparents is 67 years, that of the parents is 35 years and that of the grandchildren is 6 years. What is the average age of the family?

    (a) $28\dfrac{4}{7}$ years       (b) $31\dfrac{5}{7}$ years

    (c) $32\dfrac{1}{7}$ years       (d) None of these

12. There are two shopkeepers selling the same article at the same price for same quantity. One day, first shopkeeper offers a price discount of 25% for the same quantity whereas second shopkeeper offers 25% more quantity for the same price. From a customer's point of view, which deal is better?

    (a) 1st shopkeeper's deal
    (b) 2nd shopkeeper's deal
    (c) both are equal
    (d) cannot be determined

13. A sum was put at simple interest at a certain rate for 2 years. Had it been put at 1% higher rate, it would have fetched ₹ 24 more? The sum is

    (a) ₹1200    (b) ₹1500    (c) ₹1800    (d) ₹2000

14. *A*, *B* and *C* enter into a partnership. They invest ₹40,000, ₹80,000 and ₹1,20,000 respectively. At the end of the first year, *B* withdraws ₹ 40,000, while at the end of the second year, *C* withdraws ₹ 80,000. In what ratio will the profit be shared at the end of 3 years?

    (a) 2 : 3 : 5           (b) 3 : 4 : 7
    (c) 4 : 5 : 9           (d) None of these

15. Avinash covered 150 km distance in 10 hourse. The first part of his journey he covered by car, then he hired a rickshaw. The speed of car and rickshaw is 20 km/hr and 12 km/hr respectively. The ratio of distances covered by car and the rickshaw respectively are :
    (a) 2 : 3            (b) 4 : 5
    (c) 1 : 1            (d) None of these

16. A cistern has two taps which fill it in 12 minutes and 15 minutes respectively. There is also a waste pipe in the cistern. When all the three are opened, the empty cistern is full in 20 minutes. How long will the waste pipe take to empty the full cistern ?
    (a) 10 min          (b) 12 min
    (c) 15 min          (d) None of these

**Directions** (Qs. 17 - 18) : *Read the given passages and answer the questions based on them.*

### PASSAGE - 1

Some religious teachers have taught that Man is made up of a body and a soul: But they have been silent about the intellect. Their followers try to feed the body on earth and to save soul from perdition after death: But they neglected the claims of the mind. Bread for the body and virtue for the soul: These are regarded as the indispensable requisites of human welfare here and hereafter. Nothing is said about knowledge and education. Thus Jesus Christ spoke much of feeding the hungry, healing the sick, and converting the sinners: But he never taught the duty of teaching the ignorant and increasing scientific knowledge. He himself was not a well-educated man, and intellectual pursuits were beyond his horizon. Gautam Buddha also laid stress on morality, meditation and asceticism, but he did not attach great importance to history, science, art or literature. St. Ambrose deprecated scientific studies and wrote, that discussing the nature and position of the earth does not help us in our hope for life to come. St. Basil said very frankly and foolishly, 'It is not a matter of interest for us whether the earth is a sphere or a cylinder or a disc'. Thomas Carlyle also followed the Christian traditions when he declared that he honoured only two men and no third: The manual labour and the religious teacher. He forgot the scientist, the scholar and the artist. The cynics of Greece despised education at last.

17. What have the religious teachers taught in the past?
    (a) That man is made up of body only
    (b) That man is made up of soul only.
    (c) That man is made up of bubbles
    (d) That man is made up of body and soul together

18. What is food for the soul?
    (a) Bread            (b) Virtue
    (c) Vice             (d) Education

### PASSAGE-2

Successfully adjusting to one's environment leads to happiness. War at a universal level destroys the weaker people, who are the most unable to adjust to their environment. Thus, war at the universal level puts weaklings out of their misery and allows more space for their predators to enjoy life in a better manner. As those actions have to be performed which maximise the level of happiness of the greatest number, war at a universal level should take place.

19. What response would the author of the above discussion come up with, in the case of the objection that the weaklings far exceed strong people?
    I. He would respond with the statement that the person making the objection is a weakling.
    II. He would respond by saying that weaklings will be miserable, no matter what happens.
    III. He would respond with the statement that the strong would be frustrated if the weaklings are not destroyed.
    (a) I only          (b) II only
    (c) III only        (d) II and III

20. The author's discussion would be greatly influenced if he agreed to which of the following?
    I. Technology could change the environment.
    II. War at the universal level would be an integral part of the environment.
    III. It is possible for the strong to survive without suppressing the weak.
    (a) I only          (b) II only
    (c) III only        (d) I and III

### PASSAGE - 3

Tagore's foremost objection to nationalism lies in its very nature and purpose as an institution. The fact that it is a social construction, a mechanical organization, modelled with certain utilitarian objectives in mind, makes it unpalatable to Tagore, who was a champion of creation over construction, imagination over reason and the natural over the artificial and the man-made: 'Construction is for a purpose, it expresses our wants; but creation is for itself, it expresses our very beings.' As a formation, based on needs and wants rather than truth and love, it could not, Tagore suggests, contribute much to the spiritual fulfilment of mankind. To him, race was a more natural, and therefore acceptable, social unit than the nation, and he envisioned a 'rainbow' world in which races would live together in amity, keeping their 'distinct characteristics but all attached to the stem of humanity by the bond of love'.

21. What was Tagore's objection towards nationalism?
    (a) It is a political construction
    (b) Mechanical organization
    (c) Anti-utilitarian
    (d) None of the above

22. What according to Tagore is the difference between creation and construction?
    I. Creation is mechanical, construction is organic.
    II. Creation is natural, construction is artificial.
    III. Creation is essential to human beings, construction is utilitarian.
    IV. Creation is individual, construction is collective.
    (a) I and II        (b) II and III
    (c) III and IV      (d) III only

23. The metaphor of rainbow is used to describe
    (a) a multi-cultural society
    (b) a rich society
    (c) a multi-racial society
    (d) an ancient civilization

**Directions** (Qs. 24-25): *Study the following information carefully and answer the questions given below:*

Following are the conditions for selecting personnel Manager in an organization:

The candidate must

(I) be a graduate with at least 50% marks.

(II) have a postgraduate degree/diploma in Personnel Management/HR with at least 60% marks.

(III) not be more than 35 years as on 1. 6. 2017.

(IV) have post qualification work experience of at least five years in the Personnel/HR division of an organization.

(V) have secured at least 45% marks in the selection process.

In the case of a candidate who satisfies all the conditions EXCEPT

(i) at (III) above, but has post-qualification work experience of at least ten years, the case is to be referred to the Director – Personnel.

(ii) at (IV) above, but has post – qualification work experience as Deputy Personnel Manager of at least three years, the case is to be referred to President – Personnel.

In each question below are given details of one candidate. You have to take one of the following courses of action based on the information provided and the conditions and sub-conditions given above and mark the number of that course of action as your answer. You are not to assume anything other than the information provided in each question. All these cases are given to you as on

1. 6. 2017.

**Mark answer** (a) if the candidate is to be selected

**Mark answer** (b) if the information provided is inadequate to take a decision

**Mark answer** (c) if the case is to be referred to the Director – Personnel

**Mark answer** (d) if the case is to be referred to the President - Personnel

24. Anant Joshi has been working in the personnel department of an organization for the past six years. He was born on 7th November 1985. He has secured 60% marks in post-graduate degree in personnel management. He has also secured 55% marks in both graduation and selection process.

25. Mohan Bajpai was born on 10th April 1983. He has secured 55% marks in graduation and 65% marks in post- graduate diploma in personnel management. He has been working in the HR Deptt, of an organization for the past six years after completing his post-graduate diploma.

26. In the question given below is a statement followed by two assumptions number I and II.

An assumption is something supposed or taken for granted. You have to consider the statement and the following assumption and decide which of the assumptions is implicit in the statement.

**Statement:** "I have not received telephone bills for nine months inspite of several complaints"A telephone customer's letter to the editor of a daily.

**Assumption:** I. Every customer has a right to get bills regularly from the telephone company.

II. The customer's complaints point to defect in the services which is expected to be corrected.

Give answer:

(a) if only assumption I is implicit.

(b) if only assumption II is implicit.

(c) if neither assumption I nor II is implicit.

(d) if both assumptions I and II are implicit.

27. If 'air' is called 'green', green is called 'blue', 'blue' is called 'sky', 'sky' is called 'yellow', 'yellow' is called 'water' and water is called 'pink' then what is the colour of clear sky ?

(a) Yellow     (b) Water

(c) Sky     (d) Blue

28. A father is 5 times as old as his son. His son is 6 years old. After how many years, will the father be 4 times as old as his son?

(a) 2 years     (b) 5 years

(c) 6 years     (d) 4 years

29. One morning Savita set out from home to fetch water in the direction of the Sun. After some time she turned to her left and then to her right. After some time she turned to her right again. Now which direction is she facing?

(a) South     (b) West

(c) East     (d) North

30. In a question paper, there are 12 questions in all out of which only six are to be answered. Six questions have an alternative each. Each question has four parts. How many questions including parts are there in the question paper?

(a) 24     (b) 48

(c) 72     (d) 96

31. In a certain code language, **"SURGEON"** is written as **"QLHDURV"** and **"CORNER"** is written as **"OHKULF"**. How is **"SHADOW"** written in that code language?

(a) DRTERS     (b) TRADEV

(c) UQBCFU     (d) TFBCPX

32. Find the missing number.

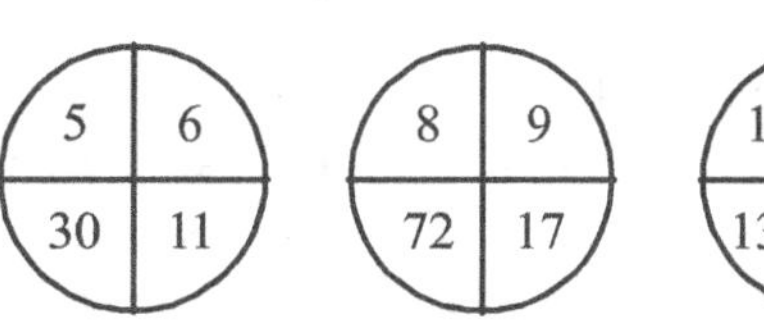

(a) 10     (b) 12

(c) 14     (d) 16

33. A beats B by 100 m in a race of 1200 m and B beats C by 200 m in a race of 1600 m. Approximately by how many metres can A beat C in a race of 9600 m?

(a) 1600 m     (b) 1800 m

(c) 1900 m     (d) 2400 m

34. On 6th March, 2005, Monday falls. What was the day of the week on 7th March, 2004?
    - (a) Tuesday
    - (b) Monday
    - (c) Friday
    - (d) Sunday

35. A garden is 24 m long and 14 m wide. There is a path 1 m wide outside the garden along its sides. If the path is to be constructed with square marble tiles 20 cm × 20 cm, the number of tiles required to cover the path is
    - (a) 1800
    - (b) 200
    - (c) 2000
    - (d) 2150

36. 2 cm of rain has fallen on a sq. km of land. Assuming that 50% of the raindrops could have been collected and contained in a pool having a 100 m × 10 m base, by what level would the water level in the pool have increased?
    - (a) 15 m
    - (b) 20 m
    - (c) 10 m
    - (d) 25 m

37. Find the sum of all numbers in between 10–50 excluding all those numbers which are divisible by 8. (include 10 and 50 for counting.)
    - (a) 1070
    - (b) 1220
    - (c) 1320
    - (d) 1160

38. In an examination 70% of the candidates passed in English, 65% in Mathematics, 27 % failed in both the subjects. If 248 candidates passed in both the subjects, then find the total number of candidates.
    - (a) 200
    - (b) 400
    - (c) 300
    - (d) 100

39. The number of words from the letters of the words BHARAT in which B and H will never come together, is
    - (a) 360
    - (b) 240
    - (c) 120
    - (d) None of these

40. 5 Indian and 5 American couples meet at a party & shake hands . If no wife shakes hands with her husband and no Indian wife shakes hands with a male, then the number of hand shakes that takes place in the party is
    - (a) 95
    - (b) 110
    - (c) 135
    - (d) 150

41. A speaks truth in 75% of the cases and B in 80% of the cases. In what percentage of cases are they likely to contradict each other in stating the same fact?
    - (a) 15%
    - (b) 20%
    - (c) 5%
    - (d) 35%

**Directions** (Qs. 42 - 51) : *Read the following passages and answer the questions based on them.*

### PASSAGE - 1

In a free country, the man who reaches the position of leader is usually one of outstanding character and ability. Moreover, it is usually possible to foresee that he will reach such a position, since early in life one can see his qualities of character. But this is not always true in the case of a dictator; often, he reaches his position of power through chance, very often through the unhappy state of his country.

42. The passage seems to suggest that
    - (a) a leader foresees his future position.
    - (b) a leader is chosen only by a free country.
    - (c) a leader must see that his country is free from despair.
    - (d) despair in a country sometimes leads to dictatorship.

### PASSAGE-2

Really, I think that the poorest he that is in England has a life to live, as the greatest he, and therefore truly, I think it is clear that every man that is to live under a government ought first by his own consent to put himself under the government, and I do think that the poorest man in England is not at all bound in a strict sense to that government that he has not had a voice to put himself under.

43. The above statement argues for
    - (a) distribution of wealth equally among all
    - (b) rule according to the consent of the governed
    - (c) rule of the poor
    - (d) expropriation of the rich

### PASSAGE-3

The despotism of custom is everywhere the standing hindrance to human advancement, being in unceasing antagonism to that disposition to aim at something better than customary, which is called, the spirit of liberty. The spirit of improvement is not always a spirit of liberty, for it may aim at forcing improvements on an unwilling people; and the spirit of liberty, in so far as it resists such attempts, may ally itself locally and temporarily with the opponents of improvement; but the only permanent source of improvement is liberty. We have a warning example in China - a nation of much talent and, in some respects, even wisdom, owing to the rare good fortune of having been provided at an early period with a particularly good set of customs. They are remarkable, too, in the excellence of their apparatus for impressing, as far as possible, the best wisdom they possess upon every mind in the community, but they have become stationary- have remained so for thousands of years; and if they are ever to be further improved, it must be by foreigners. They have succeeded beyond all hope in making a people all alike, all governing their thoughts and conduct by the same maxims and rules; and these are the fruits.

44. According to the passage, the paradox of tradition versus progress lies in which of the following statements?
    - (a) The spirit of improvement is not always the spirit of liberty.
    - (b) Custom is antagonistic to change.
    - (c) Progress cannot happen without change and custom is imperilled by change.
    - (d) It is the spirit of liberty that leads to a break from custom.

45. The author cites the example of China to show that
    - (a) it is a nation of much talent and wisdom
    - (b) it must have been at the head of the movement of a progressive world.
    - (c) conformity can lead to stagnation.
    - (d) Chinese customs are the basis for the remarkable progress it has made.

46. According to the passage, which of the following statements is not true?
    (a) The east has not progressed because custom is deeply entrenched there.
    (b) European culture with its noble antecedents can never become stagnant.
    (c) The East must have been original at one time.
    (d) The West considers itself morally superior to the East.

### PASSAGE - 4

The spiritual interlocutor interacts without preconceived notions. The good discussant receives without barriers and responds in a heightened state of understanding. The shedding of constructs becomes at once a spiritual and a humanist pursuit. Most of us, by force of one word habit, introduce our experiential and intellectual baggage into our interactions with people. This not only distorts our understanding of the material reality, but inhibits our spiritual growth as well. We stew in our 'here and now' boxes, unable to elevate ourselves as a bird would.

Yet, the validity of experience should not be discounted. Experience should be assessed with a certain heightened objectivity for one to draw the right lessons for one's actions. So detachment should be seen as a means to arrive at that state of balanced understanding. It does not preclude pain and compassion; but it discards obfuscation and hypocrisy. Creativity is said to spring from the angst of experience. Often the outpourings of a tortured mind make for great literature and painting. Ironically, existential pain can bring about work of transcendental quality. The beauty and simplicity of Khalil Gibran's The 'Prophet' is testimony to the literary virtues of spiritualism. The spiritual world is a rich, fulsome, loving nothingness that opens up the heavens, not a musty blankness.

Compassion could liberate us from the boundaries of the mind. The house-holder looks after the family out of a sense of duty and affection, which in due course becomes second nature. The mental and emotional universe of such an individual is able to accommodate reality in virtually all its dimensions. Psychologist Eric Fromm points out that love must be all-encompassing by nature for an individual to be spiritually liberated. To love some people and resent others is not real love.

47. Which of the following will be a suitable title for the passage?
    (a) Spiritual Equality
    (b) Limitations of the Intellectual
    (c) Creativity and Spirituality
    (d) Being Spiritual

48. "It does not preclude pain and compassion; but it discards obfuscation and hypocrisy." When paraphrased, how will the given sentence read?
    (a) Experience does not prevent pain and compassion but rejects disguise and insincerity.
    (b) Detachment does not prevent pain and compassion but rejects disguise and insincerity.
    (c) Detachment does not prevent pain and compassion but rejects complication and pretense.
    (d) Experience does not prevent pain and compassion but rejects complication and pretense.

### PASSAGE - 5

When we speak of the "probability of death", the exact meaning of this expression can be defined in the following way only. We must not think of an individual, but of a certain class as a whole, e.g., "all insured men forty-one years old living in a given country and not engaged in certain dangerous occupations". A probability of death is attached to the class of men or to another class that can be defined in a similar way. We can say nothing about the probability of death of an individual even if we know his condition of life and health in detail. The phrase "probability of death", when it refers to a single person, has no meaning at all.

49. Which of the following conclusions can be drawn from the passage?
    1. Singular, non replicable events can be assigned numerical probability value.
    2. Probability calculation requires data of the class of people or of events.
    3. The data about a class of events can be used to predict the future of any specific event
    (a) 1 only        (b) 2 only
    (c) 1 and 2       (d) 2 and 3

50. Which of the following statements would the author(s) disagree to the most?
    The outcome of a boxing match to be held in Los Angeles between two boxers, Joe and Mark, belonging to two different boxing clubs can be analysed and an outcome can be assigned a numerical value:
    (a) If assessment of boxers' current fitness levels and their strengths is done by experts.
    (b) By analysis of outcomes of fights between the boxers belonging to the two clubs.
    (c) By analysis of outcomes of fights between the two boxers at different venues.
    (d) By comparing outcomes of fights between the two boxers against same opponents.

### PASSAGE-6

A country under foreign domination seeks escape from the present in dreams of a vanished age, and finds consolation in visions of past greatness. That is a foolish and dangerous pastime in which many of us indulge. An equally questionable practice for us in India is to imagine that we are still spiritually great though we have come down in the world in other respects. Spiritual or any other greatness cannot be founded on lack of freedom and opportunity, or on starvation and misery. Many western writers have encouraged the notion that Indians are other-worldly. I suppose the poor and unfortunate in every country become to some extent other-worldly, unless they become revolutionaries, for this world is evidently not meant for them. So also subject peoples.

As a man grows to maturity he is not entirely engrossed in, or satisfied with, the external objective world. He seeks also some inner meaning, some psychological and physical satisfaction. So also with peoples and civilizations as they mature and grow. Every civilization and every people exhibit these parallel streams of an external life and an internal life. Where they meet or keep close to each other, there is an equilibrium and stability. When they diverge, conflict arises and the crises torture the mind and spirit.

51. The passage mentions that "this world is evidently not meant for them". It refers to people who
    1. seek freedom from foreign domination.
    2. live in starvation and misery.
    3. become revolutionaries.

    Which of the statements given above is/are correct ?
    (a) 1 and 2      (b) 2 only
    (c) 2 and 3      (d) 3 only

52. Consider the following assumptions :
    1. A country under foreign domination cannot indulge in spiritual pursuit.
    2. Poverty is an impediment in the spiritual pursuit.
    3. Subject peoples may become other-worldly.

    With reference to the passage, which of the above assumptions is/are valid ?
    (a) 1 and 2      (b) 2 only
    (c) 2 and 3      (d) 3 only

53. Find the number of triangles in the following figure :

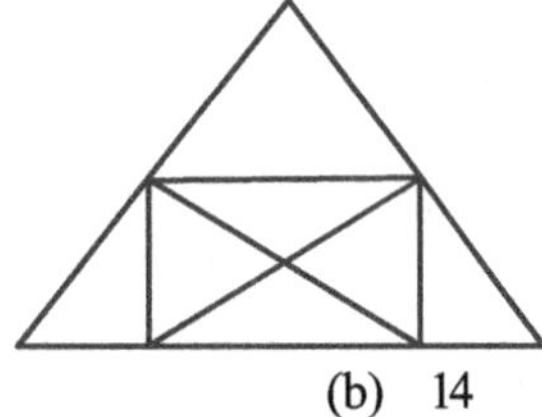

    (a) 8      (b) 14
    (c) 10      (d) 12

54. From the given answer figures, select the one in which the question figure is hidden/embedded.

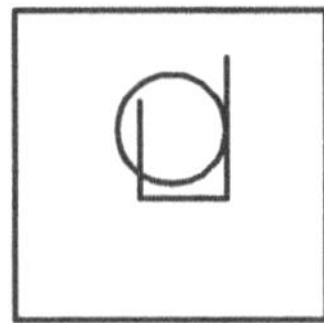

(a) 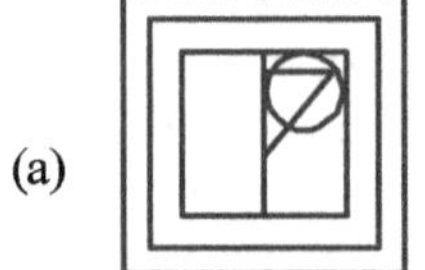      (b) 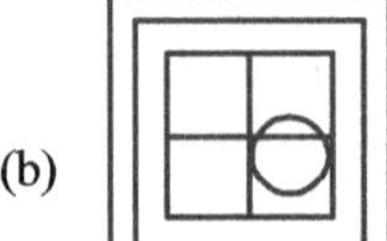

(c) 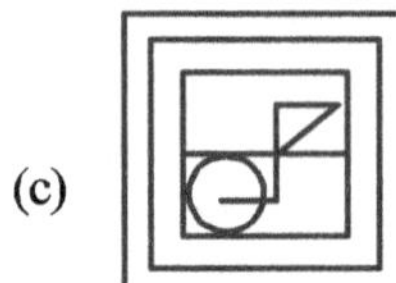      (d) 

55. Which answer figure completes the form in question figure ?
    **Question Figures :**

**Answer figures :**

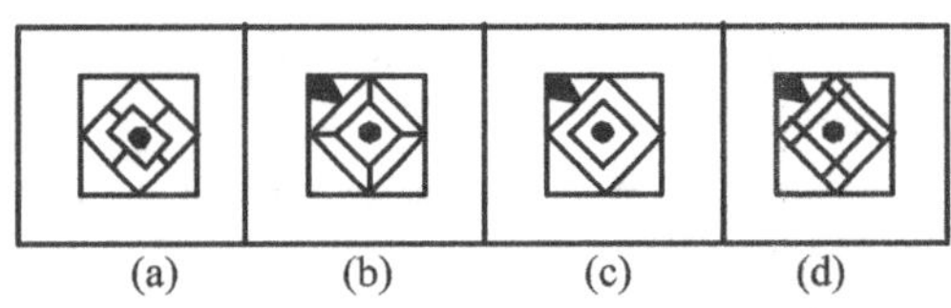

(a)      (b)      (c)      (d)

56. Four positions of a cube are shown below. Which colour is opposite to white colour in the given cubes?

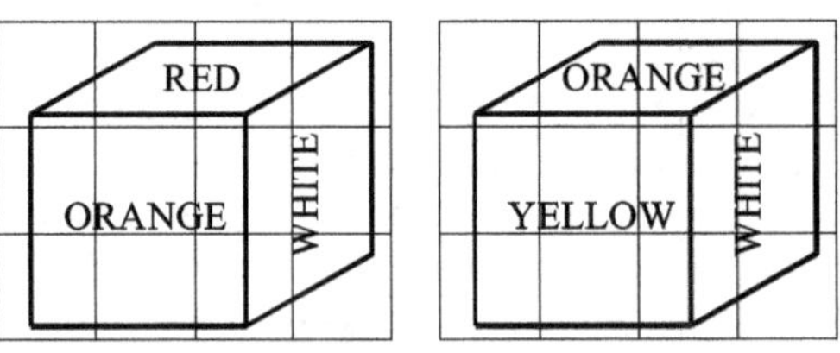

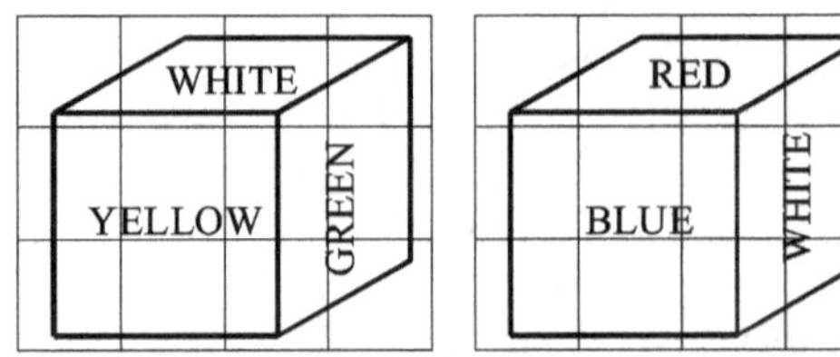

    (a) Orange      (b) Blue
    (c) Red      (d) Yellow

57. Four positions of a dice are given below. Identify the number at the bottom when top is 5.

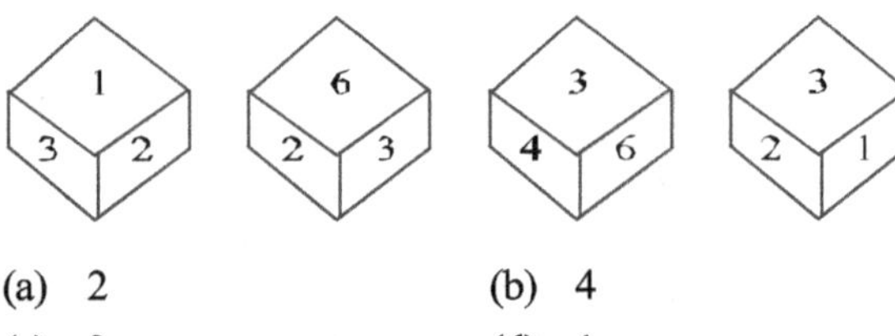

    (a) 2      (b) 4
    (c) 3      (d) 1

**Directions (Qs. 58 - 59) :** *In each of the following questions, a statement is given followed by two conclusions I and II. Give answer :*
(a) if only conclusion I follows;
(b) if only conclusion II follows;
(c) if either I or II follows;
(d) if both I and II follow.

58. **Statement :** Population increase coupled with depleting resources is going to be scenario of many developing countries in days to come.

    **Conclusions :**
    I. The population of developing countries will not continue to increase in future.
    II. It will be very difficult for the governments of developing countries to provide its people decent quality of life.

59.  **Statement :**  Yes, I know honesty is the primary concern for discharging the duties of a police officer and my officers are aware of this — Statement of police commissioner of city S.

**Conclusions :**

I.   The statement of police commissioner of city S is absolutely right.

II.  The statement of police commissioner of city S is not absolutely right.

**Directions** (Qs. 60-63): *Read the following table carefully and answer the given questions.*

**Table shows the performance of six batsmen**

| Name of Batsman | Number of matches played by batsman in the tournament | Average run scored by batsman in the tournament | Total balls faced in the tournament | Strike Rate |
|---|---|---|---|---|
| A | 20 | - | - | 160 |
| B | 16 | 55 | - | - |
| C | - | 60 | 400 | 120 |
| D | - | - | - | 80 |
| E | 10 | 70 | 800 | - |
| F | - | - | - | 70 |

(i)   Strike rate = (Total runs scored/total balls faced)×100

(ii)  All the batsman could bat in all the matches played

(iii) You have to calculate the missing value and give the answer accordingly.

60.  If the respective ratio between the balls faced by D and F is 4 : 5, then by what percent did F score more than D?
(a) 5.27%   (b) 9.675% (c) 8.57%   (d) 9.375%

61.  If the runs scored by E in the last three matches of the tournament are not considered, his average decreases by 15. If the runs scored by E in 8th and 9th match are below 100 and no two scores among these three scores are equal, then is the minimum possible run scored by E in the 10th match?
(a) 115      (b) 116      (c) 117      (d) 118

62.  Total balls faced by A is 600 less than the total runs made by him, then what is the average of A in the tournament?
(a) 70       (b) 75       (c) 80       (d) 85

63.  B faces equal number of balls in first eight matches and the last eight matches in the tournament. If his strike rate in first eight and last eight matches of the tournament are 80 and 96 respectively, then what is the total number of balls faced by him in the tournament?
(a) 500      (b) 400      (c) 1000      (d) 800

64.  200 people were surveyed to find out their hourly wage. 100 people had college other 100 were those who had not completed high school. The following graph gives number of people and their hourly wages.

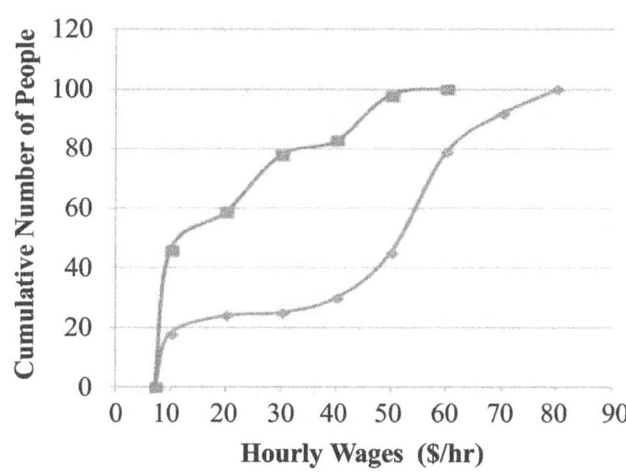


Approximately what percentage of 'people with college degrees' have hourly wage range $50-$60?
(a)   50%                    (b)   35%
(c)   45%                    (d)   44%

**Directions** (Qs. 65-70) : *Answer the questions based on the passages.*

### PASSAGES - 1

Poverty measurement is an unsettled issue, both conceptually and methodologically. Since poverty is a process as well as an outcome; many come out of it while others may be falling into it. The net effect of these two parallel processes is a proportion commonly identified as the 'head count ratio', but these ratios hide the fundamental dynamism that characterises poverty in practice. The most recent poverty reestimates by an expert group has also missed the crucial dynamism. In a study conducted on 13,000 households which represented the entire country in 1993-94 and again on 2004-05, it was found that in the ten-year period 18.2% rural population moved out of poverty whereas another 22.1% fell into it over this period. This net increase of about four percentage points was seen to have a considerable variation across states and regions.

65.  Which of the following is an **assumption** which is **implicit** in the facts stated in the above paragraph ?
(a)  It may not be possible to have an accurate poverty measurement in India.
(b)  Level of poverty in India is static over the years.
(c)  Researchers avoid making conclusions on poverty measurement data in India.
(d)  Government of India has a mechanism to measure level of poverty effectively and accurately.

### PASSAGES - 2

In 1998 more citizens from the country of Monrovia migrated from Monrovia to neighbouring Abstania than during any prior year. In 1998 the number of reported violent crimes in Abstania increased dramatically over 1997. The unavoidable conclusion is that Monrovians who migrated from Monrovia to Abstania were responsible for this increase.

66. Which of the following statements, if true, would most seriously weaken the claim that Monrovians were responsible for the increase in violent crime in Abstania during 1998?
    (a) During 1998 more violent crimes were reported in Abstania than in Monrovia.
    (b) In 1998 no Monrovians migrated from either Monrovia or Abstania to any country other than Monrovia or Abstania.
    (c) In 1998 the number of unreported violent crimes in Abstania increased as well.
    (d) In 1998 fewer Monrovians migrated from Monrovia to Abstania than from Abstania to Monrovia.

### PASSAGES - 3

A drug that is very effective in treating some forms of cancer can, at present, be obtained only from the bark of the Raynhu, a tree that is quite rare in the wild. It takes the bark of approximately 5,000 trees to make one pound of the drug. It follows, then, that continued production of the drug must inevitably lead to the Raynhu's extinction.

67. Which of the following, if true, most seriously weakens the above conclusion?
    (a) The drug made from Raynhu bark is dispensed to doctors from a central authority.
    (b) The drug made from the Raynhu bark is expensive to produce.
    (c) The Raynhu generally grows in largely inaccessible places.
    (d) The Raynhu can be propagated from cuttings and cultivated by farmers.

### PASSAGES - 4

Mobile technology has played great role in growth and development of society. Earlier cellphone was used as a medium of conversation only. Now mobile phones also support a wide variety of other services, such as, texting, email, internet access etc. The price of mobile phones is also decreasing and people are being encouraged to buy a mobile phone set at a cheaper rate. The mobile technology and smartphones have the capabilities of handling video calls, sharing large files. Mobile technology had made it more efficient to conduct business. Video calls and taking photographs have become possible as mobile phone has in built camera. Therefore, there is no need to carry around a camera everywhere you go.

68. Which of the following cannot be inferred from the given information? (An inference is something that is not directly stated but can be inferred from the given information)
    (a) One can share photos and videos via mobile phones provided that the other person has a similar device.
    (b) Many features are being added to mobile phones now-a-days
    (c) The other features of mobile phones are used as useful as the built in camera
    (d) Mobile phones can be used for purposes other than making calls

### PASSAGES - 5

Supermarkets are growing at a fast pace than Kirana Stores. Kirana Stores are such places where customer go to purchase their necessities. In place of five Kirana stores one or two supermarkets are being established. It has been found that customers' requirements are looked after by trained staff. It has been found that food products are low life products which are manufactured from local manufacturers. These products are typically purchased by the customer on the assurance. The markets is appealing to supermarkets and retail outlet owners are setting up their business in other areas where there are less Kirana stores.

69. Which of the following can be a good argument in favour of shopping, from Kirana stores instead of supermarkets?
    (a) People prefer supermarkets because they offer a larger range of products. i.e., products other than FMCG and they can buy everything under one roof.
    (b) People end-up buying other irrelevant things along with those on their shopping lists in Supermarkets and then they have to stand in long queues at the billing counters.
    (c) Most Kirana stores are closed atleast one day in a week whereas supermarkets are open 365 days a year.
    (d) Kirana stores do not accept debit and credit cards.
    (e) Very few Kirana stores sell products at a bargained price.

### PASSAGES - 6

The company's coffee crop for 1998-99 totalled 8079 tonnes, an all time record. The increase over the previous year's production of 5830 tonnes was 38.58%. The previous highest crop was 6089 tonnes in 1970-71. The company had fixed a target to be realized by the year 2000-01, and this has been achieved two years earlier, thanks to the emphasis laid on the key areas of irrigation, replacement of unproductive coffee bushes, intensive refilling and improved agricultural practices. It is now our endeavour to reach the target of 10000 tonnes in the year 2001-02.

70. Which one of the following would contribute most to making the target of 10000 tonnes in 2001-02 unrealistic
    (a) The potential of the productivity enhancing measures implemented up to now has been exhausted.
    (b) The total company land under coffee remained constant since 1969 when an estate in the Nilgiri Hills was acquired.
    (c) The sensitivity of the crop to climatic factors makes predictions about production uncertain.
    (d) The target-setting procedures in the company have been proved to be sound by the achievement of the 8000 tonne target.

**Directions** **(Qs. 71 - 74) :** *Attempt these questions based on the passages given against each.*

### PASSAGES - 1

The argument for liberalisation which answers the worries of the Left parties about the possible trade deficits created by the opening up of the Indian economy goes thus: 'In today's economic scenario, where there are many trading countries, the trade between two specific countries need not be balanced. The differing demands of goods and services and the differing productive capabilities of the same among different countries will cause a country like India to have trade deficits with some countries and surpluses with other countries. On the whole, the trade deficits and surpluses will balance out in order to give a trade balance'.

71. Which of the following conclusions best summarises the argument presented in the passage above?
    (a) Left parties need not worry about trade deficits in India since its trade will always be in balance even though it runs a deficit with a single country.
    (b) India's trade deficits and surpluses with other countries always balance out.
    (c) The Left parties in India should not be concerned about India's trade deficits with specific countries because they will balance out in the long run.
    (d) None of these

### PASSAGES - 2

Psychological research indicates that college hockey and football players are more quickly moved to hostility and aggression than are college athletes in non-contact sports such has swimming. But the researchers' conclusion—that contact sports encourage and teach participants to be hostile and aggressive—is untenable. The football and hockey players were probably more hostile and aggressive to start with, than the swimmers.

72. Which of the following, if true, would most strengthen the conclusion drawn by the psychological researchers?
    (a) The football and hockey players became more hostile and aggressive during the season and remained so during the off season, whereas there was no increase in aggressiveness among the swimmers.
    (b) The football and hockey players, but not the swimmers, were aware at the start of the experiment that they were being tested for aggressiveness.
    (c) The same psychological research indicated that the football and hockey players had a great respect for cooperation and team play, whereas the swimmers were most concerned with excelling as individual competitors.
    (d) The research studies were designed to include no college athletes who participated in both contact and non-contact sports.

### PASSAGES - 3

Acme brand aspirin claims to be the best headache relief available on the market today. To prove this claim, Acme called 10 people and asked them their thoughts on headache relief products. All 10 of them stated that they unequivocally use Acme brand aspirin on a regular basis and that they believe it to be the best headache relief available on the market today.

73. Which of the following would most weaken this argument?
    (a) Acme brand aspirin is highly addictive.
    (b) The 10 people called were married to the company's top 10 executives, and they were coached on what to say.
    (c) Most people choose to suffer silently through their headaches and take no medicines whatsoever.
    (d) This survey was conducted by an independent company.

### PASSAGES - 4

The centre reportedly wants to continue providing subsidy to consumers for cooking gas and kerosene for five more years. This is not good news from the point of view of reining in the fiscal deficit. Mounting subventions for subsidies means diversion of savings by the government from investment to consumption, raising the cost of capital in the process. The government must cut expenditure on subsidies to create more fiscal space for investments in both physical and social infrastructure. It should outline a plan for comprehensive reform in major subsidies including petroleum, food and fertilizers and set goal posts.

74. Which of the following is an inference which can be made from the facts stated in the above paragraph ?
    (a) India's fiscal deficit is negligible in comparison to other emerging economies in the world.
    (b) Subsidy on food and fertilizers are essential for growth of Indian economy.
    (c) Reform in financial sector will weaken India's position in the international arena.
    (d) Gradual withdrawal of subsidy is essential for effectively managing fiscal deficit in India.

75. How many natural numbers are there which give a remainder of 41 after dividing 1997?
    (a) 2                      (b) 4
    (c) 6                      (d) None of these

76. A number is *interesting* if on adding the sum of the digits of the number and the product of the digits of the number, the result is equal to the number. What fraction of numbers between 10 and 100 (both 10 and 100 included) is *interesting?*
    (a) 0.1                    (b) 0.11
    (c) 0.16                   (d) 0.22

77. 11 friends went to a hotel and decided to pay the bill amount equally. But 10 of them could pay ₹ 60 each, as a result 11th has to pay ₹ 50 extra than his share. Find the amount paid by him.                      [*SSC-Sub. Ins.-2014*]
    (a) ₹ 105                  (b) ₹ 110
    (c) ₹ 115                  (d) ₹ 120

78. In an exercise room some discs of denominations 2 kg and 5 kg are kept for weightlifting. If the total number of discs is 21 and the weight of all the discs of 5 kg is equal to the weight of all the discs of 2 kg, find the weight of all the discs together.
    (a) 80 kg                  (b) 90 kg
    (c) 56 kg                  (d) None of these

79. In a mixture of milk and water the proportion of water by weight was 75%. If in the 60 gm mixture, 15 gm water was added, what would be the percentage of water ?
    (a) 75%                    (b) 88%
    (c) 90%                    (d) None of these

80. A number of couch potatoes were asked 'How many hours of Nintendo did you play yesterday?' The distribution is summarized in the bar graph below. Select the statement that correctly describes a relationship between measures of central tendency for this distribution.

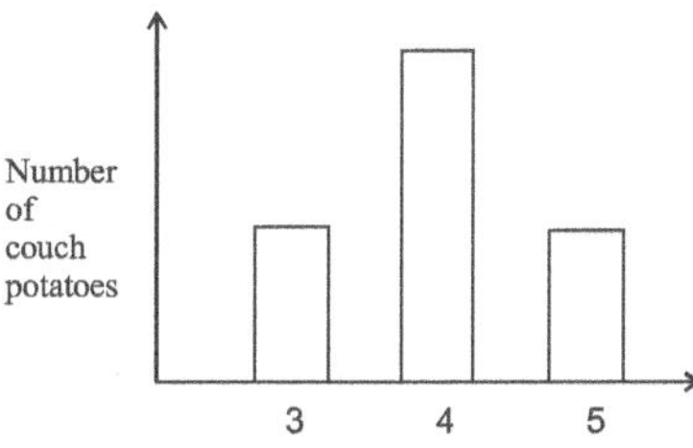


    (a) The median is less than the mean.
    (b) The mode is greater than the mean.
    (c) The mode is equal to the median.
    (d) The mean is greater than the mode.

# SOLUTIONS

1. (c)

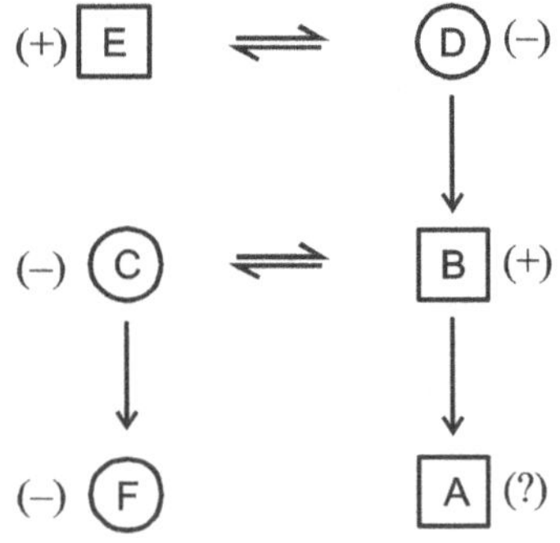

$$71 \quad 78 \quad 99 \quad 134 \quad 183 \quad 246$$
$$+(7\times1) \quad +(7\times3) \quad +(7\times5) \quad +(7\times7) \quad +(7\times9)$$

2. (d) As, gender of A is not given, so we can not determined the number of female in the family

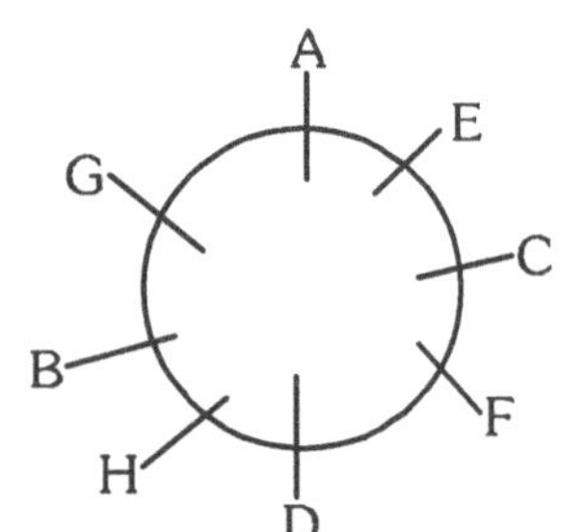

$(+)\ \boxed{E} \rightleftharpoons (D)\ (-)$

$(-)\ (C) \rightleftharpoons \boxed{B}\ (+)$

$(-)\ (F) \qquad \boxed{A}\ (?)$

As, gender of A is not given, so we can not determine the number of female in the family.

3. (d) Initial Position is V1 V2 V3 V4 V5 V6

Now from the 1st condition: V2 V5

From 2nd condition V6 V4 and none of them at position number three hence, they cannot be at 1st three places.

From 3rd condition V5 V1 V3

At 5th place even numbered book is placed.

From these information we can conclude that:-

V2 V5 V1 V3 V6 V4 hence, (d) is correct.

**Solution for 4 – 8:**

Row 1.   ↓   P    V   S    T   R   Q

Row 2.   ↑   C    F   A    E   B   D

4. (d)
5. (a)
6. (b)
7. (b)
8. (c)
9. (d) Third to the left

10. (c) A makes 1 rev. per sec

B makes $\dfrac{6}{10}$ rev per sec

C makes $\dfrac{4}{10}$ rev. per sec

In other words A, B and C take 1, $\dfrac{5}{3}$ & $\dfrac{5}{2}$ seconds to complete one revolution.

L.C.M of $1, \dfrac{5}{3}$ & $\dfrac{5}{2} = \dfrac{\text{L.C.M. of } 1,5,5}{\text{H.C.F. of } 1,3,2} = 5$

Hence, after every 5 seconds the red spots on all the three wheels touch the ground.

11. (b) Required average

$$= \left( \frac{67\times2+35\times2+6\times3}{2+2+3} \right)$$

$$= \left( \frac{134+70+18}{7} \right) = \frac{222}{7} = 31\frac{5}{7} \text{ years.}$$

12. (a) Let SP of 1 kg article = ₹ 100
For 1st shopkeeper
SP of 1 kg article = ₹ 75
For 2nd shopkeeper
SP of 1.25 kg article = ₹ 100
SP of 1 kg article = ₹ 80

13. (a) Let the sum be ₹ $P$. Then,

$$\Rightarrow \quad \left[ P\left(1+\frac{10}{100}\right)^2 - P \right] = 1260$$

$$\Rightarrow \quad P\left[ \left(\frac{11}{10}\right)^2 - 1 \right] = 1260$$

$$\therefore \quad \text{Sum} = ₹\ 6000$$

So, S.I. = ₹ $\left( \dfrac{6000\times4\times5}{100} \right)$ = ₹ 1200

14. (b) $A : B : C = (40000 \times 36) : (80000 \times 12 + 40000 \times 24)$
$: (120000 \times 24 + 40000 \times 12)$
$= 144 : 192 : 336 = 3 : 4 : 7$

15. (c) The average speed of Avinash

$$= \frac{150}{10} = 15 \text{ km/hr}$$

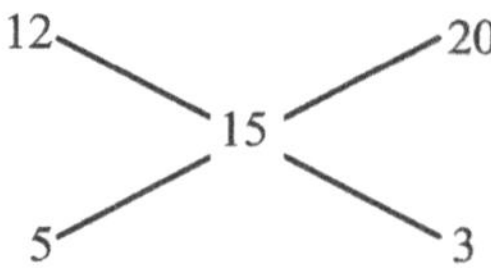

It means the rickshaw took 5/8 and car took 3/8 of the total time i.e., the ratio of time taken by rickshaw to car is $5:3$

So the ratio of distances covered by rickshaw to car is $5 \times 12 : 3 \times 20 \Rightarrow 1:1$

16. (a) Work done by the waste pipe in 1 minutes

$$= \frac{1}{20} - \left(\frac{1}{12} + \frac{1}{15}\right) = -\frac{1}{10} \quad [-\text{ve sign means}$$

emptying]

$\therefore$ Waste pipe will empty the full cistern in 10 minutes.

17. (d)
18. (b)
19. (d) In case of the objection that the weaklings far exceed the strong people, the author would come up with the response that the weaklings will be miserable no matter what happens and that the strong would be frustrated if the weaklings are not destroyed.

20. (a) The role of technology is not talked about in the passage. So if the effect of technology on environment is taken into account then the author's discussion would be greatly influenced.

21. (b) Tagore's objection regarding nationalism was that it is a mechanical organization.

22. (b) According to Tagore, creation is natural and essential to human beings, while construction is artificial and utilitarian.

23. (c) Metaphor of rainbow is used to describe a multiracial society.

**Solution for (24-25):**

| Q. No. | I | II | III/(i) | IV | V |
|--------|---|----|---------|----|----|
| 24 | √ | √ | √ | √ | √ |
| 25 | √ | √ | √ | √ | – |

24. (a)

25. (b)

26. (d) Both are imminent positive outcomes assumed.
27. (c) The color of sky is blue. But blue is called sky. Hence, option (c) is correct choice.

28. (a) Son's age = 6 yrs.
Father's age = 30 yrs.
Let 'x' be the yr. after which father will be 4 times as old as his son.
According to question
$30 + x = 4(6 + x) = 30 + x = 24 + 4x \Rightarrow 6 = 3x.$
x = 2.
Hence, require year is 2 yrs.

29. (a)

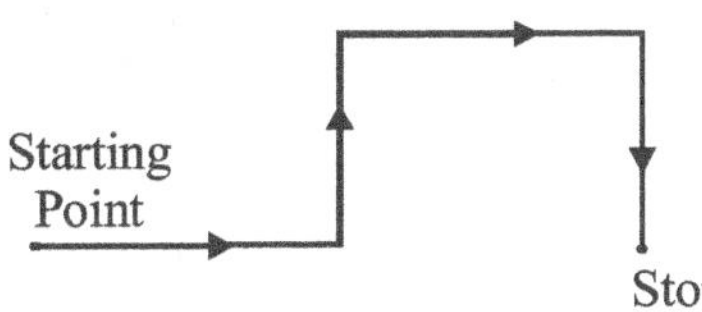


Now, Savita is facing south direction

30. (c) $(6 + 12) \times 4 \Rightarrow 18 \times 4 = \boxed{72}$

31. (b) As,

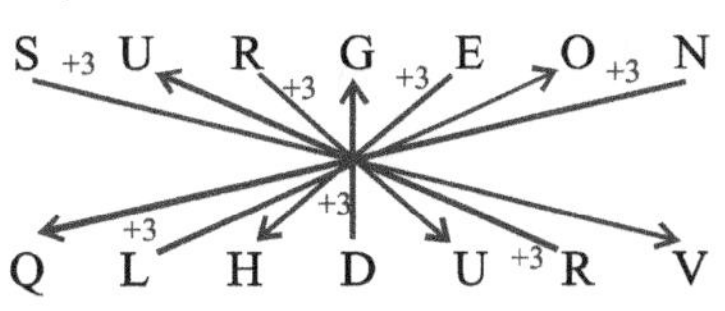


and

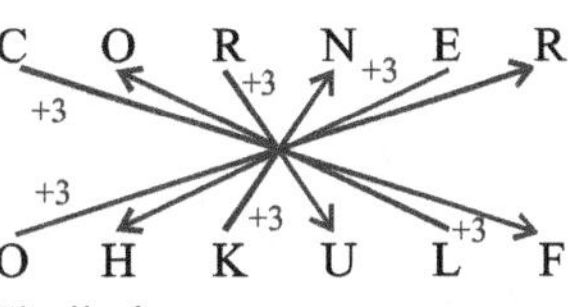


Similarly,

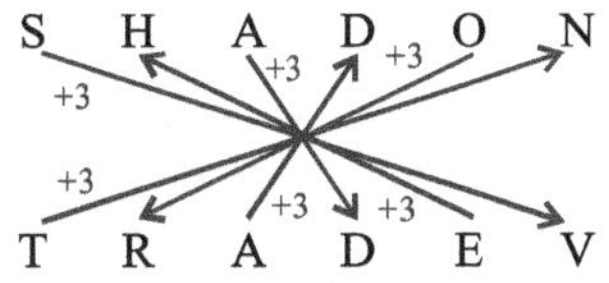


32. (b) The pattern is :
$5 + 6 = 11$ and $5 \times 6 = 30$
$8 + 9 = 17$ and $8 \times 9 = 72$
$11 + 12 = 23$ and $11 \times 12 = 132$

33. (c) Ratio of speeds of $A : B = 12 : 11$
and ratio of speeds of $B : C = 8 : 7$
Therefore ratio of speeds of A : B : C
$= 96 : 88 : 77$
So in 9600 m race A will beat C by 1900 m.

34. (b) 6th March 2005 = Monday

Then, 6th March 2004

= Monday – 1 day = Sunday.

{$\because$ 2004 is a leap year but it does not cross 29th February of 2004, so only 1 is taken as odd day}.

6th March 2004 = Sunday

7th March 2004 = Monday.

35. (c) Given, length of garden = 24 m and
breadth of garden = 14 m
$\therefore$ Area of the garden = $24 \times 14$ m$^2$ = 336 m$^2$.
Since, there is 1 m wide path outside the garden
$\therefore$ Area of Garden (including path)
$= (24 + 2) \times (14 + 2) = 26 \times 16$ m$^2$ = 416 m$^2$.
Now, Area of Path = Area of garden (inculding path) – Area of Garden
$= 416 - 336 = 80$ m$^2$.
Now, Area of Marbles = $20 \times 20 = 400$ cm$^2$
$\therefore$ Marbles required $= \dfrac{\text{Area of Path}}{\text{Area of Marbles}}$

$= \dfrac{80,0000}{400} = 2000$

36. (c) Volume of rain that is to be collected

in a pool $= 2 \times 1 \times 10^{10} \times \dfrac{1}{2} = 10^{10}$ cm$^3$ = $10^4$ meter$^3$

Volume of pool $= L \times B \times h$
$10^4 = 100 \times 10 \times h \Rightarrow h = 10$ m.

37. (a) The answer will be given by:

$$[10 + 11 + 12 + ....... + 50] - [16 + 24 + ... + 48]$$

$$= 41 \times 30 - 32 \times 5$$

$$= 1230 - 160 = 1070.$$

38. (b) Let the set $E$ and $M$ represent students who passed in English and Mathematics respectively.

$$n(E \cup M) = (100-27)\% = 73\%$$

$$n(E \cup M) = n(E) + n(M) - n(E \cap M)$$

$$73\% = 70\% + 65\% - x\% \Rightarrow x\% = 62\%$$

Now. $62\% \equiv 248$

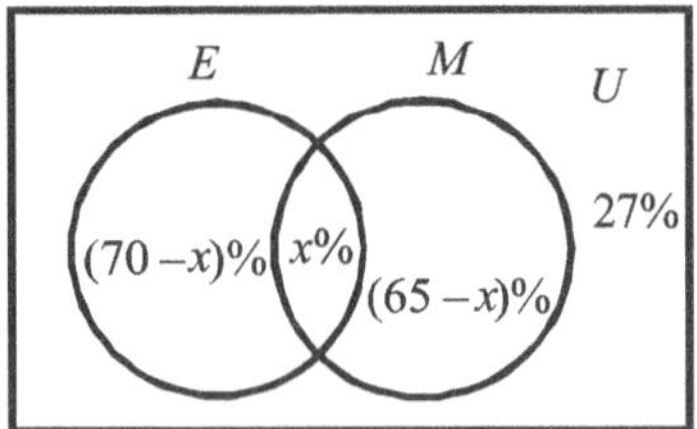


$$\text{Total number of candidates} = \frac{248 \times 100}{62} = 400$$

39. (b) There are 6 letters in the word BHARAT, 2 of them are identical.

Hence total number of words with these letter = 360

Also the number of words in which $B$ and $H$ come together = 120

∴ The required number of words = 360 − 120

$$= 240$$

40. (c) Total number of hand shakes = $^{20}C_2$

No Indian female shakes hand with male

$$= 5 \times 10 = 50 \text{ hand shakes}$$

No American wife shakes hand with her husband

$$= 5 \times 1 = 5 \text{ hand shakes}$$

∴ total number of hand shakes occurred

$$= {}^{20}C_2 - (50 + 5) = 190 - 55 = 135$$

41. (d) Contradiction can occur if A speaks truth and B lies, B speaks truth and A lies.

So, required probability

$$= 0.75 \times 0.2 + 0.8 \times 0.25 = 0.35$$

$$\text{Req}\% = 0.35 \times 100$$

$$= 35\%$$

42. (d) The passage denotes that despair sometimes leads to dictatorship in a country.

43. (b) The passage argues for the rule according to the consent of those who are governed.

44. (a) The paradox is stated in option (a). It is stated in the passage that improvements cannot be forced on a unwilling people, hence the spirit of improvement is not always the spirit of liberty.

45. (c) The author cites the example of China to show that they have stagnated because they tried to make a people all alike which implies that conformity can lead to stagnation.

46. (b) European culture can never stagnate is not true because the author warns that if they try to impose the Chinese type of uniformity in Europe, it too will meet the same fate, which indicates that it may also stagnate.

47. (d)

48. (c)

49. (b) The paragraph talks about probability of a certain class as a whole. According to the author the probability of an individual has no meaning at all. So (1) can not be concluded. (2) clearly follows as it talks about a class of people or of events. (3) can not be concluded as it is out of context. It talks about prediction whereas the passage talks about probability.

50. (a) The outcome can be assigned only if we have data belonging to some class. (b) offers data from the fights among various boxers of the 2 clubs. (c) offers data from the flights between the 2 boxers at various venues. Similarly (d) also provides data of some class. But in (a) we do not have any such data so the author would disagree to it.

51. (a) Only statements 1 and 2 are true as people who turn revolutionary are not 'other wordly'; unless world shows the contradiction.

52. (c) Only assumptions 2 and 3 are valid as for achieving anything great one has to be free of worries of basic needs and should be mentally as well as physically free.

53. (c)

54. (c) 

55. (b)

56. (b) Blue colour is opposite to white colour in the given cubes.

57. (c)

58. (b) With the limited resources and overpopulation it is very hard to provide decent quality of life. Hence II follows.

59. (c) Either the commissioner is absolutely right or he is not.

**Solution for (60-63):**

60. (d) Runs scored by D $= \dfrac{80 \times 4}{100} = \dfrac{32}{10} = 3.2$

Runs scored by F $= \dfrac{70 \times 5}{10} = \dfrac{35}{10} = 3.5$

So Required% $= \left( \dfrac{3.5 - 3.2}{3.2} \times 100 \right)\%$

$= 9.375\%$

**61. (d)** Total runs scored by E in 10 matches

$= 70 \times 10 = 700$

Total runs scored by E in 7 matches if last three matches are not considered) $= 7 \times 55 = 385$

So Total runs scored by E in last three matches $= 700 - 385 = 315$

Minimum run in 10th match, it means maximum run in 8th and 9th are below

100 and no two scores are equal.

So, run scores in 8th and 9th match are 98 and 99

**So Run scored in 10th match**

$= 315 - 197 = 118$

**62. (c)** Let average of A $= x$

So total runs scored $= 20x$

And no. of ball faced $= 20x - 600$

According to question,

Strike rate $= \dfrac{20x}{20x - 600} \times 100$

$\Rightarrow 160 = \dfrac{20x}{20x - 600} \times 100$

$\Rightarrow 8 = \dfrac{x}{20x - 600} \times 100$

$\Rightarrow 160x - 4800 = 100x$

$\Rightarrow 60x = 4800$

$\Rightarrow x = \dfrac{4800}{60} = 80$

**63. (c)** Let B played $x$ no. of ball in first eight and last eight matches

So Run scored by B in first eight matches

$= \dfrac{80 \times x}{100} = \dfrac{4x}{5}$

and runs scored by B in last eight matches

$= \dfrac{96 \times x}{100} = \dfrac{24x}{25}$

According to question,

$\dfrac{4x}{5} + \dfrac{24x}{25} = 16 \times 55$

$\Rightarrow \dfrac{20x + 24x}{25} = 880$

$\Rightarrow x = \dfrac{880 \times 25}{44} = 500$

$\therefore$ Total no. of ball faced by B in the tournament

$= 500 + 500 = 1000$

**64. (b)** Number of people with hourly wage up to $50 is 45. Number of people with hourly wage up to $60 is 80. Hence number of people whose hourly wage lies in range $50 – $60 is about $80 - 45 = 35$. Since 100 were surveyed, the required percentage is about 35%.

**65. (a)** It may not be possible to have an accurate poverty measurement in India.

**66. (d)** The argument relies on the unstated assumption that Abstania's Monrovian population either remained stable or increased during 1998. However, (d) provides that this population actually declined in 1998, despite the influx of Monrovians. Given that the number of Monrovians residing in Abstania decreased while the crime rate increased, (d) reduces the likelihood that it was Monrovians who were responsible for the increase in violent crime in 1998.

(a) provides no information useful in evaluating the argument. Whether (a) strengthens the argument depends on addition considerations as well, such as: the total population of Monrovia compared to Abstania; whether the Monrovian population increased or decreased in each country during the year; and whether the crime rate in Monrovia increased or decreased during 1998.

(b) actually *strengthens* the argument. By providing evidence that number of Monrovians residing in Abstania increased in 1998, (b) makes it more likely that Monrovians were responsible for the increase in violent crime that year.

(c) actually *strengthens* the argument, by affirming the essential premise that the number of violent crimes in Monrovia increased dramatically during 1998.

**67. (d)** (d) provides an alternate source of the Raynhu bark. Even though the tree is rare in the wild, the argument is silent on the availability of cultivated trees. The author of the argument must be assuming that there are no Raynhu trees other than those in the wild, in order to make the leap from the stated evidence to the conclusion that the Raynhu is headed for extinction. The option (d) weakens the assupmtion - 'there are limited Raynhu trees' - by saying that there are other ways as well for the propogation of Raynhu. The other answer choices all contain information that is irrelevant. Note that the correct choice does not make the conclusion of the argument impossible. In fact, it is possible that there may be domesticated Raynhu trees and the species could still become extinct. Answer choice (d) is correct because it makes the conclusion about extinction less likely to be true.

68. **(e)** From the given information we cannot infer option (e)

69. **(b)** Option (b) strengthens the statement.

70. **(a)** (a) is the best option as according to the passage the achievement of the 8000 tonne target was made two years earlier. Now, the achievement of 10000 tonnes would be unrealistic as the company would have exhausted all the enhancing measures implementing, the previous endeavour.

71. **(d)** The first statement uses the word 'always', which makes it out of context as per the argument presented. Similarly the second statement is useless as it also uses the word 'always'. The third statement is not correct as it talks only about the trade deficit only and surplus is not mentioned.

72. **(d)** The research studies were designed to create discrimination, so as to present college athletes from participating in both forms of the competition.

73. **(b)** Answer choice (d) actually strengthen the argument – which is the opposite of what the question asks you to do. Answer choice (c) is completely irrelevant to the argument. Acme could still be the best product, even if most people don't intend to use it. Answer choice (a) certainly does not bode well for the quality of Acme's aspirin, but it is nonetheless possible that competing brands are even more addictive. Answer choice (b) is correct. It weakens the passage's argument by undercutting its implied assumption that a sample of 10 people must give accurate results.

74. **(d)** Consider the following lines of the passage:

   "The government must cut expenditure on subsidies to create more fiscal space for investments in both physical and social infrastructure".

75. **(c)** Let us assume that the quotient is Q and divisor is D. Using the condition given in question, 1997

   $$= QD + 41$$

   $$\Rightarrow QD = 1956. \text{ Now } 156 = 2 \times 2 \times 3 \times 163$$

   Number of required natural number $= {}^4c_2 = 6$.

76. **(a)** Let the numbers be the form $10x + y$

   According to question

   $$10x + y = x + y + xy$$
   $$9x = xy$$
   $$\therefore \qquad y = 9$$

   The numbers are $19, 29, 39, 49, 59, 69, 79, 89$ and $99$ total of 9 numbers

   Hence the required fraction $= \dfrac{9}{91}$

   $$= 0.099 \approx 0.1$$

77. **(c)** Let total bill would be ₹ x

   Each one decided to pay $= ₹\left(\dfrac{x}{11}\right)$

   10 friends could pay $10 \times 60 = ₹\,600$

   According to question,

   $$600 + \dfrac{x}{11} + 50 = x$$

   $$650 = x - \dfrac{x}{11} = \dfrac{10x}{11}$$

   $$x = \dfrac{650 \times 11}{10} = 715$$

   Amount paid by $11^{th}$ friend $= \dfrac{715}{11} + 50 = ₹\,115$

78. **(d)** Let the total number of discs of 2 kg and 5 kg be 'a' and 'b' respectively.

   Then, $a + b = 21$ and $5b = 2a$

   Solving the above two equations, we get $a = 15, b = 6$

   $\therefore \qquad$ Weight of all discs together

   $$= 15 \times 2 + 6 \times 5 = 60\,\text{kg}$$

79. **(d)** Weight of water in the mixture of 60 g water

   $$= 60 \times \dfrac{75}{100} = 45g$$

   weight of water in the mixture of 45 g water

   $$= 45 + 15 = 60\,\text{g}$$

   $\therefore$ Percentage of water $= \dfrac{60 \times 100}{75} = 80\%$

80. **(c)**

## GRAPHS

A graph is a diagram showing the relation between typically two variable quantities. i.e., a graph is a representation depicting the relationship between two or more quantities.

The two variables are represented on the abscissa (x-axis) and the ordinate (y-axis).

Thus the graph is usually a figure (line, chart, point, curve, trace or a plot) in the X-Y plane made by joining a few points in this plane. These points in the plane are known as ordered pairs (x, y).

### Applications

Graphs can be used to represent a function, a scientific process, an economic process, etc.

A graph can be used to represent a model for knowledge representation and reasoning.

## REPRESENTATION OF A GRAPH

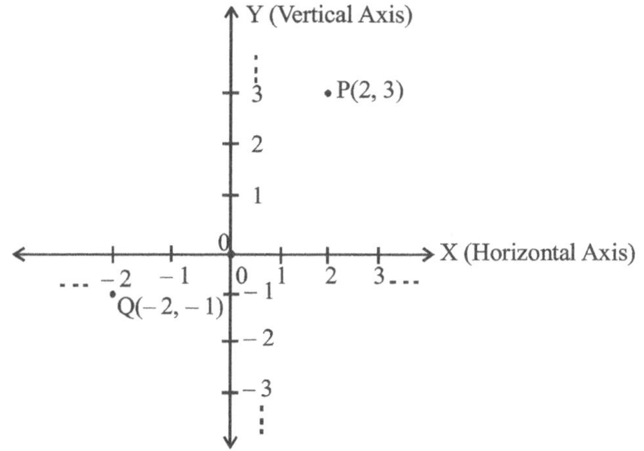

**Fig. :** *x and y axes of a graph*

The point O represents the origin. Both the axes are perpendicular to each other.

On the right hand side of the origin of the x-axis, the value of numerals is positive while that on the left hand side are negative. Similarly, on the y-axis, the values above the origin are positive while that below the origin are negative.

Point P(2, 3) on the graph is located at 2 units of the x-axis from the origin towards the right hand side and 3 units of the y-axis upwards from the origin.

While point Q (–2, – 1) on the graph is located 2 units on x-axis to the left of the origin and 1 unit on the y-axis below the origin.

Let us now understand with the help of a few examples what type of graphs may appear to test our knowledge.

## 1. INCREASING GRAPH

The increasing graph shows as one quantity increased other quantity also increases. This type of graph may be of 2 types – linear or non-linear.

**(i) Linear Graph** is a graph that shows a directly proportional relation between 2 quantities and is denoted by a straight line.

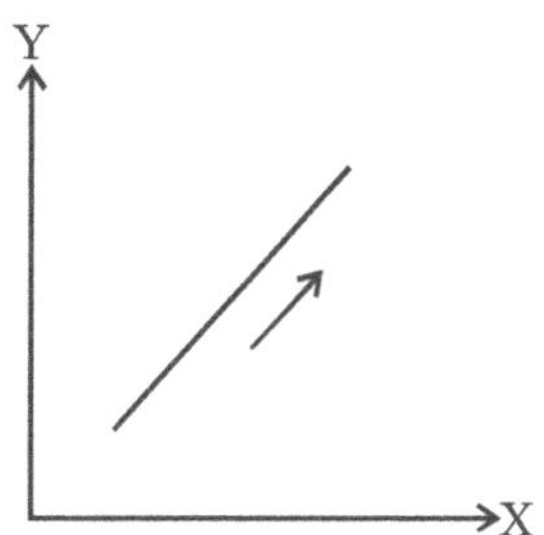

**Fig. :** *Linear increasing graph.*

In this graph the value of x is increases when value of y increases.

**(ii) Non-linear Graph** is a graph that does not show a fixed pattern of increase or decrease.

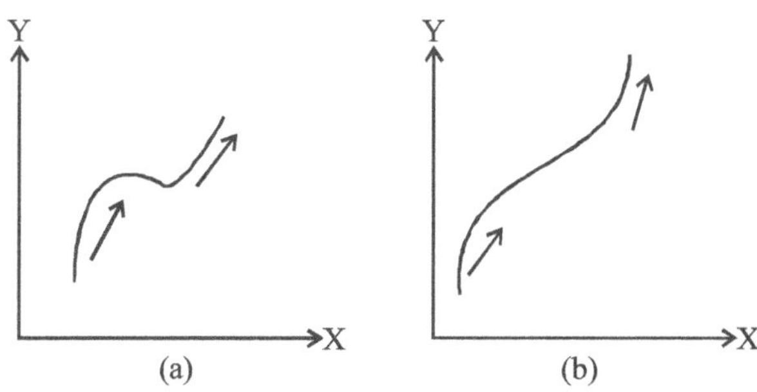

**Fig. :** *Various types of non-linear increasing graphs.*

**Graph (a)** shows an overall increase but there is a small dip in the graph which indicate decrease. The graph but does not show a fixed pattern between X & Y.

**Graph (b)** shows an increase in both X & Y but without a fixed pattern of dependency.

## 2. DECREASING GRAPH

The decreasing graph shows when one quantity increases then other quantity decreases and vice-versa. This can also be divided into two types - Linear & non-linear.

## (i) Linear Decreasing Graph

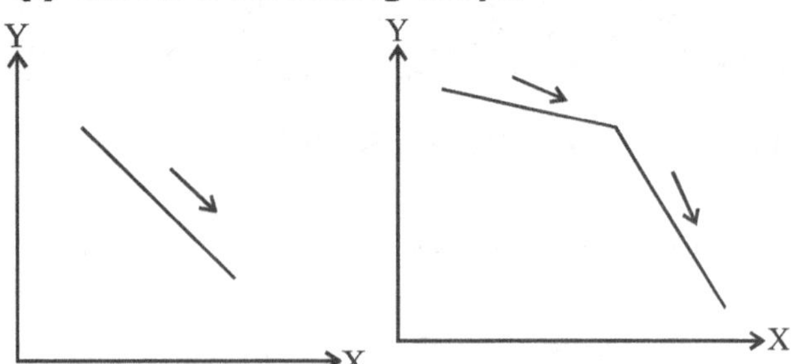

**Fig. :** *Linear decreasing graph*

In this graph, when x increases, y decreases.

## (ii) Non-linear Decreasing Graph

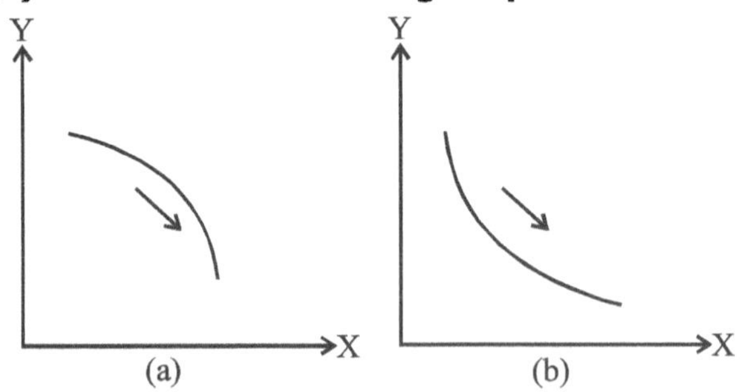

**Fig. :** *Various types of non-linear decreasing graphs.*

**Graphs (a) & (b)** are 2 curves showing decreasing non-linear relationship.

### Illustration – 1

**What happens when an Air conditioner is switched on in summers in a room having temperature of 45°C (assuming all the other factors governing the working of an AC like filters, refrigerants etc. are in a perfect condition)? Explain with the graph.**

*Solution :*

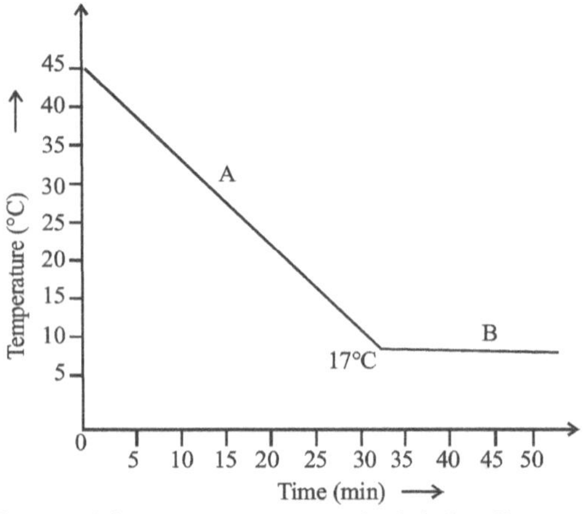

The graph has 2 parts - A & B - both being linear curves.

In a summer afternoon when a room is at 45°C (temperature shown by y-axis), it takes about 30-35 minutes (time shown by the x-axis) to cool down the room the minimum temperature to which the temperature drops to in a regular AC is about 16-17° C.

Thus the temperature drops from 45°C to 17°C a total time span of about 35 minutes, i.e., at time, t = 0 min. temperature = 45°C while at time, t = 35 min. temperature = 17°C, therefore, the curve A shows a linear decreasing graph.

In case of curve B, there is no further decrease in the temperature with increasing time, so curve B can be known as either an increasing time graph or a constant graph.

## 3. CONSTANT GRAPH

The constant graph is a curve which shows constant value of one quantity while the other quantity may increase or decrease.

### (i) Increasing Constant Graphs

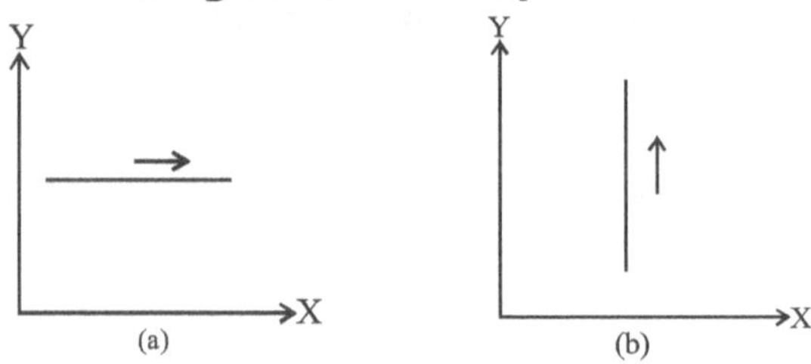

**Fig. :** *Increasing constant graphs.*

**Graph (a)** shows a constant value of y while an increasing value of x.

**Graph (b)** shows a constant value of x while an increasing value of y.

### (ii) Decreasing Constant Graphs

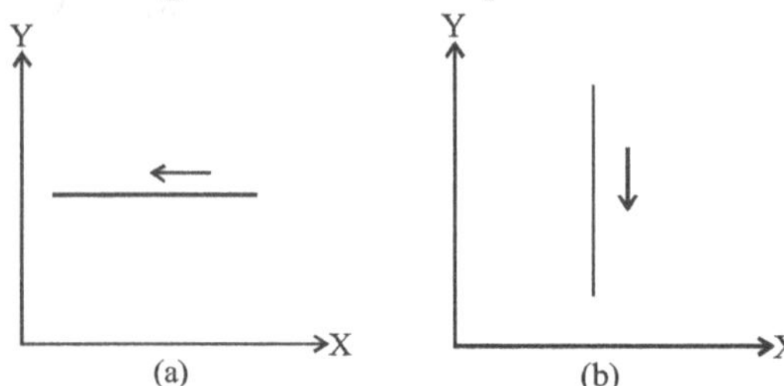

**Fig. :** *Decreasing constant graphs*

**Graph (a)** shows a constant value of y while a decrease in the value of x.

**Graph (b)** shows a constant value of x while a decrease in the value of y.

## 4. UNIFORM GRAPH

A uniform graph is a curve shows uniform pattern of increase or decrease or constant curve.

A linear graph is an example of a uniform graph.

### Illustration – 2

**The given graph shows a distance - time curve for a man where distance is given on the Y-axis while time is shown on the X-axis. Explain its uniformity.**

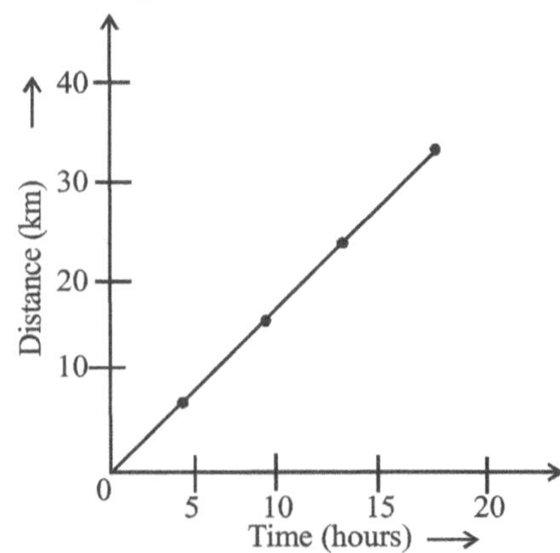

*Solution :*

We can observe from the given graph that for every 5 hours of time passed, 10 km of distance is covered by the man. This pattern is maintained further on as well. The man covers in the next 5 hours (10 – 5 = 5), 10 km (20 – 10) again and similarly does till 40 km and 20 hrs.

Thus this type of journey will be called a uniform journey, i.e., every point denotes 10 km covered in 5 hours.

## Illustration – 3

**An object moves with a constant velocity in a certain direction. For this object, draw 2 graphs - (1) Distance-time graph and (2) Velocity-time graph.**

*Solution :*

**(i)** It is given that the object moves with a constant velocity,

which means, as $\text{velocity} = \dfrac{\text{distance}}{\text{time}}$, the distance

covered by the object in the time taken will be uniform, i.e., the distance covered for each equal interval of time will be equal. Let us assume that the object started from rest (velocity = 0 m/s) and covers 10 m every second.

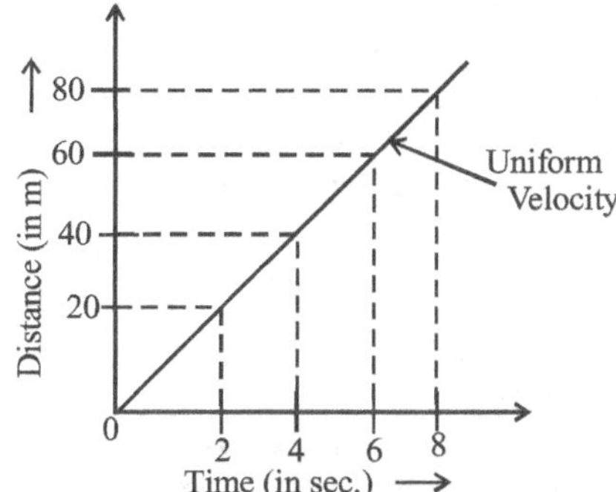


**Fig. -1:** *Distance-time graph*

Therefore, constant or uniform velocity here is

$$\text{velocity} = \dfrac{\text{distance}}{\text{time}}$$

For 0 to 20 m, $\text{velocity} = \dfrac{20}{2} = 10\,\text{m/s}$

For 20 to 40 m, $\text{velocity} = \dfrac{40-20}{4-2} = \dfrac{20}{2} = 10\,\text{m/s}$

For 60 to 80 m, $\text{velocity} = \dfrac{80-60}{8-6} = \dfrac{20}{2} = 10\,\text{m/s}$

**(ii)** Since the given uniform or constant velocity = 10 m/s, therefore the graph is given as :

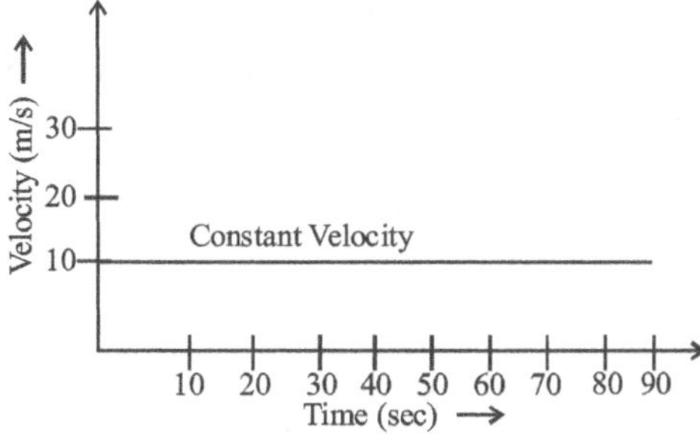


**Fig.-2 :** *Velocity-time graph.*

## Illustration – 4

**In winters, when the temperature of water is about 10°C at a certain place, what happens when the geyser is switched on to heat up this water. Explain with help of a graph.**

*Solution :*

When there geyser is turned on, the temperature of water (at 10° C) will start rising in a linear relationship with time in usual cases, the geyser heats water uptil 60-70° C after which the geyser thermostat switches off the heating element in the geyser.

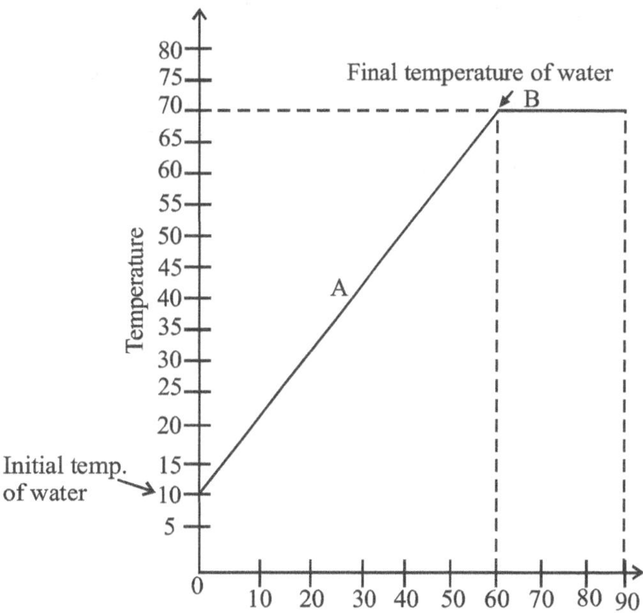


To obtain this temperature a usual geyser takes about one hour and then switches off the heating element after which the temperature is maintained at 70°C. (1st – write up sequence)

Graph explanation

**Curve A** shows uniform increase in temp. of water with time. In 60 minutes, the geyser heats up the water to 70° C.

**Curve B** Shows the constant temperature (Or maintaining of temperature) till the taps are not opened or water is not taken out.

# 5. COMBINED GRAPH

## Illustration – (5-9)

**Directions:** *Study the given graph Speed-Time and answer the following question.*

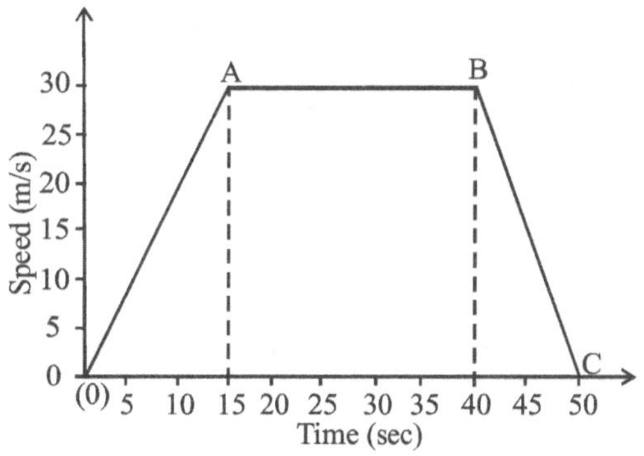

**5.** What is the maximum speed of the person who's Speed-Time graph is given ?
   (a)  30 m/s        (b)  10 m/s
   (c)  40 m/s        (d)  5 m/s

*Solution :* **(a)**

Clearly, the graph shows that the maximum speed of the person is gained at point A, i.e., maximum speed = 30 m/s gained at t = 15 s

**6.** For how long does the given body accelerate?
   (a)  10 sec        (b)  30 sec
   (c)  40 sec        (d)  15 sec

*Solution :* **(d)**

The body gained speed i.e., accelerated only upto 15 seconds, after which it moved with a constant speed.

**7.** What is the total distance covered by the body between points A and B ?
   (a)  400 m        (b)  450 m
   (c)  750 m        (d)  250 m

*Solution :* **(c)**

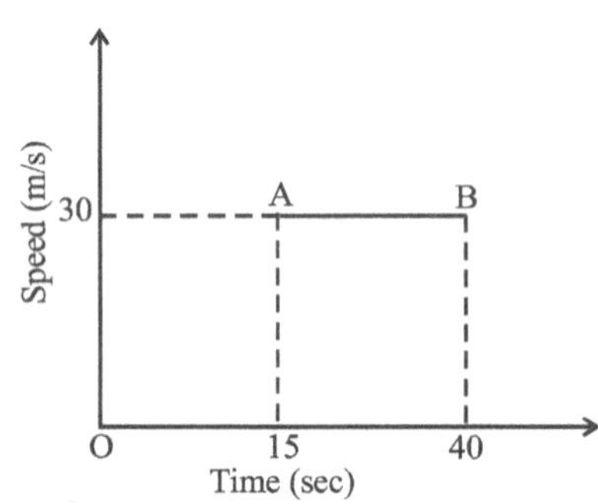


From A and B, the body maintain a constant speed of 30 m/s. The body reaches pt. A at 15 s and pt. B at 40s, therefore it covers the distance between the two points A & B within 40 – 15 = 25 seconds. Hence

distance covered = speed × time
$$= 30 \times 25 = 750 \text{ m}$$

**8.** The process of retardation of the body occurs between points
   (a)  O and A        (b)  A and C
   (c)  O and B        (d)  B and C

*Solution :* **(d)**

Retardation of a body means negative acceleration, i.e., when the speed of a body reduces with increase in time. Hence, retardation occurs between points B and C from 40 to 50 seconds.

**9.** What is the acceleration of the body from O to A ?
   (a)  30 m/s$^2$        (b)  5 m/s$^2$
   (c)  2 m/s$^2$         (d)  15 m/s$^2$

*Solution :* **(c)**

From O to A, the body's initial speed $(u) = 0$ m/s while at A the final speed $(v) = 30$ m/s. The body travels from O to A in 15 seconds. Therefore, by using formula

$$a = \frac{(v-u)}{t}$$

we can find the acceleration of the body from the graph:

$$\therefore a = \frac{30-0}{15} = \frac{30}{15} = 2 \text{ m/s}^2.$$



Consider the following velocity-time graph. It shows two cars starting simultaneously on parallel roads.

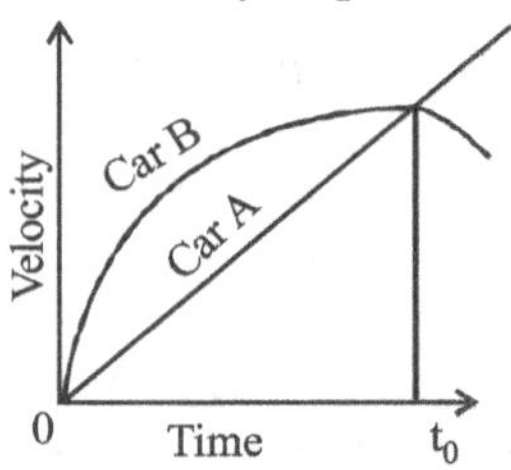


With reference to the above graph, which of the following is correct ?
   (a)  Car B travels with a uniform speed.
   (b)  The distance covered by both the cars in the given time is equal.
   (c)  Car A covers more distance at time at units than Car B.
   (d)  Car B has a greater initial acceleration than that of Car A.

*Solution :* **(d)**

Option (a) is incorrect because Car A and not Car B travels with uniform speed (increasing).

Option (b) & (c) are incorrect because

distance = speed × time

which will be different for both the cars at each moment; only at time $t_0$ will their distances covered be same as velocity of both cars in equal and time $(t_0)$ is also the same.

For option (d), acceleration $= \dfrac{\text{velocity}}{\text{time}}$ which is greater for Car B before $t_0$.



Consider the graph & information given in the above example, which of the following is NOT correct ?
   (a)  Car B has an initial acceleration greater than that of Car A.
   (b)  Car B is faster than Car A at all times.
   (c)  Both cars have the same velocity at time $t_0$.
   (d)  Both cars travel the same distance in time $t_0$ units.

*Solution :* **(b)**

Before $t_0$ Car B travels faster than Car A, at $t_0$ both the cars travel at equal speed (as they intersect to $t_0$) while after $t_0$, Car A will travel faster than car A.



**Directions:** *Read the passage given below, study the graph that follows and answer the three items given below the figure.*

During a party, a person was exposed to contaminated water. A few days later, he developed fever and loose motions. He suffered for some days before going to a doctor for treatment. On starting the treatment, he soon became better and recovered completely a few days later. The following graph shows different phases of the person's disease condition as regions A, B, C, D and E of the curve.

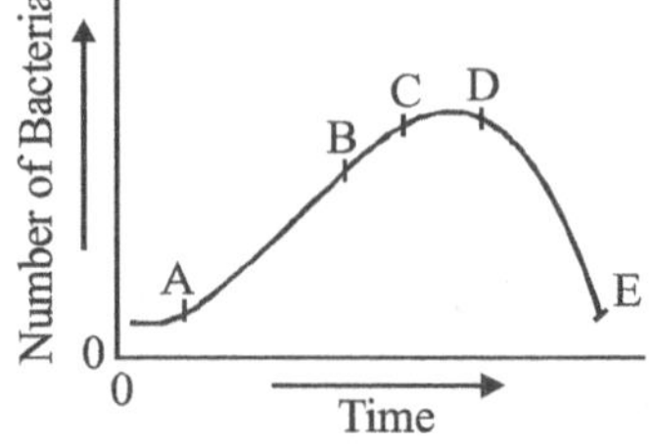

**12.** **Which region/regions of the curve correspond/ corresponds to incubation phase of the infection ?**

(a) A only

(b) B only

(c) B and C

(d) No part of the curve indicates the incubation phase

*Solution : (a)*

As the term incubation means the development of an infection, the graph clearly shows that region A is the part of the curve that shows presence of bacteria and development of the infection.

**13.** **Which region of the curve indicates that the person began showing the symptoms of infection ?**

(a) A (b) B

(c) C (d) D

*Solution : (b)*

As the no. of bacteria begin to rise drastically, the symptoms of the infection would certainly occur, so region B is the region that shows symptoms of infection.

**14.** **Which region of the curve indicates that the treatment yielded effective relief ?**

(a) C

(b) D

(c) E

(d) The curve does not indicate the treatment

*Solution : (c)*

As the no. of bacteria begin to fall in region E, the person is certainly getting treated effectively for relief in his/her condition.

**15.** **Which region(s) shows that the person went to the doctor for the treatment ?**

(a) D only

(b) D and E

(c) A only

(d) No part of the curve indicates going to the doctor

*Solution : (a)*

Somewhere in region D, he went to the doctor as the no. of bacteria begin to fall in this region itself.

**16.** **Which region shows the person was healthy ?**

(a) A only

(b) A and D

(c) A and B

(d) No part of the curve shows a healthy phase

*Solution : (d)*

Since the curve starts with region A where the person already has a certain number of bacteria, therefore, there is no region that shows the person in a healthy state.

# MEAN, MEDIAN, MODE

Mean, median and mode are the three measures of central tendency of the data.

## MEAN

Mean is actually the average. An average of a group of numbers (or data or values or observations) is a number that is the best representative of the group of numbers because it tells a lot about the entire numbers of the group.

$$\text{Mean of a group of numbers} = \frac{\text{Sum of all numbers}}{\text{Number of numbers}}$$

Thus if A is the mean of n numbers $a_1, a_2, a_3, ..., a_n$; then

$$A = \frac{a_1 + a_2 + a_3 + ... + a_n}{n}$$

$$\Rightarrow a_1 + a_2 + a_3 + ... + a_n = A.n$$

Hence, Sum of numbers = (Number of numbers) × (Average)

For example, average of 6 to 10 natural numbers

$$= \frac{6 + 7 + 8 + 9 + 10}{5} = \frac{40}{5} = 8$$

### Some Important Results About Mean

(i) If each observation is increased by 'a', then the mean is also increased by 'a'. If $\overline{x}$ is the mean of $n$ observations $x_1, x_2, ...., x_n$, then the mean of observations $(x_1 + a), (x_2 + a), (x_3 + a), ...., (x_n + a)$ is $(\overline{x} + a)$.

(ii) If each observation is decreased by 'a', then the mean is also decreased by 'a'. If $\overline{x}$ is the mean of $n$ observations $x_1, x_2, ...., x_n$, then mean of observations $(x_1 - a), (x_2 - a), ...., (x_n - a)$ is $(\overline{x} - a)$.

(iii) If each observation is multiplied by a non-zero number 'a', Then, mean is also multiplied by 'a'.

If $\overline{x}$ is mean of $n$ observations $x_1, x_2, ...., x_n$, then mean of $ax_1, ax_2, ....., ax_n$ is $a.\overline{x}$.

(iv) If each observation is divided by a non-zero number 'a', then, mean is also divided by the non-zero number 'a'.

If $\overline{x}$ is mean of $n$ observations $x_1, x_2, ...., x_n$, then the mean of

$$\frac{x_1}{a}, \frac{x_2}{a}, ...... \frac{x_n}{a}, \text{ is } \frac{\overline{x}}{a}.$$

## MEDIAN

Median of a set of numbers (or data or values or observation) is the middle most number (or data or value or observation) in a set of numbers, when the numbers are arranged either in ascending or in descending order of their magnitude.

### Method to find the median

When the numbers (or data) is arranged in ascending or descending order, then median is calculated as follows:

(i) When the number of data (n) is odd, then the median is the

value of the $\left(\frac{n+1}{2}\right)^{th}$ data.

(ii)    When the number of data (n) is even, then the median is the mean of $\left(\dfrac{n}{2}\right)^{th}$ and $\left(\dfrac{n}{2}+1\right)^{th}$ data.

i.e. median $=\dfrac{1}{2}\left[\left(\dfrac{n}{2}\right)^{th} \text{data} + \left(\dfrac{n}{2}+1\right)^{th} \text{data}\right]$

### Illustration – 17

**The monthly salaries (in ₹) of 10 employees of a factory are: 12000, 8500, 9200, 7400, 11300, 12700, 7800, 11500, 10320, 8100. Find the median salary.**

**Solution:**

Arranging the observation in ascending order:

7400, 7800, 8100, 8500, 9200, 10320, 11300, 11500, 12000, 12700

Total number of observations $(n) = 10$ (even)

$\therefore$ median $=\dfrac{1}{2}\left[\left(\dfrac{n}{2}\right)^{th}\text{observation}+\left(\dfrac{n}{2}+1\right)^{th}\text{observation}\right]$

$=\dfrac{1}{2}\left[\left(\dfrac{10}{2}\right)^{th}\text{observation}+\left(\dfrac{10}{2}+1\right)^{th}\text{observation}\right]$

$=\dfrac{1}{2}\left[5^{th}\text{observation}+6^{th}\text{observation}\right]$

Median $=\dfrac{1}{2}\left[9200+10320\right]=\dfrac{19520}{2}=9760$

Median Salary $=$ ₹ 9760

### MODE

The mode of a group of numbers (or data or observations) is that number (or data or observation) which occurs most frequently i.e. which comes maximum number of times.

### Illustration – 18

**Find the value of mode of the following data**

      **50, 70, 50, 70, 80, 70, 70, 80, 70, 50**

**Solution:**

To find mode, we prepare ungrouped (or discrete) frequency table.

| Observation | Frequency |
|---|---|
| 50 | 3 |
| 70 | 5 |
| 80 | 2 |

In the above table we see that observation 70 is repeating maximum number of times i.e. frequency of 70 is maximum. Hence the mode of the given set of observation is 70.

### Relationship Between Mean, Mode and Median

$$\text{Mode} = 3\,\text{Median} - 2\,\text{Mean}$$

### Illustration – 19

**If the value of mode and mean is 60 and 66 respectively, then find the value of median.**

**Solution:**

Mode = 3 Median – 2 Mean

$\therefore$ Median $=\dfrac{1}{3}(\text{mode}+2\,\text{mean})=\dfrac{1}{3}(60+2\times66)=64$

## SYMMETRICALLY (OR NORMALLY) DISTRIBUTED DATA

If we represent the given data through bar graph, and the left side of this bar graph is the mirror image of its right side. Then the data is called symmetrically (or Normally) distributed data.

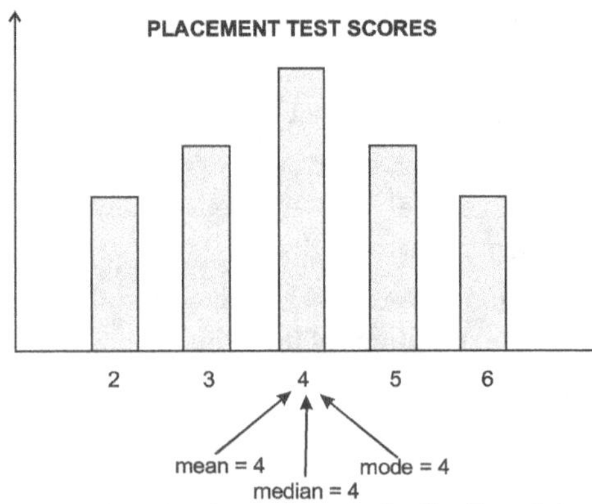


Mean, median and mode of a symmetrically distributed data are always same. This is the typical property of symmetric distribution of data. i.e. for a symmetrically distributed data,

Mean=Median=Mode

## SKEWED DISTRIBUTION OF DATA

The distribution of data which is not symmetric is called skewed distribution of data.

Skewed distribution of data are of two types:

(i)    Data skewed to the Left

(ii)    Data skewed to the Right

### DATA SKEWED TO THE LEFT

If in a distribution of data 5 is given once, 6 is given twice, 7 is given thrice, 8 is given four times, 9 is given seven times and 10 is given eight times, then its bar graph will be as shown below.

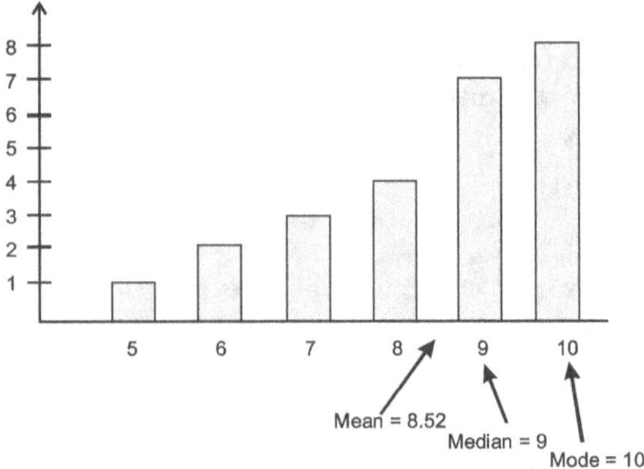


The bar graph above is an illustration of a special kind of data distribution. The distribution has the property that in every case, as the values increases, the frequencies increases as well. This means that on the bar graph, the columns get taller as we look from left to right. Such type of distribution of data is called **skewed to the left**. Here we see that the mode (10) is the greatest of the three measures of central tendency, the mean (8.52) the least of the three measures of central tendency, and the median (9) is in between. This illustrates a typical property of data which is skewed to the left. Hence for the distribution of data to be skewed to the left,

**Mean<Median<Mode**

# DATA SKEWED TO THE RIGHT

If a distribution of data are repersented by the bar graph in which as values increases, the frequencies decreases as well. that is if in the bar graph, the columns get shorter as we look from left to right, then the distribution of data is called **skewed to the right**.

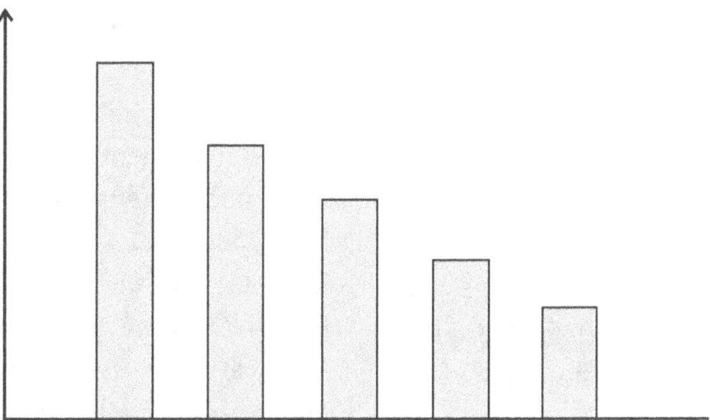

Hence for the distribution of data to be skewed to the right

**Mean>Median>Mode**

**Note:** there may be exceptions of this trend

## SUMMARY
**Typical Relationships Between Mean, Median and Mode**
**For Three Special Distributions**

| Data Distribution | Graph | Relation between mean, median and mode |
|---|---|---|
| 1. Skewed to the left | | Mean < Median < Mode |
| 2. Normal | | Mean = Median = Mode |
| 3. Skewed to the right | | Mean > Median > Mode |

---

**Illustration – 20**

If the mean of the numbers $27 + x$, $31 + x$, $89 + x$, $107 + x$, $156 + x$ is 82, then the mean of $130 + x$, $126 + x$, $68 + x$, $50 + x$, $1 + x$ is

    (a) 75     (b) 157     (c) 82     (d) 80

**Solution.** (a) Given,

$$82 = \frac{(27+x)+(31+x)+(89+x)+(107+x)+(156+x)}{5}$$

$$\Rightarrow 82 \times 5 = 410 + 5x \Rightarrow 410 - 410 = 5x \Rightarrow x = 0$$

∴ Required mean is,

$$\bar{x} = \frac{130+x+126+x+68+x+50+x+1+x}{5}$$

$$\bar{x} = \frac{375+5x}{5} = \frac{375+0}{5} = \frac{375}{5} = 75$$

**Illustration – 21**

The median of a set of 9 distinct observations is 20.5. If each of the largest 4 observation of the set is increased by 2, then the median of the new set

    (a)    is increased by 2
    (b)    is decreased by 2
    (c)    is two times the original median
    (d)    Remains the same as that of the original set

**Solution.** (d) Since $n = 9$, then median $= \left(\dfrac{9+1}{2}\right)^{\text{th}} = 5^{\text{th}}$

observation

Now, last four observations are increased by 2.

∵ The median is 5th observation, which remains unchanged.

∴ There will be no change in median.

### Illustration – 22

A set of numbers consists of three 4's, five 5's, six 6's, eight 8's and seven 10's. The mode of this set of numbers is

(a) 6　　　　(b) 7　　(c) 8　　(d) 10

**Solution.**　(c)　Mode of the data is 8 as it repeated maximum number of times.

### Illustration – 23

The graph below shows the distribution according to height of a group of jockeys at a south Florida horse track. Select the statement that correctly describes a relationship between measures of central tendency for this distribution.

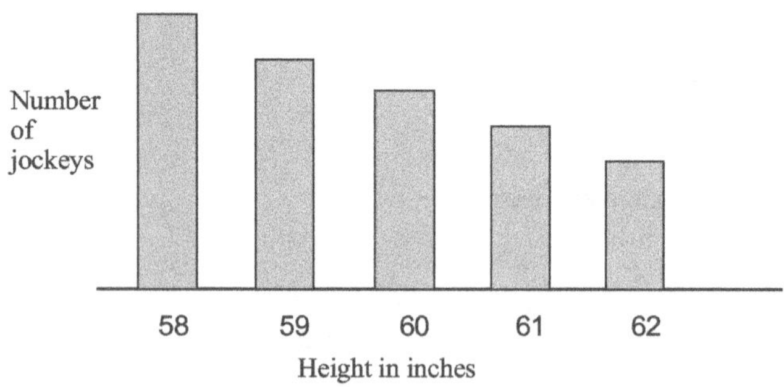


(a) The mean is less than the mode.
(b) The mode and the mean are the same.
(c) The median is greater than the mode.
(d) The median and the mean are the same.

**Solution: (c)**

This is an example of data **skewed to the left.** In this distribution we know that the mode is 58, because 58 is the value under the tallest column. But 58 is also the smallest value in this distribution. This indicates that both the mean an median should be greater than 58 (because in any collection of numbers that are not all identical, the average will be greater than the smallest number and less than the largest number). Hence the choice (c) is correct.

### Illustration – 24

The graph below shows the distribution of a group of garages according the number junk cars in their garages. Select the statement that correctly gives a relationship between measures of central tendency for this distribution.

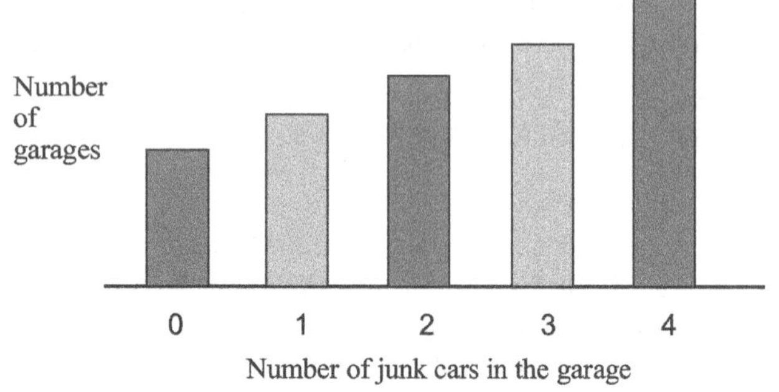


(a) The mean is the same as the median.
(b) The mean is less than the mode.
(c) The mode is less than the mean.
(d) The median is less than the mean.

**Solution: (b)**

This is an example of data **skewed to the left.**

It is easy to identify the mode: the mode is 4, since 4 is the value under the tallest column.

Notice also that 4 is greatest number in this distribution. This indicates that the mean and the median should both be less than 4 (because in a collection of numbers that are not all identical the average number must be larger than the smallest number and smaller than the largest number).

We see that choice (b) is correct.

### Illustration – 25

ABC company is soliciting donations to fund natural clamity in Kerala. More than half of his donations have been in the amount of ₹ 500. The others have been equally divided among values of ₹ 250 and values of ₹ 750. Select the statement that correctly gives a relationship between measures of central tendency for this distribution.

(a) The median is greater than the mean.
(b) The mean is less than the mode.
(c) The mean is equal to the median.
(d) The mode is less than the median.

**Solution: (c)**

Although we don't know exactly how many donations have been collected, we have enough information to draw a useful bar graph summarizing the distribution. The bar graph will show three values. 250, 500 and 750. Since half of the donations are in the amount of ₹ 500, the column above the value 500 will be as tall as the other two columns combined. Moreover, since there were exactly as many ₹ 250 donations as there were ₹ 750 donations, the column above the value 250 will be the same height as the column above the value 750. The bar graph looks like this:

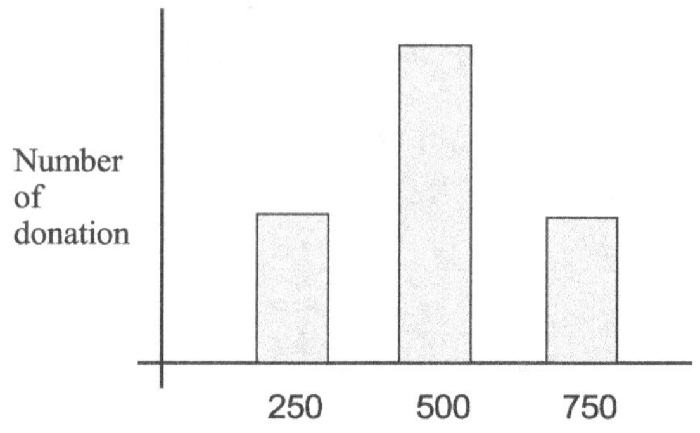


Recall that this an example of symmetrically (or normally) distributed data, So the mean, median and mode are all equal.

We see that choice (c) is correct.

# Exercise

**1.** Consider the following distance - time graph. The graph shows three athletes A, B and C running side by side for a 30 km race.

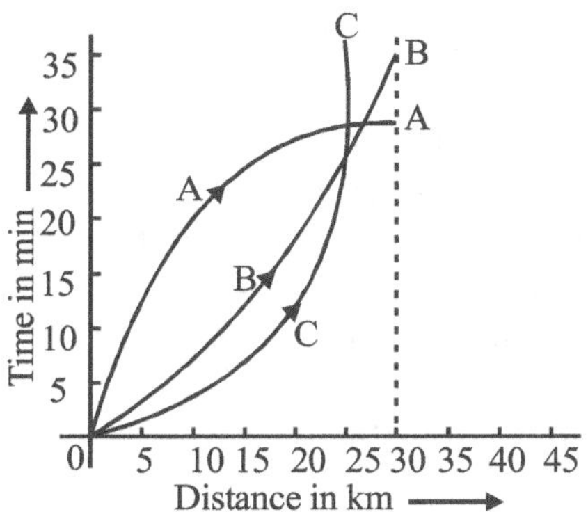

With reference to the above graph, consider the following statements :
1. The race was won by A.
2. B was ahead mark of A up to 25 km mark
3. C ran very slowly from the beginning.

Which of the statements given above is/are correct ?
(a)　1 only　　　　　　　　(b)　1 and 2
(c)　2 and 3　　　　　　　 (d)　1, 2 and 3

**Directions (Qs. 2-3):** *Manufacturing Exports and Trade Balance (in percent of GDP)*

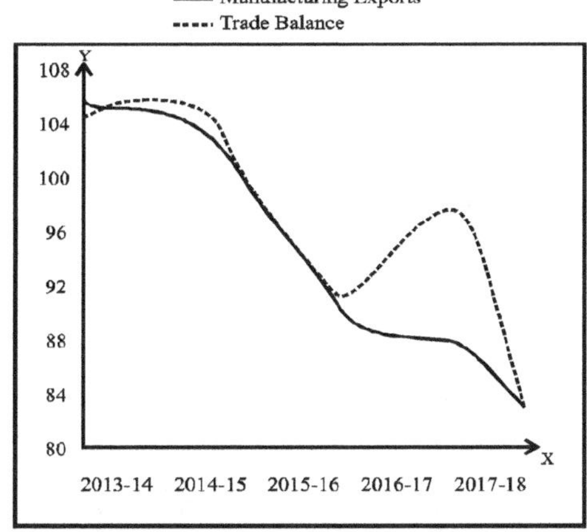


**2.** With reference to the above graph. Consider the following statements
1. Manufacturing exports are continously decreasing.
2. There is increasing behaviour of trade balance from 2015 to 2017.
3. Reviving manufacturing and making the sector internationally competitive should be the twin goals.
4. The share of manufacturing in GDP has not improved.

Which of the statements given above is/are correct?
(a)　(1), (2) and (4)　　　　(b)　(1) and (2) only
(c)　(1), (2) and (3)　　　　(d)　(2), (3) and (4)

**3.** From the graph, which one of the following can be Concluded?
(a)　Trade balance is directly proportional to the manufacturing sector.
(b)　Trade balance is inversely proportional to the manufacturing sector.
(c)　Trade balance does not depend on the manufacturing sector.
(d)　None of the above

**Directions (Qs. 4-5) :** *Read the following graph carefully and answer the questions carefully.*

**Agriculture: Real GVA and Real Revenue**

**(Crops: 2014 = 100)**

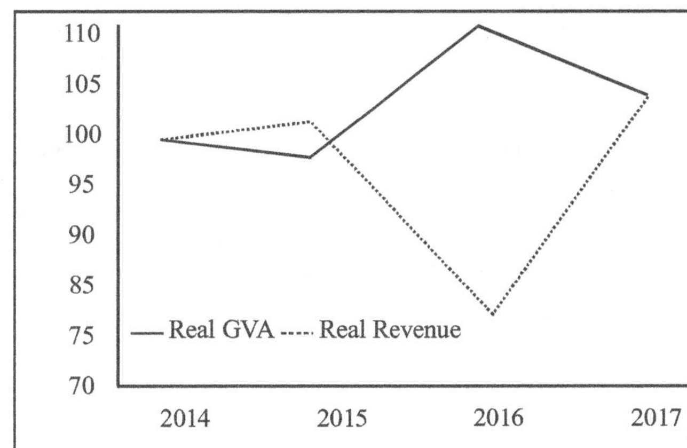


**4.** With reference to the above graph, which one of the following statements is not correct?
(a)　In 2014, 2015 and 2017, the level of real agriculture GVA and real agriculture revenue has remained same.
(b)　Real revenue in year 2016 might be impacted with weak monsoon.
(c)　The government's laudable objective of addressing agricultural crisis consequently requires.
(d)　In 2014-17, the agricultural revenue is inversely proportional to agricultural GVA.

**5.** From the graph, which one of following can be made?
(a)　The year interval 2015-16 shows the highest growth in the level of real GVA.
(b)　The year interval 2016-17 shows the highest growth in the level of real revenue.
(c)　Both (a) and (b)
(d)　None of the above.

**Directions (Qs. 6-7):** *Contribution of Contingent Liabilities to (in percent of GDP)*

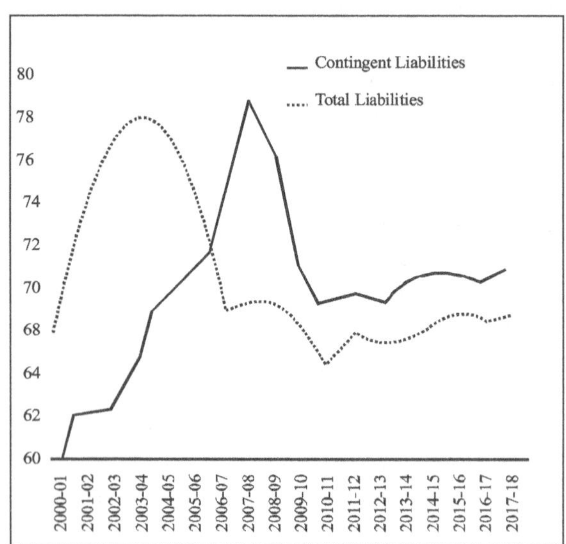

**Contribution of Contingent Liabilities to (in percent of GDP)**



**6.** With reference to the above graph, which one of the following statements can be concluded?

(a) There is no contradictory behaviour between contingent liabilities and total liabilities.

(b) Total liabilities are always directly proportional to contingent liabilities.

(c) Both (a) and (b)

(d) Neither (a) nor (b)

**7.** With reference to the above graph, which one of the following statements is correct?

(a) Total liabilities and contingent liabilities are the maximum at the same instant of time.

(b) Total liabilities and contingent liabilities are the minimum at the same instant of time.

(c) Total liabilities and contingent liabilities are the maximum and minimum at the same instant of time.

(d) Total liabilities and contingent liabilities are the maximum and minimum at the different instant of time.

**8.** For the data 2, 9, $x + 6$, $2x + 3$, 5, 10, 5 if mean is 7, then mode is

(a) 3      (b) 5      (c) 9      (d) 10

**9.** If number 6, 8, $2x - 5$, $2x - 1$, 15, 17, 20 and 22 are in ascending order and its median is 14 then the value of x will be

(a) 14      (b) 7      (c) 15      (d) 20

**10.** In a test of 50 marks, 16 students got the following marks:

48, 38, 49, 37, 43, 50, 37, 42, 48, 44, 47, 48, 45, 40, 46, 42

The mean, median and mode of the marks are respectively,

(a) 43.5, 45.5, 48      (b) 44, 45.5, 48

(c) 43.5, 44.5, 48      (d) 44, 44.5, 48

**11.** If the median of $\dfrac{x}{7}, \dfrac{x}{5}, \dfrac{x}{6}, x, \dfrac{x}{4}, \dfrac{x}{3}, \dfrac{x}{2}$ is 8, then the value of $x$ is __________.

(a) 8      (b) 24      (c) 32      (d) 48

**12.** The mean of three positive numbers is 10 more than the smallest of the numbers and 15 less than the largest of the three. If the median of the three numbers is 5, then the mean of squares of the numbers is

(a) $108\dfrac{2}{3}$    (b) $116\dfrac{2}{3}$    (c) $208\dfrac{1}{3}$    (d) $216\dfrac{2}{3}$

**13.** The mean marks of boys and girls in an examination are 60 and 65 respectively. If the mean marks of all the students in that examination is 62, then the ratio of the number of boys to the number of girls is

(a) 2 : 3      (b) 3 : 2      (c) 122 : 127      (d) 5 : 62

**14.** A number of cats were asked 'How many birdies did you eat last month?' The distribution is summarized in the bar graph below. Select the statement that correctly describes a relationship between measures of central tendency for this distribution.

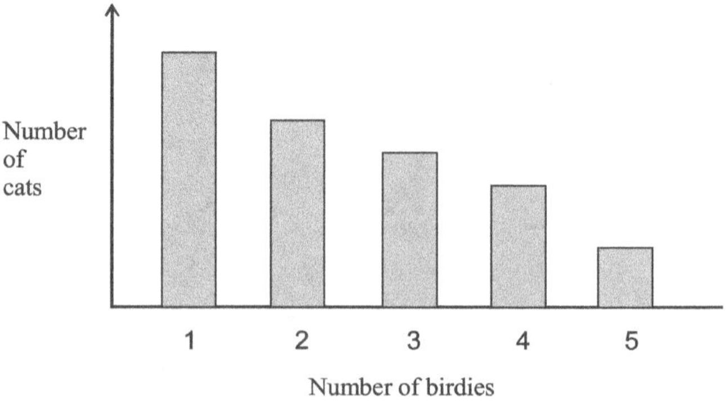



(a) The mode is greater than the median.

(b) The mode is greater than the mean.

(c) The mode is equal to the mean.

(d) The mean is greater than the mode.

**15.** A number of Spurrier fans were asked 'How many times will Coach throw his visor next week?' The distribution is summarized in the bar graph below. Select the statement that correctly describes a relationship between measures of central tendency for this distributions.

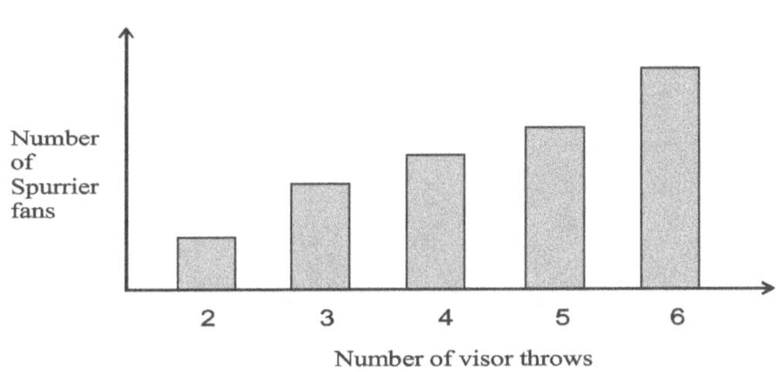



(a) The mean is greater than the median.
(b) The median is equal to the mode.
(c) The mode is greater than the mean.
(d) The mode is less than the mean.

16. A number of couch potatoes were asked 'How many hours of Nintendo did you play yesterday?' The distribution is summarized in the bar graph below. Select the statement that correctly describes a relationship between measures of central tendency for this distribution.

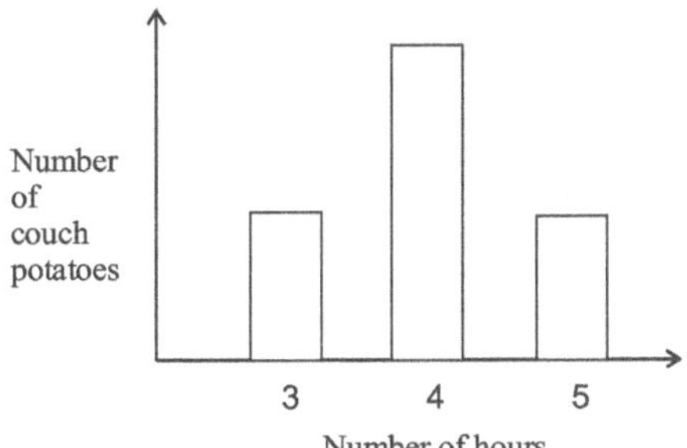



(a) The median is less than the mean.
(b) The mode is greater than the mean.
(c) The mode is equal to the median.
(d) The mean is greater than the mode.

17. If the mean of the observations $x$, $x + 3$, $x + 5$, $x + 7$ and $x + 10$ is 9, the mean of the last three observations is

(a) $10\dfrac{1}{3}$       (b) $10\dfrac{2}{3}$

(c) $11\dfrac{1}{3}$       (d) $11\dfrac{2}{3}$

18. If $\overline{x}$ is the mean of $x_1, x_2, ......, x_n$ then for $a \neq 0$, the mean of $ax_1, ax_2, ......, ax_n, \dfrac{x_1}{a}, \dfrac{x_2}{a}, ......, \dfrac{x_n}{a}$ is

(a) $\left(a+\dfrac{1}{a}\right)\overline{x}$       (b) $\left(a+\dfrac{1}{a}\right)\dfrac{\overline{x}}{2}$

(c) $\left(a+\dfrac{1}{a}\right)\dfrac{\overline{x}}{n}$       (d) $\dfrac{\left(a+\dfrac{1}{a}\right)\overline{x}}{2n}$

19. The mean of 100 observations is 50. If one of the observations which was 50 is replaced by 150, the resulting mean will be
(a) 50.5       (b) 51
(c) 51.5       (d) 52

20. The mean of six numbers is 30. If one number is excluded, the mean of the remaining numbers is 29. The excluded number is
(a) 29       (b) 30
(c) 35       (d) 45

# Solutions

## ANSWER KEY

| 1 | (b) | 2 | (c) | 3 | (d) | 4 | (d) | 5 | (c) | 6 | (d) | 7 | (d) | 8 | (c) | 9 | (b) | 10 | (d) |
|---|-----|---|-----|---|-----|---|-----|---|-----|---|-----|---|-----|---|-----|---|-----|----|-----|
| 11 | (a) | 12 | (d) | 13 | (b) | 14 | (d) | 15 | (d) | 16 | (c) | 17 | (c) | 18 | (b) | 19 | (b) | 20 | (c) |

## DETAILED EXPLANATIONS

1. **(b)** Since $x$ axis shows the distance and $y$ axis shows the time, hence lower graph will show faster athlete and higher graph will show slower athlete. Height of A's graph is the lowest, hence, the race was won by A. Height of B's graph is lower than A's graph up to 25 km, hence B was running faster than A up to 25 km. The height of C's graph is the lowest from the beginning, hence he run very fastly from the beginning, Hence statement 3 is not correct.

2. **(c)** From the graph, it is clear that manufacturing exports show continuously decreasing pattern whereas trade balance increases from 2015 to 2017. As a result, the share of manufacturing in GDP has improved slightly. However the international competitiveness of manufacturing has not made great strides, reflected in declining manufacturing export-GDP ratio and manufacturing trade balance.

3. **(d)** From the graph, it is clear that trade balance is neither directly proportional nor inversely proportional to the manufacturing sector.

4. **(d)** From the graph, both the curves intersect at 2014, 2015 and 2017. So the level of real GVA and real revenue has remained same in 2014, 2015 and 2017. Real revenue in 2016 has decreased. Therefore. there is a possibility of week monsoon impact and government's efforts are required. Here, revenue is not inversely proportional to GVA.

5. **(c)** From the graph, it is clear that the highest growth in real GVA occurs in the year interval 2015-16 whereas the year interval 2016-17 shows the highest growth in the level of real revenue.

**6.** **(d)** From the graph it is clear that in 2003-08, total liabilities decreases while liabilities is increasing. So, there is contradictory behaviour between them and total liabilities are not always directly proportional to contingent liabilities.

**7.** **(d)** From the graph, it is clear that total liabilities are maximum at 2003-04, whereas contingent liabilities are maximum at 2007-08. So total liabilities and contingent liabilities are the maximum at the different instant of time. Also, total liabilities and contingent liabilities are the minimum at the different instant of time.

**8.** **(c)** Mean $= \dfrac{2+9+x+6+2x+3+5+10+5}{7} = 7$

$3x+40 = 49 \Rightarrow x = 3$

$x+6 = 9 \Rightarrow 2x+3 = 9$

Data (2, 9, 9, 9, 5, 10, 5) and Mode $= 9$

**9.** **(b)** $6, 8, 2x-5, 2x-1, 15, 17, 20, 22$

$\dfrac{2x-1+15}{2} = 14 \Rightarrow 2x+14 = 14 \times 2 = 28$

$2x = 28-14 = 14 \Rightarrow x = \dfrac{14}{2} = 7$

**10.** **(d)** Marks of 16 students are

$37, 37, 38, 40, 42, 42, 43, 44, 45, 46, 47, 48, 48, 48, 49, 50$

$\text{Mean} = \dfrac{\text{Sum of observations}}{\text{Number of observations}} = \dfrac{704}{16} = 44$

$\text{Median} = \dfrac{\text{8th observations} + \text{9th observations}}{2}$

$= \dfrac{44+45}{2} = 44.5$

Mode $= 48$ as it occurs maximum number of times.

**11.** **(a)** Given observations are $\dfrac{x}{7}, \dfrac{x}{5}, \dfrac{x}{6}, x, \dfrac{x}{4}, \dfrac{x}{3}, \dfrac{x}{2}$

Given Median $= 8$

Since number of observation is odd

$\therefore$ Median $= \left(\dfrac{7+1}{2}\right)^{\text{th}}$ obs. $=$ 4th obs $= x \Rightarrow 8 = x$

**12.** **(d)** Let the three numbers be a, b and c such that $a > b > c$

According to the given condition

$\dfrac{a+b+c}{3} = c+10 = a-15 = k$

$\Rightarrow \quad c = k-10$

Also, $a = k+15$

$b = 5 \ (\because \text{Median} = 5)$

We know that, $a+b+c = 3k$

$\Rightarrow \quad k+15+5+k-10 = 3k \ \text{Þ} \quad 10 = k$

Thus, $a = 25, b = 5, c = 0$

$\therefore \quad$ Mean of squares of the numbers

$= \dfrac{25^2+5^2+0^2}{3} = \dfrac{650}{3} = 216\dfrac{2}{3}$

**13.** **(b)** $\Sigma b = 60m, \ \Sigma g = 65n$

$\dfrac{\Sigma b + \Sigma g}{m+n} = 62 \quad \Rightarrow \Sigma b + \Sigma g = 62(m+n)$

$\Rightarrow 60m + 65n - 62m - 62n = 0$

$\Rightarrow -2m+3n = 0 \ \Rightarrow 2m = 3n \ \Rightarrow m:n = 3:2$

**17.** **(c)** We know, mean $= \dfrac{\text{Sum of all the observations}}{\text{Total no. of observation}}$

$\Rightarrow \text{Mean} = \dfrac{x+x+3+x+5+x+7+x+10}{5}$

$9 = \dfrac{5x+25}{5} \Rightarrow x = 4$

So, mean of last three observations is

$\dfrac{3x+22}{3} = \dfrac{12+22}{3} = \dfrac{34}{3} = 11\dfrac{1}{3}$

**18.** **(b)** Given $\dfrac{x_1 + ..... + x_n}{n} = \bar{x}$ .....(i)

$\Rightarrow \dfrac{ax_1 + ... + ax_n}{an} = \bar{x} \Rightarrow \dfrac{ax_1 + ... + ax_n}{n} = a\bar{x}$ .....(ii)

Also, from (i), we have

$\dfrac{\dfrac{1}{a}x_1 + .... + \dfrac{1}{a}x_n}{\dfrac{1}{a}(n)} = \bar{x}$

$\Rightarrow \dfrac{\dfrac{x_1}{a} + .... + \dfrac{x_n}{a}}{n} = \dfrac{\bar{x}}{a}$ .....(iii)

So, the mean of $ax_1, ........, ax_n, \dfrac{x_1}{a}, ........., \dfrac{x_n}{a}$

is $\dfrac{a\bar{x} + \dfrac{\bar{x}}{a}}{2} = \dfrac{\bar{x}}{2}\left(a + \dfrac{1}{a}\right)$

**19.** **(b)** $\bar{x} = 50$

$\Rightarrow \dfrac{\Sigma x_i}{100} = 50$

$\Rightarrow \Sigma x_i = 5000$

As, 50 is replaced by 150.

Thus,

New, $\Sigma x_i = 5000 - 50 + 150 = 5100$

New, $= \dfrac{5100}{100} = 51$

**20.** **(c)** Sum of 6 numbers $= 30 \times 6 = 180$

Sum of remaining 5 numbers $= 29 \times 5 = 145$

$\therefore$ Excluded number $= 180 - 145 = 35.$